Memory, Violence, Queues

Lu Xun Interprets China

Memory, Violence, Queues

Lu Xun Interprets China

Eva Shan Chou

ASIA PAST & PRESENT

Published by the Association for Asian Studies, Inc.
Asia Past & Present: New Research from AAS, Number 9

Asia Past & Present: New Research from AAS

"Asia Past & Present: New Research from AAS," published by the Association for Asian Studies, Inc. (AAS), features scholarly work from all areas of Asian studies. In addition to scholarly monographs, translations, essay collections, and other forms of scholarly research are welcome for consideration. AAS aims to support work in emerging or under-represented fields.

Formed in 1941, the Association for Asian Studies (AAS)—the largest society of its kind, with approximately 8,000 members worldwide—is a scholarly, non-political, non-profit professional association open to all persons interested in Asia.

For further information, please visit www.asian-studies.org.

© 2012 by the Association for Asian Studies, Inc.

All Rights Reserved. Written permission must be secured to use or reproduce any part of this book.

Published by:
Association for Asian Studies, Inc.
825 Victors Way, Suite 310
Ann Arbor, Michigan 48108 USA
www.asian-studies.org

Library of Congress Cataloging-in-Publication Data

Chou, E. Shan (Eva Shan)
Memory, violence, queues : Lu Xun interprets China / Eva Shan Chou.
p. cm. — (Asia past & present: new research from AAS ; no. 9)
Includes bibliographical references and index.
ISBN 978-0-924304-68-2 (pbk. : alk. paper)
1. Lu, Xun, 1881–1936. I. Title.
PL2754.S5Z637 2012
895.1'35—dc23

2011043238

Cover Art: P. A. Staynes (1875–1953), ROI, RI, *Near Peking*. Watercolor, 22.5" x 30". Collection of the author.
Cover design, Ida K. Chou, M. Arch.

Contents

Acknowledgements / vii

Introduction / 1

Chapter One / 19
    Renewing a Seminal Literary Figure
        A Brief View of the Writing
        A Narrative of the Life
            The Life in This Study
        Memory, Violence, Queues: The Approach of This Study
            Queue
            Violence
            Memory
            The Chapters in This Study

Chapter Two / 52
    Cutting His Queue: Nationalism, Identity, and Other Unknowns
        The Firsthand Evidence: Photograph and Poem
            Changes From
            After
        The Event Itself
        The Queue Becomes a Symbol
        Lu Xun in Japan circa 1903
        Conclusion: "No More Than Things on Pieces of Paper"

Chapter Three / 99
    The Literary Afterlife of the Queue: A Closer Look at the Years 1920–22
        Establishing a Group of Works: Three Stories and Two Essays
            "Storm"
            "A Story about Hair"
            Titles
            Two Essays
            "The True Story of Ah Q"
        Biographical Connections: Political Violence and Writing
            1917: A Coup in Beijing
            1920: A Battle outside Beijing
            The 1933 Preface: Storms (fengbo) in the 1910s

Violent Deaths and Literary Limits
"Storm"
"A Story about Hair"
"The True Story of Ah Q"
Conclusion

Chapter Four / 145
The Life of a Poem, 1903–36
1931 and the Five Martyrs
Implications: The Other 1931 Poem
Implications: The Other Classical Poems
1926 and the Photograph of Self
Coda: 1936
Conclusion

Chapter Five / 181
In the Hands of Others, 1934–36: The Visual Materials
The Visual Materials
Material by Lu Xun
Lu Xun Responds: Particularity and Universality
"Not a Single Queue Looks Naturally Grown"
"What Does Ah Q Look Like?"
In the Hands of Others: Lu Xun Acquiesces in the Redefinition
Style
Subject Matter
Choice of Media: Woodcuts and Cartoons
The Background of the Artists
Conclusion: New Art Woodcut and New Literature

Conclusion / 222

Appendix A / 233
"Inscribed by the Author on a Small Likeness": Dating the Evidence; the Meaning of *shenshi* in Line 1

Appendix B / 239
Illustrators and Illustrations of Lu Xun's Fiction and His Person, 1934–36

List of Characters / 255

Finding List for Lu Xun's Writings / 259

Illustration Credits / 263

Notes / 265

Works Cited / 298

Index / 317

Acknowledgments

It is a pleasure to be able to thank in print the many people who have helped me over the years of this endeavor. That many names recur from my previous project testifies to a happy continuity in life that cannot be taken for granted, while new debts bear witness to the pleasant aspects of life's many changes. I record here my gratitude to Cynthia Brokaw, Cheng Pei-kai, Sally Church, Susan Daruvala, Ronald Egan, Susan Chan Egan, Sean Gu, Patrick Hanan, Joanna Handlin Smith, Huang Ying-che, Jeffrey Kinkley, Wolfgang Kubin, Perry Link, Victor Mair, Joseph McDermott, David McMullen, Stephen Owen, Morris Rossabi, Murray Rubinstein, Arthur Waldron, and Pauline Yu. Bonnie McDougall was always receptive to reading my articles and always gave prompt and thoughtful responses. Dennis Grafflin was a staunch reader of many chapters just after they emerged from their initial incoherence. Raoul David Findeisen kindly took me to see Käthe Kollwitz's Berlin neighborhood of Prenzlauer Berg before its present gentrification. Yen Chuan-ying enabled me to obtain records of many images that I needed to consult. Xiaobing Tang generously shared his practical experience on some logistical points. The acute observations of the late James Robert Hightower at the beginning of this project have retained their pertinence to the end.

I thank the anonymous reviewers of this manuscript, whose suggestions improved its arguments, presentation, and tone in important ways. Theirs is the generous expenditure of time and expertise that underlies the principles of peer review.

At my home institution, City University of New York's Baruch College, I owe much to my former dean Myrna Chase and to my colleagues Paula Berggren and Roslyn Bernstein. The constancy of their confidence in my work over many years allowed me to begin and then lay aside a second book on Du Fu, to move forward twelve centuries, and to explore a new interest in a series of articles before developing the arguments that form this study. This rare academic luxury is founded on their support.

A fellowship from the Harry Frank Guggenheim Foundation first encouraged me to attempt a study in which literary writings, political history, and individual biography are joined in the issue of violence. A Kluge

Fellowship at the Library of Congress gave me a chance to explore the visual and cultural history of the queue. Over the years, grants from City University of New York's Research Foundation and Professional Staff Congress provided a much-appreciated series of 3-credit releases from a 21-credit teaching load. A term as Visiting Scholar at Cambridge University, Trinity College, afforded ideal conditions in which to make inroads on a new project and to read proofs. I am grateful to all these institutions for their support.

The staffs at many libraries gave vital assistance: the Library of the Sinological Institute at the University of Heidelberg, the Lu Xun Museums at Beijing and Shanghai, the libraries at Yale, Harvard, Stanford, Cornell, and CUNY Baruch, and the New York Public Library. Jonathan Wilson, publications manager at AAS Publications, resourcefully saw this work from submission through to publication. Janet Opdyke's copyediting and Gudrun Patton's layout skills kept on track the countless details in text and illustrations.

I also owe a large debt to the many translators of the several genres of Lu Xun's writings. Though for reasons of consistency, I have mostly translated anew in quoting, I have learned much from consulting the choices that my predecessors have had to commit to the printed page. The debt to translators and translations, however, is greater than that of consultation alone, for readers and the authors in question benefit as well. Ultimately translations are the means by which the meaning of significant figures can reach beyond their linguistic boundaries, and by the same token, they are the means by which we can make the legacies of other cultures some part of our own. It is my hope that this study will lead non-Chinese-language readers to turn, or return, to the available European-language translations as a source for the words of a powerful writer.

Finally, I would like to mention gratefully friends and family: Christie and Chris Wilbur, Carol Munroe and András Riedlmayer, Elizabeth Perry, Wendy Zeldin, Virginia Mayer, Alice Cheang, my sisters May, Ida, and Ana, and my nephews and nieces on both sides. Ida in particular turned her architectural expertise to the question of cover design. Early on, in a gesture of confidence, my husband, Richard McCarrick, gave me the P. A. Staynes watercolor used on the cover. Our daughter, Heather, offered aesthetic advice and technical help. Sadly, my mother did not live to see me follow in the steps of her pioneering study of Ding Ling. To her memory and to the memory of her mother, from whom history had too early separated her, I dedicate this work.

Introduction

In the late 1910s, at a time when China's existence as a sovereign nation was coming under ever-increasing pressures, a group of the new elite issued calls for the creation of a new literature for China. These men (for they were nearly all men) were writers, editors, and professors who had been educated in "Western learning." They founded the magazine *New Youth* (*Xinqingnian*) and published in it many declarations on the need for a new culture, to be given voice by a new literature. This literature must be radically different from the genres, content, and language of tradition, they declared, because China must reject the outmoded contents of its tradition or perish. Such an agenda was not exactly wholly new, despite their rhetoric, at least not in its intent to reform the nation. Since China's defeat at British hands in the first Opium War in 1842, six decades earlier, and even more so since its jolting, more recent defeat by Japan in 1895, there had been many endeavors to join literature in a vital way to political and social reform. In the previous generations, Yan Fu (1853–1921), Lin Shu (1852–1924), and Liang Qichao (1873–1919) were vastly different men who nonetheless all held that the way ahead for the struggling nation was linked to a new kind of writing.[1] The founding of *New Youth* in 1915 marked a new reopening of the struggle to realize such a program. In the intervening decades, changes in political and social conditions had created a hospitable environment for a large variety of print cultures to develop and flourish, among which the energetic enterprises of Commercial Press, the publisher of both Yan Fu and Lin Shu, constituted a one-company sampler of what could be commercially viable.[2] The proposals advanced for New Literature and the periodicals founded to bring them to fruition took their place in this new print culture. This time the program of a serious literature both survived and flourished in an expanded print world, and both New Literature and the New Culture Movement acquired the status of proper nouns.

A member of this new elite, Zhou Shuren, using the pen name of Lu Xun, wrote the earliest works of fiction and essays for this avowedly iconoclastic program, and they brought him to the forefront of the culture it sought to foster. His first work, "Diary of a Madman," published in 1918, was a startling piece of fiction that exemplified newness in every way. Told by a madman who thought people were plotting to eat him, the protagonist's diary entries record his growing realization that many people were being eaten and his final, disquieting knowledge that he, too, might have eaten human flesh. Such a work, influenced by European models of the recent nineteenth-century past, was new in both its message and the literary style employed. From these models came the sustained metaphor (here of China as a society governed by cannibalism); the consistency in the exposition, plotting, character development, and voice; and finally, the use of the vernacular language. As Lu Xun later observed, even before the message of his early stories in *New Youth* was understood, their language and style fascinated young readers.[3] In the years after "Diary," more amazing stories followed, equally charged in message and new in style, and to these were added equally innovative essays.

In a brief span of time after "Diary," other writers rapidly emerged, new magazines were founded, and new readers came from the increasing number of new-style schools that were being established. In a matter of years, this activity carved out from the varied kinds of print culture a role for New Literature that was based on an ideology of social and moral criticism rather than on a commercially successful product. It established the feasibility and prestige of the vernacular as the medium of an elite literature and by this success sought to displace and expand the role performed by the literature of the classical language. In Pierre Bourdieu's terms, the New Literature had captured the cultural and symbolic capital of the traditional elite in a literary field that had greatly expanded.[4] As Bourdieu's idea of the literary field suggests, the context for this rapid development was much larger than the literature itself: the changes in social and economic conditions that gave rise to the new elite also promoted a commercial culture and mass culture that dwarfed the output of *New Youth* and other like-minded publishers. Furthermore, one could argue that in a modern, industrializing economy the vernacular was bound to replace the classical language, as was already happening sporadically in practical communications venues such as newspapers. Yet the specific step of establishing the vernacular language in the realm of serious literature was effected by the practitioners of New Literature. On this basis, they claimed the high moral ground of a reformist literature, one dedicated to high artistic goals and consciously modeled on European exemplars. The claim was aided by the fact that soon after, popular usage applied the broader name of May Fourth Literature to it, thereby connecting the literature to the large social-political May Fourth Movement.

Early on, Mao Dun, an activist and later a writer of the New Literature, introduced the term *creative writing scene* (*chuangzuo tan*), to name this elite slice of print culture.[5] *The literary world* (*wenxue jie*) was another term. Though quantitatively small, this literature survived through the great political changes of the succeeding decades. We need not subscribe to the claim of monolithic eminence for this literature nor to the enlightenment claims of its May Fourth era to see that its activities left a lasting mark on literary history. The writings, periodicals, and newspaper supplements that were produced in self-identification with this agenda stood at the beginning of a still-continuing and identifiable body of writing that Bonnie S. McDougall and Kam Louie have termed "the modern canon." This is the literature, together with its "forms, hierarchies, and languages," to which they provide a guide in *The Literature of China in the Twentieth Century*.[6] This is the literary world that this study, focused on Lu Xun, takes for its arena.

At the time of Lu Xun's death in 1936, the literary world—his literary world—was, by every measure, considerably larger and more complicated than when he had begun to write two decades earlier, but he remained its dominant figure. Political divisions were perhaps the most determinative factor in its complication. Two parties, Nationalist and Communist, emerged as forces that provided competing ideologies that the regional warlords of the 1910s had not afforded. Many cultural figures took positions that both created and sharpened the divisions among themselves and their publications. After some hesitation, Lu Xun threw in his lot with the Communist Party, but his influence among the educated remained great on a national basis across political allegiances. His brief returns to Beijing, in 1929 and 1932, drew large crowds for each of his lectures. In the 1930s, the students at teachers' colleges in Shandong and Hebei provinces, according to their later recollections, were reading Lu Xun more than any other writer.[7] At his death, the outpouring of accolades came from every figure in the cultural world, and his funeral was covered by publications of every political stripe.

Yet, despite his preeminence, today his position has become harder to define. Normally the passage of eight or nine decades since the death of a major figure will see several rounds of differing evaluations as both literature and society change over this long length of time. The writer may experience an eclipse for some period, or perhaps a devaluation. When he or she is taken up again, the interest of readers and critics may shift to different aspects of his or her life and achievement, for new studies in every era are to some degree a reflection of their own time. Moreover, given the passage of time, the author's writings can be seen against the perspective of literature produced in the intervening decades, whether developing from or against the writings or ignoring them.

This has not been the situation with Lu Xun. His reputation did not experience any of these shifts in fortune. Instead, his domination was asserted within Communist-controlled regions before 1949 and extended by policy after the establishment of the People's Republic of China when it lasted until the liberalization that took place in the late 1980s. The Stalinist system of control in literary, artistic, and educational fields developed during World War II in the Communist base of Yan'an was extended to the entire nation and ensured that independent, public interpretations of Lu Xun were silenced. There were also no natural developments in new writing to place him in a historical position as a writer of the 1920s and 1930s, for only members of the Writers' Union could publish, and they could publish only socialist realism. One could no longer speak of any literary or cultural factors that contributed to his standing. Rather, to talk about published work on Lu Xun in these fifty years is really to open a window on different phases and goals in the exercise of political control under the People's Republic of China. As Gao Xudong writes, "Since 1948 Lu Xun has been ceaselessly simplified and deified."[8] A cult of personality, which had been evident in his lifetime, hardened into an official cult in which every conceivable anniversary was marked. Many Lu Xun museums were established: in Shanghai in 1951, in Shaoxing in 1953, and in Beijing in 1956. Each had its collection, archives, and research institute and each substantially expanded over the decades. Guangzhou and Xiamen, where he lived for only a few months, also each has a Lu Xun museum. In some ways his status is analogous to Pushkin's standing in the former Soviet Union and now in Russia. Pushkin's supreme popularity in his own lifetime and the tsarist century following was a cultural phenomenon that the Soviet Union and its successor, Russia, took and transformed into an official cult and put to useful ends on various anniversaries of his birth, his death, the dedication of a monument, and other occasions.[9]

With Lu Xun, the time frame was much contracted compared to Pushkin's two centuries. Official appropriation of his legacy began at once, with his death in Shanghai. The Communist Party, then an outlawed underground organization whose urban activities were most concentrated in Shanghai, orchestrated his funeral through Feng Xuefeng, their agent and his friend and disciple, planning the wake, the pallbearers, the speakers, the route of the funeral procession, and the burial. The funeral banner termed him "Soul of a People" (*minzu hun*), and so he was to be through innumerable books and articles. In Yan'an, a Lu Xun Academy of Literature and Arts was established in 1938, and in 1940 Mao Zedong lauded him in the highest terms, calling him "the greatest and most courageous standard-bearer of this new cultural force, . . . the chief commander of China's cultural revolution, . . . the bravest and most correct, the firmest, the most loyal and the most ardent national hero."[10] This praise ensured that Lu Xun would be the supreme literary figure, at least as long as Mao's own star was in the ascendancy.

Mao's praise became an absolute guideline for published scholarship and, through textbooks and readers, for the nation as a whole. For a half century, the first step in writing on any topic (after quoting Mao) was to determine its proper class basis. During the radically politicized decade of the Cultural Revolution, 1966–76, when the novels of even the redoubtable Mao Dun, with his impeccable Communist credentials, were forbidden, Lu Xun was the only author whose works remained in print or who could even be safely mentioned. (There was also a favored, living handful of writers then under the direct patronage of Mao and his allies.) The official line was clear: Lu Xun always fought against feudal oppression; his early life showed an instinctive sympathy for the masses; his early writings illustrated the same instinctive sympathy for the oppressed; like others, he became disillusioned with the bourgeois revolution of 1911; when he did ally himself with the Communists, he overcame petit bourgeois tendencies he had possessed; and his consequent class awareness was to be seen in all his many activities in the Shanghai decade.[11] Several generations of scholars worked under these pressures. The areas that did not compel one to fabricate views were archival and biographical data and essential tools such as annotations and indexes, and these scholarly endeavors made valuable progress. Many useful compilations along topical lines were made: Lu Xun in each of the cities in which he lived, foreign writings mentioned by him, and many other such topics that became very useful once independent thinking became publishable.[12]

During this time, although critical writings outside China were not under such strictures, the weight of the distortions in China and of its definitions of the issues always had to be dealt with and countered. In any case, as it happened, in academia, the scholarly study of modern and contemporary literature, as opposed to classical literature, was slow to develop. With some notable pioneering exceptions, academia did not take up recent writings until the late 1970s. Thus, in the case of Lu Xun, extensive studies outside China in fact began at about the same time as they were freed up in China.

Lu Xun's history gives rise to two opposite questions: whether his writings would have survived for so long without official enforcement; and the opposite question, whether such rigidity might have harmed his legacy. It is not possible to answer the first, counterfactual question, although the example of Pushkin suggests that the qualities that made for the original impact have staying power whether or not political support is brought to bear. Regarding the second question, whether state rigidity harmed his legacy, for many this must have been the case. The critic Jing Wendong describes two generations of deadening indoctrination: his own when his elementary schoolteachers rendered Lu Xun totally boring to him; and their generation, for, he later realized, they themselves were only recent high school graduates who had been taught "a few [rote] axioms" during the Cultural Revolution with which to instruct their students.[13] Yet there was another side to enforced adulation, for private views became sharper because individually developed, though information on his continuing influence had to await the recollections of readers once they could speak. As was true in the 1920s and 1930s, Lu Xun's subtlety and his antiauthoritarian stance drew devotion from those who discovered them despite the deadening official approbation. Wang Xiaoming, a future biographer (b. 1955), writes of how they aided his solitary growth: "The thinking in them was so deep and the writing so forceful that they entered deep into my soul and consciousness. In those ten plus years [of the Cultural Revolution], whenever my growing awareness encountered some troubling aspect of the world, I would think of Lu Xun."[14] This is a remarkable echo of the influence of the unsponsored Lu Xun of the 1920s, when his writings were avidly sought out, especially by the young. Likewise, Jing Wendong, quoted above, later learned on his own to appreciate Lu Xun. Indeed, as an adult, he counted many colleagues who, like himself, had come to a personal admiration for Lu Xun, in the colleagues' case for the grim solace they found in the temperament and experiences of the older Lu Xun, a "common bitter stance toward society" and "a succor in their darkest moments."[15] These personal accounts exemplify the discoveries that his fiction and essays enabled readers to make on their own, in the face of official interpretations.

This situation finally changed in the late 1980s. The developments that advanced our ability to understand this influential figure can be thought of as being of two types, both far-reaching in their effects. One was political and came about when decentralization in all areas of control allowed some latitude in publicly expressed opinions. By chance, in the West, Leo Ou-fan Lee's pioneering study of Lu Xun was published at this time (1987) and provided an extended demonstration of how an insightful study could steer clear of the issues and theses that had hitherto seemed essential to understanding Lu Xun. About the same time, Lee's editorship of a collection of Lu Xun studies brought together important non-Chinese-language scholarship on many aspects of Lu Xun studies.[16] Within China, calls came for "a return to Lu Xun himself" from critics such as Wang Furen.[17] As the understated Chen Shuyu, whose own publications on Lu Xun were always meticulously factual, remarked in 2000 of the contrast, "Many assumptions about Lu Xun, then axiomatic, have become outdated with the passage of time and the change in circumstances."[18] Interesting studies appeared in China that took part in and contributed to scholarly debate worldwide, from Wang Xiaoming's very personal reading of Lu Xun to the wide-ranging intellectual-psychological studies of Wang Dehou and Wang Hui, and much more.[19]

But half a century of coercion could not be undone simply by the removal of enforcement. In many instances, the pendulum has swung hard the other way. Reevaluation has led many to the presumption that the myth of Lu Xun is all myth, so that the rebuttal of these and other blanket assertions about, for example, Lu Xun's complicity in his posthumous monopoly has consumed much scholarly energy. Gao Xudong has gathered together the work of some of the most vehement critics, including those who, as Gao describes it, want to "remove the halo from Lu Xun's head," to blame him for not having received the Nobel Prize, to lay responsibility for some of the extreme features of the Cultural Revolution on his words, and so on. (Gao defends Lu Xun.) Lin Qingxin also surveys exposé writings that propose, variously, that Lu Xun was "an autocratic character," a purveyor of "an orientalist view of Chinese culture," and "a fabricated national hero." Liu Yukai provides details on many points on which Lu Xun is nowadays condemned, reprinting the major items and incorporating the responses of others in his rejection of these demolition jobs, as does Chen Shuyu in two recent works.[20] The "desanctification" of Lu Xun is well under way.[21] Many of these views make for lively reading, evincing the preemptive critical rhetoric and expressive personalities of a kind unseen since the egoism of the animated 1920s. The view of the critic and novelist Hu Yinqiang, who imputes much of this revisionism to careerism, suggests another parallel with that freewheeling period.[22] At the least, such debunking endeavors illustrate the complications of writing about a figure whose legacy, inside and outside China, is still being rethought.

The other development since the late 1980s is a scholarly one and can be summarized as the growth of cultural studies as it encompassed and altered literary studies. Its impetus stemmed from Antonio Gramsci's idea of culture as the inculcation of an ideological consensus among its members. In literary studies, this meant a conception of literature as a function of large and complex relations among groups and individuals rather than the product of individual lives. Bourdieu mapped these relations in an anthropological approach that removed the hierarchy of literary evaluation as a first feature of historical analysis and replaced it with the idea of a space, a literary field, whose positions are occupied by agents who bring certain traits and capacities to their roles.[23] Its application to Republican China by Michel Hockx likewise provides a model that is not primarily dependent on judgments of relative merits or, more broadly, on the moral evaluation of literary movements such as had elevated the May Fourth writers.[24] In literary-historical terms, it has been clear for a while that a person becomes a canonical writer, *the* canonical writer, owing to a host of circumstances besides the writing itself.

In a parallel scholarly development, a comprehensive rethinking of the overall May Fourth Movement got under way that inevitably affected emblematic figures like Lu Xun. Specifically, their role in accounts of literature of the late 1910s and early 1920s is shrinking, and shrinking with it is our view of their dominance of the first decades of modern culture. As Hockx puts it, "[I]t is time . . . to remove the 'May Fourth' paradigm from the study of modern Chinese literature."[25] Narratives of the heroic and inevitable ascendancy of enlightenment and its literature, views that were put forward as early as 1924 by Hu Shi, are seen as a writing of the past in the service of New Literature.[26] The ten-volume landmark collection *The New Literature of China: A Comprehensive Anthology*, published in 1935–36, was intended by the May Fourth stalwarts to contain the best of their writings from 1917 to 1927 and to be an authoritative summation of an epochal literary period.[27] Now it is possible to see it as an enterprise that both included and excluded by creating a canon and asserting its triumphal progress. As Lydia Liu puts it, "[T]he crux of the claim to legitimacy lay ultimately in the high-powered collective (male) image [it] was calculated to project."[28] Similarly, a collection of articles originating in a 1994 conference is unequivocally titled *The Appropriation of Cultural Capital in China's May Fourth Project*.[29] As for the work marginalized by *The New Literature of China*—that is, the popular press, magazines, and film, the whole consumer-oriented world of commercial communications, as well as the evolving massification of literature (*dazhonghua*) on the left—a large body of studies has now joined Perry Link's pioneering work in *Mandarin Ducks and Butterflies*. Among them is Denise Gimpel's enlightening study of *Short Story Monthly*, which argues that this magazine, even before it was taken over in 1920 by New Literature advocates, already had the credo of teaching new ideas through literary means, though in its case the medium was the old-style love plots in classical language.[30] One of Link's terms, *urban popular fiction*, is flexible enough to embrace a class of writings that, like New Literature, is directed at the new urban population but both predates and survives next to it, having bridged the transition from classical to vernacular language. Previously marginalized works of many kinds are being uncovered and reinstated in the record, not only work by the nonelite but work by the nonpolitical. Besides popular fiction, this includes work by intellectuals who, as Susan Daravula wrote of Zhou Zuoren, "rejected the idea that the mission of literature was to help . . . overcome [China's] inferiority and enable the constitution of a modern Chinese nation."[31] Today May Fourth Literature is situated as only one of many competing ideologies of the time, vying with traditional and nonpolitical writings such as Zhou Zuoren's on the one hand and with popular press and films on the other.

Yet in terms of Lu Xun, there does not have to be a contradiction between focusing on a figure quintessentially identified with the May Fourth paradigm and a scholarly expansion of the frame of reference. It is already happening. In a work focused on Lu Xun, Ni Moyan, using the interesting source of the five reports issued by the Association of Qing Empire Students [in Japan] from 1902 to 1904, places Lu Xun's first years in Tokyo (1902–4) in the context of other Chinese students there.[32] One effect is to remove the possibility of narrating Lu Xun's activities in heroic terms (which he himself never did). As is known, but as Ni shows in great detail, in 1902–4 Tokyo was home to a disproportionate number of the first generation of political and military leaders in the Republic whose activities far outran Lu Xun's. Other areas in which the framework for studying Lu Xun is much enlarged include studies of his income, his finances, and his job at the Ministry of Education (which he held from 1912 to 1925). These shed light on the nitty-gritty of how he made a living and provide a data point in the social history of how well-received writers might make a living.[33] His personal life has also been examined in larger contexts, for example, in Bonnie S. McDougall's study, which uses his relation to Xu Guangping to develop the parameters of a concept of privacy in the modern Chinese context. Some studies in this area are, as might be imagined, more mixed in motives and quality, but the many complications of his home and personal life can be linked to the opening up of personal lives that many in his and the next generation experienced as shown in Haiyan Lee's study and, to a lesser degree, they also provide a glimpse of the lives that were shed along the way.[34] The economics of the small-press magazines he and his young followers founded, the lines of patronage, the developing programs of publication—these topics, formerly treated in studies whose tone tended to render Lu Xun unique, now place him more firmly in the literary practices of early modern writing. The many interesting questions that arise cumulatively have the effect of placing Lu Xun closer to the other practitioners of the craft of writing and of identifying May Fourth Literature as one stream among many. The difference is that this need not be feared as diminishing a figure or a movement but can be intellectually welcomed.

Aside from the tussles among specialists, Lu Xun's writings continue to play a significant part in public discourse in many arenas. His continued inclusion in textbooks means that he remains a potent common reference point for the educated. In the Tian'anmen Square Incident of 1989, which ended a period of official toleration of dissent, the college students quoted from "Diary of a Madman" and "In Memory of Liu Hezhen" in the rallying cries and manifestoes that punctuated the months-long demonstrations in the square. After the protests were ended by armored military forces, with deaths in numbers that are still uncounted today, the earliest memorial writings quoted again from Lu Xun and used his words as the titles of their collections.[35] Sixteen years later, in 2005, another vivid example came when the essay "In Memory of Liu Hezhen" was again invoked to indict a government that carried out violence against its own people. This time the government had violently suppressed farmer demonstrations in many provinces. This use of government force had been completely censored from the news, roads to the villages had been blocked, and communications were cut off. Within China, only on Internet bulletin boards were these one-sided struggles publicized and then only for a brief time before they were shut down. On one Internet bulletin board, contributors discussed "In Memory of Liu Hezhen" as a means of expressing their anger and frustration. Interestingly, the site that used this transparent screen lasted slightly longer online.[36] These poignant instances of Lu Xun's continued influence are spontaneous in a way that the official policies of the previous half century were not, but it should also be noted that, like official policies, they show a standardized, narrow selectivity about the meaning of Lu Xun's writings that is an outcome of state-produced educational materials.

At various levels of government, Lu Xun continues to be a valuable name. There are the establishment awards and institutes named after him but also more enterprising ventures, a proposal once to make a Lu Xun wine, for example, although that was shot down. The city of Shaoxing has created in three-dimensional solidity a "Luzhen" (one of his two fictional locales) as a theme park populated by reenactors.[37] Finally, a recent development threatens this common language, which is already narrower than it might be: his inclusion in textbooks is undergoing changes, of which the most unpromising is a decrease in the number of selections. The reasoning in official educational circles is not known, but outside speculation ranges from dumbing down to the desire to prevent continued access to common reference points to, most benignly, the need to make space for more recent writings.[38]

The psychological marker of the new millennium and the centennial mark of many key events of the late Qing, early Republican era have produced many titles that are variations of the ideas of a new Lu Xun for the times or a Lu Xun for the new times.[39] Like them, this study seeks a renewal of his legacy, although that is not pegged to a milestone. Its context is indicated by my subtitle, *Lu Xun Interprets China*. This allows a critical distance from his views while placing the emphasis on the greatest goals of his writing. In both fiction and essays, Lu Xun sought to offer his readers a usable understanding of China from which to proceed. In addition, in his classical poetry of the 1930s he revealed, largely for private circulation, a more tormented view of the nation and the role of the individual. This study analyzes a number of these influential writings under a subtitle that implicitly places his efforts among those of other interpreters of China, literary and otherwise, who had similar goals and it implicitly sets his work alongside other interpretations of China in other types of undertakings. Readers who are primarily interested in ways of understanding China rather than in Lu Xun specifically should thus find this framework relevant to their interests, for his vast influence deserves a readership much beyond literature.

There are many ways to look at how Lu Xun interprets China. The approach of this study is named in the elements of its title: *Memory, Violence, Queues*. It proposes that these elements can provide unusual access, via his written views, to both the stated and the unexpressed dimensions of these views. Of the three, memory and violence have been frequent topics in literary and cultural studies, whereas the queue is almost never discussed. This study aims to shed new light on the two familiar topics both in themselves and by joining them with the phenomenon of the queue and treating the three as interconnected factors. Their recurrent appearance in Lu Xun's life and writings proves to be a fruitful starting point for the investigations in successive chapters. Moreover, each feature is shown to undergo changes over the course of his lifetime: violence in the objective world, and memory and the queue in their subjective meanings and values. An overview of these features is provided in chapter 1. This study is not a comprehensive survey or analysis of Lu Xun's works but intends to provide an integrated view of a writer by selecting, as needed, from all the genres in which he wrote, from all time periods, and from works of different degrees of familiarity.

Regarding the subtitle, *Lu Xun Interprets China*, this study does not take that interpretation to be unitary. That the elements of memory and violence, and the significance of the queue all change over time is sufficient to ensure that his views changed. Rather, each chapter presents a certain interpretation of China that Lu Xun makes in particular works at a particular point in time, even though what he had to say was often retrospectively smoothed out and read in a more consistent way. After a first chapter that is necessary to lay out the complicated territory of writing about Lu Xun, the chapters move forward in selected time segments beginning with his student days in Japan in 1902 and ending with his death in 1936. Within each period, the chapter selects writings whose analysis allows access to his unstated attitudes and feelings concerning China. In chapter 2, the focus is on a time when anti–Qing dynasty activities, whose base was then in Japan, awakened a response in him that was both action—he cut his queue in 1903—and writing (a poem and a number of essays, in classical language). Action and writing are analyzed together. The next chapter moves ahead fifteen years to the early years of the May Fourth Movement, when the new elite was establishing its web of cultural production in a Beijing that was controlled by the dictatorship of first Yuan Shikai and then Duan Qirui. This chapter shows that certain essays and short stories, including his most famous work, "The True Story of Ah Q," can be read as a sustained effort on his part to bring into fiction, in a significant way, China's major political events of both the present and the recent revolutionary past. In this and the final two chapters, his memory connects the present to the past in a way that can be traced in the writings. Chapter 4 moves on to the last years of his life, when he lived in Shanghai. It shows how the 1931 executions of five young writers who became known as the Five Martyrs, victims of internecine conflict between the Nationalist Party and the banned Communist Party and within the Communist Party, are connected to the poem of 1903 and thus to the past. This connection brings about a rereading of the essays and classical poems Lu Xun wrote in the 1930s to reveal aspects of life and work in a Shanghai that was divided among foreign concessions while a war with Japan loomed. Chapter 5 focuses on his last two years, 1934–36. This chapter introduces new material consisting of depictions by others of his fiction and his person during those years and uses it to interpret the activities and writings of his last years. In the four chapters that follow the introduction, the material and approach change as the material requires. Continuity is provided by the common elements of memory, violence, and the queue and by the kind of insights yielded by the material. The framework outlined here allows a different choice of writings than convention suggests, permits new insights into his creative process as his life changed over time, and, not least important, restores historicity to his interpretations of China.

The corollary to "Lu Xun interprets China" is "China interprets Lu Xun." For a writer of his stature and chosen subject matter, the latter is inevitable, and this aspect will inevitably have a role in the analyses here. Both in his lifetime and afterward, his readers asked much of him as a public figure. As his stature grew, increasing numbers and factions of readers and diverse literary and political movements contested for their own perspectives on the meaning of his writings, on which he remained nearly completely silent. After his death, the Communist Party took over the interpretation, with results whose ramifications are even now embedded in interpretations and difficult to sort out.

A final question to consider in undertaking a new study of Lu Xun is how he can be situated in the context of world literature. It is obvious that on the world stage he does not have nearly the omnipresence that he has in China among the educated. To embark on a non-Chinese-language study is to make some kind of claim on attention outside China greater than what he has now, in particular a claim on the English-reading world, given the language of this study. Such a claim can safely rely on his high literary qualities and his pivotal cultural role at a critical historical time. This is the reliance implicit in many literary studies, including this one. The question, however, is more problematic when regarded from the reader's side: what kind of attention can the world spare for an unfamiliar figure from the past? One difficulty faced by a retroactive project such as this is that there is nothing in communal world memory to revive from the 1920s and 1930s of his writing life.

Today knowledge of Lu Xun is most reliably found in anthologies aimed at college courses, themselves a direct outcome of scholarly attention. Quicker to expand their purview of the past than other arbiters and tasked with including traditionally omitted categories, in this case, modern Asian literature, college anthologies have given Lu Xun and other writers a more secure spot than is found elsewhere. This is not a trivial measure, for anthologies and courses deal in a continual canonization process while operating within strict limits of curricular space and time, but the consequences of inclusion will be slow to have an effect in the wider world. Outside the classroom, among the general educated public, knowledge of Lu Xun has reached a higher level than at any previous time, in step with China's considerable and increasing importance to the United States and the world, in cultural matters as well as economic. Today English-language references to Lu Xun abound. In Ian Buruma's wide-ranging works, for instance, Lu Xun is a frequent touchstone. The contemporary American novelist Ha Jin is well known to be an admirer, as are the British writer Ma Jian and the Japanese Nobel Laureate, Ōe Kenzaburō. In the current boom in films and translated novels from China, directors and writers also frequently refer to Lu Xun in their interviews with Western media. Australia, geographically closer to China, has a prime minister who opened his keynote speech at Beijing University in 2007, where Lu Xun had taught, with an extended discourse on Lu Xun's pertinence to China. In 2008, Lu Xun's essay "Remembrance in Order to Forget" was read on the radio by actors and poets in Germany, Slovenia, and Hungary in an annual literary commemoration against "the political lie."[40] The next year, on the twentieth anniversary of the Tian'anmen Square Incident, many reports outside China— it was not marked inside China—featured interviews with participants who repeatedly quoted his words, as they had twenty years earlier. Examples like this suggest that the audience for Lu Xun is wider than a solely academic one.

A practical difficulty with getting Lu Xun wider recognition than the fragmentary evidence above is that it has to be retroactively achieved. He is sometimes put forward as China's entry into the world stakes of great writers, but lacking the branding of a Nobel Prize in Literature, there is no quick method for substantiating this to readers unacquainted with his name. It is too late for a simple shorthand like the Nobel, which, although its actual charge is much vaguer, is popularly felt to bestow a "best writer" status on its recipient.[41] During Lu Xun's lifetime, the Asian slot in European attention was taken by India's Rabindranath Tagore (1861–1941), whose reputation was aided by his extensive travels in Europe and America (with a short, controversial visit to China in 1924) and confirmed by his 1913 receipt of the Nobel Prize in Literature. After Tagore, there was no more space for an Asian until well after World War II, when Japan's Kawabata Yasunari (1899–1972) was made laureate in 1968. From the pre–World War II era, in terms of world literature, Tagore is the sole Asian writer who has a reputation that can be revived rather than created.

For Lu Xun, there was a moment in 1926 when that card of international recognition might have turned up. His novella "The True Story of Ah Q" was translated into French, and a comment on it was made by Romain Rolland, himself a Nobel laureate in literature in 1915. As reported by the translator, Jing Yinyu, Rolland said, in a letter to *Europe: revue mensuelle*, the magazine he edited that subsequently published Jing's translation, "The story of Ah Q is a superb work of art, the proof being that I felt it was even better on the second reading, The miserable appearance of the pitiful Ah Q lingers in my memory."[42]

Although words to this effect were relayed by more than one source and widely quoted in China, this fragment of literary history might have moldered, except that in the 1980s two trends met to renew interest in this moment. On the one side was an obsession, a "Nobel complex," in which obtaining the validation of the Nobel in literature was, as Julia Lovell writes, "promoted to a level of official policy" on a par with securing the Olympics or World Cup and entry into World Trade Organization.[43] Caught up in this trend, Romain Rolland's comment was inflated into a near brush with world literary history. It seemed to be lent substance by the information that Lu Xun received, via three intermediaries, an inquiry from the Swedish Academy. (We know this only from a letter he wrote to the final contact, if a contact is what he was.)[44] On the other side was the debunking of the author that had begun with the same loosening of political control in the 1980s. Here critics were happy to cite Lu Xun's responses, which, to them, show that he was almost angling for a Nobel and thus lacking in lofty disinterest. They point to energetic measures that were undertaken in China to promote Romain Rolland and by extension Rolland's words on "Ah Q," seeing in them Lu Xun's influence.[45]

Nonetheless, the evidence is so fleeting and so many stars would have had to be in alignment, not to mention the active cooperation required of a notoriously self-willed author, that this latter-day contretemps in Lu Xun studies, as is often the case, turns out to tell more about the interpreters than their subject.

It is true that, to some degree, Lu Xun was known outside China in his lifetime, for beginning in the mid-1920s there were translations into English, French, Russian, and Japanese. For the most part, however, his international champions tended to be confirmed leftists active in political circles, an indication of how his 1927 choice to ally himself with the Communist Party came to direct his reception. While he was alive, his supporters in English-language translations were leftists or communists such as Edgar Snow, Nym Wales, and Agnes Smedley.[46] His translators into Russian came from the center of the communist movement, and, as Irene Eber notes, they found him not sufficiently proletarian in his stance.[47] The Japanese situation was somewhat different. There initial interest in Lu Xun also came from left-wing and communist writers, but in Japan the task was to rekindle interest among the educated in a culture that had formerly been important to their worldview. Thus, when the leftists were suppressed, academics were predisposed by tradition to succeed them in taking an interest in Lu Xun.[48] All in all, despite these translations, if Tagore is used as a point of comparison, it is clear that in his lifetime Lu Xun's name was not nearly at the same level of international recognition.

To return to what kind of attention can be obtained for a figure like Lu Xun, current discussions concerning the idea of world literature are pertinent. In *What Is World Literature?* David Damrosch takes as his starting point Goethe's vision that "the epoch of world literature is at hand" and finds that nearly two centuries later the obstacles encountered by any work seeking an entry point are even greater. He suggests that rather than focusing on the makeup of world literature, we think of it as "less a [fixed] set of works than a network," "a mode of circulation and of reading" that includes "all literary works that circulate beyond their culture of origin." In this model, "works of literature take on new lives as they move into the world at large," at which point they are "reframed in . . . translations and . . . new cultural contexts." An interesting aspect of his model is its calm acceptance of a divorce between an author's original contexts and language and his current circulation in the world through translation. Indeed, Damrosch makes the stronger argument that "far from inevitably suffering a loss of authenticity or essence, a work can gain in many ways" in translation.[49] Milan Kundera, writing in a similar vein, gives a warning from an author's perspective that is consistent with this push: if his work cannot cross national or linguistic boundaries, this is a limitation that "reduces the entire meaning of a work to the role it plays in its homeland."[50] In this formulation of world literature, a critical study (as opposed to a translation) may hope to guide the ways in which an author is received in the new culture.

World literature as a network: this is what Lu Xun and many others in the Republican era practiced. In the nineteenth century, their Qing-dynasty predecessors had begun the translation of works from, chiefly, Europe, translations that introduced new information and ideas. Intellectuals of the succeeding Republican era who were Western oriented accelerated this pace. The influential intellectual role the West played in China over these several generations is a major topic in scholarship. Lu Xun was one of many in the first decades of the twentieth century who, beginning in their student days, sat and read and wrote letters to get more to read, gathering to them a web of all the wonders of the world, artistic, literary, political, and more, as can be seen in, for example, Theodore Huters's *Bringing the World Home*. They were importing, and translating, world literature and employing art objects from the world in order to join it. The same New Literature people who wrote the essays and fiction designed to galvanize their fellow Chinese also did the translations of figures such as Henrik Ibsen, Anton Chekhov, Fyodor Dostoyevsky, and many others to replace the Confucian heroes. A current version of this phenomenon is brought up in Mark Gamsa's remark about today's writers, who, after a gap of seven decades, again see "no need to apologize for ignoring native literature." A common view of the China of this early era has been unidirectional, for it is seen as struggling with the impact of the West. With regard to literary figures, however, we can see Lu Xun and his contemporaries as participating in world culture. In this case there is a place for Chinese literary history among world literary histories. As Raoul Findeisen puts it, East-Asian European interliterary communication in the late Qing-late Meiji periods" may offer "a model for globalized literature," and the example of its actors may "serve as a moral incentive."[51] Although the range of Lu Xun's references was remarkably wide, he was not uniquely alert.[52] Many intellectuals of these decades took as a natural goal the acquisition of a deep familiarity with the canons of Western culture. For those who were creative writers, their range was not a mere display of erudition but spoke to an interior life that could not be satisfied only by the examples found in national literature. Today this situation is familiar from the examples of writers as disparate as Milan Kundera and Ōe Kenzaburō, and in the next generation Orhan Pamuk, who have readily found kindred qualities in the cultures of other traditions.

Moreover, the comprehensiveness of such interests at the turn of the previous century is indicated by the way the attention of Lu Xun, his contemporaries, and their predecessors was not turned to literature alone. From the beginning, the magazines they founded included artwork, in particular introducing the artistic heritage of the West. In his classic account of his resolve to leave medical school, Lu Xun names both literature and art as the means he believed would alter men's thinking. "At that time," he wrote, "I thought that naturally this would be done through the promotion of literature and art (*tui wenyi*) and so I thought to promote a literature and art movement (*wenyi yundong*)." His next sentence makes this joint goal even clearer, for he writes of how in Tokyo at the time "no student was studying literature or art (*wenxue he meishu*)."[53]

When it came to creative writing, Lu Xun was again among many in the May Fourth period and beyond whose productions were a response to this living network of literature from other nations. Both when he began his writing life during his years in Japan and again when he resumed it in 1918, he consciously created in the context of other literatures. His writings in Japan, then mostly translations, culminated in the selection of writers from Eastern Europe in his and his brother's 1908 *Anthology of Fiction from Foreign Lands*. Twelve years later, when he began writing again under more receptive conditions, he created his fiction chiefly with reference to the techniques and qualities and density of emotion to be found in his European models. Furthermore, it is probably a characteristic of the value that Damrosch suggests is added to literature encountered in translation that Lu Xun was drawn to foreign literatures for reasons wider than literature itself: from the beginning he felt that literature was a profound, even a necessary, component of understanding the world, so much so that, like Ōe today, he later quietly moved away from fiction to a more direct confrontation with the world.

These considerations suggest that there is a certain ready-made historical place in world literature for Lu Xun. This relates to his position in the time of his nation. There are writers who stand at the juncture of their nations' transition from traditional hierarchies to industrialized ones or from colonialism to nationhood. The works of such writers give incisive expression to the issues raised in that transition, often by exposing the abuses and contradictions in that society or by capturing the confusions that arise for individuals caught in its wake. The writers themselves become emblems of the nation that emerged. Language is also critical: the writer's work comes at a time when reform of the language or the creation of a usable vernacular has become urgent. Lu Xun was such a writer for China. In these terms, world literature provides many analogous figures among whom we may place Lu

Xun. To name only those that he himself admired in his youth, we find the figures of Alexander Pushkin (1799–1837) and Nikolai Gogol (1809–52) of Russia, Adam Mickiewicz (1789–1855) of Poland, Sándor Petőfi (1823–49) of Hungary, and Jose Rizal (1861–96) of the Philippines. Lord Byron (1788–1824), in his role as a champion of Greek independence, is a variation on that pattern. Except for Rizal, all are cited in his 1907 essay "The Power of Mara Poetry."[54] The place he occupies in world literature is parallel in historical terms to these other figures, all esteemed in their own cultures for similar reasons. Moreover, since Lu Xun's time, the era of decolonization has brought to the world's attention many more such pivotal figures. As countries emerged from their colonial definition into an uncertain nationhood, writers who addressed issues of national identity, often from exile (Nigeria's Chinua Achebe [b. 1930]) or prison (Indonesia's Pramoedya Ananta Toer [1925–2006]), continue into the present a role largely familiar in its parameters. To place Lu Xun in the line of these writers, which stretches back a century before his own time and forward into our own, is to provide him with peers at a high level. Like them, his role can be continually clarified by the attention of dispassionate studies.

1

Renewing a Seminal Literary Figure

Lu Xun was the first and in time, the most prominent of a remarkably creative group of activists who in the late 1910s and early 1920s sought to bring about fundamental cultural and social changes through the creation of a modern literature. The earliest activists produced the rationale and the publishing infrastructure for a new literature, while it was Lu Xun's fiction and essays that, beginning in May 1918, led the way and came to hold the attention of readers in the most intense manner. His fiction used character types recognizable from society but never seen in its literature in the simultaneously realistic and metaphorical style that he employed. His earliest stories indicted the backwardness and passivity of the "national character" and the hypocrisy of the prevailing Confucian ethic in works whose tone, point of view, and structure were all new. Their thrust was electrifying, their language and forms no less so. After an initial period of puzzlement, they struck a highly responsive chord in his readers. His essays, for their part, beseeched, excoriated, and harangued his countrymen to recognize their responsibilities as humans and as Chinese. They took on a full range of social and cultural issues while introducing an intense, vernacular style mixed with classical elements that has come to be known as the Lu Xun style. As the fundamentally new nature of his writings in the Chinese context was recognized, their effect became vast. Characters like Ah Q from the novella "The True Story of Ah Q" and phrases like the sarcastically used "national essence" quickly became a shorthand for the condition of a backward China in a modern world and gained a permanent place in modern consciousness. The young were especially responsive. Many stressed their sense of personal discovery in comments such as "There is the desert; then there is Lu Xun," and "I read them all once, sometimes twice, as they came out."[1] Over the nearly two decades that followed the first story, this intense sense of recognition on the part of readers was consolidated by further fiction, essays, and short memoirs, works that caught and defined many of the political and social turning points as they arose in the new nation. Well before his death in 1936 and despite the deep political divisions that had opened up within the new elite, Lu Xun had become the most prominent literary figure of the emerging modern China.

The New Literature that was thus inaugurated grew quickly, as new authors and periodicals appeared and literary associations were formed at an accelerating pace. It covered every literary genre and spilled over into the political and social activism of the May Fourth Movement, which began the following year when, through boycotts and demonstrations in cities nationwide, students and merchants announced their intention to play a role in the national crisis. In literature, the term *May Fourth Literature* came to be used as often as *New Literature*, the words summing up a fervent, creative period. As the most influential and earliest figure of this remarkable time and generation of writers, Lu Xun indeed occupies a unique position at a certain pivotal juncture in China's history and in literature.

His uniqueness was the sum of many factors of talent and timing, but certainly one key was his singular ability to convey a view of China that did indeed galvanize his readers, "awakening" them, as he put it, from their sleep in an iron house that threatened to suffocate them. He was able to use new language and literary forms to render situations of profound human reality that were at the same time clearly metaphorical of China. At its simplest, his short fiction exposed as pious claims and hypocrisies the social relationships by which traditional Chinese society organized itself. Such indictments were revelatory to his readers and supplied the moral fulcrum for their own lives and developing views. Writing in 1941, Chi-chen Wang invokes the intense sense of personal connection between Lu Xun's writings and his and his brother's struggle to break free. On the dedication page of his translation of the fiction, this is how he recollects the effect of reading Lu Xun.

> [He was the writer] whom we both admired above all other Chinese writers, ancient and modern, and who did more than any one else to clear the Road to Life of the weeds of tradition and of the traps and pitfalls that man-eating men set for the young, the unwary, and the helpless.[2]

(Evidently Wang's older brother, like the oldest brother in Ba Jin's *Family*, whom we will meet later, died trapped, young, unwary, and helpless.) Such heartfelt testimony gives us a glimpse of an era when words from the avant-garde centers of Beijing and Shanghai could reach directly into traditional families and create in their young a different set of goals.

The next two sections in this chapter provide an overview of Lu Xun's writings and a narrative of his life. They contain information that is well known to Lu Xun specialists and available in English in studies such as the excellent ones by Leo Ou-fan Lee and David E. Pollard.[3] Whether or not to restate this information, even in a purposeful restatement, is always a difficult decision. Its inclusion here is owing to a variety of reasons. One is that even a monograph needs to begin at some point near the baseline, with the difference that a monograph accelerates quickly to specialized analyses, as this one will. These sections are also useful for readers who are interested in Lu Xun for nonspecialist reasons and will need some organized reminder of the facts and dates that are pertinent to this study. I also want to provide the basic information with emphases that are useful for this study. The specialist will see that the account picks its way among the many possible approaches to exploring his life and work while emphasizing, as a prelude to the analyses of the later chapters, the author's portrayals of China. A final reason is that writing about Lu Xun is complicated territory. For historical reasons, there is no such thing as a plain summary of either his writings or his life. The account of his life offered here illustrates this important point. Unless one lists only a chronology of dates and events, any narrative of Lu Xun's life is dogged by the history of his reception and the consequent controversies. The one presented here thus also serves as a sampling of the problems and methodologies of writing about Lu Xun.

A Brief View of the Writing

Lu Xun's fiction was nearly always more than its simplest level of exposure and indictment, although it was never missing this layer. The complex participation of his characters in their own fate is only one of many features by which his work hinted at difficulties in the optimistic dreams of new goals. Many of his stories contain tragedies in which the difficulty of assigning blame shows that the arrangements under which a society operates cannot be simply swept away by being shown up as self-serving.

Lu Xun's first piece of writing, however, was not like this, for it had a simple, effective message. In its brief span, "Diary of a Madman" brought readers to see in a damning and comprehensive way the cannibalism that is Chinese society.[4] The story is told through the diary entries of a madman who thinks that people are plotting to eat him and gradually realizes that others have already been eaten before him. Neighbors, their village headman come in from the country, the physician brought to see him, and finally even his brother say things that betray their cunning plans. All things need to be researched, he knows, and so he begins to search the histories for further cases of cannibalism, but he finds that his history contains no dates. Its pages are covered with only the words *humaneness* (*renyi*) and *morality* (*daode*). As he peers at them all night long, he begins to see seeping through the lines the words *eat people* (*chiren*). In this way, the author creates the metaphor that all of Chinese history is an undated stretch of cannibalism veiled by the sacred values of *renyi* and *daode*.

Although its message was simple, "Diary" was not immediately understood. Its technique of seeing the truth solely through the delusions of a madman was too strange to a readership whose experience in Western literature in translation ran to the lengthy direct narratives of Alexandre Dumas and Jules Verne. By contrast, Lu Xun drew his models from the dark, dense short stories of Eastern European writers, whose stories, as Lu Xun observed in 1920, seemed to be over before they began.[5] Even so, readers of *New Youth* had a sense that something was waiting to be understood. Mao Dun, who was twenty-two at the time, described its mesmerizing effect on him: he felt a sense of invigorating stimulus, of emerging into light after long darkness, of an indescribable sad kind of happiness. He was like someone who liked to eat peppers and felt that the hotter they were the better.[6] Light after long darkness, sad kind of happiness, hot peppers—these are his effective similes for an instinctive groping toward understanding. Their very newness satisfied a kind of longing.

During the same period, on the essay front, clearly stated attacks directed at established social compacts supplemented this enigmatic story. The essays, also published in *New Youth* under the deceptively spontaneous heading "Random Thoughts," showed a China whose vaunted cultural values were empty, self-serving conveniences: the value of chastity in widows is forced on them by men who benefit from the prestige bestowed, the desire to have sons is a gloating credit to oneself, and pride in "national characteristics" is mere self-congratulation.[7] Commonplace observations now perhaps, but they were eye-opening then. In the same essays, with amazingly direct sincerity, he urged that his readers "swear to get rid of the meaningless suffering that blights our lives," that children be brought up carefully "for the modern world," and that the characteristics one takes pride in must be carefully chosen. Such advice must have been inspiring to his young readers. To quote Mao Dun again, he said that while he could not understand the fiction, the essays fired him up and motivated him to keep an eye out for this remarkable name, Lu Xun.

In the same issue of *New Youth* in which "Diary" appeared, Lu Xun published, under the pseudonym Tang Si, three vernacular-language, free-verse poems that concerned another facet of the rejection of traditions, that is, they addressed the question of what to place in their stead.[8] Interestingly, the poems' answer was that some kind of personal freedom should be sought in the area of love. The poems, however, never caught on as far as readers were concerned, and Lu Xun himself only wrote a few more in the vernacular language. In the 1930s, when he began to write poetry again, it was in traditional verse forms and the classical language, and they were nearly all privately circulated.

In any case, after "Diary" came "Kong Yiji." Already with this second story, complexities enter Lu Xun's portrayal of society. Named after the title character (actually a mocking nickname given him), this work shows readers the pathos and harshness of failure in traditional China, where only one route, holding office, was acceptable for the gentry. Kong, who has the same surname as Confucius, has failed the examinations for office many times and now does odd copying jobs for the gentry. He steals from his employers to pay for drink and is beaten when caught. This story is more complex than "Diary" in that it exposes both human nature and Chinese society, for it shows a world where all participate in a kind of natural cruelty. The gentry, who are unseen, are vindictive: near the story's end, when Kong has been once again caught stealing, speculation is that the gentry beat him all night and that is why his legs are broken. But they are not the only ones. At the tavern, the story's setting, everyone is part of the cruelty: the customers amuse themselves trying to get Kong to admit to the cause of his injuries; the owner leads the fun to amuse his customers; the children spot him as an easy touch for cadging aniseed beans; and the young helper at the bar, who is the narrator, instinctively spurns the defeated man's attempt to teach him to read a few words useful for keeping accounts. This story, reported to be Lu Xun's favorite,[9] contains many more complexities than does the allegory of "Diary." People are not divided between the eaters and the eaten, although this is the interpretation provided in Chinese textbooks.

Beginning with these two works, a string of outstanding fiction that gave varying, mostly grim, portrayals of China further opened Lu Xun's writing career. With one exception, "A Story about Hair" (see chapter 3), his earliest short fiction became thoroughly familiar to readers, and the briefest allusions to its characters and settings were instantly recognized. Four especially are frequently anthologized ("Kong Yiji," "Medicine," "Hometown," and "The True Story of Ah Q") and are included in textbooks from elementary through college levels. "Medicine" is an intricately structured story with a simple plot in which a poor father and mother must plan to benefit from the execution of a revolutionary because they have been persuaded that his fresh blood, used as medicine, can save their son. Considering only the portrait of China in this story, we see that it is a society in which both the victim and the beneficiaries are among the innocent, while in the center are the callous, who enjoy the importance of being present at and making deals about exciting events. "Hometown" tells of a narrator, an intellectual who, as Lu Xun had, returns to his hometown to move his family to Beijing and sees again a childhood friend, then a peasant farmer's son and now a peasant himself. His efforts to talk him are met only with respectful replies. This is a China that puts in place unbridgeable separations. At the story's end, it is not clear that he can persuade himself that things will be different for the next generation.

Lu Xun's most important work of fiction, "The True Story of Ah Q," presents the most complex view of China. It was published under a new pseudonym, Baren (meaning man from Sichuan), so readers of the initial installments could not rely on their built-up knowledge of the works of "Lu Xun." However, halfway through the installments, Mao Dun provided a key that linked it to familiar purposes: "I kept feeling that Ah Q was familiar, and then, ah yes, I saw that he was the crystallization of the Chinese character!"[10] After the last installment was published, Zhou Zuoren provided further assistance: "We see written out the great fundamental weakness of the Chinese people."[11] The crystallization of the Chinese character is a village layabout and odd-job man who prides himself on transforming defeats into "spiritual victories" and on other self-deluding stratagems. Many events and situations are developed around Ah Q in the novella, culminating in the arrival of the 1911 Republican Revolution to the village, a farce that indirectly leads to Ah Q's death. Almost immediately, the words *Ah Q-ism* and *Ah Q type* entered the language as criticism and self-criticism.

The energy of iconoclasm and exposure in these stories captured the readers of New Literature. The young people of Ba Jin's 1933 novel *Family*, set in the May Fourth period in Chengdu, Sichuan, illustrate the excitement this break engendered among the young elite. In one of its first chapters, two brothers go to their eldest brother's office carrying the latest issue of *New Tide* (*Xin chao*), founded at Beijing University in 1919. They have secured the last copy in Chengdu because the newsstand owner has been keeping it for them. Their female cousin comes to the office, and together they pore over it avidly. In earlier scenes, the brothers had told her with excitement that a new teacher the next year will be a man named Wu Yu. "You know," they said, "his essays have been published in *New Youth*." This is insider May Fourth information indeed. Wu Yu was a native of Chengdu and did indeed publish in *New Youth*. In fact, his first essay analyzed "Diary of a Madman" at a time when it was still not well understood. His title, "Eating People and Ritual Propriety," emphasized the story's metaphor: ritual propriety equals eating people.[12] In *Family*, there is another vignette depicting the enthusiasm of the young where Ba Jin portrays the female cousin carefully studying the letters column in *New Youth* in her room, imitating its prose style and copying its punctuation.[13] Placed at the novel's beginning, these several scenes set the stage for each of the three brothers' struggle to free himself from the suffocating demands of the family. The three brothers and their cousin, like Chi-chen Wang and his brother quoted above, search for "the freedom and independence to which he was stranger all his life," and, like Wang's brother, they draw inspiration from New Literature. The name of the magazine *New Youth*, which had sought Lu Xun's contributions, contains both of those components, new and youth, and declared their break with tradition. *New Tide* declared the same with its English title, *Renaissance*. The influence of the New Culture Movement described in *Family* shows that Lu Xun's works were part of the greater history of how new forms of dissemination and consumption created a common culture with which the new elite identified themselves.

After five years, Lu Xun collected fifteen short stories into *Call to Arms* (*Nahan*).[14] The accolades for the collection were euphoric. By this time, an active literary world had come into existence. As early as in the May 1921 issue of *Short Story Monthly*, Mao Dun was able to begin a quarterly survey of the new writing. He reported that from April to June, counting just what he had seen, there were in existence more than 120 works of fiction (probably short stories) and 8 play scripts and that these numbers represented a one-third increase over the figures for the quarter before.[15] In this much more populated world, *Call to Arms* was nonetheless hailed as a unique marker.

> The short story collection has been published for which we must rewrite the history of Chinese literature, for this volume is its "epochal demarcation." We in Shanghai have already seen it; we have seen that cover of vermillion red and those four characters: "Nahan" and "Lu Xun."[16]

Like the young people in *Family* who study every feature of their magazines, this passage shows that the elements of newness were not limited to the words alone: the very design and color of the cover (which incidentally were Lu Xun's) were received as part of the comprehensive break with tradition. Today it is still sometimes reproduced as a design element on the covers of new printings.

After *Call to Arms*, short stories and essays of great influence continued to come from his pen. The stories increased in profundity, notable examples being "New Year's Sacrifice," "Upstairs at the Tavern," and "The Loner," but beneath their increasing technical and moral complexity, the view of traditional society as one that stifled lives and trapped or killed its members was already in place. In 1926, eleven more were collected in a second anthology, *Hesitation* (*Panghuang*). Not every work in the two anthologies is in this serious vein. Short fiction that exemplifies other aspects of his wide technical and thematic range includes "Regret for the Past," a tragedy of modern love recounted through the male protagonist's self-deluding memory, and "Soap," a domestic comedy in which again the male protagonist is the self-deceiving person.

The two collections *Call to Arms* and *Hesitation*, small as they are, form the core of his high standing and great influence. With *Hesitation*, the fiction ceased, or at least fiction as it was classified by critics and readers until the late 1990s when the 1935 collection *Old Tales Retold* began to receive more critical attention. This last anthology, as the title indicates, contains imaginative retellings of traditional myths and anecdotes, eight in all. With the rise of critical attention, it began to be referred to as the third collection of Lu Xun's fiction, and so it is, though fiction of a very different sort than that included in *Call to Arms* or *Hesitation*.[17] Lu Xun himself used the term *yanyi* to describe these embellished myths ("romance," as in historical romance), whereas he used *xiaoshuo* for the other two collections (xiaoshuo in its modern, Japanese loanword sense, means "modern fiction" or "short fiction").[18] On the basis of his distinction, in this study *fiction* will refer to the first two collections, sometimes further specified as *xiaoshuo* fiction. Because of its late date, both in Lu Xun's lifetime and in comparison with the dates of the other two anthologies, *Old Tales Retold* is only beginning to exert an influence in the interpretation of Lu Xun and, as it happens, does not enter the purview of these chapters. If we look at only the *xiaoshuo* fiction, we see a certain asymmetry in that it took up only eight years of Lu Xun's writing life, while the essays continued for a further ten years until the week before his death.

Early in 1926, the year in which *Hesitation* was published, something happened that directly injected violence into Lu Xun's life and had the effect of consolidating his personal stature as a writer. On March 18, 1926, many students held a demonstration in Beijing against the Duan Qirui government, protesting its weak response to Japanese territorial demands. Afterward a large group went on to demonstrate in front of the main government office. As they massed there, the gates to the courtyard were closed, soldiers opened fire, and forty-seven students were killed and hundreds wounded. One of the dead was a student of Lu Xun's at Beijing Women's Normal College. For her he wrote "In Memory of Liu Hezhen," an essay that became the most influential commemoration of the massacre and the beginning point for all later accounts of the national outpouring of grief and anger. "The darkest day of the Republic," he termed that day.[19] He condemned a government of "murderers" who killed women and children in acts of "evil and cruelty" that were "beyond imagining."[20] From this point to the end of his life a decade later, his personal standing, his many essays, and the frequent reprints of his two fiction collections kept such views continually and influentially before the public.

Lu Xun's essays, which he also began to write in 1918, continued until the week of his death, carrying out their separate but coordinated work with the fiction, for they expressed in topical terms what the fiction conveyed via characters and plot. He compiled a first collection of the essays in 1925, entitled *Hot Air* (*Refeng*), and a second in 1926, entitled *Unlucky Star* (*Huagai ji*). Then in 1926–27, with the help of "some friends who collected, copied, and proofread, using up time that can never be retrieved," he undertook a number of retrospective projects.[21] He collected his writings in Japan from twenty years earlier into *Grave* (*Fen,* 1927), adding also more recent ones. Also in 1927, he published the ten memoir-style essays of *Dawn Blossoms Gathered at Dusk* (*Zhaohua xishi*) and the dark and often obscure prose poems of *Weeds* (*Yecao*). Once settled in Shanghai, many more collections followed, fourteen before his death plus two posthumous collections for a total of sixteen.[22] Individual essays had more influence than the volumes in which they were collected. Some anthology titles were in themselves masterly and influential. For example, the sardonically titled *Semi-concession Anthologies* (*Qiejie ji*) was an allusion to the several foreign concessions into which Shanghai was divided (*qie* and *jie* are each half of the characters that make up *zujie*, "concessions") and also an allusion to his home on the edge of the Japanese concession. The sixteen volumes of essays, by virtue of being nearly all topical, make up a continuous chain of commentary on China.

In a different category but still constituting an interpretation of China are the classical poems, nearly all of which were written either before 1912 or after 1930. They draw on the vein in traditional poetry that takes the poem to be an expression of a felt connection between its author and the affairs of state. Lu Xun's poetry of the 1930s (the subject of chapter 4), nearly none of it made public, gave voice in a parallel manner to some of what his fiction and essays expressed in their different capacities.

A Narrative of the Life

The most influential narrative of Lu Xun's life has long been his own, a situation whose problems for critic and biographer are obvious. Why they cannot be completely escaped will become apparent in the biographical sketch below. As mentioned earlier, the difficulties are an unavoidable aspect of reading or writing about Lu Xun.

The shaping narrative came in the preface of the 1923 *Call to Arms*, with some influential contributions from the memoir essays of *Dawn Blossoms Gathered at Dusk*. In this preface, he sketched his life from his childhood in the provincial city of Shaoxing to that decisive moment in 1918 in Beijing when he took up his pen to write his first pieces for *New Youth* using the pseudonym Lu Xun. He told of certain events from his childhood and young adulthood that deeply affected him and set him on paths that led, eventually, to his vernacular literary writings.

This information marked the point at which he became a public figure. Publication had made the name Lu Xun well known, but the personal information attached to it only became widely known with the preface. Until then, even five years into the New Literature, only a few insiders knew any more. Even at Peking University, then the center of New Literature activism, where he was engaged in 1920 to teach the history of traditional Chinese fiction, the average student did not initially know that their teacher, Zhou Shuren, was Lu Xun.[23] Indeed, the next year, in a lengthy correspondence with a hopeful writer, he was able to lay a deliberate false trail: he wrote, probably in response to a direct query, that Lu Xun was not an unusual name (i.e., it need not be a pseudonym) and there might well be such a person.[24] With the preface, however, he became, at forty-three, a public figure.[25] His stories, already the favorite of educated youths, were now supplied with an identifiable person and a personal history behind the pseudonym. Moreover, the personal history provided was an affecting one of introspective, searching growth, imparting the pathos of an individual story to the metaphor of China in those years. Readers understood the several starts, the changes in direction, and the halting steps of his pre-writing life to be a metaphor for the troubled passage of China into a world that contained other nations, other histories, and more practical forms of knowledge. They took to heart his account, in Marston Anderson's fine wording, of "the awakening, deferral and eventual expression of the moral purpose that informs his fiction" and his "personal investment in their composition."[26] His progress toward New Literature and its related goals as recounted in the preface came to be emblematic of the necessary turn to modernity: he had rendered his life as a recapitulation of China's recent history and identity. A still-nascent movement drew justification from the facts of his own life as readers came to understand them. The resulting narrative created a vast personal influence for him that was extended to his characters. Because the other sources on these years are also retrospective, such as those of his brothers and his friend Xu Shoushang, and, moreover, are further distanced in time, his own narrative has long been treated as all the more authoritative. The preface is the quintessential example of Lu Xun's powerful mythmaking in transforming facts into meaning.

The personal wellsprings of writings that had a declared public purpose were thus fixed in the reader's mind at the same time as Lu Xun's introduction to the public as a personality. Every incident of the brief life story contained in the preface became iconic. Its web of loaded information was reinforced by the ten essays of *Dawn Blossoms Gathered at Dusk*, essays that expanded on incidents briefly touched on in the preface and added new material. They include, for example, an account of his traditional education and teacher, his childhood immersion in the lore and customs of the countryside, his father's long illness, and, from the Japan years, a kind professor at Sendai Medical School (Fujino) and a classmate (Fan Ainong) who died young and was in some respects a prototype for the title character in "The Loner." Even after much more became known about these antecedent years through research, none of the core incidents could be omitted without seeming to render the biography incomplete. The importance of the autobiographical writings as firsthand sources is overshadowed by their respectful treatment as sacred text. Moreover, this being Lu Xun, many compendia have been made of his other, incidental autobiographical remarks. These are very convenient for reference, but they tend to follow helplessly in the stream of his narrative of his life.

During the five years of writing that culminated in *Call to Arms*, Lu Xun had been gaining devoted readers at an accelerating pace. Once a life story could be attached to the name Lu Xun, especially one of metaphoric resonance, he became a public figure of unusual attention, and the milestones, activities, and decisions of the rest of his life took place on the public stage with public meaning. In this new public stage, information from his pen constituted only one of many contemporary sources, and his selection and interpretation of events were also only one among many, for the preface and *Dawn Blossoms* essays concern only his life before 1918. From the biographer's viewpoint, therefore, an understanding of his life after he became a public figure presents more standard issues in biographical interpretation when compared to his life before 1918.

Given this situation, the narrative of his life is presented here in two parts. For the pre–Lu Xun decades, an account has to accommodate both the dominance of his own narrative and the literary historian's need to evaluate. For this part, therefore, I first give a brief outline and then elaborate it with a glossed account of his own selection of events. In this way, for the prewriting years, it is possible to work with, rather than around, the received stories. For the years when he was Lu Xun, of great influence and fame, my account is straightforwardly chronological, with an emphasis on the features that are pertinent to this study.

First, the bare outline. Our author was born Zhou Zhangshou in 1881, the eldest of three surviving sons of a gentry family in the city of Shaoxing, in the province of Zhejiang.[27] His early education was traditional, both in content and in manner, beginning first, as with other gentry families, in the clan's own school and at eleven in a private Shaoxing academy. From the beginning the curriculum, incremental in its demands, was directed solely toward preparation for the imperial examinations and through them entry into the official service that underpinned the fortunes of the gentry class. A change came in 1898, when he persuaded his mother (his father had died) to allow him to go to Nanjing, where he enrolled first at the Jiangnan Naval Academy, then at the Army Academy's School of Mines and Railways, from which he graduated in 1902. Both institutions had been established by the Qing court to teach new, non-Confucian subjects, though apparently with limited effectiveness. He then went to Japan, the country to which Chinese students then looked for training in "foreign things" (*yangwu*). He was in the first class sent by the Liangjiang viceroy, who oversaw the Army Academy. In his first two years, he attended a preparatory program, as all Chinese students did. (He went home briefly and took part in an arranged marriage to Zhu An.) After two years, he enrolled in medical school in Sendai in the far north of Honshu island but left his medical studies after two years and returned to Tokyo. He finally returned to China in 1909. In all, he was a little over seven years in Japan, the last four not enrolled in formal programs. In China, after initial teaching positions in Hangzhou and then in his hometown of Shaoxing and a brief stint as a principal, he was recommended in 1912 to a position in the new Ministry of Education in Nanjing under Cai Yuanpei, established by the new Republic after the fall of the Qing dynasty. This proved to be the logistical element he needed. When the Republic moved its capital to Beijing that year, he moved north with the ministry. In that city he lived until 1926. It was in Beijing, in 1918, that he began to write for *New Youth*, then the main outlet of the iconoclastic vanguard. In 1926, he left Beijing, and after brief stays in Xiamen on the southeast coast and Guangzhou in the south, he settled in Shanghai with Xu Guangping, a former student, with whom he had a son, Haiying, born in 1929. In that city they he lived for the last decade of his life (1927–36).

The early years of any writer hold great interest. Who was the person who grew into this writer? What were his formative influences? Questions like these are all the more intriguing when a person with this life story turns out to be Lu Xun, who from his first work had a distinctive and fully formed style. How are we to understand the many years before the age of thirty-eight? What were the intellectual and literary influences? Among these and many more questions, the 1923 preface in effect persuaded readers that the young man seen in these recollections became the author of these works. Let us first see, therefore, the elements of the portrait he provided.

The life story presented in the 1923 preface, like everything Lu Xun wrote, is both vivid and brief (a bare six pages in English translation). There is one vignette each for childhood, youth, early adulthood, and so on. The unifying thread is stated in the opening paragraph. It involves one of the themes of this study, memory.

> Although it is said that memories can bring happiness, sometimes they cannot but cause a sense of loneliness. Of what use is it to allow the threads of one's spirits to be tangled in lonely days that are already past? Yet somehow I cannot completely forget these memories, and a part of what I cannot forget has become the source of these stories in *Call to Arms*.[28]

He laid out the axioms immediately: he is the kind of person who has memories that cause loneliness, yet he cannot discard them. The events recounted in the preface are those he cannot forget, while the stories of *Call to Arms* find their source in the same haunting events. This self-portrait of irreducible psychological components would not be surprising in something like Yu Dafu's short story "Sinking" (*Chenlun*), which caused a sensation with its self-absorbed, romantic portrait (interestingly, the two writers were to become close friends in Shanghai during 1927–33). However, in a writer whose stated goal was a public one, a "call," he said, "to awaken" his fellow Chinese, such an emphasis typically joined an intense temperament with national issues.

The first vignette is from childhood. Lu Xun tells how "for more than four years," while his father was ill, he was the person sent by the family to go almost daily to the pawnshop ("where the counter was twice my height") and from there to the pharmacy ("where the counter was my height"). The prescriptions, being from a famed practitioner of traditional medicine, required expensive, arcane ingredients ("cicadas with their original mates, sugar cane that had seen three years' frost"). The relative heights of the store counters give the impression that, at least at the beginning, he must have been a child sent to perform adult tasks (although pawnshop counters are above the heads of even adult customers). This is an image permeated with the scent of a memory that does not forgive or forget. It is left to Zhou Zuoren to tell us that his brother was fourteen when his father fell ill and sixteen (by Chinese count) when he died, not so much a child. As for the traditional physicians, there were two, and if the father had edema (*shui zhong*) a swelling of the tissues, there were several possible causes, all still difficult to manage today. Although this does not address the unscrupulousness implied, it is the case that there were and are many conditions that cannot be alleviated.

Such experiences educated the youngster in the ways of the world. "Those who have come down in the world soon learn what the world is like," he writes. In the fiction to come, all the characters show great sensitivity in the gauging of status and power: Ah Q and his fellow idlers sense the smallest shifts in their standing with each other; the landlady in "Regret for the Past" intuits the illicit relationship of the lovers and shows them a cold face. Lu Xun next states the result of this awareness—"This caused me to want to seek a different kind of people"—and this sentence serves as the transition to his departure for Nanjing in 1898. This is the first of the several instances in the preface where the author uses an intense emotion to pass over other autobiographical information.

There was more to the world's disdain than a father's illness, however. What Lu Xun does not mention and Zuoren later tells us is that in the year before the father's illness, 1893, the grandfather had been imprisoned for attempting to bribe the chief examiner in the provincial imperial examinations in Shaoxing. The arrest threw the family into turmoil; various family members, including at times the young Shuren, were dispatched to live in Hangzhou, where the grandfather was imprisoned, and look after him. He lived under a death sentence that was yearly postponed, most likely with bribes, and was only released in 1901. By then the young Shuren had entered an institution of "foreign things" in Nanjing and was only a year away from his graduation. These factors, which surely contributed to the family's decline, are omitted. A further interesting factor, impossible to integrate with this type of information, though it is given in a well-known place (in *Dawn Blossoms Gathered at Dusk*), is the role of one Mrs. Yan. A neighborhood woman who did not play by the rules and for that reason a complex source of interest to the youngsters, or at least to Lu Xun, Mrs. Yan, in the last episode Lu Xun describes of her, was likely the source of rumors that he had stolen from his mother. He began to feel guilty and, with the same decisiveness as in the preface, says, "All right. In that case, let me leave!"[29]

For the Nanjing years, an effective touch is a list of the kinds of liberating knowledge to be found there: "For the first time, I heard of the subjects of natural sciences, arithmetic, geography, history, drawing, and physical training." Except for physical training, which has its separate modernization rationale,[30] we may note that all are subjects that can be verified against observation or allowed countries other than China their own identities, displacing China from the center. Biology was not taught, but works on anatomy and chemistry gave him an inkling of modern medicine. The list of subjects in science provides him with the moral trajectory to jump to his decision some years later, in Japan, to study medicine. "It was what I learned in those young years," Lu Xun wrote, "that caused me [when I was studying in Tokyo] to register for a medical school in the north of Japan." Omitted are his graduation, the decision to study abroad, the first two years of study there—surely unsettling years—and all the accompanying new experiences. Instead, he summarizes to point a moral. Lu Xun's account provides the additional context of the choice of a modern field of study. He said he dreamed of helping patients like his father, "who had suffered so much from the wrong treatments." This has always been a common motivation among those who choose medicine, but he links it morally to the earlier vignette of the charlatans who treated his father.

Nevertheless, the young medical student left in his second year at Sendai Medical School. It is typical of Lu Xun's narrative mastery that, without diluting the impact of the first decision, he can, in the next paragraphs, give an equally powerful account of the undoing of that decision. This famous turning point occurred in 1906. The bacteriology professor used lantern slides in his lectures, and at the end of class he also showed slides of current events. In 1906, they were slides about Japan's recent victory in its war against Russia over control of Manchuria. One day he showed a slide of the beheading of a Chinese spy by Japanese soldiers in China. What disturbed the medical student about the sight was not the beheading so much as the passivity with which the other Chinese in the frame, strong and healthy looking, stood about and watched. "Before the academic year was out," Lu Xun's account in the preface says, "I had returned to Tokyo, because after that incident, I no longer felt that medical studies was an urgent issue, for when a nation's people are feeble and witless, then no matter how able-bodied they are, they are only fit to be an ineffectual audience, to be bystanders."[31] As will be seen later, this gripping account of a vivid lesson learned was not questioned for more than fifty years, though to some it is now a litmus test of credulity.

So the student left the study of medicine. But to cure minds was not so simple. His return to Tokyo after this epiphany did not lead to an obvious course of action. He did have one plan: together with Zuoren, who had arrived that year, and Xu Shoushang, he founded a publication with the declarative name *New Life* (*Xin sheng*). They had purchased the printing paper and had planned some of the content, including the cover, which reproduced an oil of an allegorical figure, "Hope," by the English painter George Frederic Watts, but their plans did not come to anything, owing, Zuoren said, to lack of finances and personnel.[32] The project was met with indifference. Approval, the preface said, "would have encouraged us," and disapproval "would have galvanized us." Indifference was worse than either. It was more than a decade before Lu Xun picked up the thread of writing (*wen*) again, this time to embark on the course that would place him in history. What happened in these intervening dozen years, which were in fact the years of his early manhood, is subsumed under a web of related words: *loneliness* (*jimo*) four times; *sorrow* (*beiai*) two times; and, once each, *sorrow* (*beizhuang*), *pointlessness* (*wuliao*), and *pain* (*tongku*). The only specific item mentioned is the *New Life* project. Otherwise, a mood poem of words glides over a large number of changes and searches for a meaningful occupation: four further years in Tokyo, a return to China, two to three years of teaching, and six years in Beijing before he began to write in 1918. This web of words passes over the changes in countries and cities and all the long years of "loneliness" with the kind of metaphorical, psychological language he later used in the prose poem collection *Weeds*.

This was his story up to that evening's conversation in 1918. Presented as pivotal, the exchange is described at greater length than any other incident in the preface. It was with Qian Xuantong (1887–1939), who came to call that evening. He was one of the editors of *New Youth* and from the same circle: he knew the Zhou brothers from their Japan days, he already had Zhou Zuoren as contributor to *New Youth*, he and Zuoren were both professors at Beida, and now he was able to engage the older brother's attention in a way that yielded results. Qian found him at his chief occupation in those years, copying inscriptions from steles and rubbings. "I was thinking, maybe you could write something," Qian said, his words trailing off. Lu Xun sensed that he knew the situation: "No one came to praise, and at the same time, no one opposed it." He recalled his own venture: "Perhaps they were feeling the loneliness." The exchange that followed between the two men contains the famous metaphor of the iron house. Lu Xun proposed that the Chinese were like people who were asleep and about to suffocate in an iron house that had no doors or windows. He asked, is it kinder to let them sleep or to wake them in the hope that they can yet find a way out? Qian urged the latter course. In the end, Lu Xun conceded to a series of negative suppositions: since the future had not yet arrived, one could not say that it was impossible to have hope. So he agreed to contribute to *New Youth*, in situation so like his own, failed *New Life*.

There is more to his first thirty-eight years than this, of course. To produce accounts less dominated by the preface and the supplementary information in *Dawn Blossoms*, biographers have both added to and qualified them. In particular, the more dramatic vignettes have been toned down by the addition of more facts. The pawnshop and pharmacy counters were mentioned earlier as a case in which he was not as young as the poignant image of their heights implies. Furthermore, the Zhou family, though fallen on hard times and using pawnshops, still had some of its land, which was not sold until Lu Xun moved the family to Beijing in 1919. The visit from Qian Xuantong, which in any case was made primarily to see Zuoren, also shows an elision that increases its effectiveness: Qian visited in August 1917, while Lu Xun's first contribution was not made until May 1918. Such vivid moments are, unsurprisingly, as much rhetorical as faithful. They can be and have been modified by sensible biographers, although biographies that merely pad out his version remain plentiful.

Among the many pieces of information in the preface that can be queried, there is one that has been seriously challenged. The challenge captures in a nutshell a situation that repeatedly faces studies of Lu Xun, including this one, and so I consider it more fully now. This is the lantern slide episode at Sendai Medical School in which the author supplies a vivid and neat—too neat—account of why he turned from medical studies to literary work. In the slide at issue, a Chinese spy is executed by Japanese soldiers while other Chinese passively look on.

For decades, the episode was cited as the pivot point of his search for a way to be of use, as the moment when he personally learned about what he later excoriated as the Chinese "national character." Although this is still the case in nonscholarly accounts, within Lu Xun studies there is no agreement about how to read this episode. The challenge is the more pointed because, unlike the other vignettes in the preface, here a question is raised about whether the incident ever happened or even could have happened. Once the veracity of this episode is put in play, it brings into question the moral edifice of Lu Xun's writing, and sides are chosen very quickly.

Information in autobiographical accounts is fair game for verification. In this case, the question was first raised in the 1970s by a professor at Sendai who found a cache of lantern slides from 1905 that concerned the Russo-Japanese War but that did not contain a slide of Lu Xun's description.[33] Did such a slide exist? Could it have been borrowed or rented from elsewhere? (Somehow the possibility that it has been lost or broken is not considered.) Was Lu Xun exaggerating or (supply your verb) to point a moral? Wang Xirong summarizes the many lines of inquiry that follow on a question so jolting in its implications. They include Lu Xun's two other accounts of this episode, which differ in their details[34]; his use of the word *dianying* for what he saw (today *dianying* only means "film") and what format that word indicates; interesting third-party information on the attention attracted by the professor's slide projector; the advertisements in contemporary Sendai newspapers showing that news slides of the Russo-Japanese war were rapidly produced and disseminated; the existence of many sets of such slides and the popularity of slide shows; and, finally, the xenophobia that pervaded the city.

(Lu Xun was one of only two Chinese at Sendai Medical School.)[35] Besides laying out these considerations, Wang tells his readers that he came across a photograph of a similar scene in a Korean pictorial magazine but misplaced it.[36] Given all the rich information uncovered about war news circulation at the time, the fact that a slide quite likely existed but is not now at Sendai does not seem like damning evidence.

Yet this question concerning unascertainable causes has turned out to be a litmus test, with those who find some level of reality in it thought of as played for fools. Strong voices speak for total debunking. As Lin Qingxin puts it, "in Foucault terms," critics look to take apart Lu Xun's "grand narrative" and discover the "base origins" that lie in the place of the "holy origin."[37] The strength of these views gives one a sense of how totalistic was the era of control to which they were reacting. A painting at the Beijing Luxun Museum that imagines the young medical student leaving in righteous anger, with his movement and pose modeled on socialist realist works, sums up the adulation that was required for so many decades. It has happened more than once that a scholar from China would say to me emphatically, apropos of nothing except that the topic was Lu Xun, "You know all that about the slide is nonsense," using the word *nonsense* in English. For such informants, the unmasking of the incident as a lie is an axiom of Lu Xun studies and must be conveyed to a possible innocent.

It is possible to look at this crucial moment in nonconfrontational ways by reflecting on the larger situation. This may smooth out the author's sharp contrast without having to call him a liar. Leo Ou-fan Lee captures the sense of the situation when he says that the incident "by itself was not enough . . . it served merely to bring into sharp focus the many frustrations he had accumulated over these two years." Furthermore, Lee points out, the young student did not leave the medical school "before the term was out" (as he claimed in the preface) but "at the end of [that] second year" (as he says in "Mr. Fujino").[38] Wang Xirong emphasizes the important point that Lu Xun had followed several quite different paths since his graduation from the School of Mines and Railways in 1902, and medicine was only one.[39] Dong Bingyue is of the view that the Sendai years, especially as captured in "Mr. Fujino," make up a narrative of many components, which is best understood as part of Lu Xun's overall "solitude" while in Japan. Dong reads the immediate elements of the slide scene—the strong-looking Chinese and their pathetic mentality—in relation to the poor opinion Lu Xun had of the only other Chinese student at Sendai, who was big and strong but failed four classes in each of his first two years and was dropped from the rolls.[40] To these suggestions I will add that the ethos and structure of medical training are so consuming that in order to leave that intense group identity a medical student needs a clearly enunciated reason, which the slide episode could have provided. This can be contrasted with other fields of study, such as Natsume Sōseki's protagonist's in *Kokoro*. In the continental European fashion, he could delay doing any work for his humanities degree at Tokyo Imperial University until the last months before his graduation, when he shut himself up and wrote his thesis. By contrast, the curriculum at Sendai Medical School for the second term of the second year contained eleven subjects (Wang lists them) and, as Lu Xun mentioned, one-third of the students in Mr. Fujino's anatomy class failed (as did he, by seven-tenths of a point).[41] Finally, there was the inducement that his brother Zuoren was to come to Tokyo that year after his graduation from the Naval Academy. That summer Lu Xun came home from Sendai, and they left for Tokyo together.

His life after he became a public figure is more quickly told, for although it is crowded with actions and events, the biographer's necessary selectivity is not controlled in the same way by the author's own intense vignettes. Here it is in brief from 1918. He was prodigiously productive. Besides the fiction, there were the essays, which filled sixteen volumes. His activities other than writing began slowly, but soon he had an enormous workload that continued up to the time of his death. He began to write in 1918 and took his first steps into the machinery of literary production in 1921, when he and Mao Dun embarked on an ambitious translation project for *Short Story Monthly*, which under Mao's editorship had been remade as a vehicle for New Literature. With younger followers, he also founded periodicals and societies, and the latter usually involved book or periodical publishing. His work in both translations and periodicals continued until he died. The translation took up a huge amount of his time, as it also included commissioning, correcting, editing, proofreading, and writing prefaces for the translations of others. With the periodicals, which all operated on a financial shoestring, the work was also huge, his efforts multiplied by the fact that all were short-lived. He also oversaw the illustrations that accompanied the periodicals and his and others' book publications. In many cases, he designed the covers himself, giving expression to his long-standing interest in illustration and graphic design. Finally, he began to teach, with contracts, first at Beijing University, starting August 1920, and then at Beijing Women's Normal College (where Xu Guangping was a student).[42] His lecture notes drew on his earlier research into traditional vernacular fiction, a field then untouched except by Hu Shi, with whom he corresponded on the subject, and these lectures became *A History of Chinese Vernacular Fiction*, the first work of its kind. These activities are just from the Beijing years.

In August 1926, he left the capital. In doing so, he left behind fourteen years of personal and professional history. The proximate cause was the March 18th Incident, in which forty-seven students were killed by government forces during a demonstration. The many essays he wrote on that event—bitter, sorrowful, and accusatory—placed his name on a government list, and that August, after two on that list were assassinated, he left Beijing. Two other major changes are marked by his departure. One was in his personal life. Xu Guangping accompanied him as far as Shanghai (his mother and wife remained in Beijing), and, although from there they proceeded to take teaching positions in different cities in early 1927 he joined her in Guangzhou and later the same year they left for Shanghai, where they set up a home together.[43] After Lu Xun's death, Xu became the conservator of his papers and reputation. The other major change was political. Beginning in 1927, Lu Xun made a new search for meaning and purpose in literature, and after wide reading and thought, by January 1930, he felt ready to declare, using Marxist terminology, that literature must be revolutionary and revolutionary literature meant proletarian literature.[44] The next month he associated himself with the founding of the League of Left-Wing Writers. This step in his evolution, though not his last, sealed his posthumous fate as a revolutionary icon.

In Shanghai, Lu Xun found himself much in demand in all the activities of a complex literary world. He was also caught up in constant negotiations over the roles that the Communist Party hoped he would play in their plans. Operating on the Left in a city under Nationalist control, he was often in some political danger, although his young associates were, of course, much more vulnerable. He did not teach, although he again held, for nearly four years, a position in education that provided a stipend, secured for him by Cai Yuanpei. The essays continued while his other interests and activities multiplied. Many more young writers came under his sponsorship, including notable writers of the next generation such as Xiao Jun and Xiao Hong. An important new interest was art, specifically woodcuts. To promote the genre, he founded periodicals, secured and published examples from abroad, mentored young artists, wrote prefaces for exhibitions, and much more (see chapter 5). An important private activity at this time was classical poetry, which he began to write again. In sum, the Shanghai years were a time when he was as much a literary figure as a writer.

In such a biography, there are many questions to ponder. As this sketch shows, Lu Xun's creative life lasted eighteen years, for he began late and died at fifty-six. Within this time span, the *xiaoshuo* fiction-writing years were even shorter, 1918–25 (the last story is dated November 1925) and the number of works is small: twenty-five short stories in all, of which only one, "The

True Story of Ah Q," is long enough to count as a novella. This is a large reputation to be founded on a small body of work written in the first eight years. We could ask how it happened that the readers built up the author, or we could ask about the nature of the author's creativity since he wrote fiction for so short a time. Lu Xun never gave an explanation; among critics, there are occasional conjectures and lately some denigrating comparisons (not a Proust, nor García Márquez, nor Faulkner is one put-down).[45] Yet to have had a relatively brief creative period, if that is brief, is no shame. The same could be said of Wordsworth, for instance, even though his poetry increased in quantity in later years. That a handful of extraordinary fiction and several dozen essays exerted an influence beyond their size is itself a considerable achievement.

But it is also possible—and this is the view that will be an underlying thesis here—that the description of Lu Xun as a literary figure should be considered as having arisen from historical convenience. It is not clear that his life can be accurately portrayed as that of a writer. Cultural studies and the ideas of canon formation have shown that influence and reputation are historically contingent. These ideas can also be employed to support the further view that the very terms of his reputation, as at bottom a literary one, are an outcome of the chance historical situation that the new elite was most receptive to the genres of prose literature and do not fully coincide with his own sense of his possibilities. A theme of the chapters here is that he was a person who had talents in many directions and felt his obligations in other areas. He was interested in different things at different times in his life. It happened that New Literature was the first area in which he made his mark, and it was one that the new elite was primed to boost at the time he did it.

The Life in This Study

This study is chronologically arranged, with each of the chapters after this one focused on a brief segment of Lu Xun's life and on certain writings from that time. They begin with the first two years in Japan (1902–3) during which he cut his queue; proceed to the eighteen months in 1920–22 that ended with the installment publication of "Ah Q"; move on to the deaths of the Five Martyrs in 1931, one of whom, Rou Shi, was very close to him; and end with the last two years of his life (1934–36), when art began to assume the visible importance in his life that it had always held for him. As it happens, each chapter covers about a two-year span of time. The biographical coverage is not comprehensive; nor is the objective to provide a comprehensive analysis of the writing by genre or period. Instead, the analyses hope to bring a different kind of clarity to what would otherwise, at this level of detail, be biographical minutiae. Each chapter aims to obtain insights into the author's manner of thinking and writing, which is based in that moment but has far-reaching implications. To do so, the analysis focuses on the space where the writing intersects its contexts, which are a mix of political, personal, cultural, and ideological forces as they act on the author. It probes for what the works of the imagination chosen in each chapter can reveal about its author, especially what they can reveal that is not otherwise knowable, to bring out features of his thought and psychology that are not otherwise accessible. The approach is akin to taking a core sample in order to obtain a cross section of information that penetrates to some depth. It is from this complex of imponderables that his interpretations of China emerge. Their bases in a particular time and place are traced here.

Memory, Violence, Queues: The Approach of This Study

The materials of a writer are many. One consideration in making a selection is whether a productive exploration is possible. This study identifies three elements as topics that in diverse guises both give rise to and find expression in Lu Xun's writings throughout his life. These are memory, violence, and queues. The queue was a style of hair imposed on its male subjects by the Qing dynasty and, as mentioned above, one that Lu Xun discarded soon after he arrived in Japan. It had, however, a persistent, elusive afterlife in his mind: its infrequent but always charged occurrences in his writings are followed through the chapters of this study. The element of violence, which is familiar in historical studies, has entered literary studies as well, for example, in David Der-wei Wang's *The Monster That Is History*. This study focuses specifically on political violence—on the imprisonment, deaths, and terror, or the threat of them, that were a feature of politics throughout his lifetime—rather than, for example, on the psychological violence that Marston Anderson invokes in his finely argued section on Lu Xun entitled "The Violence of Observation."[46] The third element, memory, is probably the most familiar one, both in cultural studies and in connection with Lu Xun. This familiarity may obscure the extent of its influence in his work. For this reason, the complex role of memory is laid out below at the greatest length. Just the listing of the three elements as a writer's raw materials already suggests something about this particular writer's mentality. Analyzing their varied presence in his writings will provide a new means of access to the nexus of his psychology, imagination, and technique. Following are overviews of the three elements in his life, providing a background for the chapters, which focus on defined segments of time.

Queue

The least-investigated of the elements, the queue, was imposed on Chinese men by the Qing dynasty when it conquered China in 1644 and was abolished by the Republic nearly three hundred years later in 1911. Lu Xun cut his at a time when it was still against Qing law. By the time he began to write, the queue had been, at least officially, an artifact of the past for some years. In his fiction, it is a prominent trait of his most famous character, Ah Q, and also forms the plot for the satire in "Storm." The ready recognition of these two occurrences, coupled with the generally heroic interpretation of his action in cutting his queue, has produced a narrow understanding of the queue's significance to Lu Xun. The general view of the matter is that the queue equals oppression, early cutting equals defiance, and the 1911 revolution settled the queue's fate.

Lu Xun did not, however, write of the past in such clear terms. For one thing, his own experience was complicated. After he cut his queue in Japan, he was home in Shaoxing in 1903 and 1906. In 1909, when he returned to China permanently, he still had two more years to go until 1911. Aside from the law, in social terms, in the early part of this period especially, people were not used to the "baldheaded" look. He used a false queue, perhaps on more than one visit, then at some point gave that up. Even in 1909, at a school that taught modern subjects like chemistry, mathematics, and English, he got strange looks from the principal for his short hair. Lu Xun never recounted his experiences in the plain manner used here, but he also did not create a stirring, upbeat story that took the reader from oppression to enlightenment. As the successive chapters show, the meaning of the queue persisted, on varying levels, throughout his life. At the moment he cut it, the forces acting on him were socially and politically complex (and deserving of narration), but the action itself seemed to have been quickly undertaken and not particularly fraught (chapter 2). That the social and political forces of this moment were complex has survived in historical materials not directly connected to him, as we will see. More than this moment in time, what has lingered are the aftereffects, when he went back to China, first on visits, then permanently in 1909, that gave the queue potency in his writings. It was not personal experience alone that caused it to become a complex signifier for different things at different times and always connected to political violence.

The queue was not a gimmick. It was not inherently amusing or vaudevillian, although it was that too, as the characters Sevenpounder and Ah Q famously demonstrate. Lu Xun put on display their comic dilemmas, but behind the show, his subtle deployment of this improbable symbol encompasses the loss of lives in the anti-Qing movements and all political violence (chapter 3). With the passage of time, the queue style of hair was no longer seen, and it went from being amusing to merely odd. The personal knowledge of it placed him in a certain generation, and what such a strange artifact could signify becomes one issue that he ponders when illustrations of his fiction by young people brought home the queues's incomprehensibility (chapter 5).

Violence

This study focuses on the violence of political events, as opposed to broader categories of physical, psychological, or metaphorical violence. Its chapters stress that violence is the aspect of the many political movements in China that strikes deepest with Lu Xun. What has been called his patriotism or nationalism or the struggle against feudalism can be seen as a response to the violence. This approach is not an analysis of "political violence as reflected in his writings." Instead, the chapters show that a continuing purpose in these writings over many years is to convey the tragedy of wasted human life. If the emphasis is placed on political events, then critical attention tends to be directed toward determining the degree and nature of Lu Xun's political involvement. In this study, by contrast, attention is shifted to the violence that accompanied political events, to the arrest, imprisonment, and deaths that were dealt out to many Lu Xun knew and the fear all lived under. This study thus highlights the degree to which contemporary political violence is an active factor in many of his works, whether fiction, poetry, or essay.

In Lu Xun's lifetime, there was never a period without political violence. If we begin our survey only from the time that we are certain he was aware of it and limit ourselves to those incidents that affected him or were witnessed by him, the following are some of the major historical movements. All are either explicitly mentioned or form the essential background in these chapters. At the beginning, during his years in Japan, the political violence pertinent to him had its source in the Qing court and the political movements against it. He arrived in Japan shortly after it had begun to serve as a refuge for Qing dynasty reformers and anti-Qing revolutionaries and when reform and revolutionary activities and debates were spreading from seasoned activists to the increasing number of Chinese students in Japan. Among those who subsequently fell victim to political violence that the young student knew or heard at public meetings in Tokyo were Zou Rong, the author of the incendiary pamphlet *Revolutionary Army*, who died in prison in 1905; Zhang Binglin, arrested with Zou Rong, who survived imprisonment to display further acts of courage; and Qiu Jin, who was executed in Shaoxing in 1907 after botched plans for an uprising. All three recur in Lu Xun's writings. In 1909, Lu Xun was back in China, and here we have the 1911 Republican Revolution, which he witnessed in its Shaoxing form. One of his characters, N in "A Story about Hair," recalls the many unknown dead and the dead in unknown graves, all forgotten. There is also the young revolutionary from the Xia family who dies offstage in the story "Medicine." Except for the Second Revolution of 1913, the violence of organized military action is largely absent from Lu Xun's writings, even though the establishment of the Republic was followed by fifteen years of open warlord rivalries. When he moved to Beijing the year after the revolution, it was the seat of the northern provisional government, headed first by Yuan Shikai, then by Duan Qirui. Frequent demands on Beijing for further concessions, made by the imperialist powers, added another factor to the political tensions. These were the years of increasing student activism, first shown on a large scale in the May Fourth (1919) demonstrations. The deaths of student demonstrators in the March 18th Incident were mentioned above. After he left Beijing, he was in Guangzhou during exactly the months in which the Nationalist government carried out a surprise purge throughout the cities of the south against its nominal ally, the Communist Party, and killed many, including, in Guangzhou, students Lu Xun knew.

Lu Xun left for Shanghai in 1927, the same year in which the Nationalists' Northern Campaign was able to bring all of China under at least nominal central control. During the ten years he lived in Shanghai, the Nationalist capital was in nearby Nanjing. Its military attempts to suppress the Communists, now an underground party, took place in the provinces, where they had established soviets, while in the city the suppression took the form of intelligence and police work. Frederic Wakeman has documented in detail the intelligence and counterintelligence work on both sides; the assassinations and betrayals, secret arrests, and executions; and the mass graves dug up on the information of defectors.[47] At this point Lu Xun had openly allied himself with banned associations such as the League of Left-Wing Writers; a disciple, Rou Shi, was secretly killed in prison; a colleague, Yang Quan, was assassinated; and the young woodcut artists, who sought his patronage, all suffered persecution. The replacement of political violence with open military war occurred in 1931 when the Japanese occupied Manchuria (Lu Xun watched the mobilization activities of students in Shanghai) and again when the Japanese attacked Shanghai in a brief but devastating war in January 1932. The wider war, which came one year after Lu Xu's death, was clearly on the horizon.

Memory

Memory is a well-known feature of Lu Xun's psychological makeup and his writings. I take time here to sketch its outlines because in chapters 3 and 4 I show that it plays a pivotal and hitherto unnoticed role at certain points in his life and his writings. In chapter 3, the writings that culminated in "The True Story of Ah Q" and in chapter 4 the revival of a poem from his youth at a dark moment in his maturity both rely on the tenacity of his memory.

Lu Xun wrote often about the place of memory in his writings. The earliest and most influential examples are his remarks in the preface to *Call to Arms*. Previously, we saw how in that preface the invocation of memories at the beginning is the unifying thread for an account of his life. Here we look at the other end of memory's connection, which is with fiction, and at how his statement that a part of his memories "has become the source of these stories in *Call to Arms*" encouraged the conviction of readers that "real people, places, and events [have] turned into characters, settings, and scenes."[48] Then we will see how, when we take a longer range of time, the situation regarding memory is more complicated than his summary in the preface has it.

To begin with, here is the opening paragraph, which was quoted earlier as his narrative of his life. Now we read it in the context of the fiction it encompasses.

> Although it is said that memories can bring happiness, sometimes they cannot but cause a sense of loneliness. Of what use is it to allow the threads of one's spirits to be tangled in lonely days that are already past? Yet somehow I cannot completely forget these memories, and a part of what I cannot forget has become the source of these stories in *Call to Arms*.

Lu Xun's fiction, particularly the best-known short stories, tends to bear out this description of memory as its source. Like the events of his life that he provides in the preface, many of these are set in the past, generally in a time before or just around the 1911 revolution. "Diary of a Madman," "Kong Yiji," "Tomorrow," "White Light," and "Village Opera" are set in a traditional China at an indefinite period before 1911, while "Medicine" and "The True Story of Ah Q" are set more specifically in a time just before the revolution. Even when the stories are set in the present, they often have protagonists who face moral dilemmas that have their roots in the past. "Hometown," "New Year's Sacrifice," "Upstairs at the Tavern," and "The Loner" are all like this. In "Hometown," the protagonist finds on his return, as Lu Xun did in life, that a childhood friend named Runtu, the son of an occasional household servant, now greets him humbly. The narrator cannot forget that as children he had been the admirer, the other the hero, and this disparity darkens his visit and his journey back to Beijing. Both "Upstairs at the Tavern" and "The Loner" have frame narrators who listen to an old friend (in the former) or watch an old friend (in the latter) as they, the friends, confront the contrast between youthful ideals and present conditions. In these and more stories, memory and the conflicts they cause the protagonists are the more powerful because Lu Xun describes them as lingering. Their traces follow the protagonists into adulthood and a different world, and take them back to theirs.

Reinforcing the pull of memory is the stories' setting in the countryside of Lu Xun's youth, a removal in space added to that of time from the author's present of Beijing. Readers soon saw that to an unusual degree his fiction was rooted in the materiality of the watery countryside that lay about Shaoxing. The fictional village of Weizhuang, the country town of Luzhen, and his slice of Shaoxing are vivid settings for characters who come to seem correspondingly real. In several stories ("Hometown," "New Year's Sacrifice," "Upstairs at the Tavern") the intellectual protagonists are shown as having returned on a visit to a south where they no longer have a home. This resembles Lu Xun's situation, as he, too, had closed up the family home in the south. He never returned, however, after he moved his family to Beijing, a discrepancy with the latter stories that needs to be factored into their interpretation. The fictional returns likely indicate that for certain kinds of themes he needed the south of his early years and that the pressure of this gave the setting a certain material veracity.

So marked is this feature of memory in Lu Xun's fiction that in 1928, when the Communist Party, sensing an opportunity in his essays and speeches for his conversion, sought to bring him into line by, oddly enough, attacking him, the notable role of the past in his fiction was the point on which he was considered vulnerable. Writing for the Creation Society (Chuangzao she), whose members had newly switched from being aesthetes to being radicals, the critic-poet A Ying called him out of date. In "Ah Q's Age Is Dead and Gone," he declared in an opening salvo, "Lu Xun is not a spokesman for our time. [F]or the past ten years, he has not been able to represent literary trends in China!"[49] Of course, once Lu Xun threw in his lot with the Left, his use of the past became proof of the length of his battles against feudalism.

Despite the seeming rightness of memory as a key to the author and his writings, the situation was more complicated than its expression in the 1923 preface. This can be seen in what he wrote about memory after his departure from Beijing in August 1926. The prefaces of the two essay collections that immediately followed, *Grave* and *Dawn Blossoms Gathered at Dusk*, show his altered view of the past and writing, alterations that are rooted in events of political violence, primarily the March 18th Incident of that year and the

Nationalist purge of April the next year. These words also serve as a preview of the ingrained role of memory in this study.

A change is first seen in the preface to *Grave*, written in October 1926, which is notably apologetic about the author's tendency to treasure the past. This is one of the passages.

> Although I know very well that the past is already past, . . . still, I cannot bring myself to be so resolute. I want to sweep up the residual grains and make of them a small, new grave, on the one hand to bury them and on the other hand to make a memorial. I will not worry that soon they will be trodden level again, nor can I worry about it.[50]

Grave was his third collection of essays, but the first to include writings from before the rise of New Literature. For this volume, Lu Xun reached far back into the past and included four essays he wrote while in Japan—nearly twenty years earlier and in the classical language. Although they are of great interest to readers today, in contemporary terms this truly was the past: in some ways, *Grave* is not a misnomer. The image Lu Xun uses minimizes even that name. A grave has a mounded shape, a few feet high: the image shrinks his collection to only a "small" grave, and even that is soon to be "trodden level" by time. In a postface, written the next month, he is at further pains to excuse the classical-language essays as being only a quirk, specifically adding that they do not support the assertion of some that to write well one needs to be grounded in the classics. Why publish things that need so much excusing? "I still thought to use this chance to look at the traces of a time in the past," he wrote. "In this small mound is buried none other than a body that once was alive."[51] He seeks to give his past self both a burial and a memorial.

The preface to *Dawn Blossoms Gathered at Dusk*, dated May 1 of the next year, shows a further change that can be attributed to yet one more episode of directly witnessed violence. Most of it, like the preface to *Grave*, reveals both his desire to put memory away from him and its Proustian necessity to him. Added now, however, is the sense that a fresh experience of political violence has made it necessary to have no memory. This is the transition from the direct, elegiac "In Memory of Liu Hezhen" of 1926 to the impossibility of the future in "Remembrance in Order to Forget" of 1933.

The major portion of this brief preface is like *Grave*'s in describing a relation to memory that is unbreakable and conflictive.[52] It begins with a wry thought about publishing a volume of memoirs: "When a person reaches a point when he has only memories left, then life could be counted as meaningless." Why retain memories when they can turn you into someone so pathetic? He is, he says, a person who is helpless under the force of memory. He knows, or he has since found out, that the fragrance of the beans and vegetables of his childhood does not stand up to an adult experience of the same foods, that only in his memory do they still retain their original fragrance. "Perhaps," he writes, "they have beguiled me my whole life and caused me to look backward a great deal." Does this mean that he is finally, at this writing, free of the beguilement of memory? He phrases the ensnarement as a thing of the past: "At one time, it used to be that the memory often came to me of the greens I had sometimes eaten in the countryside." Yet we see that even now the names are bewitching, for he names the foods: lotus roots, lohan beans (the snack the youngsters cook up in "Village Opera"), aquatic shoots, and muskmelon. And the sensation is still vivid: "They caused me to be enveloped by the sense of home." He tells readers that, although he wrote the first two essays in settled circumstances, the others were written while he was in hiding in Beijing after March 18 and in the uncongenial setting of Xiamen. Perhaps this was by way of excusing the attraction still exerted by long ago senses, but in the main his tone is one of lingering perplexity.

The changed attitude that leads ultimately to a phrasing such as "Remembrance in Order to Forget" is in the preface's first paragraph. The paragraph builds up to the conclusion that "today, even this 'waking' is not possible," alluding to an essay entitled "Waking."[53] Why waking is not possible now and what this means require some unpacking. This is the passage

> Yet there comes a time when even memories are not to be had. [But] in China the literary world will proceed apace in its patterns, and the affairs of the world will continue their swirl. A few days ago, as I left Zhongshan University, I thought of four months ago when I was leaving Xiamen University. When I hear the sound of airplanes overhead, I remember how a year ago the planes daily circled above the city of Beijing. At that time, I had written an essay called "Waking." But today, even this "waking" is not possible.

This is a series of connections between present and past, all but one violent. While the world carries on its routines unperturbed, the present for him is the time of "a few days ago," when he was "leaving Zhongshan University," in Guangzhou. Unsaid was the purge of Communists that caused him to leave, for he had resigned in protest ten days earlier when the university did not aid the students arrested and later executed by the Nationalists. Xu Shoushang and Xu Guangping had also resigned. (The past this reminded him of was his departure from Xiamen, which was ultimately personal, to join Xu

Guangping, and is pertinent here only as the paragraph's pattern of past and present.) The warplanes overhead in Guangzhou were those of Chiang Kai-shek's Nationalist forces. The warplanes overhead in Beijing are remembered from the previous year when, as he describes it in "Waking," "Every morning, airplanes, carrying orders to eject their bombs, fly above the city walls of Beijing, like students coming to class." [54] These were the planes of Zhang Zuolin's Fengtian army attacking the Feng Yuxiang forces that then held the city.

Finally, we come to the "waking" that was possible then and not possible now. The essay "Waking" was written in Beijing about a month after the killings on March 18. It takes its title from a momentary hope he had felt on waking. That day, restless in his grief, he had decided to work on the manuscripts from young people that were piled on his desk. "As the sun went down, in the steady light from the lamp," he wrote, "the figures of the young people one after the other passed quickly before me." He drifted off. When he suddenly started awake, he found that the cigarette in his hand was still lit and was sending up "small summer clouds of smoke" in which could still be seen the "indistinct shapes" of the young people of his dream. He had loved the young people, he said, both those who had died and those he feared would meet with death in the future, and the reason is that "they cause me to feel that we are still living among humans." Last year, even with such sorrows, it was possible to wake to the indistinct shapes of the young dead, to briefly feel oneself with them and "living among humans" again. "Today," in Guangzhou, after the latest bout of violence against the young, "even this 'waking' is not possible."

"When a person reaches a point when he has only memories left, then life could be counted as meaningless." Subsequent events prove that there can come a worse time, when memories cannot provide even a slender comfort. Yet this was not the end of Lu Xun's discoveries, for in a way, to be sentient is to have a memory. New memories are added to existing ones and interact with the present as he is writing. These accumulating layers are the interest of this study throughout.

The Chapters in This Study

In this study, each of the next four chapters pursues a separate argument, unified by the elements of the title. In chapter 2, "Cutting His Queue: Nationalism, Identity, and other Unknowns," the queue *is* the topic, as the title indicates. The years discussed, 1902–3, cover the first years of the young student in Japan, during which the newcomer from China encountered many new political and social experiences while the country he came to was itself in the throes of great changes that had brought its first taste of military power. Cutting his queue was one expression of Lu Xun's reaction to his new situation. Violence comes in with the final line of a poem associated with this action, in which he declares his readiness to die for his countrymen: "I would offer up my blood for the [descendants] of the Yellow Emperor." This line leads us to examine the spirit of such fervent intentions among students at this time and the general situation of Chinese students in Japan in these two years. Memory is involved when we examine how both Lu Xun and others later touch on the queue cutting or, what is even more interesting, how the period before that is obscured, the time when he still had a queue. By focusing on one incident and its material byproducts and contextualizing them in relation to his contemporaries, it is possible to take the queue as symptomatic of changes in his early years of maturity and to enlarge the framework to include some of his other early writings.

Chapter 3 focuses on the eighteen-month time span in 1920–22 that ends with the serial publication of "The True Story of Ah Q." In this period, almost his only writings are three short fictions and two essays. All but one feature the queue prominently, and all display internal connections unusual in his writings. The short stories include his single most famous work ("The True Story of Ah Q"), one that is well known ("Storm"), and one that has almost never been noticed ("A Story about Hair"), while the two essays are nearly unknown. Treating the five works as a group leads to insights into an author who is vulnerable to external, violent events and the memories that they stir up and whose response is to make a prolonged effort over these eighteen months to create fiction that responds to these burdens. It proposes that the works came into existence as a result of contemporary violence, in this case a battle that took place just outside Beijing in July 1920. It further proposes that the three stories are linked by the author's several attempts to convey the fact of violence, especially the deaths of young people during anti-Qing rebellions. In these works, we see the author making a sustained effort to find different approaches to using literature to awaken the Chinese to their world. The creation of "Ah Q" will always be considered an important time in his writing career: this chapter additionally sketches in some features of personal retrospection and artistic motivation in the period.

Chapter 4 proposes that there is a connection between Lu Xun's 1903 classical-language poem from the queue-cutting episode and a 1931 experience of violence, the deaths of the young writers known as the Five Martyrs, who were betrayed by another communist group, arrested by the British, and executed by the Nationalists. One of them was his disciple Rou Shi. Memory comes into play when we see that this connection shows that Lu Xun never forgot this poem of his youth and now invests it with a new, though wholly private, layer of meaning. The private revival of this 1903 poem, "Inscribed by the Author on a Small Likeness," affects the interpretation of the well-known commemorative essay "Remembrance in Order to Forget" and the (untitled) classical poem that it includes ("Though accustomed to"). I suggest also that the revival of this poem opens the door to the whole category of classical poetry that he began to write again in the 1930s. Other moments in the life of this poem, from 1926 and 1936, are also identified. In sum, this work, uniquely placed in Lu Xun's life, throws new light on how his personal and literary responses are interwoven in the 1930s, a period that is important both in his life and in the political history of China.

Chapter 5 moves to the period 1934–36 and a different medium—illustrations and his responses to them. The illustrations chosen are those that depict characters from Lu Xun's fiction and also woodcut portraits of him. This visual material, whose earliest known examples appear around this time, is seldom seen and has not been organized or used in Lu Xun scholarship. In them, the queue features prominently because his best-known characters are placed in settings that date from before the 1911 Republican Revolution and so they all wore queues, which had to be depicted. It came down to his memory versus their imagination. As with the earlier chapters, political violence stood in the wings: every characteristic of woodcut artists and some cartoonists courted danger—their associations, medium, subject matter, intent, and message. Censorship, arrest, and imprisonment were thus constant threats for the artists. Some met with these fates; many more were driven out of their chosen course.

Chapter 5 uses the visual material to examine a reflexive question and reveal a pattern in Lu Xun's outlook. His responses to the illustrations give us a glimpse of his view of his legacy, and we also see that one pattern of his last years, which continue to be full of activities, is to look both backward and forward. The two are related. The illustrations in effect treat his work as history, and this is the stimulus for him to look back to the time settings of his fiction when the queue was normal, now a quarter century in the past, and forward to consider the question of the legacy of the work that has such characteristics. During these years, when there was more writing behind him than ahead of him, his connections with young artists, especially through his active promotion of woodcuts, were all forward looking. We see that they represent a new stage in his continual search for ways to convey the reality he saw in China.

Individually, chapters 2–5 focus on key months and years. Taken together, they span Lu Xun's entire life, from his early years as a student of new subjects in Japan to his last years as a national figure in Shanghai. While not a biography, they provide a view of certain important moments in both the life and the writings that have in common the themes of queue, violence, and memory. In terms of the writing that constructed his interpretation of China, the chapters show major works in a new light, make relevant some minor works largely overlooked, integrate some of the classical poetry into that interpretation, and bring to light fundamental relations between works of different genres that have been largely treated separately.

It may be that the following passage from an essay written in Lu Xun's last year, "This Too Is Life,"[55] gives the implicit consent of the author for others to go ahead and find connections between his life and the often scrappy, fighting work, and to discern connections even in unmarked, ordinary moments of his life. In this passage, Lu Xun suggests that even a fighter, which he "has never been," might have trouble acting on principles on every occasion. He gives the deliberately silly example of how a fighter might be thirsty and want to eat some watermelon while other people want him to contemplate how the cut-up watermelon is a symbol of China's partition by imperial powers. It is true, Lu Xun says, that everything is potentially a symbol, including the watermelon one eats. On the other hand, we cannot have every action refer to larger questions; we should be able to eat a watermelon in a "quiet, normal way." Then he considers the two sides of the question again in a more abstract way, and this is where his words can relate to Lu Xun studies.

> In truth, the daily life of a fighter does not consist entirely of things that could be sung of or wept over. Yet at no point does it not touch upon things that can be sung of or wept over. This is the truth about a fighter.

Fighters cannot live their lives in the forefront of battle all the time, for a person's life, even a fighter's life, can be pretty unremarkable on a daily basis. But in the end, even the unremarkable aspects of that life are a part of the fighter. This has been the finding of the present study.

2

Cutting His Queue: Nationalism, Identity, and Other Unknowns

Zhou Shuren, as he was then known, cut his queue in the spring of 1903, a year after he arrived in Japan to further his studies. He was twenty-three by Chinese count (twenty-one by Western count until his birthday in September), and his identity as Lu Xun lay fifteen years in the future. Even further in the future, after his death, lay the half century of party-enforced apotheosis that endowed with iconic status every aspect of his life, including this incident and the primary evidence customarily associated with it.

This chapter probes this action of his youth by reconstructing it in two contexts, first for its significance in the life of a man who was now just a youth but was later to be the foremost writer of modern Chinese literature, and second for its interest as a case study of a transitional time for the queue style of hair in the history of China. The analysis also reveals how the episode is a concise example of the way an action of his youth, though shared by many of his cohorts, is heroicized in Lu Xun studies and how he both obfuscates and explains it in later years. In the earliest years of the twentieth century, which is our focus here, the queue was still mandated by the Qing dynasty for all its male subjects, but its rejection on political and cultural grounds had begun. Thus the individual decision of a young student, partially reconstructed, may serve as an instance of a complex phenomenon that today is still primarily understood in political terms but needs a cultural history as well.

The young student's decision to go to Japan was the last in a series of steps that took him, in outlook and geography, increasingly farther from his traditional home in the provincial city of Shaoxing and the countryside that lay so close about it. In his first step, leaving Shaoxing for Nanjing, as he did in 1898, he left behind the study of Confucian texts with tutors in a clan school and discovered, as he later wrote, "such subjects as physics, arithmetic, geography, and physical education." By the time he graduated in 1902 from the School of Mines and Railways (the certificate survives), he had advanced a great deal in learning of the wider world.[1] Among the things he had read or owned were the progressive Shanghai newspaper *Subao*; Adam Smith's *Wealth of Nations* and Thomas Huxley's *Evolution and Ethics*, both translated by Yan Fu; *Renxue* by Tan Sitong, recently executed for his part in the Hundred Days Reform; a series entitled *Science* (*Kexue congshu*); and a two-volume work on the Meiji Restoration.[2] After graduation, he received a place in the first contingent of students sent by the viceroy of Liangjiang, who oversaw the Jiangnan Army Academy, for further studies in Japan. In the event, he remained in Japan for more than seven years, and when he returned to China in 1909, he was a mature man of twenty-eight.

In Japan, Lu Xun wrote half a dozen essays and made several translations that give us a glimpse of the range and types of knowledge that were his interest. All were published in magazines founded by Chinese students, mostly along lines of provincial affiliation. The writings fall into two distinct periods. His second year in Tokyo, 1903, saw three essays and a number of translations, and 1907, his second year after his return to Tokyo from Sendai, saw four essays and a number of translations. The 1903 essays were "Soul of Sparta," an account of Thermopylae with many revealing interpolations; "On Radium" (discovered five years earlier); and "Outline of Chinese Geology."[3] (The last was followed in 1906 with the coauthorship of a book on Chinese mineral resources.) In 1903 he also translated parts of Victor Hugo's *Les Miserables* and Jules Verne's *Journey to the Moon*, in each case with a postface. These earliest writings show that the young student already trended in the direction of reaching people with knowledge that is both concrete and more far reaching than initially apparent. They also show that at this point science formed an important part of that knowledge. As he wrote later, it was at Kōbun that he first learned that water was made up of hydrogen and oxygen and how to locate on a creature's anatomy the point where the body ended and the shell began.[4] For the second of these periods, 1907, besides the four essays, he translated with his brother H. Rider Haggard and Andrew Lang's 1890 novel *The World's Desire*.[5] This work, a fantasy spurred by recent archaeological finds, sends Odysseus to Egypt after the Trojan War, where he witnesses the dealings between the pharaoh and Moses. One can see in this weaving together of Greek, Egyptian, and ancient Near Eastern civilizations that the materials held multiple attractions for Haggard and Lang and indeed for anyone interested, as the young Lu Xun must have been, in large syntheses of mythology, science, and the history of man. But by the next year, 1908, Lu Xun had turned entirely from science and the science in science fiction to the literary writings of Eastern Europe. They became the next source for his translation of knowledge: a work about the Hungarian poet Sandor Petőfi; a number of translations that were never published; and what was, in retrospect, a landmark two-volume translation done with his brother, *Anthology of Literature from Foreign Lands*.[6]

Concerning these early writings by the student, Wang Hui's studies have especially deepened our appreciation of their continuities with the Lu Xun he became. Using the thought-provoking dates of 1903–24 for one major section, Wang focuses especially on the continuities in paradoxes and contradictions in the author. This interest means that the essays from 1907 receive more of his attention than do those of 1903.[7] The theoretical interest of this chapter will be in the opposite direction: rather than seeking continuities, it will isolate as much as possible Lu Xun's experiences during his first year or so in Tokyo so as to leave open the possibility of large changes on the part of the young student. For this reason 1903 will be of primary interest, in particular, the political contexts for two of the essays, "Soul of Sparta" and "Outline of Chinese Geology." The kind of general and scientific knowledge they contained was, by the early 1900s, a major component of the student publications in Tokyo. In the 1920s and 1930s, to speak of continuities for a moment, Lu Xun still saw translation as a rapid and necessary way of establishing a basic core of knowledge. In the 1920s, this was primarily knowledge of literature; in the 1930s, he added art woodcuts, so we see him continuing with a philosophy and practice he had established almost from the beginning.

During his first two years in Japan, Lu Xun lived in Tokyo, enrolled at the newly founded Kōbun Academy, the newest of a number of institutions that prepared Chinese students for matriculation at Japanese institutions of learning (registrar's records survive).[8] Kōbun provided an introduction to the sciences and mathematics and also provided classes in the Japanese language (weekly syllabus survives). In April 1904, he graduated from the academy (the certificate survives) and went on to Sendai Medical School.[9] He left after two years without completing his degree. Over the next years, he, his brother, and Xu Shoushang lived in a number of boardinghouses in Tokyo, embarked on a number of self-directed schemes, and collaborated on a number of literary projects. Xu returned to China in the spring of 1909 to take up a position as dean of Zhejiang Normal College. In the summer of that year, Lu Xun followed him and was appointed a teacher at the same college.

In considering the young student's queue, we focus on the first two years of this eight-year period, Lu Xun's time at Kōbun Academy. This is perhaps the time of the most intense transformations for the overseas student, who was encountering new information and experiences in a country that was itself undergoing rapid political and social changes that were straining its society.

His first two years also coincided with an increase of anti-Qing activities among the Chinese in Japan. These were newly reorganized by veteran activists to reach students and were further intensified by the heightening of tensions between Japan and Russia in their dispute over control of Chinese territories in the northeast. The result was that the nature and scope of political activism suddenly increased. Yet the traces of our student in these two important years are faint. The administrative records from Kōbun Academy for registration and graduation were mentioned above. In other areas, particularly regarding political activities that would seem to be connected with queue cutting, very little can be learned. These two years saw the beginning of political activism among Chinese students. They convened several large assemblies and passed resolutions on the successive territorial and economic demands made by the French, Russian, and Italian governments upon the Qing court. Other meetings that marked ceremonial occasions, such as (lunar) New Year's Day in 1903, turned into a series of anti-Qing speeches. Finally, many demonstrations were held to protest against specific schools that detained students on account of their political activities.

Lu Xun's role in these activities was far from prominent. Later he never gave out any information on these points. In the recollections of the 1960s from contemporaries of that time, it is hard to say whether there is anything to show that Zhou Shuren would later become Lu Xun. Two memoir essays from 1961, for example, by Shen Diemin, who was among Lu Xun's dormitory roommates and must have been at least eighty years old by then, attempt to specify which meetings the young Lu Xun attended and whether he joined certain revolutionary groups.[10] His description of Lu Xun's political activities amounts to the first two meetings of Zhejiang Students Association with Lu Xun agreeing to join, and he adds an account of the group and its plans. Shen also says, vaguely enough, that while at Kōbun, Lu Xun was secretly connected to revolutionary friends, opposed "reform" because he felt it was bound to fail, and vowed to be "a general of revolution." Another classmate remembers some serious words from him.[11] A third classmate, Zhang Xiehe, one of six students sent by the School of Mines and Railways, has similarly vague recollections.[12] The fact that they remain fragments when these memoirs must have been solicited shows the difficulty of pinpointing concrete actions.

Ni Moyan, who has detailed each of the student meetings and strikes in these two years, has shown that, at the most, Lu Xun attended two of the largest assemblies and perhaps a third one. Concerning the writings, as we will see in a subsequent section, Ni proposes a deeper commitment, for he connects "Sparta" and "Geology" with two of the most rousing political issues of these student assemblies: "Sparta" in response to Russian demands and provocations in Manchuria, and "Geology" in response to Italian demands for mineral rights in Zhejiang.[13] That the response took the form of writing was to typify the later Lu Xun, while the lack of recordable overt political actions was also to hold true during the May Fourth Movement.[14] By contrast, the record of activism is quite clear for many of his contemporaries, including, to take a person close to him, Xu Shoushang. The fact is that in general Lu Xun cannot really be distinguished from other serious young men studying in Tokyo. On the other hand, it is possible to make a distinction, as Lu Xun later did, between himself and a frivolous group of students who had a good time "singing under the trees" in Ueno Park and "cooking up home-style beef stews in their rooms."[15] The most lasting outcome of the first two years is not his participation or nonparticipation in political activism but the deep friendship that formed between him and Xu Shoushang. This friendship was to last to the end of their lives and to be, at least for Lu Xun, an uncharacteristically uncomplicated bond.

Against this background of student activism, the assumption of critics and biographers is that cutting the queue is de facto a political act. Certainly the political motivations have proved more easy to articulate than cultural or social ones, for the anti-Qing rationale against the queue is better documented than the cultural reasons. As it is formulated regarding the young Lu Xun, the view is that he vehemently (*yiran*) cut off his queue. At the same time, the accounts are either very brief or very padded, showing that little can be easily added to the quick, political gloss of "vehemence." This chapter aims to go beyond the view of this act as a political declaration by exploring the contexts of these events and by adding to the artifacts relating to them. Its first section expands the question of what the poem and photograph mean by introducing pertinent evidence from the year before and the year after the young student cut his queue. The next sections examine questions of symbolism: what did it mean to cut his hair in 1903 and in Japan? Both factors—the year 1903 and the location Japan—are important, for they shift the focus from the person to the cultural and political forces acting on him at this time, in this place. One impediment to recognizing further relevant material has been a reluctance to associate the great figure of Lu Xun, even in the guise of the young Zhou Shuren, with the backward trait of a queue, even when it is soon to be (defiantly, as all would have it) disposed of. Yet Lu Xun's interpretation of China in this early year, which is a snapshot at one particular time, may not be continuously applicable throughout his life.

The Firsthand Evidence: Photograph and Poem

Two striking pieces of evidence are commonly associated with cutting his queue. Both were produced close to the time, though neither can be precisely dated. These are a photograph that shows him with his hair cut short and a four-line poem containing fiery patriotic sentiments that is inscribed on its back. The combination of photograph and poem into one artifact makes them especially effective. Although little other material of equivalent relevance appears to exist, several other contemporary items can be brought to bear.

The photograph in its surviving print (fig. 2.1) is 4 x 2 ½ inches.[16] It shows the young student in a military-style jacket, presumably the uniform of the Kōbun Academy. The poem that goes with it is a seven-character quatrain.[17] It survives in calligraphy from 1931, when Lu Xun wrote it out again. Here it is, with a translation.[18]

靈台無計逃神矢　　風雨如磐闇故園
寄意寒星荃不察　　我以我血薦軒轅

My mind has no wish to avoid the arrows of the gods
The winds and rains [of political disorder], black as boulders, darken my old home
I entrust my thoughts to the star of a cold night, the king does not understand,
I would offer up my blood for the [descendants] of the Yellow Emperor.

The overall ardent and nationalistic tone of these four lines is clear. The verbs, especially, are strong and unwavering: "no wish to avoid [his fate]" and "would offer up my blood." Although the verb-object of line 3, "entrust my thoughts," may seem nonactive, it is also strong, for the entire line is based on the exalted, allegorical political vocabulary of *Chuci* (Songs of the South), the fourth-century BCE poetry anthology identified with the patriotic Qu Yuan. In spite of these unambiguously fervent assertions, however, there are unresolved meanings and references in every line. This is especially the case for line 1 because it uses a new word, *arrows of the god* (what god? what arrows?), which has given rise to wildly different glosses, for example, from the two people closest to Lu Xun, Xu Shoushang and Xu Guangping. Less dramatically, the references of lines 2 and 3 are also not known, although their political import is clear. We know line 2 refers to political disorders but not whether the poet has specific ones in mind, nor do we know what advice he harbors in line 3 that is not heeded (and not heeded by whom?). Such uncertainties typically beset traditional poems, which were written for oneself or shown only to close friends, but they are not obstacles to the poem's usefulness in this section. In the section "Lu Xun in Japan circa 1903," I suggest an interpretation of line 1, while appendix A summarizes the issues of dating and interpretation. Here we have need of only its obvious features: the overall ardor and nationalistic tone and the final line with the passionate avowal of the young student's willingness to die for his countrymen.

We know that the poem and photograph existed back-to-back because he gave them in this form to Xu Shoushang.[19] To his brother he apparently sent the photograph alone, for Zuoren's *Diary* notes the receipt of it on April 10 but makes no mention of a poem—he usually copied such things into his diary.[20] This is probably an indication that the poem was not yet written and that the intimate connection between poem and photograph was made later, in the copy for Xu. Neither photograph survives. A print must have remained in his possession, for Lu Xun was most likely the one who put it into circulation in 1926.[21] The Beijing Lu Xun Museum has reconstructed the evidence as a postcard-sized souvenir with photograph and poem on the two sides. The photograph and the 1931 calligraphy are reproduced in figures

Figure 2.1. "Photograph with Hair Cut Short," so named by its subject. Courtesy of Beijing Lu Xun Museum.

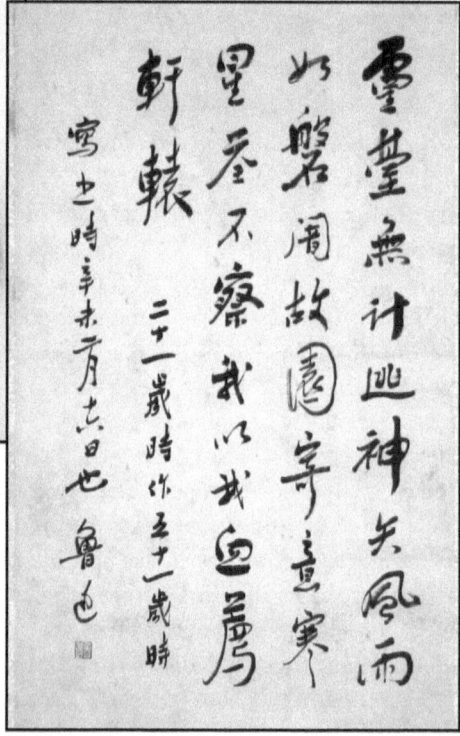

Figure 2.2 The poem known as "Inscribed by the Author on a Small Likeness," as written out in 1931 by its author. Courtesy of Beijing Lu Xun Museum.

2.1 and 2.2 so you can imagine the poem and photograph back-to-back. (The proportions must have been altered to create the souvenir.)

The photograph and poem are referred to by the names used by their recipients. "Photograph with Hair Cut Short" (duan fa xiang) comes from Zhou Zuoren's diary entry, recorded when he received it, and presumably so named on the basis of Lu Xun's accompanying letter.[22] This was brought by a friend from Japan, and Zuoren's entry for that day lists the many items he received including books and another photograph (this is described as a group shot of the student body at Kōbun). Although the universal identification of the "Hair Cut Short" photograph with the one pictured here is conventional, still it was the earliest surviving studio photograph in Lu Xun's possession and he preserved it over the years. The name that Zuoren uses, relying on his brother's information, increases the photograph's significance since it tells us that it is more than a school identification. As for the poem, it is untitled, as classical-language poems often are. Its descriptive name, "Inscribed by the Author on a Small Likeness" was used by Xu Shoushang in an essay written two months after Lu Xun's death.[23] He quoted the poem, and this marks its first publication, that is, it began to exist as something other than a handwritten copy.

Since Zuoren does not mention a poem, it was likely absent from the print sent to him. This strongly suggests that it was not yet written, that the photograph and poem were separate acts of self-identification spread over a brief period of time, and that the photograph came first. Lu Xun had no need to give Xu a photograph since he saw Xu every day, and in fact, as we will see, Xu recollected seeing him right after he cut his queue. Once Lu Xun had a poem to give to Xu, he did, significantly, elect to put it on the back of a photograph. This in turn increases the significance of the poem, which, if it were not inscribed on a photograph, would be just another poem of self-expression, though a powerful one. Once the photograph and poem are joined, they constitute an act of self-definition and draw our attention by means of their dramatic nature. That he put them together for his closest confidant reinforces this import.

The question is, then, what is the identity captured here? The answers supplied have all been political ones. Interestingly, however, Lu Xun's then closest confidants, Zuoren and Xu, later provide mild formulations. Zhou Zuoren offers only the connection of "revolutionary thinking bore fruit and he decided to cut his hair," while Xu focuses not on the act but on a story about when he saw him afterward: "I remember that day, . . . he came into our study."[24] It is those who came after who employ a primarily political tone in a formulation such as "He vehemently cut off that queue, which symbolized the reactionary control of the Qing dynasty." "Vehemently" (*yiran*) is used by nearly everyone in describing this act.[25] Such a word shows how, backed by the existence of photograph and poem, the queue cutting is interpreted solely as political defiance and thus as a foreshadowing of the future great literary figure.

Although this view of the evidence—that political symbolism is intended—must be sound, several provisos should be noted. One is that, aside from the connection of the quatrain to the photograph, Lu Xun never once claimed political intent for himself in cutting his queue. His remarks came down to the idea that it was no big deal. Over the years, he said, "There wasn't anything extraordinary about it, it was just because it was too inconvenient" (1920), "I left it behind in Japan, giving half to the hostel maid and half to the barber" (1935), and "I was not like Zhang Taiyan, a man of Yue with the Yue temperament . . . in my case, it was simply inconvenient" (1936).[26] This studied casualness cannot be wholly sincere, but it does show that to describe the act as *yiran* overlooks at least his deliberately self-disparaging statements. Another important counter to the political emphasis is that the sheer newness presented by the evidence is an important quality. The two gleam with newness, the photograph as much as the poem, due to the short hair, of course, but also to the Western (Prussian) military-style school uniform adopted in Japan, which signaled a new-style school oriented to new curricula. The poem, too, is all new, despite its classical language and form (no other language or form was available to him in 1903) and despite the way the intense political sentiments also fit into the Confucian concern for the state that is a traditional theme of lyric poetry. One of its deliberate novelties is to fit into a mere four lines a smorgasbord of many traditions: intense Daoist self (*lingtai*) plus a totally new word, *shenshi* (both in line 1); anguish expressed in Confucian vocabulary (line 2); the heightened solipsistic patriotism of Qu Yuan from the Chu culture of the south (line 3); and, in line 4, use of the archaic "Xuanhuang" to refer to the Yellow Emperor. Lu Xun never did say what the neologism *shenshi* might mean; what he did mention in later years was his love of novelty in vocabulary in those years. His style in the essay "Sparta" (also 1903), he wrote, was influenced by Yan Fu (1853–1921), the pioneering translator of the exciting new ideas in Thomas Huxley's *Evolution and Ethics*, especially his use of transliterated sounds for new concepts, resulting in coinages "that are probably understood only by me now."[27] Newness in a culture that values the old has a political dimension, but a heady sense of freedom can be very personal.

To provide fuller contexts for photograph and poem, I propose that we ask what these brave pieces of evidence represent a change *from*. And were there developments, changes, *afterward*? There is no reason to assume that Lu Xun had always held this view, nor that his later life contained a fulfillment of it. If nothing else, his young age argues against this. Thus two threads of analysis are pursued below: first, when was this heroic stance acquired and can we trace what preceded it; and, second, was it ever discarded, and if so, when?

Changes From

There is general agreement that the poem and photograph are stirring and mark a new stage in the young student's consiousness. At the same time, there is general reluctance to consider the question of what they are new *from*. This disinclination, widely held, was most pronounced during the decades of systemic Communist Party control and, in terms of the young Lu Xun before 1903, most striking in the visual interpretations. This section begins by briefly considering a few of them, for visual art is particularly suited to revealing to us our own tendency to feel both that something in his consciousness or character may distinguish him even at a young age and that possession of a queue is somehow inconsistent with that consciousness. Whereas this dual attitude need not obtrude in verbal works, in the art that illustrate his pre-1903 years, the queue could not be avoided. In the very search for solutions we see cultural forces at work to which we still subscribe to some degree and, in the art considered here, political forces as well.

These are artists of great talent and training whose works in other subject matter and whose prominence both amply testify to their abilities. In their encounter with a subject matter that must be positively portrayed, we see that the connection of the debased style of the queue with the great man was a sensitive question both to the cultural bureaucracy and in social attitudes. One solution seen in the art is to include the queue but in such a way that it cannot be discerned. Thus in a well-known print by Yang Keyang (b. 1914) (not shown), the boy Lu Xun, out to purchase medicines for his father, is shown to the viewer three-quarters from the back, but his black queue lies on a black vest, from which it cannot be distinguished, and furthermore his person is in the shadow. In another well-known print, this a black-and-white by Zhao Yannian, the young student, leaving home to study in Nanjing, turns his head away from the viewer to bid farewell to his mother, who is standing in the family compound's gateway. This is a pose that might permit a view of the queue, but it happens to lie on the other side from the viewer. In both prints, the naturalness of the pose, together with the strong converging diagonals of the composition and the high artistic achievement, conceal the artists' concealment of the queue.[28]

A more common solution shows the young subject from the front. Though the queue is then not an issue, a further touch is often added: the other required part of the queue style, the shaven part in front, is made smaller and shaded a bit so that it is minimized. A quick glance would give the impression merely of closely cropped hair, itself perhaps a style unusual for the time but one much softened from a band of shaven surface all around the head. This is the case in a watercolor (artist not named) that also shows the moment of leaving home for Nanjing (fig. 2.3). In this lovely portrayal of a youth on the verge of adulthood, there is some heroism that would be especially at odds with a queue, for this young Lu Xun, walking towards the viewer from the gateway of the family compound, has just passed two members of the gentry who are clearly criticizing his intent to study "foreign things," but he strides on firmly, his expression resolute. The same softening of the frontal area is seen in two oil paintings, one of the young student when he arrives in Nanjing (artist not named) (fig. 2.4) and one when he is on board ship for Japan by Zhang Zuying (b. 1940) (not shown). In both, the setting is energized by clouds and a distant horizon, vigorous settings for an awakened-looking hero who could have already written the patriotic poem. It is only at a lower level of skill that we see the issue sidestepped by changing the facts rather than softening them. Thus we have an illustration that shows him embarking for Japan with his hair already cut (fig. 2.5).[29] Finally, depictions

Figure 2.3. The young Lu Xun leaving for Nanjing, artist unnamed, watercolor. In the collection of Beijing Lu Xun Museum.

Figure 2.4. The young Lu Xun arrives in Nanjing, artist unnamed, oil. Source: Ouyang Wenli, ed., *Pictorial Biography of Lu Xun*.

of Lu Xun as a boy in his mother's home village or with the country boys who were sometimes his companions are less subject to such remedies, perhaps because the young age absolves him of accountability. Yet, often the queue is softened by making the picture as a whole the subject matter, for example by depicting a countryside landscape in which the friends are relatively small figures. Han Heping's watercolor illustrations of "Hometown" include one that sets the young Lu Xun and his friend Runtu in such a gentle landscape.

Owing to their great skill, these images, which are works of art in their own right, make an imprint on our minds that demonstrate the hold that cultural constructs of the queue still has on us. In instructive contrast to all these examples, there is no such hesitation when it comes to depicting Ah Q. For him, the queue is as much the symptom of his Ah Q-ness as it must be kept at a distance from his creator. In Liu Jian'an's portrait (fig. 2.6), for instance, the queue is almost a personality in its own right.[30]

The self-defination encapsulated in the photograph and poem is one moment in a series of moments that make up a life. What kinds of snapshots might have preceded this one? One possibility is that Lu Xun might have been strong and emphatic all along, as Xu Shoushang for one seemed to have been. Xu arrived in Tokyo in September 1902, and that same day, "impatient with coiling up my hair," he and his classmate Han

Figure 2.5. The young Lu Xun, on board ship to Japan, hair already cut short. Courtesy of the New York Public Library.

Figure 2.6. Liu Jian'an, Ah Q. Gift of Professor and Mrs. Theodore Herman, Picker Art Gallery, Colgate University.

Qiangshi had their queues cut off.³¹ Xu was also almost immediately engaged in political activism, and, unlike Lu Xun, his name is readily found among the political records of this time. Aside from a passing mention of his queue cutting in an essay on Lu Xun, however, Xu said no more about his own case. It may be that he had fewer financial considerations. Although he was also sent by the Zhejiang provincial government, his family was well off—"Mr. Lu Xun often said that even in their student days, Mr. Xu was already wearing western clothes made of smoke-gray wool"—and he might not have needed the government stipend.³²

As it happens, we have solid evidence for a different kind of person in a period shortly before this moment marked by the "Hair Cut Short" photograph and poem. It is evidence from the young Zhou Shuren himself, and it is a completely parallel set of evidence from Japan in the year before. In 1902, he had produced *another* combination of photograph plus poem. Furthermore, we know that this was a combination from the start, for this set was also sent to his closest confidant, in this case his brother Zuoren in a letter of June 8. This would be two months after his arrival (Xu did not come until September). The 1902 set provides a contrast that sharply emphasizes the newness of the 1903 set. This one also has not survived in its original back-to-back state. Only the poem is extant, separately preserved through Zuoren's copy of it in his diary entry of June 16, from which *LXQJ* collects it.³³ No print of the photograph has turned up. From line 3 of the poem, however, we know that the photograph shows the student in the uniform of Kōbun Academy. He sent three prints home. On the back of the one intended for Zuoren, he wrote this poem.

會稽山下之平民　　日出國中之遊子
弘文學院之制服　　鈴木真一之攝影
二十餘齡之青年　　四月中旬之吉日
走五千餘里之郵筒　達星杓仲弟之英盼

An ordinary person who lived below Kuaiji Mountain
A wanderer who one day departed his country
The uniform of Kōbun Academy
A photograph from Suzuki Shin'ichi
A youth of twenty-some years,
On a lucky day in the middle days of April,
A missive traveling more than five thousand *li*
Will reach the resplendent countenance of my middle brother Xingbiao.

This poem is completely different from the quatrain he was to write within the year. There every line expresses utterly serious sentiments. Here we have lightness and a lack of portentous concerns. The style matches the easygoing, rhythmic gait derived from its seven-character, old-style (*qiyan gushi*) form, which is folk in its origins and here is not densely packed with meaning. It uses just one playful device seven times in eight lines: in the first seven lines, each line is a noun phrase (no verbs) in which the last word is the noun that is modified by all the preceding words. (In English translation, this is reversed: the noun comes first, or nearly first, in each line.) The ending couplet is a sentence that partially preserves the pattern: line 7's final word is a noun (missive), but it is also the subject of the next, final line. To go with this closing variation, the ending also contains an exaggerated piece of diction, "my brother's resplendent countenance" (*yingfen*). This lightness is laborious to point out but playful to read. The lines also skillfully provide information (on the school uniform, name of the photography studio, and date, in lines 3, 4, and 6) that the recipient, his brother, would not otherwise know.

The points shared by the two sets of poems paired with photographs are just as important. Here, too, the author sketches a portrait of himself, though a very different one: an ordinary person (pingmin), a Kōbun student, and a youth. The lines show his sense of the great changes taking place—in Kuaiji in China versus at Kōbun in Japan, a distance of five thousand *li*. In both years, he takes stock of these changes in both photograph and poem. He sees no disparity in employing the same format twice. Change cannot occur in a straight line. The 1902 poem and photograph, so much not a part of any straight line, is difficult to fit into studies of the author's classical poetry.[34] Even its placement in *LXQJ* as the very last of the creative writings signifies its marginality.

A poem captures only a moment, and this lighthearted moment is difficult to generalize.[35] Easier to bring out are the serious stages in the young student's life. Indeed, each step he took out of the comparative backwaters of Shaoxing introduced new information to his ken. Four years earlier, even the short distance between Shaoxing and Nanjing had caused him to discover something of China's situation in the larger world, information that he passed on in a letter home to family. According to Zuoren's diary, in Hangzhou (on his way to Nanjing), Lu Xun saw in the newspaper *Knowledge of the New* (*Zhixin bao*) a map of China divided among "the five countries of Great Britain, Japan, Russia, France, and Germany, and describing their plan to proceed up the Yangtze to take Baimen and thence to divide [China's] land."[36] In January of 1902, four months before he left for Japan, the early death of a classmate at the School of Mines and Railways brought forth a somber reflection that begins: "When a man dies, / He hates only that his ambitions are unfulfilled"

男兒死耳 恨壯志未酬.[37] When we read this, it assimilates "naturally" to our conception of the young student and the type of classmates he might have had, for its sentiments are serious and public spirited. On his departure for Japan, he received a set of farewell poems expressing similarly stirring expectations. "The great ambitions of a heroic man are difficult to probe / As he goes forth to the distant land of Japan" begins the first quatrain presented to him.[38] (Lu Xun appears not to have responded with a poem, for Zuoren records only the friend's three poems.) By contrast, the jaunty poem he wrote and sent to his brother four months later is hard to assimilate to our portrait of the young student even though he gave it the additional force of inscription on a photograph.

Now we consider the other piece of 1902 evidence, the photograph. In its absence, what can we deduce about it? Lu Xun arrived in Tokyo on April 4, and by the end of the month he had enrolled in Kōbun Academy. The photograph was taken in this month (line 6) by the well-known photography studio Suzuki Shin'ichi (line 4). We do not know exactly what he looked like, but from line 3 we know it shows him in the uniform of Kōbun Academy. But think: what else does it show? A queue, of course! It undoubtedly showed its author with his hair still in a queue. First of all, since in April 1903 Zuoren records a photograph his brother sent showing what his short hair looks like, earlier photographs *must show Lu Xun with a queue!* Furthermore, it is probable that besides wearing his uniform he was also wearing its cap, as is the common practice, for Zhou Zuoren recollects its absence in the (short-haired) photograph he received the next year: "He had a new one taken *without the cap* [emphasis added] and sent it to me to show what he looked like."[39] Now, if he had a cap on in this 1902 photograph, there are a number of ways he could have worn his hair: he could have had it unbraided and coiled loose and flat under the cap, in a facsimile of short hair; he could have coiled the plaited queue under the cap; or, in a third style, he could have placed the cap directly over the queue. Zhou Zuoren tells us which of the three styles was, at some point, employed by his brother when he says that, like other students who sought to minimize the distinctive look of the queue, he initially unbound his hair and wore it on top of his head hidden under a cap (i.e., under the school cap).[40] So Lu Xun employed the first of the three options described above. Figure 2.7 is an illustration of the last style (though not the clothing).[41]

This 1902 photograph and Zuoren's information make an interesting contrast for readers since there is a famous passage in which Lu Xun disparages the methods by which students hid their queues. In "Mr. Fujino," he describes the first two methods mentioned above.

In the park, [lounged] "students from the Qing Empire," their long queues coiled on top of their heads, [poking up] the crown of their student caps like Mount Fuji. Others had undone their queues and arranged their hair flat on their heads, so that when their caps were removed it [came down and] glistened for all the world like the lustrous locks of young ladies; and they would toss their heads too. It was really a charming sight.[42]

"The Fuji hairdo" was a standard term for the effort made to blend in, described by Marius Jansen as "a pompadoured compromise" achieved by barbers.[43] This conjunction of an unadvertised period in Lu Xun's life and his later sarcastic description of essentially the same thing shows us something about ourselves as readers and also about the author. About ourselves, it is telling that Lu Xun's description in "Mr. Fujino" is well known, but Zhou Zuoren's associated information about his initial hairstyle is not quoted in conjunction. About the author, it is equally telling that in making this vivid, cutting description he provides readers with a good target, as well as a feel-good target, in the "Qing Empire" students without any hint whatsoever that he once belonged to this group of students that wore this style of hair. What adjectives can encompass the authorial motivations that keep his personal stake oblique in the vivid sketch in "Mr. Fujino"? Lu Xun was never easy on himself, yet this is only the first instance in this study in which we see the severing of visible connections between personal experience and the much more famous fiction or essay in which a distanced account is provided, an account that is literarily so effective as to direct the reader's attention wholly toward the object described and not at all toward the author. Certainly the author's privacy has been protected.

Actually, the comments that Zhou Zuoren made over the years regarding his brother's early hairstyle are vague and sometimes inconsistent. For example, he does not seem to clearly differentiate between the very different 1902 and 1903 poems, nor between the two very different photographs, and

Figure 2.7. Queue under a new-style student cap. Source: H. Y. Lowe, *The Adventures of Wu*, 5. Courtesy of Library of Congress.

furthermore he seems to consider the distinction not that important. This is evident in a manuscript essay quoted in the *Lu Xun Chronology*.[44] He writes, of a poem, "This must have been the [defiant quatrain] written on the back of the February, 1903, 'Hair Cut Short' photograph. It could not have been on the photograph from the previous year where he was wearing the Kōbun uniform. The difference between the two photographs is only [*"only"*!] that in one he is bareheaded while in the other one he has a student cap on because on his head was still a 'Mt Fuji,' which was not that great looking." He sounds as though he finds the poems, and even the photographs, hard to keep straight. (Note two inconsistencies here with his own diary: he writes February 1903 for the "Hair Cut Short" photograph [the date is actually April] and also implies that it came with the inscription.) In another instance, in reply to a query from the critic Hu Bing in 1957, he gives the impression that the 1903 poem does not loom large in his memory. Hu Bing had asked about its date of composition, and Zuoren arrives at his answer, which is itself a range of several months, by reasoning from other, extraneous factors. His reply, as quoted by Hu, is "My recollection is that when I saw this poem, it should have been at the time he first cut his queue, which would be between *jimou* third month [i.e., April] and when he came back to China during summer vacation [August]. For if he were still wearing a queue, it would have been ridiculous for line 4 to refer to 'the descendants of the Yellow Emperor.'"[45] (He is saying that "descendants of the Yellow Emperor" specifies that it is the Han people, not the Manchus, for whom Lu Xun is willing to die.) Note that in this reply the poem is separate from the photograph.

These two contrasting sets of poems and photographs and Zuoren's vague, contradictory recollections are warnings that although the "Hair Cut Short" set is significant, it is part of a larger picture and we cannot extrapolate backward from 1903 and see him as awakened before the fact. The artists' renditions of him setting off with a determined and resolute mien for Japan do not work if you have this earlier set. The paintings and prints do not depict the person who wrote the 1902 poem and sent home three copies of the 1902 photograph. One critic who does mention the 1902 poem and photograph as a set nonetheless omits to mention that the photograph *has* to show the queue. He merely says, "After Lu Xun enrolled, he sent photographs to his family, among them one to Zhou Zuoren which had written on its back the following verse: [and he quotes the eight lines]." This despite a drawn-out account of cutting the queue a bit later.[46]

To return to Lu Xun's early Japan years, the description in "Mr. Fujino" is usually quoted to support the idea that it was witnessing subterfuges like those of his fellow students that propelled the young student to his more straightforward action. Thus the typical comment that "Lu Xun hated these ploys and thus under the stimulus of the anti-Qing movement, he vehemently (*yiran*) cut off his queue."[47] Yet some of the actual evidence is to the contrary—the queue must have been acceptable to him at least at the time he sent three prints home and even increased the photograph's importance as a memento with a poem. Indeed, in later years, there was a time when he almost disclosed that he belonged to the group that arranged their hair loose and flat under the cap: in 1936, in listing the drawbacks of the queue, which his tone implied were all petty considerations for nonheroic persons like himself, he wrote that "it was inconvenient to take off your hat," that it was inconvenient in physical education, and that it felt awkward arranged above the forehead.[48] This must have been his personal experience. (Men in physical contests or engaged in physical labor tied up their queues [fig. 2.8], but they would not have been members of the gentry.)[49]

As it happens, we do have a surviving image of our student when he still had a queue. It is a group photograph of Zhejiang students in which his head is a mere blob, identified by editors as being in the fourth row, fourteenth from the left (fig. 2.9).[50] The photograph was taken in November 1902 at the end of the meeting at which students from Zhejiang, his home province, formed the Zhejiang Students Association. The meeting also passed a resolution to publish a magazine, *Zhejiang Tide* (*Zhejiang chao*), one of many province-based patriotic student publications in Japan at this time. This was where most of Lu Xun's 1903 and 1907 writings were published. The group photograph was reproduced in its first issue, February, 17, 1903. In it he must have had a queue, as did nearly everyone else—after all, he was the first from his year to cut his. Did they then, at closer range, all look like the students he satirized, their school uniform caps perched on top of coiled queues? (Xu Shoushang, who must also be in this photograph, is one exception; he arrived in September and, as we saw, cut his hair the next day.) Magnifications have been made of Lu Xun in nearly every early group

Figure 2.8. Queues tied up during annual summer competition among soldiers – a detail from *Contests of Skill and Courage, Dianshizhai Pictorial*, 1884. Courtesy of Library of Congress.

photograph in which he appears because of their rarity, but not this one. Here is my attempt (fig. 2.10). It is hard to make out anything, but it must stand for contrast between our 1902 and our 1903 material: he went from *this* poem to *this* poem, from *this* photograph to *this* photograph.

I close this section with a different set of contrasts, which illustrate how Western-style hair is not required for an open attitude toward the outside world. Only one of many examples that can be cited even at this late (1908) date, it is interesting because it involves Cai Yuanpei (1868-1940), a half generation older than Lu Xun and later to be his lifelong patron, and because the visual evidence is so parallel. Cai went abroad to study in 1908, when he was already forty. Later to hold many important positions in the government education world, at the time of his departure, he was already a considerable figure. The first photograph of Cai reproduced here was taken in 1907, on the eve of his departure for studies in Berlin (fig. 2.11). It shows what we know: that even among the progressive elite, as late as 1907 a queue was still standard. On its back is an inscription to his younger brother noting the date and the occasion, his departure (fig. 2.12). Finally, we have photograph of Cai, taken the next year in Berlin, wholly altered in appearance (fig. 2.13).[51]

Figure 2.9. Group photograph of students from Zhejiang province, *Zhejiang Tide*, February, 1903. Courtesy of Beijing Lu Xun Museum.

Figure 2.10. Head of Lu Xun – detail of 2.9.

CUTTING HIS QUEUE : 71

Figure 2.11. Cai Yuanpei, on the eve of his 1907 departure from Beijing. Source: Cai Jian'guo, *Cai Yuanpei Pictorial Biography*, 25. Courtesy of Library of Congress.

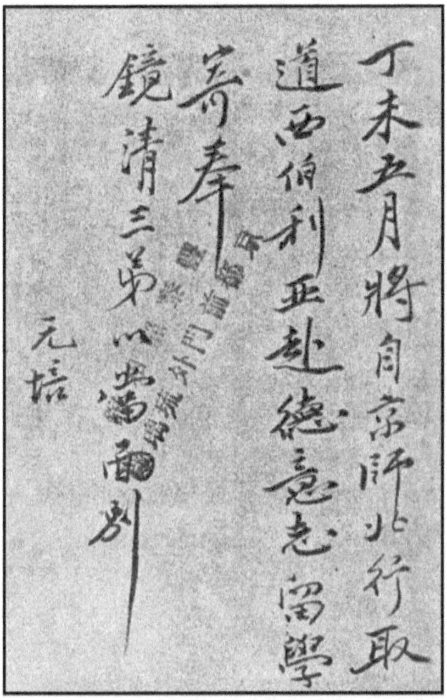

Figure 2.12. Inscription on the back of 1907 photograph. "In the 5th month of the dingwei year [1907], about to set out from Beijing northward via Siberia to Germany with the intention of studying there. Sent to third brother Jingqing in lieu of a personal leave-taking. Yuanpei." Stamped with the photography studio's name and location. Source: Cai Jian'guo, *Cai Yuanpei Pictorial Biography*, 25. Courtesy of Library of Congress.

Figure 2.13. Portrait of Cai Yuanpei in Berlin, 1908. Source: Cai Jian'guo, *Cai Yuanpei Pictorial Biography*, 25. Courtesy of Library of Congress.

After

There is no doubt that this photograph and especially the poem capture a militant time. The question is how long this radical stance lasted. David Pollard, for example, would say not long, for he is of the view that 1903 was "the year of Lu Xun's greatest militancy in Japan."[52] This seems right, but before we look at the change in his attitude we must first consider some information that adds to our knowledge of this brief period of militancy.

The first piece of information is that Lu Xun arrived in Tokyo with a goal of taking direct action in the political situation. He had initially sought to matriculate at Seijō Academy, which was then the preparatory school for the Army Officers School. This was not unrealistic: he had come to Tokyo as a graduate of a school run by the Army Academy and on a government stipend from the Liangjiang viceroy, which was funded by the Nanyang Army.[53] Entrance to Seijō was restricted to government-funded students, which he was. He must have thought his entrance highly likely, for his brother's diary records a letter written four days after his arrival stating that "any day now, he will be entering Seijō Academy."[54] Why he did not, we do not know, although it is a fact that all six graduates from the School of Mining entered Kōbun. (These two academies absorbed the greatest number of students in that year, 152 and 172, respectively, out of just over 500).[55] These connections with China's modern military, one completed and one desired, are worth noting, although it is not certain how to give them their full value. The poem is clear about Lu Xun's ardent love of country, and this is consistent with his lifelong engagement with China and the Chinese character, although that was to be very differently expressed. But the actual intention to enter a military preparatory school, when added to his graduation from one administered by the military—at the least these indicate the fluidity of the situation for him and the flexibility of a young person's outlook. As an aside, a satirical poem on the hauteur of Seijō students was attributed to Lu Xun by an old classmate and this disparagement is more often cited than his hope to enter Seijō.[56] The poem is in a triangle shape, with each line one character longer than the previous line, and thus fun to read, but any reading of it should be complicated by the above perspective and it will then be less tempting to accept the attribution.

The second item consistent with the poem's militancy is Lu Xun's essay "Soul of Sparta," published in June of 1903. An account of the Spartan defense of Thermopylae, it shares with the poem a spirit of ready self-sacrifice and soaring rhetoric. "May the spirit of the Spartan warriors last forever and ever!" the young writer declares. He points out that the path for saving the country is martial: "They must renounce the pen for the sword." He quotes Spartan women who rebuke their husbands for returning alive from the battlefield. He reproves the reader who is blind to China's fundamental flaws and internal strife: "You, apparently, have not seen countries where base slaves . . . kill their countrymen."

The question is, after this moment caught in the 1903 photograph and poem and after these frequently quoted lines from "Sparta," what happened next? The mature Lu Xun is the opposite of the speaker in the poem. He never advocated violent confrontation, for himself or others. The evidence suggests that this attitude, so evident in the 1920s and 1930s, began as soon as the next year, that the student of even a year later was different in his views. A retreat from the ardency of the last line may be one reason that Lu Xun never made the poem known, for the headlong rush to self-sacrifice in line 4 is especially contradicted in the future by his frequently equivocal writer's style and the mind behind it. First, he never again holds the view that death is a sacrifice worth making, and, second, he seldom again makes an open avowal of a position. On the first point, if we look at the adult Lu Xun, the abhorrence of the shedding of blood, even righteous blood, is an unmistakable feature of his outlook. The adult Lu Xun refused to equate blood sacrifice with the worthiness of a cause. As he explicitly said in a 1923 lecture delivered at Beijing Women's Normal College, "We have no right to urge people to sacrifice themselves" (although it is true that he adds, "And [we have] no right to stop them either" and further adds, "This choice of sacrifice is a personal one which has nothing in common with the social commitment of revolutionaries.")[57] In 1926, when students killed by government fire on March 18 included one of his, his responses were so complex that their underlying principle—that lives are precious—was not heard. His eloquent mourning was read as a validation of the students' sacrifice, but in truth his chief plea was for the dying to end.[58] He did not volunteer the blood of others, even in the form of elegies. This was again true in 1931, when the deaths of the young writers who came to be known as the Five Martyrs included his disciple Rou Shi. As Wang Dehou notes, the importance of being alive is a seemingly simple principle that is in fact subversive of many unthinkingly held tenets.[59] This is an important point about Lu Xun that is also emphasized by, interestingly, an editor at the *People's Liberation Army Daily* in a work on *Call to Arms* published by the army's press.[60]

There is evidence that this withdrawal began as soon as the following year. There was the practical matter that by June 1904 he was in medical school in Sendai, quite a different place from Tokyo's concentration of Chinese students and their many meetings and publications. Still, at the time he chose medicine, he had not wholly retreated from the idea of direct action. He thought he could do both. He had "a beautiful dream," he wrote, that he could cure people like his father and then "in times of war, could serve as a military physician."[61] Yet while he was still in Tokyo, there was a telling incident in which he refused an opportunity to act as an assassin. As he later said, "When I was engaged in anti-Qing revolutionary activities, I was once asked to carry out an assassination." He replied by speaking of his concern about his mother if he should die in the attempt, and the other party replied that a person with a divided mind would not be able to carry out this kind of task. This episode is known only from one account, told by Lu Xun to a young Japanese scholar, Masuda Wataru, who visited him nearly daily for ten months in 1931.[62] Today this story is sometimes used as evidence of his selfishness, which is then extended to other aspects of his life.[63] Interestingly, though, "Medicine" has a widowed mother left grief-stricken by the execution of her revolutionary son. At any rate, Dikötter has described 1903 in Japan as "a turning point marked by the gradual emergence of a virulent nationalism."[64] The more radical of the politicized students advocated assassinations and bombings, as was the case worldwide in the early years of the twentieth century. The plan that came Lu Xun's way would have been one of many bruited in the fervent atmosphere. Pollard makes the plainer conclusion that "he never again expressed himself willing, even by implication, to literally take up the sword and lay his life on the line."[65] Stepping back from the fervor of his poem's line 4 is consistent with other things known about the later Lu Xun, particularly his tendency to hold back from mass emotion.

Another point is that Lu Xun did not again make the absolute avowals found in this year of the quatrain and "Sparta." Nor did he ever voice such certainty in advocating action again. When he relinquished the certainty that death validated the worthiness of the cause, he did not acquire new certainties. When he came to write, his output was predicated on seeking principled paths through difficulties, but he did so without ever presuming to cast himself or his protagonists as principled persons in the mold of the speaker in this poem. This roundabout type of negation that constituted principle was a peculiar characteristic of the mature Lu Xun's power and influence. It never took the form of overt declarations. Throughout many crises in the future, this remained true and has thwarted the search for some proof of a positively stated principle behind his excoriating words. Yet, although he changed, this poem remained important to him throughout his life. This is not a contradiction. He never repudiated the poem; he simply kept it private. In chapter 4, we will examine the new meanings with which he endowed the poem as events unfolded in later years.

The Event Itself

There is no contemporary record and hence no exact date for the poem and photograph. The date is usually given as April 1903, or sometimes more generally as the spring of 1903, about a year after Lu Xun's arrival in Japan. The month of April comes from the date of his brother's receipt of the photograph, but it could hardly have been taken in April since the accompanying letter is dated the second. And the queue cutting must have occurred some months earlier than that because in the photograph (the one we have), the shaven parts of the queue style have grown in fully (which would have taken two to five months?). The *Lu Xun Chronology* places it in the month of March without giving a reason.[66]

There is only one other event whose date we can relate it to, and that has a time frame of "some time before April 1903." The event is included here even though it does not narrow the range of time, for it shows that queue cutting had many meanings simultaneously, and in this case a meaning that was not compatible with patriotic gestures. This frequently recounted incident involved an official sent with the Zhejiang delegation, named Yao Wenfu in some accounts, who, according to all, was having an affair.[67] In the radicalized atmosphere, a number of students decided to teach him a lesson. They included Zou Rong, whose *Revolutionary Army* was soon to take the patriotic world by storm, and Chen Duxiu, the future founder of both *New Youth* and the Communist Party. They cut off his queue and hung it in a doorway. Everyone went to look at this public shaming, Xu among them, and presumably Lu Xun too, since Zuoren records a letter about it on May 7, 1903.[68] As to relative timing, Xu says that Lu Xun cut his queue at some point before this; N's account in "A Story about Hair" (where all other details accurately reflect Lu Xun's life) has the same sequence (N cut his hair, *then* the womanizing official had his queue cut off).[69] As to when Yao find himself a victim, Zou was forced by his part in the prank to return to China in April, so this gives us the same date as "some time before April."

With Yao and the young Lu Xun, two instances of queue cutting of quite different meanings occurred in the same space of time. The Yao incident is cited in many places, with the writers taking the side of the young vigilantes. Some comment that this was a common measure dealt out to adulterers. Since the perpetrators all became well-known figures in history, this likely increased the fame of Yao's sorry case. A reason for choosing this particular form of vigilantism might be that cutting Yao's queue made his position as a Qing official very difficult. A possible additional reading of Yao's situation might rely on Edward Leach's thoughts on hair. Drawing on theories from anthropology and psychoanalysis that speculated that hair on the head has sexual connotations, Leach proposes that the "magical potency" of hair means its cutting in a "ritual" can equal "castration." To this C. R. Hallpike has objected that the assumed connection between hair and sex "lacks prima facie reason."[70] Leach's essay was not observationally based, but in cases like Yao's his is actually a workable hypothesis.

Yao's victimization shows that queue cutting can have sharply different meanings in the same time period. Yet another meaning is found in Xu Shoushang's 1936 recollection, where his account points to feelings that are not fiercely political. This is how he describes seeing his friend soon after he cut his queue when he came to Xu's study.

> I remember that day, after he'd cut his hair, he came to our study [assigned to ten or more students in Xu's year], on his face just a faint expression of happiness. I said, "Ah, a completely new edifice!" (*bilei yixin*). He ran his hand over his head, and we exchanged a smile. This feeling, this scene—all these years ago, and they are still fresh. This is why I said that this was my earliest memory of him and that even today it is as clear as if it were just before my eyes.[71]

On Xu's side, their lifelong friendship began with this incident. His words give a personal, affectionate context to his friend's action and show us a moment when words were not needed. The passage is almost like fiction in that feelings and motives must be inferred through the depicted outward behavior. Are we seeing happiness? A sense of release? Something else? It is interesting that Lu Xun spoke not a word, that the only comment was from Xu. Lu Xun exhibited only a behavior, "a faint expression of happiness," and, after Xu's comment, "ran his hand over his head and we exchanged a smile." Where in this scene is the political meaning? As depicted, politics comes far behind. This snapshot by Xu Shoushang suggests that more than one factor is involved, which also means the poem imparts only one of them. Because the political history of the queue is well known in outline, the poem fits into it. By contrast, factors that correlate with the subjective details—"ran his hand over his head," "we exchanged a smile"—for these, we need a cultural or social history of the queue to understand what Xu indicates about Lu Xun's frame of mind.

Lu Xun also left a charming vignette that shows almost the same physical, or apolitical, gesture as Xu Shoushang captured, but about *his* friends. This vignette is from nearly ten years later, when he was back in Shaoxing. He recalled a visit from friends soon after their native Shaoxing went over to the Republican Revolution.

Some old friends from the country, also without queues, came, and as soon as we met, they smoothed their hands over their bare heads and said, smiling from their hearts, ah, finally such a day has arrived.[72]

Like Xu's account, this has the evocative quality of fiction. It is a moment whose origin is a political event but is rendered in personal terms: "smoothing their hands over their bare heads," "smiling from their hearts." We see them act before we hear them speak. It is true that there is a political dimension in the words "finally such a day has arrived," a welcome to the new dispensation, but the happiness, the sense of release, is uppermost and might be translated into cultural rather than political history. This is what Lu Xun emphasizes in his recollection of his friends, and from this Xu might have taken his lead. In Lu Xun's final essay, incomplete on his death, he writes that after twenty-five years he still finds himself with the same physical gesture of touching the back of his head and that it was "a sign of triumph, meaning, 'After all, my queue is cut off.'"[73] Here again, the "triumph" is personal as much as political.

The Queue Becomes a Symbol

What did it mean for Lu Xun to cut his queue? The larger question is what did it mean for him to do so in 1903 in Japan?[74] Both factors—in 1903 and in Japan—draw our attention away from a focus on Lu Xun and cast it more usefully on the forces acting on him. This in turn gives us reasons to attend to a time period that turns out to be interesting in itself.

Certain questions are raised by the year 1903. Is this an "early" date? And is "early" more likely to correlate with the act as political symbolism? It is true that he did it at a time before Qing dynasty law requiring the queue could be blithely flouted. This being the case, does this mean that "early" equates to "harder" and thus to more politically meaningful? Xu Shoushang says, and consequently it is often emphasized, that Lu Xun was the first in his Jiangnan class of 1922 to cut his queue. This piece of information, itself only factual, tends to be equated with political. Yet one might ask what the role of social conformity in this political schema is. Individual actions tend to be located in a mix of political and cultural reasons, and though political reasons are easy to recite, the cultural dimensions surely cannot be absent.

The beginning and end of the history of the queue, its imposition by the Manchus in 1644 and its abolition by the Republic in 1911, are well known, but how do we mark the middle? We know that near the end of the nineteenth century calls for cutting the queue began to be heard, but where, in what must have been a rapidly moving decade, does 1902–3 fit in?

Since the earliest records, the hair of Chinese men, always worn long, had been bound in various ways on the top of the head. In the fifth century BCE, Confucius could already use bound hair (and type of clothing) as a shorthand for the civilized way of life: "If it were not for Guan Zhong, we might now be wearing our hair loose (pifa) and our clothes fastened on the left."[75] Only those who rejected or were rejected by society wore any style other than bound hair. Monks shaved their heads; Daoists cut their topknots and wore their hair loose, as did barbarians, eccentrics, outlaws, criminals, and those in mourning. (These were the same groups exempted from the queue when it was imposed.) Thus the beggar in this eighteenth-century drawing by William Alexander (fig. 2.14) has unbound hair and unshaved pate. The Taiping rebels of the mid-nineteenth century, whose depredations formed the folk stories of Lu Xun's childhood, grew their hair in defiance of the Qing and wore it loose.[76] In the 2001 film *Crouching Tiger, Sleeping Dragon*, the older hero is a good outlaw, that is, he only defies corrupt authorities, and he keeps his forehead shaved and hair braided; by contrast, the film's young hero, a bandit from the steppes, wears his hair loose and wild, which also coincides nicely with the look of the romantic individualist. There seems to be a universality to this distinction between civilized and wild on the basis of hair. Hallpike has proposed that "Long hair is associated with being outside society and the cutting of the hair symbolizes re-entering society."[77] If we substitute bound and unbound hair for his short and long hair, his schema fits the Chinese case well. In fact, Hallpike allows for this, too, for he does not insist on actual short hair and suggests that "dressing the hair may also be ceremoniously equivalent to cutting it." Certainly the bound hair of Chinese tradition is dressed hair: long hair was the norm for all, but outside society it was unbound, as with Daoists and others, and reentering society was symbolized by binding the hair.

Figure 2.14. William Alexander (1767-1816), *A Chinese Beggar*. Watercolor and grey ink over graphite. Courtesy of Yale Center for British Art, Paul Mellon Collection.

With the queue, the hair remained bound, but the method of the binding was considerably altered: the head was shaved all around the front and sides while the remaining hair was gathered in the back and braided in a queue. This was based on the Manchus' own style of hair and was intended as a symbol of subjugation. Initially resistance was very determined in some quarters, and there are records of Ming loyalists meeting with death rather than making the change and of others who chose to go into seclusion.[78] The resistance is often ascribed to political feeling, but when culture and the state are so strongly identified with each other, resistance is unlikely to be solely political. A feature so entrenched as bound hair acquires many cultural explanations for its absolute necessity. Thus in popular culture, as Weikun Cheng pointed out, "hair was believed to absorb and store spiritual power," and in Confucian thinking, the body, including the hair, was inherited from one's parents and must be kept intact.[79] The violation of that identity in the physical changes that followed the political ones had to have been deeply felt.

Nonetheless, with the passage of time, the intended symbolism of subjugation faded, and the queue became acculturated. Only under stress did the queue style of the hair separate out from general issues involving hair. Thus in Philip A. Kuhn's study of a sorcery outbreak in the eighteenth century, hair from a victim, clipped from the end of his queue, put him in the sorcerer's power, but it was initially only one of a number of personal items that made him vulnerable. Only later, when repeated attempts at suppression of the sorcery were unsuccessful, did the queue come to the foreground as a suspected symbol of opposition to the Kangxi emperor.[80] That there was general acceptance is shown by its incorporation into social customs at all levels. In portraits such as the informal one reproduced in figure 2.15 by the late Qing artists Ren Yi and Hu Gongshou of their calligrapher friend Gao Yongzhi, the queue figured as only one feature in the portrayal, less significant than the pine, rock, and other identifiers that marked the friend as one above material concerns.[81] This type of acculturation, which is anthropologically unsurprising, is shown by Ren Yi in a visually seamless fashion.

The two ends of its history—its imposition by force and its drawn-out rejection—are predicated on the queue's foreignness and not on its centuries of assimilation. It is against this background of normalcy that the gradual late Qing changes in attitude from acculturation to rejection should be seen. During the antiqueue movements and after its abolition, few among abolition's advocates pointed out its centuries of assimilation. That the queue was an integral part of one's identity could be seen in the resistance to queue cutting after 1911, for orders had to be reiterated many times on different levels of government from 1911 through to early 1920s.[82] Writing decades after the fact, Lu Xun gives an amusing account of both the assimilation of the queue and the difficulty, in hindsight, of acknowledging the long centuries when it was assimilated. "By the time I knew anything about things," he wrote,

> everyone had forgotten its bloody history and only felt that to have a full head of hair was to be a "longhaired," to be all shaven was like a monk, that one must shave a little and grow a little, that this was the only proper way to be.[83]

As always, he is factually accurate ("everyone had forgotten its bloody history") while his phrasing gainsays that information. By describing it as a shave-a-little-grow-a-little hairstyle, he asks how anyone could have gotten used to it, even though he also admits that he was "a youth of fourteen or fifteen trailing his queue behind him." (A remark in "Ah Q" similarly embeds information on customs in a way that renders them quaintly interesting. Noting the increasing number of people coiling their queues in anticipation of the revolution's arrival, the narrator observes that had it been summer people might have done so, or they might have tied them in a knot, but not now, not in autumn, so something must be happening.) To return to the essay, Lu Xun draws our attention to the assimilation, but his tone renders the customs as accommodation. The passage continues in this vein.

Figure 2.15. Ren Yi and Hu Gongshou, *Portrait of Gao Yongzhi at Age Twenty-eight*. Source: *Yiyan duoying* 10 (1980): 23. Courtesy of Library of Congress

> And then, too, many little tricks came about with the queue: a child would have a little knot with a paper flower sticking through it; the fighter in a play would hang from a pole by it and slowly blow out some smoke to show his skill; the acrobat wouldn't have to stir a finger, he would just shake his head a little and *pa-la*, his queue would jump up and coil itself on top of his head.

Poking fun at mild amusements is succeeded by serious condemnations.

> There were also practical uses: in fighting, the queue can be grabbed hold of and be very hard to get loose from; in arresting someone, the queue could be used and a rope dispensed with, and if someone was seizing many people, he just had to tie the queues together and one person could lead a whole string of men. Wu Youru's work, "Highlights of Shenjian," which is in the municipal office, shows a gendarme pulling along a miscreant by the queue, so we see that this sight has qualified as a "highlight."

Wu Youru (1840?–93?) was the chief illustrator from 1884 to 1890 of the popular *Dianshizhai Pictorial*, and in its pages, devoted to both serious news and juicy items about thefts, fights, and dead bodies floating by, can be found many illustrations of the queue used in the ways Lu Xun describes.[84] From that magazine, one illustration shows that the queue is a convenient handle in a fight (fig. 2.16), and another shows its handiness in arrests (fig. 2.17).[85]

Lu Xun also utilizes this memory in his fiction, where the difference in treatment is instructive. In "The True Story of Ah Q," grabbing hold of the queue in fighting, as in figure 2.16, is what Whiskers Wang does to Ah Q, a move painful enough for Ah Q to immediately give in (see also fig.

Figure 2.16. The queue's usefulness is seen when two men capture a thief and a third deals with him – a detail from *The Sight of Riches Spawns a Plan, Dianshizhai Pictorial*, 1884. Courtesy of Library of Congress.

Figure 2.17. The queue's usefulness is seen in a raid when, *right*, one officer holds two men by their queues while, *left*, another subdues a man by his queue – a detail from *Officials Capture Gamblers, Dianshizhai Pictorial*, 1885. Courtesy of Library of Congress.

B.18). Later, when Ah Q and Xiao D fight, each gets hold of the other's queue with the result that they are locked in an ineffectual stalemate that lasts all afternoon (see fig. 3.4). These scrapes are chiefly appreciated as amusing, sarcastic portrayals of Ah Q's identifying characteristic, his ability to discover "spiritual victories" in his defeats. It is this disturbing trait that makes up the author's damning critique of China, not the queue. By contrast, in the essay passage quoted above, the author's condemnation is directly linked to the queue: the fact that Chinese society has found, via the queue, ways to facilitate aggression against each other or, more lightly, ways to make a living at it, as with acrobats and actors, constitutes the condemnation. The indictment in the list of the many large and small ways the queue has been assimilated into daily life cannot be refuted because it lies in the sardonic tone.

By the time of the queue's abolition in 1911, memory of its assimilation had been put aside. Attitudes, at least among the Western- and Japanese-oriented elite, had become quite the opposite, and the queue was perceived as a backward feature unsuited to a nation seeking to join the world on equal terms. How the queue made its transition from an assimilated, invisible feature to anathema is a complex story that will be sketched chiefly to locate within it the time and place of Lu Xun's action. Antiqueue sentiments on the part of the Chinese have their own dynamic. As Dikötter has shown, there were many changes in Chinese views of themselves as they struggled to place themselves somewhere in the hierarchy of Western discourses of race.[86] In addition, the queue intersects at various points with the growth of Western (and Japanese) contempt, for the first disparaging view of the queue came from the outside world until finally the two views came into agreement. The situation on the Western side is simpler, a straight line downward, so this will be sketched first.

Initially, when the West first encountered China, the hairstyle so noticeable to outsiders was, in pictorial terms, rendered in a nonjudgmental way. For example, William Alexander, whose Chinese beggar we saw in figure 2.14, accompanied Lord Macartney's embassy to the Qianlong court (1792–94) and depicted the human world he encountered with a pictorially unprejudiced technique. Among his many outstanding renditions is a delicate watercolor of a young scholar (fig. 2.18). At a lower artistic level, the chinoiserie ornamental wallpaper of scholars at their leisure is similarly neutral with respect to the queue (fig. 2.19).[87] This objectivity continued in the many photographs of China taken in the 1920s, but in general did not survive outside photography for the same length of time. The world probably began to stigmatize the queue when China's weakness in the face of

Figure 2.18. William Alexander, *A Young Chinese Scholar,* 1792-94. Watercolor with graphite. Courtesy of Yale Center for British Art, Paul Mellon Collection.

Figure 2.19. A detail of Chinese parlor wallpaper. Courtesy of Winterthur Museum.

imperialist demands became unequivocally clear, first with its defeat in the first Opium War (1842), then over the next decades with the successive and increasingly damaging concessions it made in sovereign control over trading, taxes, laws, and more. Contempt for its political weaknesses was summed up and symbolized by cultural features, and caricatures of the queue became

Figure 2.20. *History Repeats Itself*, 1860. Source: Neville Edwards, *The Story of China*, 1900. Courtesy of Library of Congress

Figure 2.21. William A. Rogers, *The Most Unkindest Cut of All*, New York Herald, November 6, 1911. Courtesy of Library of Congress

common. An 1860 cartoon shows France simultaneously controlling China and Morocco; it throttles Morocco while stomping on the pigtail of China, throwing both figures off balance (fig. 2.20). Even to well-wishers, the queue symbolized what was defective about China. Thus a 1911 cartoon in the *New York Herald* saluting the Republican Revolution equated cutting the queue with the elimination of government corruption and the overthrow of the Qing dynasty (fig. 2.21). In the cartoon, a short-haired officer, dressed in a Western-style military uniform and identified by the words "New China" on his belt, is cutting off a queue labeled "long ages of graft" from a corpulent mandarin in silk robes.[88] Given these associations, one can speculate that it would have been hard for Sun Yat-sen to become the worldwide symbol of modernizing China after his 1896 detention by the Chinese legation in London if he had not previously cut his queue. Indeed, his portrait in the frontispiece of *Kidnapped in London*, which made his mission known to the world (fig. 2.22), did more than show him with the right kind of short hair (and clothing); it showed him Europeanized in his features.[89]

How the queue became a negative in Chinese attitudes is a more complicated story, for different groups advocated cutting the queue at different times; they gave different kinds of reasons, which initially were cast in practical, modernizing terms rather than anti-Qing ones, and experience outside China made a difference. In the end, antiqueue sentiment became most closely identified with the revolutionaries. A quick overview can begin with the scenes of fights and arrests from *Dianshzhai Pictorial* illustrated above, in which the usefulness of the queue shows their assimilation into daily activities. When the same commonly encountered scenes depict Europeans, however, although the same utilitarian properties of the queue are demonstrated, the texts teach a lesson about imperial domination. The first one, from *Yulun shishibao*, shows, like figure 2.16, a victim in a struggle held fast by his queue, but the text explains that a westerner at a certain address in

Figure 2.22. Sun Yat-sen, *Kidnapped in London*, 1897, frontispiece. Courtesy of Library of Congress

the "American Concession" had held his Chinese servant captive and beaten him (fig. 2.23). Another example is a 1904 illustration in Chen Duxiu's *Anhui suhua bao* (fig. 2.24). As in figure 2.17, men, in this case four, are led away by one man who is holding onto their queues. The accompanying text, however, explains that with Russia then controlling Manchuria, a Russian has seized the men for forced labor on the railroads.[90]

In the years just before the Republic was declared, there was agreement, at least among the urban elite, that the queue was to be discarded. This is also the period most fully treated in the scholarship. By this time, many efforts had been undertaken in the urban press to change popular opinion on the native hairstyle and not only for political reasons. Cartoons directed at a modern, urban readership promulgated the new view. *Shibao*'s regularly occurring feature, the cartoon square "The Contemporary Scene" (*shihua*), ran two cartoons entitled "Uses for the Queue," showing the queue in ridiculous scenarios. In one, a man ties his queue to a fan overhead and gently rocks himself while his queue works the fan (fig. 2.25). In another, two men eat at a table while their queues lift up and lower, depending on their posture, the dish covers to which the queues are tied (fig. 2.26)[91] Many of the men who produced these exhortative vignettes may have themselves just cut their hair. The editor of the paper, Chen Leng, adopted a Western style of life, cutting his queue (in 1904) and riding a bicycle.[92] Usually

Figure 2.23. *A Westerner Shows His Brutality* 西人逞兇, *Yulun shishi bao tuhua*, 1903.

Figure 2.24. *Captured to be Slaves* 捉人為奴, Pictures of National Humiliations, No. 4, *Anhui suhua bao*, 1904.

study abroad was needed, although having been abroad was not sufficient in itself. A certain cultural orientation was also needed: the Chinese who actually lived abroad as immigrants and remained in Chinese enclaves kept their queues until well after 1911.

In the years just before 1911, the general trend was clear: the queue was bound for demise. Even court officials were ready to acknowledge that certain social realities were associated with living in a world dominated by Western imperial conceptions of civilized dress. In 1910, members of the first group of students sent by the Qing government to the United States, supported by the Boxer Indemnity Fund, were instructed to prepare for their sojourn by cutting their queues and having Western clothes made.[93] (Hu Shi was one of them.) In the last months of the Qing dynasty, the National Assembly, the newly constituted monarchical parliament, was finally prepared to debate a policy concerning the queue, even as events were overtaking it.

Although the queue's days would have been numbered in any case, the Republican Revolution successfully appropriated the abolition of the queue. Even the Weizhuang villagers knew that "the revolutionaries are coming" meant the end of the queue. For their part, as we saw, Lu Xun and his cohorts found their short hair legitimated by the arrival of the revolution. For the Republican government, queue cutting was one of a number of attitudes

Figure 2.25. A man's queue fans him as he rocks. *The Uses of a Queue*, The Contemporary Scene, *Shibao*, April 13, 1910. Courtesy of Harvard Yenching Library.

Figure 2.26. Queues operate the positions of the dish covers, one up, one down. *The Uses of a Queue*, The Contemporary Scene, *Shibao*, April 13, 1910. Courtesy of Harvard Yenching Library.

and actions that were actively promulgated to create republican citizens. Its policies on hair were met with confusion and resistance as well as welcome anticipation. When cities and towns went over to the revolutionaries, entire units, especially among students, soldiers, and police, organized to cut their queues en masse. They then formed enforcement brigades and roamed the streets of cities and towns, taking the initiative into their own hands.[94] In the countryside, however, compliance was both more difficult to enforce and more heavily resisted. For example, Liu Dapeng, a gentry diarist from a Shanxi village, had had his queue cut off when in the nearby town. As Harrison describes him, "Despite considerable pressure, [he] refused to attend the new county assembly until his hair had grown back"[95]—and this was the *new* county assembly. Likewise, in 1917, some of the villagers in "Storm" had had their queues cut off and were growing them back while the tavern owner had kept his uncut.[96] Although the queue was phased out rather than abolished overnight, it was only a matter of time before it would be quite gone. This was the situation at the end of the Qing dynasty.

The time period of interest to us is the far more murky dozen years or so before this 1911 moment, a time that includes 1902–3. The relative clarity of views among the Western-oriented elite just before the revolution makes a good contrast to our point of interest. In 1902–3, things had not advanced so far. The queue was not yet the sole property of the revolutionaries, who did not exist in notable numbers compared to the reformers. Sun Yat-sen's revolutionary group, Tongmenghui, was not founded until 1905. In this time period, though discussions were limited, they were distributed across more of the political spectrum, including among the reformers, who petitioned the throne for its abolishment. In the early years of this time period, even the advocates of short hair had not yet cut their queues. Relatedly, the number of people who had been abroad still numbered just in the hundreds, among whom the handful of people who had cut their queues were to be found. Moreover, since the imperial examinations were not abolished until 1905, they were still the route to a position in the central government, and so adherence to Qing laws was important. The gathering focus on the queue as an indisputable symbol of backwardness was just beginning. It was in this interestingly murky period that Lu Xun cut his queue.

The earliest proponents of short hair were Tan Sitong and Kang Youwei, who were to become leaders of the short-lived 1898 Reform.[97] Both their proposals predate the anti-Manchu arguments of the revolutionaries and were couched in cultural and utilitarian terms that recognized the queue as a focus of Western denigration. They sought reform in clothing and calendar as well and, in Kang Youwei's case, petitioned the Guangxu emperor to set the example, as the Meiji emperor had in Japan. Tan's proposals were made in *Renxue*, published posthumously, a work owned by Lu Xun as a student. One topic Tan discussed was style of hair. He sought to ground his choice on a rational basis, arguing that the function of hair was to protect the head and world history showed there were four approaches to this: the old Chinese style of growing the hair, which protects but is inconvenient; the shaven style of monks, which offers no protection; the half-shaved style of the Manchus and Mongols, which has both of these drawbacks; and the cut style of the West. Kang, in a 1898 memorial, "A Petition to Cut the Hair, Change Clothing Style, and Change the Calendar," made utilitarian arguments in a number of areas: to conform with the customs of the world, to overcome the queue's drawbacks for operating the machinery of the industrial age, to facilitate the exercises of the New Army, to improve hygiene, and to counter the scorn the queue attracted. Neither Tan nor Kang had cut their queues at the time of their petitions. Tan was executed when the Hundred Days Reform was halted by the Cixi empress; Kang, who fled to Japan, cut his queue there. When the queue became an anti-Manchu symbol, Kang Youwei took the position that as a monarchist he would regrow his queue. It was clear that the revolutionaries had successfully monopolized the abolishment of the queue as a symbol of their anti-Manchu stance.

The earliest examples of queue cutting were not always anti-Manchu, though a few were explicitly so. Zhang Binglin (1868–1936) was an example of the latter. He dramatically cut his queue in 1900 in China and in public, and then published a defense in the revolutionary paper *Zhongguo ribao*. This occurred in the tense weeks during the 1900 Boxer Rebellion. The Boxers, with the acquiescence of the court, had besieged the foreign legations in Tianjin and Beijing. An expeditionary force under eight nations captured Tianjin on July 13 and Beijing a month later. In the weeks of crisis after the foreign capture of Tianjin, reform and revolutionary groups convened in Shanghai, but their debate was ineffectual. In protest against continued support for the monarchy at the meeting and to express his irrevocable split with the monarchy, Zhang cut off his queue. "The queue which the Europeans call a pigtail," he wrote, "was shameful and insulting." Another famous case was also early and decidedly political: Zou Rong (1885–1905), later a comrade in arms to Zhang, though nearly a generation younger, is said to have cut his on the way to Japan and thrown it overboard. (Like Lu Xun, he arrived in 1902, but he enrolled at another preparatory school.) The case of Sun Yat-sen was earlier than those of either man and also political, though in a less clear-cut way. According to the revolutionary Feng Ziyou, Sun cut his queue in 1895 at the home of Feng's father in Yokohama and changed to Western clothing. Wang Dongfang described him as "the first to cut off his queue to make a fundamental split from the Qing court." The *Biographical Dictionary of Republican China*, however, gives a pragmatic reason, saying that as a fugitive after the failed uprising in Canton that year, "seeking to disguise himself as a modernized Japanese, [Sun] cut off his queue, grew a mustache, and adopted Western-style clothing." Chiang Kai-shek (1887–1975) cut off his queue in China in 1905 (at the age of eighteen) after the Russo-Japanese War revealed starkly the Qing court's weakness in the face of foreign powers. He resolved to go to Japan to study military science, and "to convince his mother of his determination to go to Japan, Chiang cut off his queue and sent it to her." Huang Xing (1874–1931), a future revolutionary leader who entered Kōbun Academy the same year as Lu Xun, took a different approach to this principle: he did not cut off his queue until some time after he returned to China to organize revolutionary movements there; while in Japan, he kept it in order to conceal his anti-Qing stance.[98]

Lu Xun in Japan circa 1903

For Chinese students in Japan, their location was a factor on two counts. Japan had been a locus of anti-Qing feeling since such sentiments first arose in the later decades of the nineteenth century. Both reformers and revolutionaries used it as a refuge and a base for organization. Sun Yat-sen, Kang Youwei, and Liang Qichao were all based in Tokyo or Yokohama, where they published their influential newspapers and periodicals and founded the various incarnations of groups like Tongmenghui, which provided the organizational and financial resources for revolutionary plans. Thus in Japan it was possible for the queue to become a symbol of opposition to the Qing dynasty. The second factor was that Japan had increasing numbers of Chinese who came as students and then were drawn into political activism in an anti-Qing setting.

Students had first been sent to Japan in 1896 as a direct result of China's defeat in the Sino-Japanese War the previous year. According to Wang Xiangrong, "Prior to the war of 1894–95, the sending of even one student to Japan was unthinkable."[99] This first group of students numbered 13, of whom 4 went home within the month. Three years later, in 1899, there were just over 200 students in Japan. In 1902, Lu Xun's year, there were still only 500. After that, the numbers increased quickly. In 1903, they doubled, to 1,000 students, and in 1904 to over 2,000. The numbers for 1905 and 1906—the latter is the year Zhou Zuoren arrived in Japan—reached over 8,000.[100] This was the peak, however, and by 1910 the surge was over, for that year the Boxer Indemnity Fund opened up study in the United States. Although Chinese students continued to go to Japan, it was no longer the vanguard of Western education. The trend had lasted fifteen years.

From the beginning, for the students, being abroad meant subjection to the pressures of social conformity, with hair at the fore, but unlike queue cutting, which became a political symbol, there was no organized way to act on this feeling of cultural difference. The first group of students arrived immediately after the Sino-Japanese War, at the height of Japanese nationalistic euphoria over the victory, which reversed the centuries-long superiority of China. The students were, unsurprisingly, targets of this nationalist feeling. The difference in clothing was probably easily resolved, for it is likely that once enrolled they wore their school uniforms most of the time. The uniform was the token of identity for all students, judging from contemporary novels such as Sōseki's and Ōgai's. Thus, when Chinese students met with ridicule, it focused on their distinguishing hairstyle, and many writers remembered the calls of "pigtail" that followed them everywhere. Jansen quotes the memoirist Jing Meijiu on the humiliating personal questions that led him to cut his queue. An anonymous student, writing in the inaugural issue of *New Fiction* (*Xin xiaoshuo*) under the title "New Feelings on Arriving in Tokyo," lists "Seventeen Distressing Things." The first of them is "To wear the wide-sleeved jacket and one's queue onto the streets." (Under "21 Delightful Things," he lists, first, 'crossing the ocean with the wind and waves.' The second was trains.) "You saw your ugliness and felt the pain of it," Zou Rong writes, "When I touch the clothes I wear, the hair on my head, my heart aches." He further describes, presumably from imagination, the feelings of a Chinese in London, writing, "When a man with a braid and barbarian [i.e., Manchu] clothes is on the streets of London, why does everyone call out 'Pigtail' or 'Savage'?" As late as 1956, Liu Dajie remarks that any Chinese who has been a student in Japan can sympathize with the sense of national futility and anguish felt in this xenophobic situation.[101]

In Lu Xun's recollection, his initial awareness of the queue as stigma came before Japan, but it came with learning of Manchu-Han distinctions.

> What first brought my attention to the division between Man and Han was not books but the queue. . . . It was all right living in an out-of-the-way place, but as soon as you reached Shanghai, then you could not help sometimes hearing a certain English word: "Pig-tail" [English in the original]—a pig's tail.[102]

It seems that for the young person from the "out-of-the-way place," the Man-Han distinction, when it came to his attention, was directed toward the most visible, most visual, feature of Manchuness—the queue. Visual, visible—and risible—the last characteristic not challenged by the newly targeted. When would this have happened, the youngster's rude exposure? It is hard to say, as one had to pass through Shanghai both to go back and forth between Shaoxing and Nanjing's School of Mines and Railways and to depart for Japan. (After he cut his queue, Lu Xun's transit through Shanghai was a different story, one that involved the purchase of false queues.) This was his conclusion in the above passage.

> [This seemed to be] a description of a person who's grown a pig's tail on his head.... And so one gradually began to feel toward the look of that queue with the more than two hundred years' pedigree that it was not too elegant.

In these Shanghai experiences, we see that at an early date cultural stigma on a particular point came first, for which the political symbolism was learned later. As he writes, "not books but the queue" taught the distinction between Man and Han. He learned to be ashamed of the queue for social conformity reasons, and afterward came the extension to its political source, the Manchus.

For cutting off your queue to be perceived as political symbolism, several things had to happen. One was the nurturing of political activism among Chinese students in Japan. Another was that the queue had to be politicized, strongly marked as the hair of a subject people. It was experienced revolutionaries who increased student activism and made explicit the politicization of the queue. Zhang Binglin was chief among them in effectiveness. As the goals of the revolutionaries became distinct from the reformers', they came to express the revolutionary choice as an ethnic one of Manchu versus Han and, by extension, of the queue versus the rejection of it. As Kai-wing Chow has argued, in making the dichotomy, the revolutionaries gave the "Han race lineage" (Hanzu) a "semantic stability," noting also that this now stable concept is used today to dominate China's minorities.[103] On both points important milestones occurred in 1902–3, while politicization intensified, with the buildup to the 1905 Russo-Japanese War. (This suggests that Lu Xun was slightly on the early side.) The groundwork was laid with the formation of a student association in February 1902, two months before Lu Xun's arrival, and the construction of a student center (*huiguan*) that year, ironically with Qing government funds.[104] The center had newspapers and a library and was the site of large political student meetings. As Lu Xun described its role in student life, "Nearly all students who went to Japan sought first of all to acquire the new knowledge. Besides studying Japanese in preparation for entering specialized schools, people went to the Center, roamed the bookstores, went to meetings, and attended public lectures."[105]

The politicization of the queue came with the promotion of specifically anti-Manchu sentiments among the students in Japan. Lu Xun's first month in Tokyo coincided with an inspired piece of propaganda devised by Zhang Binglin for the express purpose of promulgating the idea that the Manchus were a race alien to the Han Chinese over whom they ruled and in this way to promote anti-Manchu sentiment among the students. Zhang had fled to Japan in February when he learned that orders had been given in Shanghai for his arrest.[106] He was there for only a few months, but he wasted no time. He made contact with many revolutionaries, initiated what became a decades-long on-and-off alliance with Sun Yat-sen, and notably increased student activism. Most immediately, he organized a rally, for which he chose April 26 because on that date in 1644, according to his proclamation, the last emperor of the last Chinese dynasty committed suicide after the Ming's defeat by the Manchus. Although the last Ming emperor did kill himself on this date in April, the capital had fallen not to the Manchus but to Li Zicheng, leader of a decades-long peasant rebellion. Only in June was Beijing taken by the Manchus and in October a Qing emperor installed. Zhang's canny elision of this inconvenient interregnum is of a piece with other evidence of his ability to redefine history for his audience. The proclamation was called "The Commemoration of 242nd Year of the Loss of China" (*Zhong Xia wangguo erbaisishiernian jinian*)." Although in the end the Qing government pressured the Japanese authorities to curtail the demonstrations and the meeting had to be held in Yokohama rather than Tokyo, it was a triumph of symbolic activism and stimulated the founding of many anti-Manchu associations among the Chinese students.[107] According to Ni Moyan, Lu Xun's later writings showed that he did not attend the rally on the twenty-sixth.[108] Its influence, however, is visible via *Revolutionary Army*, in which Zou Rong dated his preface from the number of years since the fall of the Ming dynasty. We know in turn that the fiery Zou Rong had an effect on Lu Xun. Xu Shoushang recollects this influence (seen also in Lu Xun's own writings): "At that time, Lu Xun was already in Tokyo, and of course he felt greatly the influence of this great revolutionary forebear."[109] We also know that Zhang retained a lifelong importance to Lu Xun. In 1906 when Zhang returned to Japan after a prison term in Shanghai, Lu Xun, Zhou Zuoren, and Xu Shoushang were among the many who attended Zhang's lectures on the apparently arcane topic of philology. Their connection continued in Beijing in the mid-1910s, and Lu Xun's final two essays in his life dealt with topics connected to Zhang's death that month.

The anti-Manchu aspect of revolutionary thought brought to notice by Zhang's campaign to mark the 242nd anniversary still required a general rise in political activism to take off. This happened the next year, in April. Political consciousness among Chinese students in Japan took a big jump when Russia presented seven demands to the Qing court that were designed to solidify Russia's control of Manchuria. This was the run-up to the Russo-Japanese War in 1905. In Japan, as in China, anti-Russia movements were organized among Chinese students, which lasted for many months and initiated the politicization of the urban elite.[110] In Tokyo, a number of large student rallies over other political issues culminated in the anti-Russia agitation and a greater number of radical actions than ever. On April 29, 1903, an all-student meeting called forth many fiery speeches. A volunteer militia of students was proposed—the Resist-Russia Militia (*ju E yiyongjun*). There were stirring calls: "This is the objective for which we should shed our blood!" and "Those who do not fear death, those who are willing to sacrifice their lives to seek life for China, sign up now, form a corps, and tomorrow we will set out." A telegram was sent to the Beiyang Army, declaring that the students were prepared to make a symbolic (i.e., deadly) resistance. The next day more than 130 signed up. They were organized into three units, each subdivided into four sections. The volunteer corps soon underwent several name changes to avoid trouble from the Qing and Japanese authorities, who not unreasonably saw the show of patriotism as a cloak for anti-Qing activities. On May 14, two students were sent as emissaries to Yuan Shikai of the Beiyang Army, and so on. In the end, the movement petered out.

Lu Xun was present at this April meeting, as was Xu Shoushang. Xu was among those who signed up for the volunteer corps, but not Lu Xun. Ni Moyan suggests that the latter did not act because the plan did not make much sense, neither the proposal to integrate the corps into the Beiyang Army, nor the idea of fighting to the death.[111] These are obvious problems with the students' excited plans, but there is no evidence that these sensible reasons were Lu Xun's. A similar situation arose in 1931 when Japan occupied Manchuria. The strong response that followed included a volunteer student militia and this time Lu Xun wrote, "Here [in Shanghai], students are organizing to train for a volunteer militia and such, but in a while this will cease of its own accord. I have seen this happen several times."[112] This was Lu Xun thirty years older, but the tendency to see too far ahead might have been present earlier.

Although he took no overt action, when we turn to Lu Xun's writings, we find that "Soul of Sparta" was written at this time, and in this essay, as we saw earlier, he called for military action in words as fiery as any made at the anti-Russia meetings. His account of Sparta's stand at Thermopylae, where three hundred Spartans "died to the last man," was published in the June issue of *Zhejiang Tide*, which also included many reports on student activities, including their anti-Russia measures. Like his quatrain, "Sparta" contains an unambiguous call for self-sacrifice. The young author writes in the preface, "Today when we read that history, it is still rouses our sense of injustice. I lay out the facts of that event to present to our youth of today. If there are men in this world who scorn to rank below their womenfolk, then there must be men who will throw aside their pen and arise! " This is not too different from the students' slogan, "Rather Death Than a Vanquished Country." The author's words were supported by the editor, Xu Shoushang: "This essay by a youth uses the story of Sparta to urge us to raise high the military spirit of our people."[113] In the event, as we saw, his belief in these bloodthirsty words was brief, and his participation in politics was expressed only in the form of writing.

If the quatrain has a separate date from the photograph, the fiery sentiments shared by the poem and "Soul of Sparta" suggests its origin in a time when politicization was increasing by the week. The period of political protest that produced "Soul of Sparta" seems a likely context for the quatrain before it found its way onto the photograph, especially because its line 4—"I would offer up my blood for the [descendants] of the Yellow Emperor"—is so consistent with "Sparta." The immediate cause might have been Russian aggression in Manchuria, but in this year every month, even every week, saw large meetings on both general and specific nationalistic issues, as well as an overall strong rhetoric on Manchu-Han distinctions, all recorded and disseminated by the many newly founded student publications. In pairing the poem with the "Hair Cut Short" photograph, the young student reflects the amalgam of large social and political issues with the freeing of the individual youth that was later to characterize the ambitions of the May Fourth Movement.

We are now in a better position to appreciate that the quatrain contains clear traces of influence absorbed in the twelve months since his arrival in Tokyo, centered on a rapid inculcation in anti-Manchu feeling joined with Han self-definition. That he absorbed this new ideology can be seen in the quatrain in two places: first, in the ideology of Han versus Manchu; and second, in a clear echo of a Liang Qichao poem. First, consider the ideology of Han. This occurs in line 4, where the people for whom the poet declares himself ready to die are called "the descendants of Xuan Yuan," the Yellow Emperor. This term, which might roughly mean his fellow Chinese, is in fact restricted to his fellow Han Chinese. As we saw earlier, Zhou Zuoren had made this point too. Dikötter provides many examples of Chinese publications in this period in Japan in which the Yellow Emperor "was elevate[ed] . . . to a national symbol" and the Han people were singled out as his descendants. Kai-wing Chow notes that the usefulness of the Yellow Emperor as the ancestor figure is that he could unify all Chinese into "one mammoth kinship group" directed against the Manchus.[114] Such sentiments are echoed here by the young ideologue: his readiness to dedicate himself to country is additionally an anti-Manchu expression.

Second, is the Liang Qichao influence. This is seen in both lines 1 and 4. Together they echo a single line from a well-known set of two poems that Liang wrote in 1901 and published in 1902 in *Xinmin congbao*, which had been founded by him in Yokohama that year. Entitled "Encouraging Myself" (自勵), the first line of the second poem reads, "I willingly offer my person as the target of ten thousand arrows." 獻身甘作萬矢的. Liang's self-sacrifice 獻身 is echoed in Lu Xun's avowal to "offer up my blood" in line 4, while Liang's resolve 甘作 to be the target of arrows 萬矢的 is echoed in all three parts of Lu Xun's line 1: the unusual word for *self* 靈台, the resolve not to avoid something 無計逃, and the arrows 神矢. When he wrote this set of poems, Liang was already a towering figure in the reform movement as a result of his role in the Hundred Days Reform. He had fled to Japan in 1898 after the Reform's collapse, when it became his base of operations. There he stayed for months at a time between the travels he undertook worldwide to promote reform and raise funds. Like many journals of this period, his *Xinmin congbao*, where the two poems were published, introduced political philosophy and historical figures to its readership.[115]

In later years, when it comes to the political zeal of 1902–3, Lu Xun's recollections have a critical tone that must encompass his own unacknowledged part in it. For instance, he describes the many students who turned to doing research in libraries for works on Ming dynasty loyalists under the victorious Qing. Of this interesting direction in student zeal—what we might think of as looking backward rather than outward—he writes that they hoped that through their research "old forgotten enmities can be revived to help the revolution." Elsewhere, with hindsight, he criticizes the prevailing idea of revolution because it amounted to only a displacement of foreign Manchu rulers by old Han rulers: "What they called revolution was in fact ethnic revolution. They wanted to take the land out of the hands of a foreign ethnicity and return it to the old owners." At the time, of course, he participated in the Manchu-Han ideology through his use of "Xuan Yuan" in the poem and for that matter in the political meaning of cutting his queue. A third comment comes even closes to home: "At that time, at the end of the Qing dynasty, among certain young people in China, the fervor for revolution was high, and a response could easily be aroused by calling for revenge and resistance."[116] The last remark is descriptive of both his poem and "Soul of Sparta," and as such it also has to include his younger self in the criticism.

The mature writer was more tolerant of the personal, as opposed to political, dimensions of that heady period, enjoying the memory of the personal freedom that often accompanies widening political horizons. Sacrifice and the lure of the heroic were in the air, and this certainly called for eloquence. Of "The Soul of Sparta," Lu Xun later singles out the language for affectionate repudiation. It "makes my ears burn now," he writes. "Did I indeed write this, I wonder?" he asks. He clarifies. "I remember," he says, that for something to be considered good writing, "you have to write things like 'undo your hair and shout,' 'carry books and walk alone,' 'no tears to dash away, great winds snuff out the candles.'"[117] "Even I am startled by my immaturity then, verging on the shameless. But, what can be done? This is certainly from me—let it go into print then."[118] This was what it was like to be young.

Yet in later years, when he weighs words against other possibilities, words are too easy.

> There were also poems and prose that were full of sorrow, but these too were no more than things on pieces of paper, and had no connection to the later Wuchang [Republican] uprising.[119]

His poem and "Sparta" surely belong to such a category of "only things on pieces of paper." It is perhaps for this reason that neither the poem nor the Sparta essay exert any influence in his lifetime. He did not publish the poem in, for example, *Zhejiang Tide*, where he published his other works, and "Sparta" was not retrieved for republication until 1934, when its style was unlikely to attract attention. In the passage quoted above, he goes on to compare words that "were no more than things on pieces of paper" to the words that came from Zou Rong's *Revolutionary Army*, probably the most influential, and incendiary, anti-Manchu tract of the time. He writes:

> If we are to speak of influence, then the millions of words cannot be compared to the straightforward, easy-to-understand *Revolutionary Army* by "Zou Rong, Foot Soldier of the Revolutionary Army."

A lot of words were written in those years, whose immaturity he admits, and they tellingly fall short when measured against Zou Rong.

Deeds survive through the medium of words, as Sima Qian has pointed out, but what are the deeds worthy of recording? Among his actions, a concrete one is that he had cut his queue and done so at a relatively early time, but he never claimed a principled basis for any action of his, including this one. The situation, however, is different for when it came to others. Lu

Xun wrote often in appreciation of the courage of others, but he did not explicitly emphasize the physical courage of principled action. Perhaps he did not want to be misinterpreted as encouraging what, given the political situation throughout his life, was inevitably a foolhardy course of action. Yet, from 1902–3 alone, he was acquainted with many who demonstrated physical courage to an extraordinary degree: Zhang Binglin, "seven times arrested and three times imprisoned" over the next decade and a half; Huang Xing, whose insouciant "rebellious Chu temperament" at Kōbun Academy presaged his future role as revolutionary leader;[120] and the twenty-year-old Zou Rong, friend and protégé of Zhang Taiyan, whose multiple rash actions ended in an early death in a Shanghai prison. Among the fellow provincials who came after him were two "revolutionary martyrs" (Lu Xun's words) who were to die in 1907 and others who were imprisoned, while against their future he places his own shallowness, recalling the silent scorn he had felt on observing their outdated elaborate manners (and hence he assumed, their attitudes).[121] His own friend Xu Shoushang was likely a quiet version of these physically valorous men: at this early point, we see that he volunteered for the militia to fight against Russia; at the end of his life in 1948, that courage was ended by assassination while he held the seemingly uncontroversial post of dean of humanities at Taiwan National University. Even within this limited but eventful span of 1902–3, the young Lu Xun had many measures of the actions and words of others to which he paid tribute. We can follow his lead in placing his actions and words in the context of the words and actions of others to which he draws our attention.

Conclusion: "No More Than Things on Pieces of Paper"

In the quatrain and photograph, the young student left a striking memento. In this chapter, I have sought to disentangle it from its accrued veneration and situate its elements—reentangle them, if you will—in possibly enlightening ways by reconstructing their original world. In turn, the issue of the queue provides a focus for exploring some effects that the many issues in the eventful years 1902–3 had on a young student.

Over the years, the writer that Lu Xun became seldom returned to the specific topic of the queue, but each time he did, it was strongly charged. If he had never written about the queue after 1903, the reasons to investigate this early moment would be much weaker. But he did. The reuse, the reappearance, even the faintness of the queue's trace in the fiction and the essays, all point to a charged topic and both direct our attention to this early moment and lead on to their later surfacing in the chapters that follow. This chapter has focused on two uneasy topics that have been relatively neglected: the queue in a time of transition and our author in this contingent moment. Regarding the queue in transition, the tendency is to look forward, to the moment of its discarding. Yet the years of its drawn-out end, when in stages people began to act on their changed attitudes, are full of interest and complexity. In this chapter, 1902–3 constitutes one of many such transitional periods. When one of the persons concerned is our author in his youth, then we can catch him in a moment when he is both a developing person and a person of his times, in other words, someone who is not exceptional. The resulting picture is not amazing, though it is fuller, but perhaps it is a contribution to Lu Xun studies to make him less singular.

3
The Literary Afterlife of the Queue: A Closer Look at the Years 1920–22

A study of Lu Xun would seem incomplete without a discussion of "The True Story of Ah Q," the most complex and influential of his portrayals of China. This chapter examines this novella and groups it with four other works, two fictions and two essays, in which the queue features prominently. By identifying and analyzing both literary and biographical contexts for this work, we are able to view "Ah Q" as part of a longer history, both personal and national, and gain a rare glimpse of the author's working methods as he finds and grapples with a large subject whose outlines emerge only gradually.

There are three parts to the argument here. The first part is to prove that the five works identified do cohere as a group. This is done on literary levels of character, theme, language, and such. It next argues that the works originate in a particular historical moment, a battle that took place outside Beijing in July 1920, which authorial memory transferred to the 1917 coup of the Pigtail General Zhang Xun. Finally, using the queue, the stories are analyzed as a series of responses to one particular feature of the times, the political violence he had witnessed since 1911. By considering them as a sequence, we can see how the author makes a number of approaches to a portrayal of China that would awake the Chinese to their world. His several attempts demonstrate a perseverance that adds up to a faith in writing—particularly fiction—that can be traced back to the later years of his time in Japan.

Lu Xun's satirical portrayals of fictional queues are well known. His most famous character, Ah Q, is essentially named for his style of hair, while Ah Q's nemesis, the Imitation Foreigner, had his lack of a queue as his single defining characteristic (although he was growing it out). In "Storm," Seven-Pounds's lack of a queue is central to the short-lived crisis that forms the story's plot.[1] In proposing a literary afterlife for the queue, this chapter argues for going beyond this satirical understanding of the queue to explore the ways in which it has serious, even somber, purposes. As satire, the works depend on the common assumption that the queue was an amusing artifact abolished by the Republican revolution, but in addition "Ah Q" and "Storm" show the permanent shadow of violence, as well as the cultural resistance that was felt against such radical change. To look at the complex picture, this chapter examines three short fictions and two essays in which the queue features prominently and the span of time from August 1920 to February 1922 in which they were written. Here is the group chronological order. The first is "Storm," written in August, 1920 and published that September in Lu Xun's usual venue of *New Youth*.[2] It is a favorite of anthologists for its clever premise, amusing problem, and neat solution. Next is "A Story about Hair," written a month later in September and published in October,1920 in a special National Day issue of *Student Lamp* (*Xuedeng*) in Shanghai. It is a puzzling story that is never anthologized and almost never analyzed.[3] Then come two short essays published on consecutive days in May 1921: "'Surrendering in Life but Not in Death'" (the title is a quotation) and "Names."[4] Finally, a half year later comes the fifth and last item, "The True Story of Ah Q," Lu Xun's best-known work.[5] Its protagonist is a hapless villager whose self-regard and misadventures very quickly gave rise to terms like *Ah Q-style* and *Ah Q-ism*. This novella-length work was published in installments in the space of ten weeks between December 4, 1921, and February 12, 1922, in *Morning Post Supplement* edited by his former student and friend Sun Fuyuan. Before the end of the series, the name Ah Q had passed into the language as an adjective.

The three short stories are remarkable among Lu Xun's fiction in that it can be shown that they are linked to each other in terms of working method and continuity of purpose. Hitherto his fiction has been praised, rightly, for its great variety, for each short story is quite different in conception and technique from the others. The other face of this variety is the critical problem of making connections among them. Thematic analyses have been a productive procedure in this regard, with rewarding analyses that focus on, for example, the figure of the intellectual, the modern woman, or the motif of the crowd. A model of the chronological development, however, has proved elusive. The grouping described here provides such an account for a brief section of his fiction-writing years. Over this period we see the author's experience of violent political events, their accumulation in his memory, and the function of the queue as a symbol of these complexities.

There are a number of unusual features about the eighteen-month time frame of the five works. One is that these five queue-related items are *nearly all* the creative writing he did during this time. It is true that in fiction there is a fourth story, "Hometown," written in January 1921 and published May 1921, but it is not about the queue, and it can be separately explained as arising from his return to Shaoxing a year earlier.⁶ The number of fictions, a total of four, is not actually small, for he was always slow there, but the small number of essays is unusual. In 1920 he wrote *no* essays, and in 1921 he wrote only five, of which two are directly relevant here. In the preface to the essay collection *Hot Air*, he remarks that he did not write much after May Fourth (1919), but then he claims he is unsure whether he did not write much or whether the essays did not survive.⁷ As Pollard notes, 1920 and 1921 were "bleak years" for essays.⁸ Another way to look at this information is that nearly everything of the little that Lu Xun wrote in this period was related to the queue. He seemed to be following a thread in some way. A final notable feature about these months is that we have very little in the way of private papers from this period. We have the diary for 1920 but not 1921, the later year having been recovered only in fragments from Xu Shoushang's copy. As for letters, only one survives from 1920, and, although many from 1921 survive, they are mostly to his brother and concerned with the minutiae of their translation projects. This paucity of private material must have many reasons, but it does make one wonder about this period in general.

For the essays, there might have been practical reasons for the scarcity. Lu Xun had, of course, his day job at the Ministry of Education.⁹ His commitments outside the ministry had vastly increased, especially in the area of translating and teaching, both of which were new undertakings. Teaching began in 1920, with a contract from Beijing University in August of that year and one from Beijing Women's Normal College in October. His lecture notes from Beijing University ultimately resulted in the substantial pioneering study, *A History of Chinese Vernacular Fiction*. Translating began with two milestones in the nurturing of New Literature: the founding of the Literary Research Association (Wenxue yanjiu hui) in January 1921, in Beijing; and its taking over of *Short Story Monthly* in Shanghai as its official publication. Although Lu Xun was not listed as involved in either endeavor, his brother Zuoren and nearly all his associates were connected with them. Mao Dun, the new editor of the reorganized *Short Story Monthly*, initiated several ambitious translation projects and, although they had not yet met, successfully enlisted Lu Xun's help with them. In these eighteen months, besides coordinating translations, he himself translated sixteen shorts stories of varying lengths and one play.¹⁰ In the end, these activities helped his reputation as a writer, especially teaching, through which he reached members of the new elite in Beijing. In effect, it prepared the way for his fame when students figured out that their teacher, Zhou Shuren, was Lu Xun. Another addition to his schedule occurred when he bought a house, refurbished it, and moved into it from Shaoxing Hostelry near the West Gate. At the end of the year, he went home to Shaoxing, closed up the family home, moved the household to Beijing, and reconstituted his immediate part of the Zhou clan there. In the new quarters, Lu Xun's living situation was cramped, for as Chen Shuyu describes it, at night he slept in a room that was really a passageway and had one rear window and no real place to write, so this might have been a factor in the scarcity of the publications.[11] Finally, for most of 1921, Zhou Zuoren was convalescing in Western Hills, and Lu Xun took on much of his brother's translating and editing work, as their numerous letters that year show. All in all, perhaps he was too busy to write. It is therefore all the more interesting to note that when he did write, what he wrote circled around this topic of the queue, which found expression in diverse forms, diversely handled.

The fact that these five works were written in such proximity to each other and to the exclusion of works on other topics during this time (with the previously noted exception of "Hometown") is the basis for the hypothesis of this chapter: what he wrote about can be thought about as manifesting itself somehow in the common feature of the queue. This is tested by looking for interconnections in two places: among the works; and in the years in which they were written, 1920–22. The connections among the works are examined first.

Establishing a Group of Works: Three Stories and Two Essays

Literary interconnections among these three stories and two essays reveal a rare instance in his fiction when Lu Xun can be seen reworking persons, situations, and rhetorical devices. I do not imply that he was trying to work toward a particular end, that, for example, "Ah Q" is the climax for which the earlier works are tryouts. It is more likely that they are all tryouts, with different technical solutions each time, and that his last attempt was "Ah Q." Why did he do this? I think it is because at this time, when he had been writing for only two years, he still felt that fiction was something that can draw people to a larger understanding of their world. When over the next years he no longer felt this anymore, he stopped writing fiction (or he stopped writing this kind of *xiaoshuo* fiction as opposed to the later *yanyi* fiction of *Old Tales Retold*). This was late 1925.

Grouping the three stories goes against the common implicit assumption that they are three distinct works. Critics tend to treat "Storm" and "Ah Q" separately, while "Hair" is only mentioned in passing if at all. There is much to support this approach, for by criteria of form, tone, structure, plot, and authorial attitude, in short, in nearly everything, the stories are quite unlike each other. They are of distinctly different natures and seem to be no more connected than any other group of three short stories. I will describe them as standing alone first and then trace their connections.

Artistically, "Storm" is a short, perfectly formed comedy and satire. As the pivot of the plot, queues *are* its point and theme. The protagonist, the boatman Seven-Pounds, lacks one, having had it forcibly cut when he ventured into town in the days of the Republican Revolution. Now it is 1917, and suddenly he needs one because the emperor has been restored to the throne in a coup. It is a temporary restoration, as it turns out, so after some fun at his expense his dilemma passes. This clever plot and the satirical opportunities it affords make "Storm" a favorite with anthologists, although critically it draws less attention, perhaps because its obvious satire and simple, almost gimmicky plot require little commentary except of the antifeudal kind that used to be standard.

"A Story about Hair" is the opposite, for it is very untidy, consisting of a motley sequence of moods and topics displayed through the monologue of a protagonist named N. Queues figure in some of the incidents in his monologue, but their significance is not clearly indicated to the reader and their relation to other parts of his diffuse but intense monologue is not clear. The parts do not add up to any recognizable fictional form, and yet they give no indication of constituting an experimental flouting of fictional rules. Fifteen years later the reader learns that the story is a kind of nonfiction, for Lu Xun gives an account of his experiences of those years that is nearly identical to N's. By then, however, it had long been mentally classified as fiction following its inclusion in *Call to Arms*.

Finally, there is "The True Story of Ah Q." To be sure, it is not primarily about queues. The role that the queue plays is more important in some chapters, less so in others. When queues do appear, readers usually feel that they already understand the scene and no special commentary on the queue is needed. An example is the way Ah Q and the gentry, on their separate tracks, both coil up their queues in anticipation of the successful Republican Revolution arriving in Shaoxing. The parallel actions seem to speak for themselves, and this is reflected in the comparative lack of commentary on queues in the voluminous Ah Q criticism.

The next task is to show that the works do form a group. In doing this, my interest is not in making a literary comparison of the three stories, finding thematic and stylistic connections, and so on. Rather, my goal is to demonstrate that the shared elements of these stories are deeper, more significant than simply an analysis of a "common themes in Lu Xun's fiction" type. The shared elements will show in what manner the queue weighs on

Lu Xun's mind and how it is through the accumulation of later experiences, particularly after he moves to Beijing, that earlier incidents in his life gain new weight. The analysis aims to show that the deeper connections in Lu Xun's mind find literary expression here.

Lu Xun himself tells readers that certain things have occupied his mind for a while. Although he does not state what they are, he does say that they exist, and he says this prominently and unambiguously in the first and last sentences of the very first paragraph of "The True Story of Ah Q." The first sentence reads, "For some years now, I have wanted to write a true account of Ah Q." And the last sentence reads, "In the end . . . I always came back to the idea of writing an account of Ah Q." So he tells us there is premeditation.

This information has tended to be overshadowed by the paragraph's humorous disclaimers. The paragraph in which these sentences are camouflaged are joking statements of history principles directed at the educated reader.

> For some years now, I have wanted to write a true account of Ah Q. But although I had this desire, I also considered how it would clearly demonstrate that I was not someone who [like one of the Sages] could establish his immortality by his words, for it is said that immortal words must record the deeds of immortal men so that the person may be made known by the words and the words be made known by the person, until gradually who is made immortal by whom is fused together. Yet in the end, as though there were an imp in my thoughts, I always came back to the idea of writing an account of Ah Q.

The paragraph immediately gives us a taste of the mock perplexity that is developed through the whole first chapter, while its humor distracts from the author's statements that his purpose has been a long-standing one.

In fact these statements are the complete opposite of how Lu Xun afterward presented "Ah Q" as an ex tempore, installment-by-installment performance; they are the opposite of his claim that he only wrote the story because Sun Fuyuan cajoled him into a contribution and that it had started out funny because it was for the humor column. His frequently quoted comment about the ending also stresses spontaneity. He says he ended it on the spur of the moment—"I killed off [Ah Q] because I got tired of it"—and since Sun was away at the time, there was no one to stop him.[12] In fact, Ah Q is already dead in the first installment, although this is mentioned only in passing: "During his lifetime everyone called him Ah Quei, but after his death no one mentioned his name again." Lu Xun knew his ending was going to include Ah Q's death, although the time and manner might still have been open.

Whatever the story of Ah Q might add up to, we should take Lu Xun at his word that he had been thinking about it "for some years now." Authorial hints of preplanning are an incentive to the literary critic. Of course so far we have only two sentences and some corroborating evidence from its first chapter. But to have a hint from the author himself to search for sources for his most famous work is encouraging. One question is how far back in time we can push his comment "for some years now." My proposal is that by studying the five works together we can find clues as to why he had been thinking about something like Ah Q and what the issues were. Their interconnections show the nature and strength of his motivation. In the remainder of this section, I will show that "Storm," "Hair," and the two essays all contain elements that we can construe as being varying attempts to grasp his topic.

"Storm"

We ask whether in retrospect the first of his three stories can support the idea that Lu Xun was working on something. At first glance, it may seem that the two stories have only the occurrence of the queue in common, but further examination shows more connections.

"Storm" is set in a river village in 1917 and takes advantage of the brief restoration of the Qing emperor, when queues were required again. Some years earlier, in 1911, Seven-Pounds's queue had been forcibly cut off when he took his boat into town to trade. When the story opens, it is suppertime, and the villagers are all preparing dinner and eating it out of doors within view and earshot of each other. Seven-Pounds is late, and when he returns, it is with worrying news of the restoration of the emperor to the throne. Soon the tavern owner, Seventh Master Zhao, comes from nearby Luzhen to confirm the news and gloat. He has let down his coiled queue, shaved his forehead, and put on a long gown for the occasion. These ominous signs are instantly understood by Seven-Pounds's wife, who is especially upset; the tavern keeper sows more panic at opportune moments; the children are rounded on and scolded; and the neighbors chime in with their views on the family crisis. The uproar finally ends with nightfall and bedtime. This is essentially the whole story. A final section takes place two weeks later, when the wife passes by the tavern and sees that the tavern owner once again has his hair coiled on top of his head. She knows her worries are over.

One of Lu Xun's rare lighthearted stories, "Storm" is, in Patrick Hanan's apt description, "a comic study in various shades of ignorance and self-deception."[13] It is structurally and thematically perfect. It is clever and economical and makes many acute observations: about what queue cutting looks like at ground level for the millions of people, not just men but also their families, who are willy-nilly affected; about how those who are safe for the moment change sides immediately (the villagers avoid the queueless man during the two weeks of danger); and about the importance of timing, better figured out by those who are little more savvy (the tavern owner). We see that political ideology operates at a level that is irrelevant to the average person. Added to these points is the author's usual adeptness at capturing key psychological moments, his good ear (the wife's harangue, her freewheeling anger), and the knowledge of rural life that some gentry absorb through their lives in the countryside. Except for its topical starting point at the 1917 coup, it seems a perfect story to explicate in entirely literary terms. In fact it is difficult to bring in external factors.

Yet there are connections with both "Hair" and "Ah Q." Common features with these two works, especially with "Ah Q," show elements in "Storm" that Lu Xun later worked out in different ways. As has often been noted, in "Ah Q," Lu Xun mentions Seven-Pounds's case. When the revolution comes to Ah Q's Weizhuang, the villagers think of what had just happened to Seven-Pounds in Luzhen as an example of the hazards of going to town when the political situation is so unsettled. But there are other connections that are not explicitly made. To begin with, we can see that Seven-Pounds is a simpler version of Ah Q. First, his life circumstances are simpler. He earns his living in a steady job rather by odd jobs. He is a family man, so his relations to others in the village are more set, not in flux. All this means that his daily life is simpler and he does not find himself constantly having to jostle for supremacy and thus needing to create the spiritual victories that give us the Ah Q-ism of "Ah Q."[14] For both characters, lying low is the most important stratagem for survival. Again, Seven-Pounds's situation is simpler. He sticks out involuntarily, mostly because his job as a boatman takes him into the city and thus got him into trouble that one time. Ah Q's work in odd jobs also brings him trouble, but more than his different jobs, it is his personality that lands him there. Every feature of it attracts friction, and he is especially apt to get into scrapes with other odd-job men, from which further trouble then flows. Simpler also is Seven-Pounds's style of hair, which is inadvertent, determined by outside forces, whereas toward the end of "Ah Q" it is a "serious" "sociopolitical" decision for its main character, who coils it up and goes out in search of his fellow revolutionaries. Seven-Pounds, who did not choose his short hair, finds his life possibly in danger, but the critical moment passes and his story remains a comedy. Ah Q chooses his coiled hair, which is a safe enough choice at that time, on that day, but his story has been growing more symbolic and he ends up dead. All in all, therefore, Seven-Pounds is a simpler foreshadowing of Ah Q. The elements that Lu Xun works out here he complicates in "Ah Q." Indeed, in retrospect, writing nearly two decades later, Lu Xun explicitly places Seven-Pounds in relation to Ah Q: "Seven-Pounds can be called Little Queue (xiao bian'er)."[15] This interesting comment is even more intriguing when we note that the one point of comparison he suggests between the two characters is in fact not true, for Seven-Pounds cannot be a Little Queue since a queue is exactly what he does not have.

Another trait Seven-Pounds has that becomes more important for Ah Q is that he and Ah Q both have roles that make them different from the others in their small, isolated communities: their work takes them to bigger places—to town—Seven-Pounds through his work as a boatman and Ah Q because he is often jobless and footloose. As a result, they both enjoy the superiority of a wider knowledge of the world. Indeed Lu Xun uses the same description of their status as big fish in small ponds. Of Seven-Pounds, he writes:

> Every morning he left Luzhen for town, returning in the evening. As a result he was up to date with all the news.

And of Ah Q, he says:

> Ah Q had been to town a few times, and this made him even more conceited.

In connection with this character trait, we can observe one point on which "Ah Q" is technically improved in terms of tone and point of view compared to "Storm." This is in the examples the author provides of the protagonists' superior worldly knowledge. Of Seven-Pounds, Lu Xun writes:

> [He] knew . . . for instance, where the thunder god had struck dead a centipede spirit, and where a virgin had given birth to a demon.

The satirical point is clear—the reader knows these are not really points that give one superiority—but the effect is not quite right. The comment seems mean-spirited. Distinctions in the social world of any group are important to the members of that group, and something must provide the basis for making distinctions. Naming these items of supernatural local lore as the distinguishing basis, however, gives an unpleasant feeling of authorial and reader superiority. Undoubtedly the author and the reader know more than Seven-Pounds and do not consider information about thunder gods and virgin births to be superior knowledge. By contrast, in the description of Ah Q on the same point of snobbery, the choice of examples is better judged. Here is Ah Q's snobbery. Having been to town, he was conceited,

> but at the same time he looked down on townspeople . . . who called a "long bench" a "straight bench," and he thought, "This is wrong, it's stupid!"

Townspeople also cook fish with shallots cut on the diagonal rather than in segments (this is actually a fancier way of slicing), and for this practice, too, Ah Q has only contempt. This is cleverer on several points, and yet it still makes the author's point well. First, Ah Q despises his fellow villagers and the townspeople "at the same time." Second, in having the basis of his superiority concern social customs rather than informational items, no objective basis for superiority is possible. His snobbery can be generalized to human nature, which is a hallmark of satire. What traveler in our own circle has not come back with the same Ah Q sense of having superior knowledge of another country's customs (e.g., salad served after dinner) and thus felt contemptuous of his stay-at-home countrymen, while still feeling superior to foreigners, since clearly salad before dinner is better.

Thus it is that in Ah Q, Lu Xun achieved a universality that is not in Seven-Pounds, so that Ah Q's qualities are endowed with pertinence to us while Seven-Pounds's qualities remain further from our experience. He had tried, the author wrote in 1925, to make Ah Q "the soul of our contemporary Chinese selves."[16] As the novelist Zhang Tianyi (1906–85) attests in an amusing account, as a priggish youngster in the late 1910s, he preferred traditional literature, but he became a reluctant convert to modern literature when, despite an initial feeling of "uneasiness," he came to realize more and more deeply after repeated readings that "my soul contains the kernel of Ah Q's soul."[17]

Seven-Pounds is a protagonist whose characteristics are both purified and rendered more complex for Ah Q. Seven-Pounds may be a first sketch, but we don't have to suppose an endpoint was in mind. In working out ideas, Lu Xun adopts a preexisting literary category of satire that covers up, so to speak, his ideas. The opportunity to deliver clever satire directed against multiple targets—against the literati in the opening passage (see next section), the tavern owner, Seven-Pounds, the other villagers—this opportunity comes at the expense of the ideas. But there is still something left over, as we shall see in the section "Violent Deaths and Literary Limits."

"Storm" is perfect, but Lu Xun has done too well. It is the most literary of the three, and that accounts for its self-contained perfection, as well as its defect of being impenetrable. It is too literary. The strongest impetus in "Storm" is the opportunity to be clever. Lu Xun produced a well-wrought story, but if we take the larger context of the three stories to be about China, then we can see that the author has not been able to incorporate serious issues in Seven-Pounds's story.

"A Story about Hair"

"Hair" followed "Storm" by only one month. It was written in response to a request from *Student Lamp* for something for a special October 10 issue to mark the founding of the Republic. (We do not know whether fiction was specified.) The proximity to "Storm" and the coincidence of subject matter, both factors external to the author, may have operated internally to pry open more things, to bring nearer to the surface events that after all had taken place a decade earlier. What Lu Xun actually ended up writing about within the general subject area of the Republic is the interesting part: as the title points out, he wrote, among other things, about the queue.

"Hair" consists of many separate topics and anecdotes that do not add up but remain separate entities.[18] It can be summarized only by itemizing. It begins as a conventional fiction: a first-person narrator speaks and makes a few observations; then a second person, N, appears and takes over the narration, which does not end until nearly the last sentence. So far, it is a conventional enough frame, especially for fiction of the late nineteenth century, where a first narrator often sets the scene and a second narrator recounts the bulk of the story. N's monologue is rambling, but his is not the revealing literary monologue of nineteenth-century fiction nor of Lu Xun's own "Diary of Madman" and (the later) "Regret for the Past." N begins with somber thoughts of the forgotten martyrs from the long years of revolutionary activities against the Qing dynasty. He then shifts gears and gives a disquisition on the history of the queue. From that he changes to an account of his own experiences on his return to China with short hair before 1911. This is the longest segment, for he describes being eyed suspiciously by relations and jeered at by strangers. His teaching appointments bring other unpleasant experiences stemming from his short hair, which he recounts. Finally, he breaks off his recollections to gives his views on a hair controversy then in the news, this time girls who are not allowed to enroll in school because they had cut their hair short. From there, he vents his exasperation at Chinese lethargy, then suddenly picks up his hat and leaves. That's it, except that it is less easy to see where you are when reading the story than this summary implies. This is understandably among the least read or discussed of Lu Xun's fiction.

What are the connections to "Storm" and "Ah Q"? First, we can say that the story takes us to a different social level than we saw in "Storm," whose highest level was the tavern owner. In this respect, the fictional world is opened up to new spheres and their different social and moral issues. "Storm" shows the experience of a villager caught willy-nilly in the conflicting demands made on him by opposing sides in history. A level above the villagers is the tavern keeper, alert enough to have it both ways. The local elite makes only a cameo appearance at the beginning: its representatives float by on a boat and exclaim over the bucolic village scene before them of villagers preparing dinner out of doors. In "Hair," the experiences of members of the new elite populate the story. These include N, the narrator, the revolutionaries whom they mourn, and the students at N's school, all of whom understand the queue in some political sense. For his part, N faces several dilemmas over the queue that are of his own making but is unfocused in his responses. The next story, "Ah Q," has all three social levels: the countryman (Ah Q and the other villagers), the local elite (the Zhao and Qian families), and in a manner of speaking, the new elite (the Imitation Foreigner).

Second is what "Hair" can tell us about Lu Xun's relation to his material when his own person is involved, for the story is actually a displaced account of his experiences as a member of the new elite. Like N, Lu Xun wore an artificial queue on his return to China from Japan; like N, he encountered derision from family and strangers alike and had unsettling experiences at the new-style school where he taught. The fact that this was not known to readers until mentioned in an essay fifteen years later—and even then no connection was made to this story—points to a personal dimension that the author has chosen not to make known.[19] If we consider the three stories linked, then "Hair" makes it clear that all the stories in the group contain an intractable personal dimension, a hidden self of the public writer, which we happen to be able to uncover.

The third connection between "Hair" and "Ah Q" stems from the autobiographical nature of "Hair." It is a transformational one: scenes depicted in "Hair" reappear in "Ah Q" in a form that is almost unrecognizable. One such scene is the long passage in which N describes returning to China with short hair in 1909.

> Who knew that it would soon be my turn to suffer over the issue of hair.
>
> When I went abroad to study, I cut off my queue. There was nothing remarkable about this, it was too inconvenient.... A few years later, because my family situation had deteriorated and required me to find a position to help out at home, I had to come back to China. As soon as I reached Shanghai, I bought an artificial queue—at that time it cost two dollars—and wore it home. My mother didn't say anything, but other people—others, as soon as they saw me, had to study it, and then once they figured out it was artificial,

they would give a cold laugh, labelling me as someone who would be losing his head. One interfering relative was going to report it, but then there was the possibility that the Revolutionary Party might be successful and so in the end he did not do it.

I thought, well, falseness is not as straightforward and open as truth, so I got rid of the artificial queue and put on western clothes and went out on the streets.

All the way, as I walked I heard the sounds of derision. Some even followed after me, calling out, "reckless idiot!" "imitation foreigner!"

So I put aside my western clothes and put on a long gown, but the abuse grew even worse.

It was at this point that, at end of my rope, I added to my equipment a cane, and after I had furiously laid about me a few times, the abuse gradually left off. It was only when I walked to places where I had not hit anyone that I would hear name-calling again.

What are N's feelings? What are the author's views? N's experiences as presented here surely elicit from readers feelings and opinions on a variety of points, but on nearly every level, questions persist that cannot be answered as the story is written. What are N's feelings? What are the author's views?

The same incident is depicted in almost unrecognizable form in "The True Story of Ah Q." The uncertainties attendant on its account in "Hair" are replaced on every point, or so they seem to be, by clear-cut satire. In "Ah Q," it is the Imitation Foreigner who wears an artificial queue and lays about him with a stick. He is a member of the Qian family, which together with the Zhao's are the two gentry families in the village. This is the related passage.

> [In the distance came] Mr. Qian's eldest son whom Ah Q thoroughly despised. After studying in a foreign-style school in the city, it seemed he had gone to Japan. When he came home half a year later his legs were straight and his queue had disappeared. . . . His mother told everyone his queue had been cut off by some scoundrel when he was drunk. . . . Ah Q, however, did not believe this, and insisted on calling him an Imitation Foreigner or Traitor in Foreign Pay. . . . What Ah Q despised and detested most in him was his artificial queue. With an artificial queue, a man could scarcely be considered human.

The accessory of the cane was also present, for when Ah Q begins muttering "Baldhead" audibly, he finds that:

> Unexpectedly, Baldhead was carrying a shiny brown cane—just what Ah Q calls a mourner's stick (*kusang bang*)—and he bore down on him. In that

instant Ah Q knew that he was in for a beating. He quickly tightened his muscles and hunched his shoulders, waiting, and sure enough *"thwack . . . thwack! thwack!*[20]

The roles are handed out in a completely different way here, and for the reader certitude replaces the earlier uncertainty. The reader is led to feel confident of his or her own viewpoint, of Ah Q's opinions, and even of the author's. The Imitation Foreigner has become a byword for hypocrisy, while his similarity to N and, through N, to Lu Xun is nearly invisible. Ah Q's derision is only what the Imitation Foreigner deserves, whereas in "Hair" the passersby who jeer at N are acting gratuitously toward a stranger. We must conclude that when Lu Xun says that "for some years now, I have wanted to write a true account of Ah Q," there is also a very personal dimension to his words.

Titles

This is a good moment to point out the close connections among the titles of the three works. We cannot know whether the connections were consciously planned, but their partial repetition does show the degree to which Lu Xun's thoughts have been circling around the same items "for some years."

First, the title of "Storm" can serve as an umbrella title for all three. *Fengbo*, which literally means "wind and waves," add up to "storm," which is a standard term for "political storm," meaning unrest or revolution. In "Storm" itself, *fengbo* is used satirically, a big term for a small and temporary scare. In "A Story about Hair," the main part of N's recollections is the period of revolutionary activities, and he recounts episodes from this time, when one's style of hair was fraught with meaning and danger. As for "The True Story of Ah Q," the final three of its nine installments concern the Republican Revolution, which arrives at the big town near Ah Q's Weizhuang and changes everything and nothing, both a tempest in a teacup and a truly destructive storm.

Second, "A Story about Hair" and "The True Story of Ah Q" have essentially the same title. This is especially clear if we insert the optional preposition *de* in the title of the latter work.

Tou-fa de gushi
Ah Q de zhengzhuan

Toufa (hair) is a synonym of the Q (queue) of Ah Q, and *gushi* (story) is a synonym of *zhengzhuan* (official biography). So the titles are made up of synonymous components: a story about hair and a story about a man called Queue.

The stylistic relation between the two titles is also parallel. In "Hair," both nouns—*toufa* and *gushi*—are tamely used; in fact one could complain that "toufa de gushi" is *too* bland, too little indicative of the actual content. By contrast, both *Ah Q* and *zhengzhuan* are fully, amusingly exploited, and neither means what it seems. The elaborate reasoning process by which the author arrives at the name Ah Q for his protagonist and at the genre of *zhengzhuan* for his proposed biography is taken to absurd lengths before he finally ends up with a title that is amazingly similar to the earlier fiction.

Two Essays

After "Hair," more than half a year passed with neither fiction nor essay. Then, on May 5, Lu Xun wrote two essays, both later connected to "Ah Q," which were published on successive days, May 6 and 7. It seems that Lu Xun's thinking had proceeded during the intervening seven months, and so it cannot be completely true that he put things down on paper because Sun's request pushed him into it.

The first essay is "Surrendering in Life but Not in Death." The title itself is a quotation. It is one situation on a list of ten in which one surrenders only outwardly while keeping one's integrity inwardly. The list is called *shi xiang shi buxiang* (Surrendering while not surrendering: ten situations) and dates from Ming dynasty subjects living under the new Qing rulers who took it as a form self-encouragement. The idea is that they only outwardly acquiesced in their subjugation, for example, in wearing the queue that was imposed. More immediately, it is a quotation from 1905 (as Lu Xun's essay notes, "15 or 16 years ago"), when the revolutionary activist Wang Jingwei (1883–1944) published an essay in which he used this phrase, averring that "the men have surrendered, the women have not; one surrenders in life but not in death." The meaning is that although they now wear queues, in death they will revert to their real, unqueued selves. Wang's essay, entitled "Minzu de guomin," was published in the inaugural issue of his Yokohama-based *Minzu bao*.[21]

Lu Xun's essay was published in *Morning Post Supplement* in the "Miscellaneous Thoughts" (*zagan*) column, under a new pen name, Feng Sheng 風聲, which he was to continue to use for several more contributions to the column. In the second paragraph, he gives a brief history of the title phrase as he encountered it in his youth, and in the next paragraphs he gives his present views. Lu Xun's essay is short and is translated in its entirety here.

About fifteen or sixteen years ago [i.e., 1905–6], I was very much taken in by the revolutionary parties.

They said, We must have revolution! Look how much the Han people do not want to be slaves, how much they think day and night of the recovery of the homeland. This dedication is incised like coppergraphs onto our hearts and bones. To give an example—they said—when Han people die and are prepared for their coffins, their queues are coiled up on the top of their heads, as was the style under the Ming dynasty. This is known as "surrendering in life but not in death."

Surrendering in life but not in death. How tragic and yet how pitiable.

In recent years, however, my superstition has begun to break up. I see many people in the obituaries today who have neither died for their country nor are fugitive subjects of the previous dynasty, who are in fact completely unconnected to the Qing dynasty, or perhaps they have in fact even eaten the "emoluments" of the Republic—but when they die, their obituaries always mention their Qing-enfeoffed titles.[22]

For this reason, I no longer put any stock in the words of the revolutionary parties. For I think: everything else was a lie, only the fact that the Han people have "surrendered in life but not in death," only this eccentricity is true.

In this essay, more openly, more deliberately than in "Hair," Lu Xun writes of his past, in particular of an idealistic period when he believed in the advocates of revolution, indeed when he even believed in their assertion of silent resistance. The essay provides proof that during this half year, after he had written two stories on the queue, he is thinking over this past and the queue in terms of political metaphor, as the revolutionary parties did and as he once did too. The queue was once, in 1644, imposed as a symbol of Manchu conquest. Over time, this meaning lost its force and the queue was assimilated into every corner of the culture. When its alien source was revived as an anti-Manchu goad during Lu Xun's early years in Japan, he along with many others learned, some years before their compatriots, to regard it as a symbol of political subjugation. But political defiance cannot always be instantly carried out—N's refusal to support his students' queue cutting is one instance—and this reality is acknowledged in the tidy saying *shi xiang shi buxiang*.

But when we place this essay with "Ah Q," we find new things in it. In the saying "surrendering in life but not in death," we see the kernel of what would become Ah Q's "spiritual victories," in which a person's triumph is invisible to all but himself. We see that a persuasive argument of Lu Xun's youth represented, in a term that was soon to come into existence, an Ah

Q-ism. Here is an example of Ah Q's thought process with which Lu Xun was personally acquainted. The assertion that one's submission is only an outward one, that true loyalty is to be found in the heart—and will find expression after death—is skewered here as hypocrisy. Calling this hypocrisy "eccentricity" is a typically brilliant move. Lu Xun says that, despite their defiance, the Han people prefer, Ah-Q-like, to wear their queue-related, Qing-bestowed honors rather than not have any and to reserve the inconvenient aspects of their principles for later. "How tragic and how pitiable," used here of these self-deceptions, are adjectives that will soon summarize Ah Q very well.

The essay Lu Xun wrote the same day is on names! Entitled "Names," and published on May 7, it shows that on the same day, Lu Xun was thinking about names in terms that would soon be familiar and funny with the novella's first installment and its disquisition on the possible characters for Ah Q's name. As is usual in his essay style, he begins with a stray thought from which he switches to his main point. So here he begins by ranking pseudonyms: he says he always checks the author's name first and if it falls into certain classes of pseudonyms, he decides right away, nope, he won't read that. He used to fear that his system was bit drastic and others would disapprove when they learned of it. But then he came across a passage by the Song dynasty literatus Yu Cheng and—here is the switch—Yu was writing about the names that people give themselves or their children. With this switch, Lu Xun is not writing about pseudonyms any more but about choosing names. According to him, Yu says that people are now giving their sons really grand names, and Lu Xun gives some examples. He, Lu Xun, then contrasts it with ancient times, when people gave themselves the opposite kind of names, derogatory ones like dogs, wild dogs, and so on, to protect against bad luck. The essay then becomes a kind of survey of names as meaning. Of course what happens is that just a few months later the narrator of "Ah Q" is deciding which grand word would be the correct character for his protagonist's formal name (*ming*), which he says is pronounced *gui*. Is it written 貴, "esteemed," the narrator asks himself? Or could it be 桂, "cassia," he wonders. He thinks that if only he knew his subject's alternate name—his *zi*, itself an elevated concept—maybe that would help him decide on a *ming* that matches the alternate name. He ends up with not even a derogatory name but a nugatory one, Q.

One more point about names. This essay marks only one stage of Lu Xun's thinking on names. The actual name he arrives at for Ah Q is prefigured in the other two stories, for none of the three protagonists has a real name. All their names are ciphers. The protagonist of "Storm" is named after his birth weight, as are all his fellow villagers; the protagonist of "Hair" is referred to by his initial N; and the protagonist of "Ah Q" is named after a letter of the alphabet. The reason for each cipher name differs and is appropriate to its story, but they are still all ciphers. In the case of Seven-Pounds, one could argue that country people tend not to have refined names of the type Lu Xun was trying to foist on Ah Q, but the author could have chosen other naming systems. Runtu, the name of his childhood friend in "Hometown," is an example of a country name that is not personalized, but neither is it a cipher. (Runtu means "earth added," so this element must have been lacking in his astrological makeup; his counterpart in life was Runshui, "water element added.") If Lu Xun had wanted to use numbers, he could have used birth order, a near-universal custom that captures human social order. But no, he gives his characters an arbitrary one, so Seven-Pounds and his fellow villagers are birth-weight ciphers (Zhou Zuoren does say it was a custom in the countryside in their youth).[23]

The protagonist of "Hair," N, has the most conventional literary reason for his name. Although it is also a letter of the alphabet, the initial is simply employed in the manner of the nineteenth-century European fiction that formed Lu Xun's earliest study of modern literature. There the names of people and places are often indicated only by their first letter. This convention also suits well the story of two colleagues in a government office, for such settings and characters are common in nineteenth-century literature.

In the third case, Ah Q only receives his alphabet name after much "research," as the author laboriously and systematically considers his possibilities, rejecting each one on the basis of elaborate sociological reasoning before settling on one that is in fact not a name but a letter of the alphabet, and foreign to boot. Ah Q is the most reduced of the ciphers. The author's decision to write his name based on its sound "spelled in the English fashion" represents not only the joke we can see but also a sleight of hand before the reader's eyes. The author's decision to use the "Western alphabet" is the joke that he shows us. He says the sound of the character's name, "spelled in the English fashion," is "Quei" and he will "abbreviate it to Q." He incidentally pokes a little fun at various current proposals for phonetic systems to represent Chinese sounds, but the upshot is that this most insular sample of the Chinese man who sneers at the people in town for their different way of cooking fish is represented by a letter of the Western alphabet. But the joke is also on readers. A word that sounds like 貴 or 桂, which the narrator says are some possible characters for Ah Q's name, is not romanized with the initial *q*. Even if you are making up your own phonetic spelling, as Lu Xun undoubtedly was and as many did in those days, nothing was romanized with a *q* at that time (the *q* in today's pinyin romanization system stands for an entirely different sound). A plausible romanization would begin with either *g* or *k*. Chuandao and his

Beijing University classmates at *New Tide* thought so. He remembers that when the first installment came out, he and other students in the magazine's office had a theory about the author and his target and thought that the author needed *q* to make a certain satirical topical reference since normally both 貴 and 桂 would begin with *k*. (Later that day Sun Fuyuan stopped by to tell them Lu Xun was the author.)[24] There is no obvious way to pronounce the spelling of *Quei* without Lu Xun first telling us that it represents 貴 or 桂. He wanted the *q*, and he got it. As for "Ah," in the end the narrator decides that the only absolutely certain element of his name is the "Ah," which will be "proof against the scrutiny of the learned." Alas, as his readers well know, "Ah" is not a name but a prefix, and while close male friends may use it with each other, it is usually only for someone younger or socially inferior. Indeed, when the revolution comes and the gentry are briefly in awe of Ah Q, Old Master Zhao timidly hails him using the more respectful prefix "Old" (*lao* 老), "Lao Q," but Ah Q does not recognize his new, better name, and finally Old Master Zhao has to call out "Ah Q" to get his attention. So no part of Ah Q's name is a name.

"The True Story of Ah Q"

Many of the connections among the two short stories and two essays have been noted already. Here I will give an account of this famous story entirely from the standpoint of the queue as a means of bringing out, from a different direction, the ways in which "Ah Q" is more complicated compared to Lu Xun's earlier treatments of the topic. Befitting a more complex story, the queue operates on more levels.

1. He is defined by the queue. The first connection, his name, or more exactly, the name the author ends up giving him has been mentioned already. Zhou Zuoren suggests the visual metaphor: the author, he writes, liked the look of the tail on the capital letter *Q*.[25] Figure 3.1, the cover of a play adaptation, captures the conflation of *Q* and the back of a man's head. There is also the visual impact of the recurring letter *Q* in a story printed in Chinese characters, where we see the pictograph of a queue cropping up in an otherwise Chinese text, as can be seen in the first installment in the *Morning Post Supplement* (fig. 3.2). In fact, Zhou says that in the first edition of *Call to Arms* only the three occurrences of *Q* on the first page have a good tail; the subsequent *Q*'s are in a different font.

With "Q," Lu Xun gives us a protagonist defined by his hair. This point cannot be overemphasized: Q is not just his name; it is his definition. Just as the sound *gui*, if written as "esteemed" or "cassia," would have placed him among the gentry, so *gui* transmuted into "Q" defines his milieu as that of the queue, a world the author proceeds to fill in for us with such matters as "spiritual victories." Qu Qiubai, in a little doodle he gave Lu Xun, also made this point when he drew Ah Q as a composite of ten *Q*s—head, body, and two per limb. He also wrote a colophon, "Steel lash in hand, I will thrash you" (*shou zhi gangbian jiang ni da*) (fig. 3.3).[26] There are two moments for this stirring song in "Ah Q": once when he is cowing everyone by alternating shouts of rebellion with roaring lines from this song, and then in his final moments when he thinks to sing it but finds his hands tied. That stops him, as he cannot gesture appropriately. (Neither time, of course, does he have a steel lash in hand: this drawing is his mental image of himself.) A man whose identity is Q, who is made up of ten *Q*s, has in his way won our confused sympathy, and this contradiction is caught in Qu's drawing.

Near the end of the novella, Ah Q by chance comes to define himself in the same terms. He is arrested for burglary and condemned to die, although he does not yet realize this. The authorities decide he should sign his name to the sentence. He says he cannot write, so he is told to draw a circle. Holding a brush for the first time and watched by all, he is anxious to acquit himself

Figure 3.1. The back of Ah Q's head outlined as a *Q*. Unidentified artist. Source: cover of playscript by Chen Baichen, *The True Story of Ah Q*, 1981.

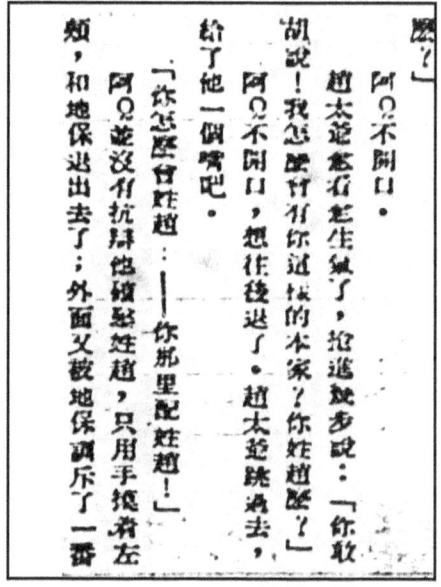

Figure 3.2. The appearance of the English letter *Q* set in type among Chinese characters – a detail from first installment of "The True Story of Ah Q," *Morning Post Supplement*, December 4, 1921.

well. He makes the circle shape slowly, and just as he is finally about to successfully close the wobbly circle, his brush swerves and he ends up with a shape like a "melon seed." The author leaves the scene there, but a not quite round shape that has a bump at one end is a bit like a head with a queue.

A reader, looking where Lu Xun points, sees Ah Q's effort as he strives to make a circle. Likewise, illustrations of this scene depict his concentrated struggle rather than the moment he shapes a

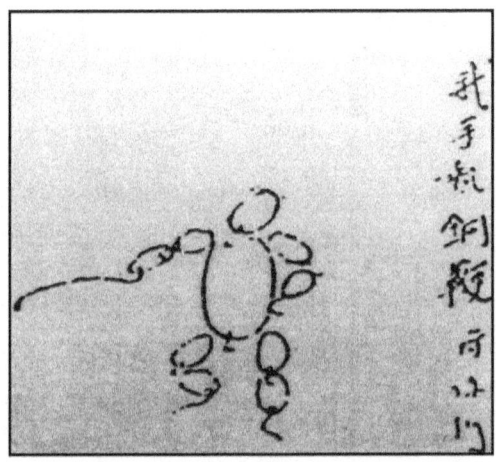

Figure 3.3. Qu Qiubai. The colophon identifies his subject matter. It reads "Steel lash in hand, I will thrash you," Ah Q's favorite song. Courtesy of Beijing Lu Xun Museum.

melon seed as his signature. This is the case with the seven illustrations, all well-known, that are included in Peng Xiaojie's compendium on "Ah Q."[27] In them, following the novella's description, Ah Q is kneeling on the ground, and the paper has been placed in front of him. He grasps the brush and leans over the paper. Four of the artists focus with great effectiveness on how his entire back is tense with the effort brought to bear on that space on the paper, and this tense curve of the back dominates their composition. As for the circle, in Zhao Yannian's work, Ah Q's hand just blocks a view of what he is attempting, while the others depict him at various stages in his effort: in Feng Zikai, the brush is poised over the paper, not yet started on its journey, while Ding Cong shows the circle close to completion. None bring Ah Q all the way around the circle, perhaps because completion is felt to imply success. As a result, we do not see an interpretation of the melon-seed shape.

2. *Ah Q's queue in the plot.* Although the author does not stress this point, all of Ah Q's spiritual victories involve fights, and they all involve his queue. The very first of the squabbles arises from his hairstyle. He is touchy about the shiny ringworm scars that form patches on his scalp and gets into fights at the least mention of them. These scars must be on the shaven part of his pate. The other fights also all involve hair: he has "his brownish queue pulled"; someone "pulled or twisted his brown queue"; and looking to get away, he "clutches the root of his queue, his head on one side." He has a run-in with Whiskers Wang, who grabs him by the queue and bangs his head against a wall. There is one that he could have won in a forfeit since his opponent, Xiao D, wants to

beg off, offering to humble himself. This is an especially metaphorical one and also involves queues. Ah Q and Xiao D face off, each grabs the other's queue while protecting his own with his free hand, and thus evenly matched, they grapple feebly "for half an hour, their shadows joined in a blue rainbow upon the Qian family wall." The symmetry, or stalemate, of figures and shadows forms the design of many illustrations of this scene, and to a degree, the design element can overshadow the metaphor of the scene as well as its comic fierceness. An example is the book cover in figure 3.4, a playscript of "Ah Q."[28] Feng Zikai and Ding Cong include the second symmetry of the shadows.

3. *Ah Q and his queue have a double in the story.* This is another way in which the novella gains in complexity over the earlier works. The second Ah Q is Xiao D. He begins as someone beneath notice, even scrawnier and more hopeless than Ah Q, though not obviously characterized by Ah Q-ism in his behavior. Then he becomes Ah Q's rival, for the Zhaos hire him to do odd jobs after Ah Q disgraces himself by propositioning their servant. Aggrieved at this, Ah Q challenges him to a fight even though he is weakened by the lack of jobs and by hunger and Xiao D "has become almost an opponent on an equal footing." As we saw above, they fight to a standstill, so now Xiao D is Ah Q's feeble equal. Then near the story's end, when Ah Q coils up his queue to join the revolution, he finds to his great irritation that Xiao D has also coiled up his queue. Finally, Xiao D succeeds to another role Ah Q once had, for significantly he is the person Ah Q sees running in the darkness when Zhao family is being burglarized. Xiao D must have been the lookout since he knows the burglarizing is going on when Ah Q asks what is happening. That had been Ah Q's job in that memorable period when he was in town and had come back with some goods to sell. Further cementing their twinship, it is for this burglary in which Xiao D is involved that Ah Q is arrested and executed.

Figure 3.4. Ah Q and Xiao D fight, evenly matched. Cover of *The True Story of Ah Q: a Literary Playscript*, unidentified artist, unidentified author. Source: Ouyang Wenli, ed., *Pictorial Biography of Lu Xun*, 414.

One interesting thing about Xiao D as the second Ah Q is his name. If pronounced as written, Xiao D (小D) has the same sound as 小弟, "younger brother." In other words, he is even called (Ah Q's) younger brother. For this reason, I use the transliteration Xiao D to emphasize the pun of "little brother." (This supposition should work even given the many regional pronunciations of Chinese words: if *D* is pronounced "in the English fashion," it matches the word in Mandarin; pronounced in German, Lu Xun's chief European foreign language, it matches the word in the Shaoxing dialect.) Like Ah Q, this name uses a letter of the English alphabet, so it, too, sticks out everywhere, while the *xiao* part, like the "Ah" in "Ah Q," is a prefix for a younger or inferior person. Another interesting point about the name is that, many years after naming him Xiao D, Lu Xun came up with a distractor about its meaning. Writing in 1934, he said that 小 D is short for 小同 (*xiao tong*, "little duplicate") for, and here he spells it out, "when he gets older, he will be just like Ah Q." It is true, as we saw above, that Xiao D will be just like Ah Q, and "little duplicate" also works to denote that. But why suggest that D stands for *tong* when *di* works? An *–ng* final does not rhyme or even come close to rhyming with the *-i* of *di*. (*T* and *d*, aspirated and unaspirated, are different sounds, but that is less important.) Maybe Lu Xun liked to put people off the scent. When he gave out this information, he was responding to a speculation that maybe Xiao D stands for 小董 *xiao dong* (also an *–ng* final), which is actually pretty good, especially for the tin-eared adaptation in which the suggestion appears and also because *dong* is a real surname, which, paired with *xiao,* can mean "minimal understanding." In any case, the authorial suggestion for "Little Duplicate" has been accepted by a 1981 playscript that describes Xiao D in the cast of characters as "in his 20s, called by others Xiao Tong."[29] A similar perception is probably behind Paul Foster's calling Xiao D Ah Q's "companion character." Foster also draws our attention to Ah Q-related pen names of the 1930s; among them, "Ah D," used in 1936, might illustrate this sense of kinship in the structure of the name; another one, Younger Brother of Ah Q (*Ah Q zhi di*) probably refers only to the creator of the pen name, not to Xiao D.[30]

4. *The absence of a queue is the other side of having a queue.* Until near the novella's end, the Imitation Foreigner was the sole representative of this advanced style of hair, and he was, as Ah Q notes, "scarcely human" without a queue. The other absences occur with the approach of the revolution to their part of Zhejiang province. First is the fear of having their queues cut off. The villagers talk of "some bad revolutionaries who made trouble by cutting off people's queues," and furthermore everyone has heard of Seven-Pounds's situation. Then as the revolution's success becomes more certain, the desire not to have a queue, or more safely, to coil it, strengthens. Three members of the Zhao family are the first to make the change. Next is Ah Q, who coils

up his queue and goes out to join the gentry in revolution. He finds them together, all wearing the silver peach pins of the new "Persimmon Oil" Party, and discussing possible offices to be had under the new system.

This is history as farce. A corresponding nonfiction account, longer in its time frame, is grimmer. As Lu Xun wrote in "'Fair Play' Should be Postponed," in Shaoxing, it was the gentry who "instantly took fright like masterless dogs and coiled up their queues on their heads."[31] They are at a savvier level than the Zhaos and Qians of Weizhuang, for, officeholders to begin with, they bided their time and used the crushing of the Second Revolution (in 1913) to return to power under Yuan Shikai and take their revenge. This was only one of the many instances in this essay in which the nimble, willing to shed the blood of others, win not only in history but in historical memory.

An interesting problem for the reader that Lu Xun does not address, except through the contrast between Ah Q and the gentry, is how to tell the sincere from the agile in these treacherous situations. Indeed, if we look at Lu Xun, there are two points on which he outwardly resembles the gentry in "Ah Q," just as earlier we saw that, like the Imitation Foreigner, he had worn a false queue and been jeered at. One is that, like the successful provincial candidate in town, he received a post under the new power: he was appointed principal of the school in which he had taught until some months earlier (though he soon

Figure 3.5. Group photograph, "Commemorative Photograph of the Shaoxing Academy Excursion to the Temple of Yu in Spring, 1911." The persimmon pin against the left shoulder is very visible on those wearing dark clothing. Courtesy Beijing Lu Xun Museum.

Figure 3.6. Detail of 3.5, the row of teachers on the left of the group. Lu Xun is the first figure from the top in dark clothing. Courtesy of Beijing Lu Xun Museum.

resigned over administration policies). Second is the Persimmon Oil Party's pin that the gentry wear, "persimmon oil" (*shiyou*) being what the villagers heard when the gentry spoke of the new Freedom Party (*ziyou*, a new word for a new idea). Lu Xun and his like-minded colleagues also wore such *shiyou* pins that year, as we see in figures 3.5 and 3.6. Cutting off the queue and wearing a pin were intended to signify something specific and political, but the use of these symbols by persons with such a range of motivations made them far more versatile in Lu Xun's hands and also gives readers an insight into an otherwise unrecorded, changeful period of his life.

The connections among the three stories and two essays outlined above represent some traces of Lu Xun's thinking and working methods over a fairly long time span, nearly two years in an eight-year fiction-writing career. This still leaves the question of what the connections mean about the works as a group, as opposed to each story's individual meaning. When he took time out from translating, managing translations, teaching, and family responsibilities, these are what he wrote. What was he working out? What issues were evolving? They are tied up somehow with queues. For a brief span of time, he crept up on this topic, or this topic crept up on him. It found partial expression in three very different stories and two essays. Let us now look at the other pieces of the puzzle. These lie in the biographical context of political violence. After that, we will trace how the connections between queues and political violence are worked out in each of the stories.

Biographical Connections: Political Violence and Writing

The first part of this section presents evidence that suggests the stimulus for this group of five items lies in contemporary battles that Lu Xun experienced and through them what he had witnessed in the preceding violent decade. The second part gives an account of his experiences in the battles of 1919 and 1920 with the purpose of explaining how the political violence in China in the years leading up to 1911 and since could be the somber topic underlying the satire of these stories.

Examining the details of Lu Xun's life in these months, I suggest that the immediate stimulus of "Storm" was the fighting that took place over a few days in July 1920, on the outskirts of Beijing, between Zhili forces, whose base was in provinces along the Yangtze River, and Anhui forces centered on Beijing and headed by Duan Qirui, who, though not premier at this moment, held effective power through his other offices. The battles began July 14 and ended on July 19 with the defeat of Duan's army. Duan had resigned his offices the previous day. This short battle of five days concluded the long-term militarized rivalries of cliques initially derived from Yuan Shikai's Beiyang Army and set the stage for the next group of rival regional powers. As Lu Xun's *Diary* records, "Storm" was completed on the fifth of the next month and sent to Chen Duxiu at *New Youth* on the seventh where it was published under the pen name Lu Xun.

How is this 1920 battle a precipitating event for "Storm," which after all was set in 1917? I suggest that Lu Xun's experience of it resembled his experience of an earlier episode of fighting, which took place in 1917, also in July, this time within the walls of Beijing. This was the brief coup that provided the plot premise for "Storm." In this year, the general Zhang Xun entered Beijing on June 14 and installed the Qing emperor on the throne on July 1. On the fourth, the heads of other, rival armies declared their opposition and assembled an expeditionary army against Zhang, which, under Duan Qirui's command, laid siege to Beijing. The fighting that took place began July 3. On July 14, Duan entered the city. This was the campaign that established Duan in power in Beijing as premier and minister of war. (In the next conflict, in 1920, he fell from power.)

One might ask, why Zhang Xun? Why not find a 1920 topic? One reason may be that he did not have a topic for 1920 whereas 1917 has an obvious one. Zhang Xun naturally brings up pigtails: he kept his after the establishment of the Republic as a symbol of his loyalty to the emperor and was known as the Pigtail General (*bianzi jiangjun*). He compelled his troops – the Pigtail Army (*bianzi jun*)[32]—to keep theirs, and after entering Beijing, he issued an edict reinstating the old style of hair. This became the plot for "Storm." Lu Xun was already sensitized to queues through his own experiences. Moreover, during the coup, he saw things he remembered. He recalled in 1934 that he "once saw his [Zhang's] Pigtail Army standing guard outside the walls of Beijing, acting in an overbearing manner towards people without a queue." Why did he not write about it in 1917? He could not, at least not in the form of "Storm," because in 1917 no one was writing in the conventions of realist European literature on which the first New Literature fiction was modeled. It may be that in 1920 he wanted to write about the fighting, and Zhang Xun from 1917 provided the handiest topic, which with Lu Xun's ready wit, resulted in a work like "Storm." Or it may be that the fighting of 1920 reminded him directly of situations that had come up with Zhang Xun, for which he had no format at the time.

That Lu Xun might have wanted to write something at this time in 1920 (as opposed to not having any writing in mind) is hinted at in the way "Storm" begins. He begins the story with an altered version of a sketch of a river village that he had already published. This may indicate that he was casting about for a way to put certain experiences into writing and by using a sketch from the previous year, he has a way of beginning it in a distancing manner right away. The sketch that is reprised by "Storm" was published in August 1919 in *Guomin gongbao*, at that time briefly under the editorship of Sun Fuyuan.[33] It depicts a summer evening in a river village described by a narrator who sees it from the middle distance. People are sitting under trees in a river village on a summer evening, fanning themselves, "a pleasant thing indeed"; men and women talk unhurriedly, telling stories; children sing or tell riddles; and—Lu Xun's typically discordant note—an old man sits by himself. The others avoid him as he is "a little deaf, a little blind, has had limited experience, and yet is opinionated" and thus annoys the others. "Storm" begins with the same idyllic description of a village scene, admired from the middle distance by some literati on an excursion, who float by. They see people preparing their evening meals out of doors, the women cooking, the children playing, the old people sitting and talking. This scene is also jarred by discordance: the narrator interrupts the literati's appreciative exclamations, zooms in, and lets us hear the quarrelling and complaining that are the constant accompaniment to this time of day.[34]

Lu Xun had also previously used the device where a short-lived panic showed people in their true hypocritical colors. This was in his 1911 classical-language fiction, "Remembering the Past," where a sudden alarm goes out that bandits or perhaps rebels are coming. A tutor and a neighboring member of the gentry confer hurriedly about plans to flee or, the opposite possibility, to placate the rebels, while another neighbor prepares to flee with his concubines. Then all return; the rumor had been started by the sight of a few dozen refugees, and refugees, as the neighbor says, are nothing, like beggars.

Another feature of "Storm" hints that, although the vehicle is satire, the author's thoughts are not really on satire. This is the fact that the setting is the countryside outside the fictional village of Luzhen in the south, whereas Zhang Xun's coup took place in Beijing. His brief tenure in power never reached beyond Beijing, the edict reinstating queues must have had limited force, and this is a river village so small that it gets its news from Luzhen. Indeed, it has to be very far from the nearest big town, for the other villagers and the tavern owner still have their queues in 1917 and in some cases are even growing them back (the latter are described as trying to look invisible while the tavern owner is sweeping triumphantly away). One reason may be that Lu Xun's rural pieces are all set in the south, the only countryside he knows, whereas his stories that are set in the north have the city of Beijing as their setting. Another reason may be that Lu Xun was also thinking about

1911 and conflated the two in some ways. Zhou Zuoren notes a couple of anachronisms in the story that seem to show that the time frame of 1911 or 1912 slips in sometimes. He points out that the hair the men in the village are trying to regrow would have been long again if it were five years later and that the daughter, who is about six in the story, could not have been old enough to cry over her father's queue if 1911 were five years in the past.[35] These anomalies would be explicable if Lu Xun's mind was also on 1911 even though he needs 1917 for his joke and his starting point.

What happened after "Storm"? The 1920 fighting served as a precipitating event for "Storm," and the others follow from the opening into the memory that it created. At the beginning, that volition was taken out of his hands because a few weeks after "Storm" was finished he received a commission from Shanghai's *Student Lamp* to write for a special October 10 issue. The general subject matter of 1911 was already specified, "A Story about Hair" was the ungainly result, and he sent it off on September 29. N's monologue in "Hair" contains a number of topics related to 1911, on the one hand fulfilling the commission and on the other presenting new elements in the author's experiences from 1911 and earlier. The story shows that Lu Xun was reviewing queues in terms of his own experiences of them, and this is reinforced by the memories mentioned in the essay "Surrendering in Life but Not in Death." The essay "Names" shows that material independent of direct personal experience was now enriching the mix. Then came "Ah Q," after which he no longer dealt with this topic in fictional terms.

The biographical stimulus proposed here centers on two incidents of battles in and around Beijing, both occurring in July. In both years, like other inhabitants of Beijing, Lu Xun, his brother, and in the second instance, their dependents were affected by the fighting. They left their home to take refuge outside the city, reported the sounds of battle, and recorded the heightened tension. There is also some mention of food scarcity. In providing, as much as possible, a thick description of Lu Xun's experiences in these few weeks, the descriptions below of the ripples of war aim to make comprehensible the influence of immediate events on his writing. They are reconstructed from his diary entries, his brother's diaries and memoirs, and primary sources such as newspaper reports collected in *Lu Xun Chronology*.[36]

1917: A Coup in Beijing

Zhang Xun entered Beijing without resistance on June 14, 1917, and ousted Li Yuanhong from the presidency. On July 1, after two weeks of uncertainty for the residents of Beijing—Zhou Zuoren said that when asked, Cai Yuanpei said that as long as there was not an imperial restoration, he would remain in his post as chancellor of Beijing University—Zhang put Puyi, the last Manchu emperor, then aged eleven, on the throne; issued edicts that gave himself positions and titles; and ordered the reestablishment of Qing dynasty government names. Duan Qirui led the combined forces that set out to relieve Beijing. On July 12, he entered the city; on the fourteenth, he resumed the post of premier from which Zhang had driven him. Zhang's reign lasted only four weeks and the restoration only two.

Zhou Zuoren, who had three months earlier joined his brother in Beijing at Shaoxing hostlery, remembered the day Puyi was placed on the throne:

> Lu Xun had got up fairly early and was preparing to go to Liulichang [the antiquarian bookdealers' district] when the son of the super at Shaoxing hostlery came in and said, "There are imperial dragon flags everywhere outside." This was not unexpected, but still, to hear it gave everyone an unhappy feeing all over.[37]

Zhou Zuoren recalls that they did not have the funds to go south or to Tianjin, as some of their colleagues planned. In Lu Xun's diary, the first indication of the restoration came on July 3 and was oblique. There he recorded, without giving a reason, his resignation from the Ministry of Education, going in that day to the ministry to bid his colleagues farewell. Notations in the diary during the month that Zhang Xun held Beijing mention telegrams of protest that arrived from the provinces and Cai Yuanpei's resignation as chancellor of Beijing University. His dairy also lists many visitors, perhaps an indication of the constant circulation of news and rumors.

On the seventh, "a hot and sunny day," he and Zhou Zuoren moved to safer quarters in the Dongcheng district of Beijing, outside the city walls to the east. That morning, his diary notes, "we had seen planes overhead." According to *Beijing Daily* the next day, the planes dropped three bombs at the palace where Zhang Xun was headquartered.[38] In Dongcheng, the brothers stayed at the Xinhua Hotel until the fourteenth. Others had made the same move. Lu Xun notes that "many people we knew were [at the hotel]," and Zuoren writes that "from the 6th onwards, many people from within the city walls came here for refuge. What people feared was not the rising waves of fighting, but the looting of the Pigtail Army." It must have been during this week "outside the walls of Beijing" that Lu Xun saw soldiers harassing commoners about their queueless hair.

On the afternoon of the ninth, Lu Xun sent a telegram to let the family in Shaoxing know that he and his brother were safe. His diary entry reads, "[That] night, there were sounds of gunfire." The next day's newspaper reported fighting between two battalions and Zhang Xun's forces.[39] For the twelfth Lu Xun's diary entry is long. He notes, of what must have been Duan Qirui's short and successful attack, that "there were sounds of fierce fighting beginning at four-thirty in the morning, not stopping until two in the afternoon. Peace was restored." This was not quite the end. On the same day, he notes that "there were a great many rumors. It was hard to find things to eat. In the evening, together with Wang Huazhu, Zhang Zhongsu and Zuoren, went to Yixing district to look for Qi Shoushan [who ran a grain store] and in that way we obtained a meal." On the fourteenth he reports, "The situation is somewhat more settled" (Duan had entered the city), and he and Zuoren moved back to the Shaoxing hostel. Zuoren recalled that sounds of gunfire continued all day, but with curiously few wounded, and rumors had it that guns were being fired into the air. They sent someone to Dongcheng for their things and learned that "the five-colored flags [of the Beiyang Army] were already everywhere." Lu Xun did not record his return to the ministry on the sixteenth. On the thirty-first, together with Qi Shoushan and Xu Jishang, he paid a call on their superior, Cai Yuanpei. This presumably was the end of the incident and its immediate effects.

1920: A Battle outside Beijing

In 1920, also in July, fighting took place outside Beijing, but nonetheless its residents were affected, and many sought refuge outside the city walls. At this point, much of Lu Xun's immediate family (mother, wife, brothers, Zuoren's wife and children, and Jianren's wife and children) had been in Beijing half a year, since December of 1919. So this new conflict involved care for a much larger brood. The battle this time involved Duan Qirui and his Anhui forces on one side and Zhili forces from the Yangtze River area on the other. Opponents had forced Duan from the position of premier, but he continued to exercise power in his other roles as head of the frontier defense force and the political organization, the Anfu Club. The battle between the two sides on the outskirts of Beijing took place on the fourteenth. Several sources, including Lu Xun's diary, record the eighteenth as the tensest day. There had been rumors that the conquering army was entering Beijing, creating much fear among the populace. On this day, Lu Xun notes, "The news is very tense. This evening, sent mother and all the women and children to Tongren Hospital in Dongcheng to take temporary refuge." The Dongcheng district, east of the city walls, had been his place of refuge in 1917 as well. As for Tongren Hospital, Lu Xun had been there almost daily since May, when his nephew Pei, Jianren's year-old son, had been hospitalized repeatedly with an infection in the lungs. Pei had been discharged on the May 13 and readmitted on the sixteenth. On the eighteenth, the entire family went to Tongren Hospital. This time the refuge was for only a day, for on the nineteenth fighting ceased with Duan's defeat. His retreating soldiers reached the station at Yongding Gate by rail. Homes and stores were looted. "The city gates were closed, patrols were added, tensions rose, and rumors flew. Many in the city sought refuge elsewhere."[40] Despite this, we find that on the morning of the nineteenth "mother and others" were home again. This was the end of the crisis for Lu Xun's family in the written records.

The battles of 1917 and 1920 were the two junctures at which rival armies that had been formed since the Republican Revolution fought in the Beijing area. At the beginning of that decade, a year after the revolution, a provisional government had been formed in Beijing under Yuan Shikai. Lu Xun's move to Beijing came during the brief months of constitutional government that followed. Soon after, Yuan's suspension of the constitution and dissolution of Parliament fractured the fragile national structure and introduced the first set of players in the shifting regional alliances and wars that were to define domestic China until the eve of World War II. In 1917 and 1920, the players belonged to factions that had devolved from the Beiyang Army, created under the Qing dynasty by Yuan Shikai on a modern, Western model. The first of these battles brought Duan Qirui, already a powerful figure, to openly-exercised power, and the second removed him from power. This was the situation as it was fought out in Beijing. Elsewhere in China, to the south in Guangzhou, in southwestern Sichuan, and soon in northeastern Manchuria, localized centers of military power pursued individual agendas that contributed to the instability of the new nation and jeopardized its nominal unity. Lu Xun and others like him were observers of this national scene, as were many newspapers in urban centers. The question now is how this observation, brought to a pitch by the personal experience of being caught up in armed conflicts, intersects with his influential writings. This is the focus of the next section.

The 1933 Preface: Storms (fengbo) in the 1910s

A preface that Lu Xun wrote for a 1933 self-selected anthology of his works provides a sense of the political events that had impressed themselves on his thoughts since 1911. It provides a different picture of the relation of his writings to politics than does the influential account of his 1923 preface to *Call to Arms*, and as such, though also often quoted, it needs to be brought more to the fore in our sense of the author. As with the 1923 preface, this one was written for an important collection, the *Self-Selected Anthology*.[41] The anthology consists of selections from the two collections of fiction, the reminiscences of *Dawn Blossoms Gathered at Dusk*, the prose poems of *Weeds*, and two retellings of traditional tales that were later gathered into *Old Tales Retold*. In his preface, Lu Xun devotes one paragraph to each of the collections from which selections are made. At their head is a paragraph on how he came to write in the first place. This is what he says:

> At that time, I was not especially enthusiastic about the "literary revolution." I had seen the 1911 revolution, I had seen the Second Revolution, had seen Yuan Shikai proclaim himself emperor and Zhang Xun attempt a restoration. When I saw all these things, I began to have questions, to become very disappointed and dispirited. . . . But because my experiences were very limited, I also began to question my disappointment, and thinking of it this way gave me the impetus to take up my pen.

Here Lu Xun provides nothing like the personal history and vivid memories that served as explanation in 1923. He does state a number of feelings: "I began to have questions," "I [became] very disappointed and discouraged," and "this gave me the impetus." In place of their source in evocative personal memories, however, he lists their source in four political events: the 1911 Revolution, when the Qing dynasty was overthrown; the Second Revolution, led by Sun Yatsen and Huang Xing in the south in summer 1913, after Yuan Shikai had suspended the constitution and Parliament; Yuan Shikai's proclamation of himself as emperor on January 1, 1916; and finally, Zhang Xun's attempted restoration of the Qing emperor to the throne in 1917. In other words, Lu Xun names four "storms" (*fengbo*) in seven years as the reasons he took up his pen. Each was unsuccessful, short-lived, and violent, a part of the fundamental instability that brought about and followed the fall of the Qing dynasty.

The 1933 preface directs our attention to the decade of the 1910s as governing the author's frame of mind when he began to write. It lays greater stress on the role that the silent years in Beijing, the years of these *fengbo*, played in his writings. These years were also mentioned in the 1923 preface, but their impact was lessened because they followed the more vivid memories of childhood and young adulthood and because Lu Xun described them chiefly as a time when he collected copies of steles and recorded them, an absorption from which Qian Xuantong's memorable visit stirred him. By contrast, the 1933 preface gives specific political reasons to pay attention to those years in Beijing. A comment by Mao Dun on "Ah Q" similarly emphasizes the intervening years of political events as the chief concern of the fiction, as opposed to personal memories. He writes that the work allows us "in seven or eight chapters . . . to know the source and causes of the troubles of the past twelve years."[42]

During Lu Xun's first five years in Beijing, the city was under Yuan Shikai's rule. Throughout Yuan Shikai's tenure, Lu Xun was employed by the Ministry of Education, in a sense a member of Yuan's government. He had come north with the ministry in 1912 when Yuan, in exchange for delivering the eventual neutrality of the imperial Beiyang Army, was made president of the new republic and forced the removal of the capital from Nanjing to Beijing, where his military power was centered. Yuan initially assumed the title of provisional president and then, after he dissolved the Parliament, of president for life. Under Yuan, as in the next year under Zhang Xun, there was a movement toward restoration of a monarchy, and on January 1, 1916, he accepted the proffered crown of emperor from his followers. Public outcry and international protests forced him to relinquish the claim two months later, but he remained in office until his death in June 6 of that year.

Recent scholarship has uncovered some of Lu Xun's activities in connection with his work in the Ministry of Education, locating ministry reports and such that make very interesting reading. In 1916, for example, his Ministry of Education work included committee work on new awards for fiction, judgments on questions concerning "quality" fiction and "low-class" fiction (shangdeng xiaoshuo and xiadeng xiaoshuo), exhibits at new institutions of higher learning, and projects associated with the Beijing Library such as construction and new sites. For November 1917, there is an intriguing instance when he and Zhou Zuoren issued under the ministry's name a review that praised a three-volume translation of European and American short fiction, *Ou Mei mingjia duanpian xiaoshuo congkan*.[43] Such work is clearly of the kind needed in the many areas to administer and encourage new types of educational and cultural activities.

Against this background of everyday duties, Lu Xun also describes another kind of reality in Beijing under Yuan. In another essay of 1933, he had this to say.

> And so it was kill, kill, kill. In Beijing, even the restaurants and hostels were full of spies. Then there were the military garrisons, where one saw young people who had come under suspicion taken in, but one never saw them walking out alive. There were the "Government Notices," where every day one can see notices posted in which [Revolutionary] Party members renounced their party, saying that they had been deceived by friends into joining the party, and only now have they woken up and are leaving the party, washing their hearts, changing their faces, and becoming good people.[44]

The opening words "kill, kill, kill" are likely a reference to the seven repetitions of the word on a monument in Sichuan erected by Zhang Xianzhong (1606–47), evidently as the motto of his bloody seven-year independent kingdom in Sichuan. Zhang Xianzhong was an early villain when Lu Xun began to read history—he was then fourteen or fifteen—though more were added as he learned more.[45] When he wrote of the terror felt by civilians under Yuan Shikai, he was living in Shanghai and seeing the same political dangers, under different authorities, for the young: this is what fear is like; the fortunate are those able to recant.

Information from Zhou Zuoren expands on Lu Xun's. According to him, under Yuan, special attention was paid to the intellectuals, whose opposition was feared. He writes that all civil officials adopted hobbies as screens: some sought women, others antiquarian hobbies. General Cai E's dalliance with a prostitute while he was planning to move against Yuan, mentioned by Zuoren, is the most famous. Zuoren suggests that Lu Xun's copying of inscriptions at this time was likewise a screen, a suggestion corroborated by Lu Xun's own comment in the 1923 preface about this hobby: "The inscriptions raised no political problems or issues, and so the days slipped quietly away." (*Lu Xun Chronology* notes that in thirteen days in March 1916 he copied the biography of the Jin dynasty monk Faxian in forty pages.)[46] Though a practical refuge from political dangers, the copying also gives some sense of his link to traditional temperaments in which political will is sublimated to artistic discipline. This is also what his former mentor Zhang Binglin chose for himself in the 1920s when he returned to classical studies, although under Yuan Shikai, Zhang did not lie low: he "dangled his big medal on his fan and [went] to the president's house to curse his treachery."[47] Zhou also says that the sobriquet (*hao*) that Lu Xun gave himself at this time, Si Tang, probably alluded to these dangerous times. It could mean the hall in which the ancients awaited death, or it could be suggesting that the gentleman (*junzi*) lived outside politics (*juyi*) while awaiting command.[48]

In this context of political intimidation, Lu Xun's role as a civil servant as it touches on Yuan Shikai must have been full of contradictions for him. An early, hopeful moment can be seen in a diary entry for National Day of 1913, on which day he mailed himself a letter in order to have that day's postal stamp; then, the following year, there is an ominous note when a national holiday was declared for Yuan's birthday, an imperial custom.[49] He was one of the delegation from the ministry that was received by Yuan the year he was sworn in as provisional president. On the day of his burial, government offices were closed. Funerary obsequies were held at government house on June 15, and Lu Xun was named the representative from the Ministry of

Education for the memorial service. In addition to official attendance, government offices were required to have their employees pay their personal respects on specified days.⁵⁰ So Lu Xun must have gone twice. In August, two months after Yuan's death, Lu Xun, in his capacity as a representative of the Ministry of Education, wrote a memo advocating the abolishment of the educational requirements promulgated under Yuan for rituals related to Confucius and Mencius, providing an interesting insight into the importance of administrative work.⁵¹

To return to these *fengbo* as the source of Lu Xun's fiction, of the four events mentioned, two are explicitly in the stories (the 1911 Revolution and Zhang Xun's coup), and a third, the Second Revolution, is implicit in the figure of Zhang Xun, who was the general who suppressed, with great brutality, that revolution in Nanjing. Thus only Yuan Shikai's claim of the throne is not an element in the fiction. Conversely, four of the twelve stories in *Call to Arms* feature revolution. Three are the stories analyzed in this chapter; the fourth is "Medicine." Lu Xun's words suggest that in them we may see the figure of death behind the face of satire. In them can be found arbitrary death and the threat of it, death for the pure exertion of power, and meaningful deaths rendered meaningless. These are the total possibilities. As he wrote of the years under Yuan Shikai, "And it was kill, kill, kill." The violence of *fengbo* is at the center of the analysis in the next section.

Violent Deaths and Literary Limits

This section is both analysis and argument. The analysis traces the theme of death and the queue through the three stories that are the focus of this chapter to bring out more consistently the somber foundation of the witty satire. The argument is that in writing of this subject Lu Xun seems to have encountered limits. On the face of it, this should not be the case. Even though in 1920–22 New Literature, of which these three stories are early representatives, had just two years of examples behind it, his study of European writers dates back farther and provided him with many models. In the *Anthology of Literature from Foreign Lands*, he and Zuoren chose authors whose topics and treatment of war and suffering were universalizing in their literary skill. Significantly, in 1920, he revisited these works, for in this year he and Zuoren reissued their *Anthology* (still in classical Chinese) with a new preface. The 1909 volumes, published with their own funds, had been ahead of their time and found no readers, but in 1920, some months before our group of five works was written, Lu Xun wrote that they had represented "an inchoate hope that literature could be used to transform mentalities, to change society."⁵² Beginning in

1920, he also returned to some of the same authors with his translation projects for *Short Story Monthly* (this time in vernacular Chinese), although he also included authors from more recent periods.

The limits that are explored here are related in some ways to what Marston Anderson examines in his chapter on Lu Xun in *The Limits of Realism*. The starting observation is similar, that "what Lu Xun constantly probed with his restless experimentation was his identity and responsibility as a writer." We have already seen that what he constantly probed in the three very different short stories is intimately connected to his "identity and responsibility as a writer." Anderson suggests that one important responsibility Lu Xun felt was the need to avoid having "representational art . . . mak[e] the victim into a mere object of the reader's curiosity or pity." He sees Lu Xun as wanting to "counter the purgative effects of representational art," which "camouflage the true nature of the reader's [complicit] involvement with the victim."[53] My time frame of two years and five works is shorter than Anderson's five years. In terms of writerly responsibility, it focuses on Lu Xun's attempts to depict violent death rather than on his attempts to expand realism. Here may be seen his gradual sense of the limitations of literature for him as a writer rather than its limitations as a too-comforting catharsis for the reader. Like Anderson's analysis, mine seeks some insight into this "restless experimentation."

Death is frequent and prominent in Lu Xun's fiction, as often noted. Altogether fifteen of his twenty-six stories feature death. Death comes to characters whom readers have met, to characters who remain offstage, and also to animal protagonists (the rabbits and ducks in "Rabbits and the Cat" and "A Comedy of Ducks"). In some plots, there is more than one death; in others, the main character dies. Most deaths occur offstage. Many critics have written perceptively of this theme of death. T. A. Hsia names it the power of darkness; Theodore Huters notes Lu Xun's preoccupation "to the point of obsession with the question of moral responsibility for these deaths," noting "the particular intensity it has" in his fiction.[54] The analysis here differs in focusing on only one type of death, death that is political or, in Ah Q's case, unexpectedly political.

Death and queues became linked once cutting off the queue became a symbol of resistance to the Manchu dynasty. In these three works of fictions, queues and death are pulled in opposite directions, queues toward comedy and death toward—well, death is not so easily comedic. The tension produces different outcomes in each story. For "Storm," the queue is clearly comedy. For "Hair," the situation is not so certain: the revolutionary youths mentioned at the beginning are, interestingly, not mentioned with their queues, although they must have had them. By contrast, later in the story N's students wish to cut theirs off, and this produces a complex situation, sardonic if not exactly comic. Finally, for Ah Q, the queue begins as political comedy and ends as a motif in his death. The presence of violent deaths in the three stories speaks to the author's struggle with the limits of his material as it intersects his temperament. The author's specific dissatisfaction with each attempt will be traced, culminating in his expression in the 1930s of the feeling that this task is not possible, at least not for him.

"Storm"

The character of Seven-Pounds in "Storm" is the first of the creations. This story of his short-lived dilemma is perfectly pitched on the one hand to satirize what high-minded legislation looks like at the ground level and on the other hand to expose the ready hypocrisy of anyone who is the least bit higher up on the power scale, such as the tavern owner, or those not in danger themselves, like Seven-Pounds's fellow villagers. The latter also receive some mild sarcasm for their nosy participation in his dilemma. The scheme is textbook satiric: a member of the lower orders provides the broad humor while the setup as a whole is a satire of society's hypocrisy and love of power.

Yet the point of the satire is ultimately serious. In this serious layer, "Storm" illustrates the caprices of the all-powerful authorities versus the powerlessness of the individual cipher. Seven-Pounds's total obscurity might save him or, equally easily, might condemn him. In the event, it is a quirk, the brevity of Zhang Xun's coup, that releases him from his fate. The satire shows clearly that being a nonentity places him at the mercy of other forces. This is a daily reality that accounts for the wife's immediate fear and the tavern keeper's immediate glee. The dark end that Seven-Pounds avoids is realized for Ah Q, his successor and distillation. Ah Q has the opposite situation: he has his queue, but he wishes to discard it and join the revolutionaries. His is the opposite fate: he meets with the capricious death Seven-Pounds avoids. When a burglary occurs in the village, he is picked up and quickly processed, and the next day he is executed. End of story.

What the setup of "Storm" cannot do—what it is not designed to do— is convey the seriousness and tragedy of death. It cannot provoke the kind of awareness that results in social action. Although Seven-Pounds' story is told as an amusing satire, his situation is not funny for him. It is in fact a life-and-death one, and thus the features of the plot are much darker than presented. For example, the tavern owner's glee is in fact triumph at the prospect of another's possible death. In others of Lu Xun's works, the same features do appear in darker versions. Thus, in both "Medicine" and "Ah Q," rapt audiences judge death on purely aesthetic grounds: did the death provide the requisite entertainment? Another example is the villagers' instinctive sensitivity to the shifts in power. This easily morphs into the bestial crowd that critics have noted is a recurring motif in the fiction; in "Ah Q," it is the crowd at the end whose wolflike eyes shine and advance toward him the moment before he is shot.

One can object that "Storm" is satire, that satire cannot take some poor devil's dilemma totally to heart without abrogating the genre, and that Lu Xun did everything he set out to do. I agree—except that there is material outside the story that suggests there were other authorial goals, which did not have a chance to be admitted because he had fixed on the genre of satire. The limitation of satire for all his purposes is that the success of the satire makes us lose sight of the gravity of Seven-Pounds's situation. "Storm" did not exhaust what the author wanted to say on the subject; it may be that he had not entirely clarified his subject matter to himself. That there was something else, Ah Q's opposite fate shows.

Of course Lu Xun was well aware that this was a matter of life and death. It simply did not come out in "Storm." We can find hints that this was frustrating to him. In a 1934 essay, he touched on Zhang Xun; he wrote that after 1911 "there was to be one more little storm (*fengbo*) over the queue, when one false move and the queue could once more become a critical issue."[55] Another indication of his frustration is that his other comments on Zhang Xun and the 1917 coup contain much greater bitterness than "Storm" reveals. Despite popular conceptions of history, which treat Zhang's coup as a blip on the screen of those years of continual civil war, and despite Lu Xun's clever exploitation of its singular feature in "Storm," which has probably helped this conception along, Lu Xun did not consider Zhang to be just an anachronism. As a military figure, Zhang was for a while a serious force on the national scene with a history of brutality. He was the general who led the troops that conquered Nanking in 1913 during the Second Revolution, and he allowed his troops to pillage and rape for three days before moving in to impose order. Only the year before this tragedy, Lu Xun had been living in Nanjing, working at the Ministry of Education. Earlier still, he had lived in Nanjing for four years as a student before leaving for further studies in Japan. He did not forget the wanton destruction of Nanjing. Nearly fifteen years later, when the city was recovered by the Northern Expedition Army in 1927, Lu Xun, in an uncharacteristically euphoric essay, rejoiced that now a memorial to the dead of 1911, destroyed in 1913 by Zhang Xun, could be erected again. In that year (1913), traveling north in his move to Beijing, his train was stopped in Zhang's territory; four or five of Zhang's men came on board, intimidated everyone, and took away someone who had crossed them.[56] Finally, as Zhou Zuoren remarked, "It was different once you lived in Beijing, where matters both large and small all developed in front of your eyes. All was closer and more real, and the impact was correspondingly greater." Zhou then describes how one effect on him and others at *New Youth*, including Lu Xun, was to accelerate their editorial commitment to advocating fundamental socio-cultural change.[57] All these connections are left out of "Storm." Such omissions may be behind Lu Xun's remark that "Storm" was the only work he knows of concerning this 1917 event.[58] This odd comment, which may be factually true but sounds like boasting, is better understood as referring to the author's sense that the coup's many consequences need to be fully recorded and properly remembered, not just by one person's output in the snappy perfection of "Storm."

"A Story about Hair"

On the heels of "Storm" came "Hair." In this story, there are two kinds of death. The first is death of the principled kind, as opposed to Seven-Pounds's accidental quandary. This type had occurred among revolutionary youths and is recollected by N, who directly states their appalling numbers and kinds. A second one intends to be principled but is lightly incurred, the example being N's students, who want to cut their queues and give no thought to the possibly serious consequences.

The first, the large number of political deaths, is mentioned near the beginning. The frame narrator remarks that today is National Day but that nowadays no one observes it. N overhears him and says that he, N, cannot bear to observe National Day because of the painful memories it brings. He then says that he cannot forget the deaths of so many who had sought to bring about National Day. The length of N's remarks clearly reflects the author's desire to include each detail and each kind of death, so I quote his words in their entirety.

> If I were to begin to commemorate [National Day], all the events before and after that first National Day would lie upon my heart and I would not be able to sit or walk calmly.
> How many people from the past will float before my eyes: youths who have gone hither and yon for more than ten years and then in unknown circumstances lost their lives to a bullet; youths who did not think of themselves and suffered for months in prison; youths who carried dreams with them and suddenly vanished without a trace, not even their bodies to be found.

> They have all lived their entire lives in the cold laughter, the cruel contempt, and the heedless scorn of society. Now their graves have long been forgotten and are gradually toppling into dirt.

The language is angry and tells readers, reminds them really, of the number of lives sacrificed to ideals in the recent past. They are victims twice over, of pitiless authority and our uncaring society.

Young lives sacrificed for principled actions is a category that lies outside the humor of "Storm," and one might suppose that here the author has found his stride. In literary terms, however, the treatment in "Hair," though wider in scope, is inadequate in a different way. In "Hair," N's dark, heartfelt presentation of large numbers of deaths constitutes a false start, for the author does not continue this thread, probably is not able to continue it. Having spoken these words, what does N say or do next? Lu Xun changes the subject: he has the narrator interject and coax N to "more pleasant topics." Thereupon the story does indeed change direction, and N switches to a brief history of the queue. From there he goes on to a number of other queue-related topics, including his own experiences of the queue. His first speech is not integrated into the story and remains an essaylike passage that holds the fossil remains of a fictional intention. As with "Storm," it is possible to surmise that Lu Xun was not satisfied with his approach.

One problem for Lu Xun if he wanted to proceed further is the immensity of the young dead within the framework of fiction. N's list goes against the main strengths of nineteenth-century fiction, which gains its effect by depicting the situation of individuals in its universal aspects. Aside from this passage, Lu Xun never again writes about the fate of large numbers of people. Among the works he had studied and translated in 1908 and again from 1920 onward, several were extraordinary depictions of meaningless deaths in wars.[59] The limits he experienced are demonstrably not limits for literature as he knew it. He began, but, in literary terms, he could not continue. There was more he would have said: his description of Beijing under Yuan Shikai—"And so it was kill, kill, kill"—indicates the force of personal experience that impelled him to write these words of N's.

Another problem might have been his sense of his own literary temperament, which was bound up with the limits set by reality. When it came to large-scale deaths, he seemed to have felt that, for him at any rate, there were limits to writing. In a 1932 letter, he tells his correspondent that he found that large-scale violence could not be recorded in literary terms. This letter was written after the monthlong attack on Shanghai in January 1932 by Japanese forces in which air strikes inflicted particularly large and new kinds of civilian devastation and local Japanese residents, with the help of Japanese troops and criminals, were organized in vigilante actions.[60] During this time, Lu Xun and his family left their home and took refuge in the International Settlement Section of Shanghai. When they returned, they found their neighborhood had been devastated by the bombing. To a correspondent, Lu Xun wrote of the inadequacy of literature.

> In the midst of fighting, I saw slaughter with my own eyes, saw extreme danger and yet was not harmed. I very much wanted to record it, but there truly is no place at which to begin.[61]

The scale of destruction was large. Among civilians, there were 10,400 missing, 6,080 dead, and 1.2 million refugees. Half the factories destroyed were in Zhabei, the area where Lu Xun lived.[62] These experiences brought him to a conclusion regarding himself, writing, and political violence: "There truly is no place at which to begin."

Lu Xun spoke of his situation alone; concerning the attempts of others, he was encouraging. To a young writer of fiction, Lai Shaoqi (later to be better known as a woodcut artist [see chapter 5]), who had sent him an illustration and a short story on the workers' movement, Lu Xun responded with encouraging advice.

> When changes and events are too momentous, we may not have the ability to capture them, but this is not a cause for pessimism. Even if we cannot give expression to the whole, we can convey a corner of it.[63]

The story Lai sent him was likely too ambitious in scope. Lu Xun's advice contains a standard literary technique, to use the particular to convey the general. This was manifestly what he himself did in "The True Story of Ah Q." He surely knew he had done this, but nonetheless he still felt unable to capture "events [that] are too momentous."

The other queue-and-death connection in "Hair" has to do with N's students. This incident provides an ambiguous intermediate ground between readers and the idealistic revolutionary dead that N described earlier. In this part, N recalls his students at the middle school where he, like Lu Xun, taught shortly before the Republican Revolution. They observe his short hair, and so they seek his advice about—really his approval of—cutting their own queues. He suggests they wait, and they leave in disgust. Where do these students fit in the scheme of things? They want to make a principled stand, to be revolutionary heroes, but have no awareness that they might be volunteering for death. They do not see the "young people who had come under suspicion taken in, but one never saw them walking out alive" and are unaware of those whom N cannot forget, all the revolutionaries who lay in forgotten graves. They have forgotten even their own hometown revolutionary dead, Shaoxing's Qiu Jin, whose execution ground and memorial they pass every day on the way to class.[64] The short human memory for the dead, a constant motif in Lu Xun's writings, here could have led to fresh volunteers for sacrifice.

Elsewhere, Lu Xun provides a psychological metaphor of the obliviousness that his writings are intended to remove. In a preface for a Russian translation of "Ah Q," he describes the distance between humans when their fates differ.

> In making humans, the Creator has been extremely clever and has arranged it so that one person cannot feel another one's physical pain. As it turns out, our sages and the disciples of our sages have emended an oversight of the Creator's and have further arranged it so that one person does not feel the mental or spiritual pain of another person.[65]

Unlike most, N has not managed to divorce himself from the pain of others, but because his is a crabby personality who relates several discreditable things about himself, it is easy to forget that, like his creator, he is unable to forget the revolutionary dead.

"The True Story of Ah Q"

The death in this story is Ah Q's. By the story's end, such is the author's skill that the death of a nearly anonymous villager with almost no place in society has taken on immense meaning. One of the ways the author achieves this is by portraying types of violent death that are then refracted in Ah Q's end. In writing this story, Lu Xun seems to have experienced no limitations, only made the fullest use of literature's resources. Yet, even though this is an amazing achievement, universally praised, the author came to have reservations, as we shall see.

First a principled death occurs offstage. It happens in town, where Ah Q has been living for some time because odd jobs for him had dried up in the village after he impulsively propositioned the servant of a gentry family. The death is described by Ah Q on his return to the village, where he flaunts his experience of the world. These include chancing to see the execution of a revolutionary youth. The youth had been led on a cart through the streets to his execution, and along the way he did not sing, as was the custom. As Ah Q opines to the villagers, this was a paltry fellow. The incident resembles the situation in "Medicine": there a revolutionary youth is also executed offstage, and there his death is also later recounted by someone (Uncle Kang) to whom a political cause is beyond comprehension and dying for it even more so.

The deaths of the revolutionary youths in "Ah Q" and "Medicine" are individualized instances of the numerous deaths that N mourns in "Hair." They represent the youths N speaks of, "who have gone hither and yon for more than ten years" and then "lost their lives to a bullet." "And so it was kill, kill, kill." As individual deaths, they illustrate the agony in N's words, but they are not depicted directly. The author has them occur offstage and has readers learn of them through the words of uncomprehending characters like Ah Q and, in "Medicine," Uncle Kang. Filtered in this way, their sacrifices are seen to be meaningless to the country they sought to help at the very moment the reader learns of them. Their sacrifices illustrate N's words: they "lived their entire lives in the cold laughter, the cruel contempt, and the heedless scorn of society."

A second violent death in "Ah Q" is the typical method of dispatching criminals. This, too, is not seen. It is described by implication when Ah Q complains about the disappointing death of the revolutionary youth. He prefers that criminals, when they are led through the streets to the execution grounds, sing their last, bold song and proclaim that they would soon return as hearty, swaggering fellows. When Ah Q describes the execution he saw in town as lacking in dramatic interest, initially the author's intent seems to be to chalk up another Ah Q-ism to Ah Q. As he wrote in 1936, "When I was young, I heard of many such cases. I always thought the scene barbarous, the method cruel."[66] When the condemned reaches the execution grounds and is killed—this is essentially the scene that revolted him in Sendai in 1904, when a slide from the news showed a Chinese man executed while many Chinese looked on. It simply omits the Japanese-Chinese dichotomy. Furthermore, as often noted, this scene is repeated in his 1925 story "A Public Example," in which onlookers crowd around a criminal, wanting to see what can be seen until he is led away.

But Lu Xun came to change his mind about the public parading of criminals. In a sense, he came to agree with Ah Q, though perhaps not for Ah Q's reasons. He felt that such a system, though a "barbarous" one, allowed the condemned a chance to give voice in his last moments of life. In that way

> he could complain of injustice, curse the officials, recount his own heroic exploits, or deny any fear of death.

A public spectacle is not the worst because there is something worse that Lu Xun had come to realize "only recently": "how bitter it is for a man to die in secret." When he lamented this, he had mind the secret execution of his young follower, Rou Shi, and also the arrest, imprisonment, and interrogation of another young follower, Cao Bai.

> I am always more distressed and worried by the death of a friend or student if I do not know when, where, and how he died. And I imagine that from their point of view to perish at the hands of a few butchers in a dark room is more bitter than dying in public.[67]

Actually, half of Lu Xun's statement—"how bitter it is for a man to die in secret"—was already in "Hair." N remembers the youths who "suddenly vanished without a trace, not even their bodies to be found." This was how Rou Shi died. He was arrested and secretly executed, buried with others at an unknown site, something Lu Xun felt was worse than the "cruel and barbarous" custom of parading criminals.

On the way to his execution, Ah Q is unable to sing the song he had finally settled on, "Steel Lash in Hand I Will Thrash You," because his hands were tied, but in his drawing for Lu Xun, Qu Qiubai presciently gave him his moment, his hands free and a weapon in one (see fig. 3.3). Two years later Qu Qiubai provided an unnervingly courageous enactment of this little drawing. He was captured in Fujian province by the Nationalists, and on his way to a public execution, he sang the "Internationale" in Russian.[68] "Complain of injustice, curse the officials, deny fear of death," all were in this extraordinary moment.

The third violent death is Ah Q's. It is a combination of the other two and in this way attains its remarkable power. Technically, his death is that of a common criminal, for he is arrested and executed for a burglary that occurred in the village. Furthermore, his attitude on the way to his death is also that of the common criminal: he wants to sing a last, bold song as he is being paraded through the streets to the execution grounds. As it turns out, he cannot decide what to sing. He considers first one song, then another, then a third. He cannot make up his mind, and when he does, suddenly he is already there and being executed. The outcome is that, if seen only from the outside, since a bystander cannot know that Ah Q is trying to decide which song to belt out, he is, in fact, just like the revolutionary youth he saw—completely silent on the way to his death, providing a poor show for those who came to watch.

In other respects as well, he has, in his own Ah Q way, become quite a bit like the revolutionary youth. Almost like a true revolutionary, both politics and queues had inserted themselves before his death. In his case, the revolution reaches Shaoxing, and in the village of Weizhuang, Ah Q is eager to join. He coils his queue, wedges it in place with a chopstick, and goes out hopefully, with visions of loot and women and of his enemies trembling in fear before him. He knows only two revolutionaries, and "one, unfortunately, had lost his head." So he goes to look for the other one, the Imitation Foreigner. The gentry, naturally, have acted faster and are already wearing the new pins of the

"Persimmon Oil" Party. They beat him for his presumption and forbid him to join them. Like the executed youth, he has chosen the revolutionary course. The death that is its endpoint is merely deferred for a few days. And like the revolutionary youth, he is executed as "an example" to others.

Later Lu Xun sometimes disparaged Ah Q's revolutionary activities, writing that "Ah Q had to make revolution because China did."[69] The story itself, however, indicates otherwise for at his death, Ah Q shows his strange affinity to the revolutionary youth. Such an extraordinary ending would seem to demonstrate the special powers of literature as a window onto reality. Yet despite his achievement, there is evidence that over time the author came to be dissatisfied with it. One reason seems to be that in the years after he wrote "Ah Q," literature had been outpaced by reality in China's continued volatile situation. He wrote, of the manner of Ah Q's death:

> I used to think that sometimes what I write is too extreme, but I no longer think so, for if I were to depict truthfully the events we see in China today, they would seem *grotesk* to people in other countries or to those of a future, better China.[70]

A distortion made for effect had become less grotesque than reality.

Conclusion

The queue is a comparatively overt, surface feature, but it turns out to increase our understanding of the stories and to direct our attention to a certain complex of thoughts, memories, and circumstances from the author's life. In the time frame 1920–22, Lu Xun's attitudes are relatively accessible through these five works. We see two factors working together: his belief in literature and his response to the violence of his time. As such, the writings do not represent the literary reshaping of events, or the aestheticization of suffering, but a faith in literature as an instrument in changing people's mind-sets. He began with the light treatment of Seven-Pounds's queue, but later the story lines became darker. At this time, two years into writing fiction, Lu Xun still believed that he could convey through literature the terrible facts of life in China and that people would come to understand and act. If we start counting from the translations of 1907, he had worked at this genre for a great number of years. He was still writing in the belief that the forms and techniques of fiction as he had seen them employed in the literatures of other nations could convey the terrors and griefs of life. Literature was a preliminary step toward doing something.

Only three years further on, Lu Xun stopped writing fiction altogether (that is, *xiaoshuo* fiction). November 1925 was the date of his last work in this genre, the story "Divorce." *Hesitation*, was published in August of the next year. That was also the month he left Beijing in some danger. This departure may have played a part, too, for he left behind an entire complex of arrangements in the literary world, including the confluence of factors that had brought him to the point of taking up his pen in the first place. It may be that Lu Xun continued to change and develop, perhaps because his world, China, kept changing and worsening. The overwhelming reception given his writings in New Literature and their special historical role at an early juncture in modern Chinese literature have fixed his historical definition as a writer. Yet in the pattern of his whole life, literature is better seen as a productive search for a way to move from understanding to action. His was a kind of holding action until people could act for themselves:

> In the future, the people who are surrounded by a high wall will be able to awaken themselves, walk out, and speak for themselves. But this is not often seen right now. So I can only rely on my own observations and with a feeling of loneliness write about them as what my eyes have seen of the lives of the Chinese people.[71]

Behind the literature was his keenly developed sense of the political scene. He closely followed political events, but it seemed to be all observation. Evidence of direct involvement does not exist, not during the Republican Revolution of 1911, not during the May Fourth demonstrations of 1919, not in the 1920s, not even during his years in the League of Left-Wing Writers (1930–36) and in spite of his use of the language of mass popularization (*dazhonghua*). His observation was sharp, intense, and engaged, but it did not extend to action. The common thread in his work was not an updated version of the political commitment of his youth but rather an abhorrence of violence, an abhorrence that was deep, consistent, and lifelong. He felt deeply the destruction of life, the erasure of the fact of life by means of orchestrated violence. He had no interest in politics in the sense attributed to him by the Communists and Marxists. His low opinion of human nature, of politics' participants, made him follow it with an unbearable fascination. He never ceased to have the capacity to be sickened by the casual casualties of politics. He never became the thorough cynic that the protagonist in the later story "The Loner" gradually developed into.

4

The Life of a Poem, 1903–36

Lu Xun's interpretations of China in this chapter take place on a nonpublic level, and his views were fully revealed only to a few intimates. This is the case even though one of his most famous essays, "Remembrance in Order to Forget," is involved. The access point for this exploration is the uncovering of a 1903 poem's importance to him long after its first writing. We saw this poem, "Inscribed by the Author on a Small Likeness," in chapter 2, where it was one of a variety of sources useful for understanding his first years in Japan. This chapter presents evidence that the poem, widely known now but known only to a few in his lifetime, was important to him throughout his life (hence the chapter's title), that its meaning for him changed and deepened over time, and that many consequences flowed from these changes.

The 1903 quatrain is given again here for convenience of reference.

靈台無計逃神矢　　風雨如磐闇故園
寄意寒星荃不察　　我以我血薦軒轅

My mind has no wish to avoid the arrows of the gods
The winds and rains [of political disorder], black as boulders, darken my
　　old home
I entrust my thoughts to the star of a cold night, the king does not
　　understand,
I would offer up my blood for the [descendants] of the Yellow Emperor.[1]

This poem became known only after his death and was widely quoted only decades later, in the 1950s. Today it is one of Lu Xun's best-known poems, especially because of its impassioned final line, "I would offer up my blood for the [descendants] of the Yellow Emperor." Since the 1950s, the poem and the photograph on which it was inscribed have been frequently reproduced, both separately and as a set. The Beijing Lu Xun Museum has reproduced the format in which he first gave it to Xu Shoushang: it sells a postcard-sized souvenir that shows the poem in Lu Xun's calligraphy on one side and the photograph, known as "Photograph with Hair Cut Short," on the other (see figs. 2.1 and 2.2).

It is natural that critical interest in them is closely tied to their original association with the youth in Japan who had just cut his queue, but the early date of those sentiments means that to extend their import, the poem has to acquire a foreshadowing function. In the 1950s, official promotion of the poem fulfilled the political imperative that Lu Xun be revolutionary and that this revolutionary spirit be traced as far back as possible. The seriousness of its sentiments makes it more suited for this purpose than the other half dozen or so poems surviving from 1903 and earlier. Although this admiration is no longer politically required, the question remains of how to bring this early poem into the whole of the life. For example, the quatrain could be read as foreshadowing some aspect of the later life but not necessarily labeling that life revolutionary. Xu Shoushang was of this opinion, for he wrote that "the achievements of the later part of Lu Xun's life could long ago be seen in that line from the poem of his youth, 'I would offer up my blood for the descendants of the Yellow Emperor.'"[2] Nearly all critics agree that the continuity of resolve with the rest of his life is its most notable feature. In a different approach, Leo Ou-fan Lee has insightfully placed it, as an object of the past, in relation to a later poem, the 1932 "Self-Mockery," also very well known, and he reads the lines of the 1932 poem as "a gentle self-mockery of his own past life."[3]

This chapter proposes another source for the poem's significance in the later part of Lu Xun's life. Just as, on its first appearance, the poem's importance to its author is unambiguously signaled by its inscription on the back of a photograph, so its importance to the author in later years is indicated in equally unmistakable ways. It is possible to sketch its changing importance over time from the beginning of his adult life in Japan to the month of his death in 1936. This much longer stretch of time displaces critical attention from certain unresolvable problems of its contemporary significance, including vocabulary and dating, to its provable importance for the author at later points in his life and, as will be developed in this chapter, the multipronged implications of this for our understanding of his thinking in the 1930s and his use of poetry in this connection. Because of changes in the meaning of this poem over such a long time span, the commonly used name for the poem, "Inscribed by the Author on a Small Likeness," which comes from the recipient, Xu Shoushang, no longer fits well, and so it will mostly be referred to in this chapter as the 1903 poem or the 1903 quatrain.

The poem's presence can be detected in three years, 1926, 1931, and 1936. Of these, 1931 is pivotal. This chapter will first show that the poem's renewed, but wholly private, significance came in connection with the 1931 arrests and deaths of the young writers known as Five Martyrs, one of whom was Lu Xun's disciple Rou Shi. Such a connection means that the poem can be informatively paired with the famous essay that commemorates these deaths, "Remembrance in Order to Forget," and with the equally famed, classical eight-line poem that it contains (untitled and identified by its first line, "Though accustomed to"). In both roles, as a renewed poem and as a silent companion to the essay's poem, the 1903 quatrain provides a deeper understanding of Lu Xun's response to this incident and opens up the larger question of his response as a writer to the political violence of the 1930s. Finally, another consequence of the poem's renewal in 1931 is to provide a framework for interpreting Lu Xun's classical poems as a phenomenon of the 1930s, which will be examined here as well.

The other significant dates for this poem briefly examined are 1926, when the photograph that accompanied the original poem was provided for publication by Lu Xun; and 1936, when he republished two political poems written by Zhang Binglin on the deaths of anti-Qing revolutionaries in prison. As we shall see, on both these occasions, Lu Xun's introduction of this material into public circulation renews, without wholly revealing, aspects of his past in the context of commentary on the present.

1931 and the Five Martyrs

The quatrain was not published in Lu Xun's lifetime; it existed only in calligraphy. The original copy that is known to have existed in his hand—the photograph-and-poem memento he gave to Xu Shoushang—does not survive. An indication of the poem's comparatively obscure stature is indicated by the fact that it was not collected until the posthumous *Second Supplement to the Collected Works (Jiwaiji shiyi)*, and that it was on another occasion misdated to 1912.[4] Interestingly, the poem was recovered not from Lu Xun's manuscripts but from an essay written on Lu Xun's death by Xu Shoushang, in which this was the first of eleven classical-language poems Xu quotes.[5] Thus this poem was only known posthumously and uncertainly.

In lieu of any originals, what we do have is the copy Lu Xun wrote out again in 1931, using a calligraphy brush, his usual writing implement (see fig. 2.2). The calligraphy sheet is large, measuring 24 x 13 inches.[6] In other words, it is *much* larger than the original photograph memento he sent and much larger than the postcard-sized souvenirs (5 ¾ x 4 inches) currently sold.[7] At such dimensions, it represented a notable gesture—of what? We shall see. The calligraphy in his hand was found among his effects, which were transferred to the Beijing Lu Xun Museum. Later editions of Lu Xun's collected works (e.g., the 1984 and 2005 editions) footnote their source to this calligraphic copy.

A look at the calligraphy copy so familiar today shows that it includes a colophon in smaller writing in the fourth and fifth columns stating that it was "composed at age 21" and is "written out at age 51" and giving a date of "*xinwei* year, second month 16th day [signed] Lu Xun" (fig. 4.1). (The two large characters are the last words of the poem.) *Xinwei* year is the year that largely corresponds to 1931. (The inclusion of this postscript renders the back-to-back souvenir anachronistic. In addition, although the 1931 calligraphy in this souvenir is signed "Lu Xun," at the time of its first writing, in 1903, he was, of course, still Zhou Shuren.) Critics have taken note of the information in this postscript but only for the purpose of dating the poem. (This information has been vexing rather than confirming [see appendix A]).

The poem reveals a different significance when we ask what it meant to Lu Xun not at its writing but at the time of its copying thirty years later. Whatever meaning it had in 1903, it acquired new meaning in February 1931 when he wrote it out again. Why did he write out an old poem? And why did he write out *this* old poem?

As a preliminary, it should be noted that obviously 1931 was a long way from 1903. One might ask whether Lu Xun accurately remembered the poem. We cannot know for certain, but in classically trained minds, memory tends to be accurate. For example, in 1926, he wrote out from memory six of eight lines he had written fourteen years earlier when he was mourning Fan Ainong.[8] Additionally, one might ask whether Lu Xun altered the poem in the rewriting. This seems unlikely, for the unknown meaning of, for example, "arrows of the gods" (*shenshi*) in line 1 remains unknown and the lost references of the other lines remain lost—he could have made it more comprehensible had he chosen to.

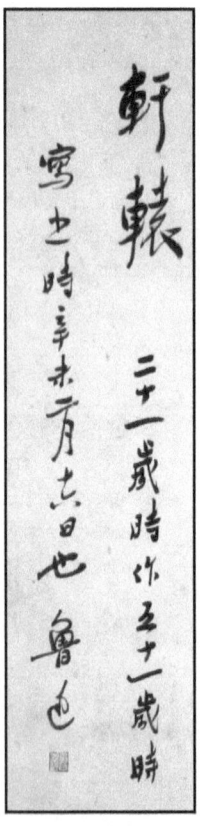

Figure 4.1. Colophon noting the date and place – a detail from the 1931 calligraphy of the quatrain in fig. 2.2. Courtesy of Beijing Lu Xun Museum.

Lu Xun notes the exact date of his calligraphy: February 16, 1931. After he wrote it out, he did not publish it; he simply kept it. He did not give a copy to Xu Shoushang, which he was to do with other classical poems that he began to write later in the 1930s. He did, as we shall see, write it out again two years later for a Japanese physician, a copy that soon went to Japan with its owner (this time he did change *shenshi* as we will see). Other than that, the poem was kept among his papers. (There was another copy that seems to have been a discarded, rough copy that will be discussed below.) Thus, even in its rewriting, it remained essentially a private poem.

What was happening at this time? Lu Xun had been living in Shanghai since October 1927. At this time, Shanghai was the center of finance, commerce, and manufacturing; the center of publishing in all its branches; the site of mass, elite, and commercial cultures; the center of Western imperial interests; and the center of domestic organized crime. Authority in police, judicial, and military matters was divided among the International Settlement, the French Concession, and Chinese Shanghai. This Shanghai, the nexus of capitalism and imperialism, created, among other things, a modern consumer society whose attractive products, energy, and hedonism have been the subject of countless studies, memoirs, and imaginary re-creations. Lu Xun did live in this Shanghai. He went to many movies and restaurants, used its advanced medicine, took its trolleys and cars, and was conversant with the products and gossip that formed the staple of the popular press. But by the time of this writing, he had become acquainted with most of the people who would form part of his several circles and had initiated the projects and activities that would occupy the remaining years of his life. In particular, in early 1930, with the founding of the Communist Party's front organization, the League of Left-Wing Writers, he became part of an identifiably leftist literary world. Although he never joined, he was listed as a member of the league's founding committee, and he gave the address at its inaugural meeting on March 2, 1930. This was a definite step for a stubborn and independent personality that the Communist Party had been carefully cultivating via intermediaries for at least two years. The practical consequences of this alliance were manifold. One is that nearly all Lu Xun's connections and activities in Shanghai had something to do with the Left: his writings, their general focus, his friends, his disciples, to some extent even his enemies. Owing to his great prestige, Lu Xun, unlike most of those with whom he associated, was able, as far as the Communist Party was concerned, to write on the subjects of his choice in the manner of his choice. His greatest problem in this area was the restrictions of Nationalist censorship rather than directives from the Comintern. The other constraints on him were more subtle. His closest associates, such as Feng Xuefeng and Rou Shi, were delegated by the party to work with him precisely because they got on with him, and guidance and persuasion came into play in the course of friendship rather than in the form of directives. A more pervasive constraint is that, with his allegiance and his consequent leftist connections, out of the complex worlds that made up Shanghai in the 1930s, Lu Xun put himself in the midst of the specific world of political conflicts. He made this choice at exactly the time when Shanghai became a major site of the struggle for power between the Nationalists and the Communists, the latter now an underground party, and when political surveillance and civilian terrorism were increasing on both sides. The Nationalists' programs of suppression were called White Terror by the Left and Red Suppression by the Right. This was the situation in early 1931. The deadly rivalries continued until the year after Lu Xun's death, when Chinese Shanghai fell to Japan. (The foreign concessions remained autonomous until the Japanese attack on Pearl Harbor.)

The entire time period on either side of this date of February 16, from late January to late February of 1931, was centered on the arrests and subsequent executions of five young members of the league. Later known as the Five Martyrs, they were among thirty-six Communist Party members arrested by British police at a meeting in the International Settlement on January 17 and turned over to the Nationalists.[9] Together with eighteen other Communists, the five were secretly executed in jail on February 7.[10] Two of them, Rou Shi and Bai Mang, were well known to Lu Xun, and in "Remembrance" he said he had been introduced by Rou Shi to a third, Feng Keng, the only woman among the five. He was especially close to Rou Shi (b. 1901), whom he called "my student," and had worked closely with him on many projects, especially the introduction of European woodcut prints to China.[11] Of the others, Li Weisen he had not known, and Hu Yebin, the lover of the writer Ding Ling, he had met only to chat with. In their letters from jail, the young writers showed courage: they looked after Miss Feng; Rou Shi asked for his editorial duties to be covered in his absence; he studied German with Bai Mang; and they asked for tin rice bowls.[12]

The betrayal and deaths of the young writers are much studied events and this is a much studied six weeks in Lu Xun's life. Yet their fate was but one set of deaths among the multitude of deaths, defections, betrayals, and assassinations on the part of both the Nationalists and Communists that characterized Shanghai in the 1930s. The assignment of blame might be regarded as complex. Frederick Wakeman has described the tactics and calculations by means of which the organizational units responsible on each side for intelligence and counterintelligence carried out their tasks, the Communist arrangements for safe houses, the defections and resultant deaths (some killed by the other side and the defectors' families by one's former side), the cooperation of Shanghai's French and British authorities with the Nationalists out of concern about communist movements in their own colonies, and directives and policies from the Comintern that governed Communist Party actions.[13] Out of this complicated tangle of reversible principles and disposable lives, the Five Martyrs were singled out as symbols of the persecution of innocents, even though rumors soon circulated, accurately as it turned out, that they had been betrayed by a rival Communist Party faction.[14] Internal disputes within the party had arisen in late 1930 and early 1931, a crisis centered on criticism of the recently ousted party leader Li Lisan and his policies. The January 17 meeting that was betrayed to the authorities was held by some who supported Li Lisan and still believed that the party's differences could be resolved by the means of debate and resolutions. The party's hand can be seen in the fact that it was these five members of the League of Left-Wing Writers whose names were made known among the thirty-six arrested and twenty-three killed and these five whose lives and fates were memorialized by the party. They must have presented more sympathetic cases for exploitation. As T. A. Hsia argues, the five were not betrayed because they were writers, but in their deaths, these still-novice writers were of much greater use than the political operatives who also attended the meeting.[15] Similarly, Lu Xun notes that they and the others were not executed as writers but as political figures: "They were members of League, but their 'crime' was likely of another type," meaning it was their party activities that brought about their deaths.[16] But for the Communist Party, they immediately became the Five Martyrs.

Lu Xun mourned them in numerous essays, the best known of which came two years later, "Remembrance in Order to Forget." As with Liu Hezhen's death in 1926, his connection with the case and his powerfully moving public commemorative words and actions played a crucial role in the elevation of the five young writers and were of paramount importance in the historical memory of this incident. His earliest public writings and actions were planned with Feng Xuefeng, who had been designated by the Comintern to act as his liaison with the league, and this connection strengthened the mutual reinforcement of Lu Xun's writings and the deaths of young writers in the minds of readers. This chapter turns to a different aspect of the confluence of writing and public events: it examines a thread in his writings about these deaths that was not public. The thread is traced by following the path of the 1903 quatrain.

With the arrests, Lu Xun's own situation, which had been of only uncertain security, became precarious. Nearly all those with whom he worked, both in his generation and the younger one, were members of the outlawed Communist Party. He used Uchiyama's Bookstore rather than his own home for receiving mail and storing his papers. In April of the previous year, he had had to leave his home when there was word that permission for his arrest was being sought. When he was given an early fiftieth birthday party at a restaurant in September 1930, preparations were careful and the guests arrived and left in discrete groups with lookouts posted outside. Furthermore, since September 1930, there had been a ban on the League of Left-Wing Writers, and orders had been issued to arrest its members.[17] Lu Xun was not a member of the league, but he was the most prominent figure associated with it. Rou Shi, known to be close to him, had also been assigned to act as Lu Xun's intermediary to the league.[18] That January it had become seditious to criticize the Nationalists in print or to publish or disseminate criticism of it.[19] The night before his arrest, Rou Shi had come to consult him on behalf of a friend about publishing contracts (a visit not recorded in Lu Xun's diary), and at the time of his arrest he was carrying a contract of Lu Xun's as a model. According to her biographer, Agnes Smedley, an American activist and, as it later emerged, Comintern spy, warned Lu Xun that Rou Shi had that document with him.[20] That night Lu Xun burned many of his papers, and on the twentieth he went into hiding with his wife and son, staying at the Japanese-run hotel Huayuanzhuang until February 28.[21] "There were some who sought to involve me in this," he wrote in a letter, "and hence I have moved my lodgings for some time."[22] In what he felt was a related move, the next day four leftist publishers were raided and works confiscated from them.[23] He wrote to let friends know that he was alive. His letter to Xu Shoushang employed names only they two would recognize, and as an additional precaution it used no punctuation, in the old style.[24] A rumor of his arrest was published in Shanghai on the twentieth, reprinted in Peking on the twenty-first, and, via news agencies, spread throughout the country.[25] It reached the papers in Japan as well.[26] "Rumors may be enough to kill—it may be that I will be arrested," Lu Xun wrote to one correspondent.[27]

What about this old poem, composed thirty years earlier and written out again on February 16? After the arrests of the young writers, "the Communist Party started a campaign to save them, but nothing could be done."[28] Nonetheless, among the writers' friends there circulated the belief that they could be ransomed. There was also the opposite rumor, that they had been taken to Nanjing and released. Both rumors are reported in "Remembrance." Two letters from Rou Shi to a friend were brought to Lu Xun. The letters make poignant reading. "It does not look as though I will be released soon," he wrote, and asked the friend to ask Lu Xun to ask Cai Yuanpei to intervene on their behalf (this Lu Xun did, but with no result), saying also that his older brother, who had come to Shanghai, should be consulted for ransom funds. In the second letter he wrote, "Sister Feng's face is swollen black and blue."

On February 7, Lu Xun received a manuscript payment of 450 yuan and gave 100 to one "Huang Houhui" to put toward the ransom. (This was actually the night they were killed.) The name Huang Houhui appears only this once in Lu Xun's works.[29] The *LXQJ* editors identify him as a Huang Su via an allusion to the *Analects*.[30] This identification makes sense, for Huang Su was a member of the League of Left-Wing Dramatists, had been imprisoned in 1930, and *was ransomed* by friends who made up the sum needed. Nine days later, on the night of February 16, Lu Xun received a payment of 73 yuan and 60 cents, and this time he gave 50 yuan to "a person from Nanjiang store" for "ransom money." This unnamed intermediary has not been identified.[31]

The night of February 16 was also the eve of the lunar New Year, traditionally a time of stocktaking, typically, for literati, by means of a poem. Lu Xun's diary notes that he asked Zhou Jianren's wife to make three meat dishes for dinner that night. Jiang Jingsan (1899–1936), an editor at Commercial Press and a frequent visitor in the early 1930s, came by and stayed for dinner. Jiang had also come to Lu Xun's home on the night of January 17, the night of the arrests. Perhaps he had been the one to bring word then, for he came several other times to Huayuanzhuang, always at night. The manuscript payment, the arrival of "the person from Jiangnan store," and the ransom contribution are recorded as occurring after the meal. Then he was alone. His lifelong habit was to write late into the night. Many New Year's poems are written in the silence of the night. On the sixteenth, he wrote out the 1903 poem. This is the copy that has been so visually familiar for the last fifty-plus years. Even though he did not go on to display it but simply kept it among his papers, he used a large piece of paper, as noted earlier. You have to clear your desk to do something like that. In hiding at Huayuanzhuang, space was very tight. It had to be an intentional, deliberate gesture. That the poem served as a kind of marker can also be seen from the postscript notation of his two ages, "composed at 21, written out at 51"; fifty-one was his new age that night with the turn of the lunar year.

In what way is it a stocktaking, and why this poem? To ask these questions essentially asks what in the poem applies to the 1931 situation, and conversely, what in the 1931 situation applies to the poem. We can start by seeing elements shared by the young student of 1903 and the imprisoned young people—the youth of the writer, the fieriness of the sentiments. The arrested youths were young, only beginning as writers. Some, such as Hu Yebin, were writers only by intention and courtesy of title (the league they belonged to was for writers). In 1903, Lu Xun, too, was at an age when he had not yet begun anything, and yet, as the poem shows, he had a fierce desire to accomplish something.

Everything about the poem is singularly apt. Each line can easily be read two ways, in its sense in 1903 and in its present application. This is especially the case because the grammar allows for an unstated subject and unmarked number and tense.

> My being has no plan to avoid . . . / Their beings had no plan to avoid . . . (line 1)
> Wind and rain darken my homeland / darken their [our] homeland (line 2)
> I entrusted my thoughts . . . no understanding / They entrusted their thoughts . . . no understanding (line 3)
> I would offer up my blood . . . / We offer up our blood . . . (line 4).

Every line is capable of a dual meaning. In its new context, we see echo, aptness, and resemblance. The young people had been steadfast, with no flinching in the face of their sufferings (line 1). (Incidentally, the unknown meaning of *shenshi* seems to be not so important now.) Disorder envelops China (line 2), now as was the case thirty years earlier, indeed all thirty years since. The young people with their great hopes and many plans for the future encountered only unheeding authorities (line 3). The last line is especially bleak. The youthful resolve so ardently expressed in "I would offer up my blood for the descendants of the Yellow Emperor" is now grimly applicable to the young: in their words, "We offer up our blood." He had just given another sum of money for them. If he knew they were in fact dead, then line 4 in particular would be couched in the past tense: "We have offered up our blood." (Note that the thread of anti-Manchu sentiment is gone.) His long-ago ideals are transferred to these young people with a grimly different outcome. The poem is changed from a young man's manifesto to a tribute by an old man to the new, young men. It is now both a young man's poem and the poem, as the postscript notes, of a fifty-one-year-old man. If he knew or believed them dead, then it is furthermore a commemorative poem.

In the essay "Remembrance in Order to Forget," there is a passage that shows the same mental habit of connection made through poetry over a thirty-year time span. There Lu Xun writes about two volumes of Petőfi that he had once given to one of the writers, Bai Mang, which had been confiscated when Bai was arrested a previous time. Bai had consulted Lu Xun on his (Bai's) translation from German of a biographical notice of Petőfi and also some poems of his, and Lu Xun had sent him his volumes, purchased "thirty years ago." They were a German translation, "not a fine edition nor expensive," but quite complete. "To me they were a kind of treasure," he wrote, "because it was thirty years ago, when I greatly loved the poetry of Petőfi, that I ordered them from Maruzen bookstore." He had had some trouble with the purchase because, he now thinks, it was too cheap a set for a special order. "Then," he wrote, he met Bai Mang and "decided to give these volumes to a young man who, as I had at that time, greatly loved the poetry of Petőfi ." As in the rewriting of the quatrain, we find threads linking the two ends of thirty years: the youthful devotion to the same poet, the inexpensive but precious volumes, the unimportant but precious poems. All are shared in common between the young man Lu Xun had been and the young people he now mourns. Lu Xun goes on to note that this time he lost another German translation that he had given Bai Mang. Typically, he masks his sorrow with a complaint about the loss of the books and casts the loss as a synecdoche of the death of their new owner.

In general, this date of February 16 is passed over.[32] A daily acquaintance in those days, Nagao Kagekazu, a Japanese guest at Huayuanzhuang, who wrote down his recollections in 1956, mentions their "long talks at night by the heated brazier" and even a false alarm that occurred "around the lunar New Year," but otherwise the days passed equally for Nagao.[33] Among commentators on the poetry, some comment on the writing out of the poem again in 1931 and some further comment on the date of February 16. All focus on the poem in reference to its author, in particular taking line 4 to be a reaffirmation of his earlier resolute stance.[34] Even Zhang Ziqiang, whose findings on other matters relating to the poem are relied on below, connects the poem to Lu Xun alone.

> Not only did he write out again his sacred vows of thirty years earlier, but at its end, he wrote out the information [here Zhang quotes the postscript]. His strong feelings, his grief, his goals. . . —all these are crystallized in this poem.[35]

Yet reaffirmation of the old sentiments, especially those involving bloodshed and sacrifice, seems unlikely. Lu Xun did not think the way he had as a youth and had not done so since soon after the time of the poem's writing. By connecting the poem to the Five Martyrs, it can be read not as an affirmation of blood and sacrifice but rather as a sorrowful tribute to the sacrifices made.

Among the dead, Lu Xun was closest to Rou Shi, and it is possible to link him most closely to the poem's new meaning. In a sense, the tribute represented by this early poem emphasizes the obvious fact of Rou Shi's importance to him. Nonetheless it is a valuable addition to see that *this* (and, as we shall see, the "Remembrance" poem) is the first of the many tributes Lu Xun paid to Rou Shi. Made in both written and visual media, each of these tributes was notable in some way, each enmeshed Lu Xun more intricately in the web of leftist activities, and each consecrated, as it were, the commitment he had already made. He left Huayuanzhuang on the last day of February, and in March he and Feng Xuefeng began to plan a new magazine, *Outpost* (*Qianshao*), intended as the official league magazine. Its inaugural issue (April 25), which in the event was its only issue, was a commemorative "Special Issue in Memory of the War Dead," its copies run off in great secrecy overnight to protect the printers. To this he contributed an unsigned "Biographical note on Rou Shi" and an elegy, "Chinese Revolutionary Proletariat Literature and the Blood of Its Vanguard," signed with the initials LS.[36] In the same month, Lu Xun, Mao Dun, and Agnes Smedley composed an English-language letter of protest that Smedley sent for publication to *New Masses*, the American communist periodical, then a monthly.[37] An essay, "The Present State of Literature and Art in Darkest China," also intended for *New Masses*, appeared in Chinese the following year.[38] To another new magazine, *Beidou* (Big Dipper), edited by Ding Ling, who with this position started to become prominent in leftist circles, he sent a more oblique tribute, a woodcut entitled "Sacrifice," by Käthe Kollwitz, for the cover of its inaugural issue.[39] Inside were photographs of the Five Martyrs. The cover's connection with Rou Shi was explained in "Remembrance" and again some years later, when Lu Xun published a fine edition of twenty-four of Kollwitz's prints.[40] Linked by Kollwitz, the whole woodcut enterprise, which he began with Rou Shi's help and which became a much bigger enterprise after his death, was imbued with Rou Shi's presence.

Out of all this material, this poem is the concealed tribute: amid Lu Xun's many activities on behalf of Rou Shi's memory, he never mentioned this poem. I have suggested that his earlier silence was perhaps because he no longer subscribed to its fiery explicitness and its acceptance, indeed its welcoming, of death. Now there is a different quality to the silence. A poem only known posthumously has a further connection to one of the most symbolically burdened cases of political violence in 1930s Shanghai. On the night of February 16, it was not enough to recall the poem: only writing it out formally could give full expression to his feelings. The size of the calligraphy and the tight quarters at Huayuanzhuang draw attention to the deliberate and formal nature of the action, the will to make the space to do it, to find the solitude in which to do it. Even though he never wrote about the actions originally associated with the poem, they had never been forgotten.

There is another copy of the poem from this time, much smaller and not well written. According to Zhou Haiying, Lu Xun's son, this copy, now in his possession, was secretly retrieved from the wastepaper basket by his mother after having been discarded by his father.⁴¹ Since Zhou was two at the time, this must be family lore. He suggests that it was discarded because there is a mistaken word in the colophon, a suggestion taken up by Ye Shusui and Yang Yanli. Wang Shijia proposes, however, that because an uncorrected facsimile of this calligraphy has now been published (earlier "facsimiles" had improved the alignment), we can see that the discarded attempt was simply not very good: two of its three lines slant noticeably to the left, the last character of the poem is very roughly written, and the date is off (fig. 4.2).⁴² The date on this one is "*xinwei* year, the last third of the month." *Xinwei* year began on February 16, but it takes four days more to reach *xiaxun*. Wang Shijia supposes this error in dating to be an additional reason why Lu Xun discarded this copy.

I wonder when this copy was made? Wang does not make a suggestion, but it is possible to think of this as a rough copy, in which case it would have been written just before the "good" copy. First, since Lu Xun was writing out a poem from thirty years ago, a lot of factors had to be worked out first. Also the discarded copy measures 17 x 7.9 inches, a bit narrower and longer than a sheet of legal-sized paper, a size that seems more like a rough copy than a discarded good copy.⁴³ (The good copy is half again as large in each direction, 24 x 13 inches.) Finally, the date, "the last third of the month" though inaccurate, is not much more misleading than the Gregorian date he did use of February 16, which obscured the fact that it was really the lunar New Year's Eve that was significant. But these are only suppositions. The matter cannot be resolved with current information.

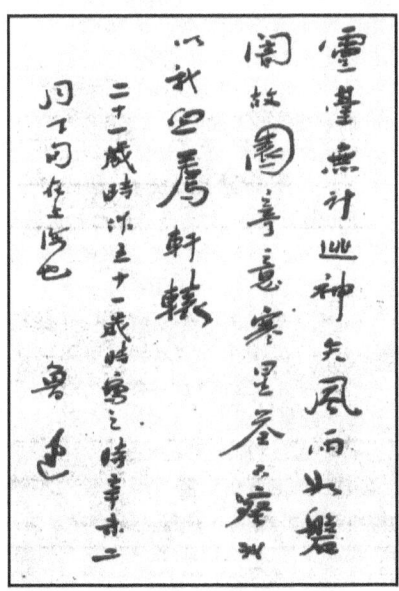

Figure 4.2. A discarded 1931 copy of the quatrain. Note the leftward slant of, especially, the first two lines. *Lu Xun Research Monthly* 9 (2007): 58.

For nearly two years Lu Xun did nothing more with the revived poem. That is, he did not publish it and, as far as we know, he did not show the copies to anyone. In one sense, this is unsurprising. Later, too, he mostly did not publish his classical-language poems. (He published his vernacular-language poems, but there were only six, published in May 1918, July 1918, and April 1919.) None of his poems predating 1918 was published; indeed, they were not collected until after his death and even then only on the second or third go-around. Only one was published by his direct action in his lifetime, the octet included in "Remembrance," which will be discussed later. Three more poems from the 1930s were published by their recipients, perhaps with his cooperation.[44]

It is interesting that Xu Shoushang seems not to have known of these two 1931 copies or at least that he did not give thought to the poem's renewed significance. It is he who brought this old poem to our attention in his 1936 essay on Lu Xun, but he did not mention 1931. He obviously valued the classical-language poems. He had many poems by Lu Xun in his possession, some were copies made by him and some were in Lu Xun's hand made at his request. As he described it, whenever he visited Lu Xun, he would ask whether he had written any more poems. Sometimes Lu Xun would show him some, which he would copy, and sometimes Lu Xun would bring out his own copies to give to him. In this way, in 1948 he had eleven more poems than the bare fourteen that the *Supplement to the Collected Works* could scratch up.[45]

Then nearly two years later, on December 9, 1932, Lu Xun wrote out the poem another time. This time it was done for someone, Okamoto Shigeru 岡本繁 (fig. 4.3), identified by *LXQJ* editors as being a physician at Shinozaki Hospital. Okamoto had often treated Lu Xun and his son Haiying. All three in the family had been sick off and on, and earlier, in September and October, the diary records more than thirty visits to this hospital. On this day, the *Diary* shows Lu Xun with his wife and son at the hospital in the morning. Later that day Lu Xun wrote out "two strips" using the Japanese term *tanzaku* 短冊 for "Dr. Okamoto" and also a horizontal piece (hengfu) for Tai Jingnong.

The diary entry does not name the "two strips" and their identity was not known until this copy came to light in 1987, when it could be matched with this diary entry. In that year, according to the Beijing Lu Xun Museum,

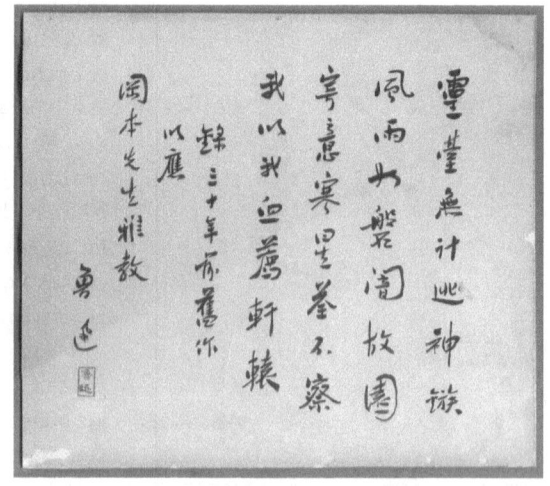

Figure 4.3. The 1933 copy of the quatrain written out for Okamoto Shigeru. Note the change of the seventh character from *shi* to *zu* (in the compound word *shenshi / shenzu*). Courtesy of Beijing Lu Xun Museum.

the physician's descendants in Japan found it in their storage building and presented to the museum in May of the next year, where a facsimile is now on permanent exhibit. It was reproduced by the museum in a 1998 publication.[46] Unlike the 1931 copy, this one is horizontal, almost square, measuring 24 cm high by 27.2 cm wide.[47] This is only a little wider than our modern U.S. standard-sized paper laid sideways, much smaller than the February 16 one. The (undated) postscript reads, "Copying out an old work from thirty years ago in response to Mr. Okamoto" (錄三十年前舊作以應冈本先生) with Lu Xun's stamp beneath it. So Okamoto had made a request. It is interesting to note that in both 1931 and 1932, Lu Xun describes the poem as having been written thirty years later, so he is clearly rounding off. Also interesting is that the vexingly unexplainable word *shenshi* 神矢 (arrows of the gods, godly arrows) in line 1 is changed in this copy to *shenzu* 神镞 (arrowheads of god, godly arrowheads), equally a neologism.

In a convincing bit of detecting and reasoning, the critic Zhang Ziqiang makes a connection between this copy of the poem and Qu Qiubai in a way that accounts for both the gift to the physician and the change of wording in line 1.[48] I give Zhang's reasoning here on how it was that Lu Xun showed this renewed poem to Qu and why this would have led to a copy for the physician. Zhang begins by noting that the complete diary entry for December 9 also includes an item related to Qu Qiubai: earlier that day he and his wife had given Haiying, then three, a Meccano set. (This extravagance of an expensive, imported toy has been made much of in accounts of the intimate friendship between these two great figures of the 1930s Left.) Zhang suggests, "Perhaps because of this toy that Qu and his wife gave Haiying, Lu Xun wrote two pieces for the physician who had been treating Haiying." I think Zhang means that the present to his son reminded Lu Xun that he had unfulfilled obligations on the child's behalf in another direction. If that is the case, the next questions are why choose this poem as one of the two to present and why change *shenshi* to *shenzu*? Zhang thinks the answers to both are still connected to Qu.

At this time, as a security precaution, Qu and his wife had moved out of their room and had been living with Lu Xun since late November. (They remained until late December.) The intimate, empathetic relation between the two men of different generations who met only that summer is well known and has many proofs. In the days they spent under the same roof, they spoke of everything, and Zhang suggests that it is now that Lu Xun showed Qu the poem he had first written thirty years before. He suggests this because we know of half of the discussion between them: on December 7, two days earlier, Qu had written out for Lu Xun a poem he had written in his youth, as it happens also a quatrain in seven-syllable lines. To this he had added a reflection somewhat longer than the poem: "To think today about such utterances of despair—they are so different they seem a world away.... Written and offered to Mr. Lu Xun."[49] Lu Xun's poem from *his* youth might have been the other part of this conversation. One result would be that two days later, when reminded of an obligation to Haiying's physician by a gift from Qu to his son, Lu Xun wrote out the poem of his youth that he had shown Qu. I would add that Qu's postscript, which shows both affection for and distance from the words of his youth, captured something of what Lu Xun felt about his own poem.

This poem and another by Qu Qiubai in his hand are held in the Beijing Lu Xun Museum. Each poem reveals supporting details for the scenario outlined above. About the poem of his youth, despite Qu's note that "the utterances of despair . . . seem a world away," the despair of the first line could easily have contemporary applicability, as Xu Guangping has noted. This two-edged pertinence, which I argued above for the 1903 poem, adds another quality shared by the two men's poems. The second poem, which Qu sent later that month, is a four-line jesting poem (*dayou shi*) with a long note explaining the newspaper item that is his target. The poem mostly makes fun of, as line 2 says, "modern fads sweeping the homeland," but the pertinent point here is the first line, which reads, "They face, not a thicket of knives, but dance halls." Qu's phrase "face, not a thicket of knives" 向刀叢 quotes from the eight-line poem (discussed next) that Lu Xun wrote at Huayuanzhuang on hearing of the writers' deaths but had not yet published in "Remembrance."[50] So that poem, so closely connected to the Five Martyrs, must have been shown to Qu, strengthening the suggestions that the 1903 poem had been.

Zhang also makes a suggestion about the change of wording in line 1 from *shenshi* (arrow) to *shenzu* (arrowhead). Now it reads "My mind has no wish to avoid the arrowheads of the gods." He points out that compared to the arrow as a whole, the head of an arrow names the part that "goes straight to the heart and stays permanently in the heart." This is interesting and can be connected to Qu. The change of wording might reflect discussion with Qu. In changing the word to "arrowhead," the author is focusing, not on the first part of the line, where the speaker is braced against an onslaught, but on the last part, the lodging of pain and grief in the heart. The fierceness and permanence of anguish is stressed; in this reprise the line reverts to referring only to the poet, as opposed to its reference to both poet and the Five Martyrs: "our minds had no wish to avoid the arrows of gods." (Note that the allusion to the arrows in Liang Qichao's poem, the modeling of his poem on Liang's, is left behind in this version.) It gives an intriguing hint of what the two men might have discussed.

The 1932 calligraphy adds to our sense of the poem's importance to Lu Xun because the change in feeling and emphasis brought in with "arrowheads" shows the lability, the continual aliveness, of poem to him. If, in addition, we accept Zhang's reconstruction of its 1932 appearance, then our view is further enriched because we are able to connect Lu Xun's grief for Rou Shi to his friendship with Qu Qiubai, both men known to be close to his heart. He gave it to others twice, once back in 1903 and now as a coded gift to one person (Okamoto) in honor of another (Qu). In sending it to Okamoto without explanation, the poem remains opaque. Except for Qu, it remains, to use Zhang's words, "this secret poem from the past that he showed no one."

There was to be one more appearance of the quatrain, this one a hint only. It occurred the next year, in the essay, "Remembrance in Order to Forget," where it is implicit in some lines he quotes from Petőfi. The lines, expressing eagerness for self-sacrifice, exactly correspond to his own youthful desire to "offer up my blood for the descendants of the Yellow Emperor," but this time it is their source in Bai Mang that renews the quatrain's applicability. While writing the essay, Lu Xun had searched for manuscripts of Bai's that might still be in his possession, but he found only Bai's copy of Petőfi's poems. In it he saw this translation written next to a poem entitled "Wahlspruch," meaning, he explained, "maxim" (*geyan*):

生命誠寶貴　愛情價更高　若為自由故　二者皆可拋！

> Life is truly precious,
> Love even more so,
> But if freedom is at stake,
> Both can be flung away! [51]

Lu Xun had with him Bai's copy because he wanted to check a translation Bai had sent against the version he had used, while in an uncanny switch, Bai had Lu Xun's two volumes, which, as we saw, was lost with Bai's earlier arrest. Looking through Bai's copy now, Lu Xun found little, "except for these four lines written in ink." One wonders with what force they struck him, with what feelings he saw that the young man who like him, had loved Petőfi's poetry, left this particular trace in his hands after death.

Implications: The Other 1931 Poem

Reading the 1903 quatrain as a commemoration of Rou Shi and the other writers must alter our reading of a famous poem that *is* known to commemorate them. Also untitled, this poem is in the regulated verse form of eight lines, in this case of seven characters each (*qiyan lüshi*). (Usually referred to by its first words, "Though accustomed to"; I will use the grammatically more convenient formulation "Remembrance poem.") The poem became widely known when it was incorporated into the powerful commemorative essay "Remembrance in Order to Forget," written on the second anniversary of their deaths, noted in his diary entry as the day on which "two years ago, Rou Shi was killed." Augmented by the essay's information on its composition and by its descriptions of the young writers, this classical poem came to readers with a clear story that made its traditional features readily comprehensible. Because the essay was widely read, the poem received wide circulation and became identified with the tragedy and his grief. More compactly quotable than the essay that contains it, it became his most famous poem in his lifetime.[52]

Though published in 1933, this poem was composed, as Lu Xun tells readers in "Remembrance," on the night that he learned of the deaths of those arrested. Thus it has always figured in our sense of these weeks as marking their most painful moment. At the same time, the poem is generally felt to have attained its full meaning when it was published in the essay. With the emergence of the 1903 poem, we can see that in its original state, as a poem before the essay existed, it is intimately connected with that early poem and that the two poems need to be read together. Furthermore, once the Remembrance poem is no longer the only poem associated with these tragic deaths, our attention is directed to the time at Huayuanzhuang in terms of all the poetry written in those weeks, and this brings up in a significant way the third poem from this period. This poem, four lines long and entitled "A Farewell to Mr. O.E., Who is Taking Orchids with Him on His Return to Japan", has a known date, February 12.[53] So in this group of three, the only undated poem is the one directly connected to learning of the deaths. Pinning down the actual date, which had seemed an abstract task for sake of exactitude, is now more pressingly related to understanding the larger poetic context of the Remembrance poem, indeed of all three poems.

The twenty-four prisoners were shot on February 7. Lu Xun does not tell us when he learned of it. He only says that one night, those on the outside "suddenly received the reliable information that Rou Shi and twenty-three other people had been executed on the night of the 7th or the morning of the 8th at Longhua prison." He knew at some point before the twenty-fourth, as can be seen from a letter written on that day, where he gives the source of his information: "It was only in reading the Japanese papers that I learned that, on the 7th of this month, a group of young people were executed by gunfire." In an earlier letter, written on the eighteenth, he seemed not to know of the deaths. Together the two letters suggest a day between the eighteenth and the twenty-fourth. On three of these days, February 19–21, Lu Xun visited Uchiyama Bookstore, where he could have seen Japanese papers, so it has generally been narrowed down to these dates.[54]

Again, Zhang Ziqiang pursues some evidence that seems convincing. He proposes that Lu Xun learned of the executions much earlier, probably within three days of their occurrence, that is, by February 10.[55] As far as the effect on the 1903 poem is concerned, its four lines can still be read with the young writers as a double subject with Lu Xun in his youth, for they can be read either as if he knew of the deaths or as if he only feared that outcome for them. The effect of a new date for the Remembrance poem will bear on the relations between the poems, including bringing "A Farewell to Mr. O.E." more to the fore. We still cannot definitely fix the three poems in a chronological relationship, but merely by freeing up the possible time for the Remembrance poem, by showing it can be moved up, our attention is redirected to the poems as a group and to considering anew the tenor of the weeks at Huayuanzhuang.

Before Zhang begins, he lifts the existing limits in time by suggesting plausible reasons why Lu Xun's letters may not give the truth about when and how he learned of the deaths. He argues that in the letter of February 18, in which Lu Xun seemed not yet to know of them, he was writing to someone in Moscow and naturally had to be careful about what he relayed. And in the letter of February 24, which gave "Japanese newspapers" as the source of his news, Zhang quotes to show that Lu Xun's correspondent, a former student who was a Nationalist, often wrote with suggestions for him to, for example, go abroad for a while, and that on his side Lu Xun was always careful to convey an air of frankness in his communications.[56]

Zhang's case is quite long, but his main line of evidence is straightforward. He shows that the connections of Hu Yebin, one of the five writers, were able to learn of the deaths only two or three days after they occurred and also suggests how their information could have reached Lu Xun. Specifically, Zhang quotes the 1950 recollections of Ding Ling, the lover of Hu Yebin and already a famous writer, who writes of her experiences and how she knew for certain by late on February 9 that they were dead and how the nature of their deaths was definitely confirmed on the tenth. The account here generally follows Zhang's with the incorporation of more details from both Ding Ling's relatively brief record and Shen Congwen's detailed 1933 memoir about her.[57] When Hu Yebin and the others were first arrested, Shen Congwen, an intimate friend of his and Ding Ling's, came to Shanghai and became deeply involved with the attempts to free him by appeals or by ransom, or at least to separate his case as a writer from the political activists arrested. He and Ding

Ling went many times to Longhua Garrison, though only on the first occasion did they catch a glimpse of Hu; on later visits, they sent in money to pay for letters delivered from within. During these weeks, Shen went three times to Nanjing to see highly placed people, both Nationalist and Communist, who sent him back to Shanghai to see yet others. The third time Ding Ling was with him. According to Shen, while in Nanjing, a letter from Shanghai gave them the news that that night (no date given) twenty-three persons had been shot.[58] Ding Ling and Shen returned by night train and reached Shanghai on the morning of February 8. That day, she sensed from the way that a jailor she knew from Longhua Garrison avoided a meeting with her that Hu must be dead. On the ninth, Ding Ling and Shen were essentially told by Shanghai friends that Hu Yebin and the others were no longer alive. By late that night, Shen had learned that they had been shot in Longhua Garrison, and on the tenth a jailor from the garrison came to see her. As Zhang points out, if someone like Shen Congwen, just returned from Wuhan, was able to obtain this information, others must have also known.

As to how such knowledge might have been relayed to Lu Xun, Zhang notes that in Shanghai, Ding Ling stayed with a contact on the Left, so her information must have reached Feng Xuefeng and others quickly. For that matter, Feng must have had his own sources, for his memoirs note that "we comrades and relatives were able to confirm [the deaths] within a few days." He was not the one to tell Lu Xun, he says, but he records being shown what must have been the Remembrance poem. He writes, "I went to see him at dusk about three or four days later" (a visit not recorded in the diary) and found him "ashen-faced." "He sat silently on the bed-platform, not speaking for a long time. Then from a drawer he took out a poem and showed it to me, and in a low voice said, 'I put together some lines.'" Feng's notation of "three or four days later" can mean the tenth or so. A bit of consistent evidence is that in "Remembrance," Lu Xun mentions a lapse of time that matches an earlier date than the twenty-fourth. Describing the efforts of those on the outside, he says, "And so this went on for about twenty days." This would take us from January 17 to February 9, consistent with an early date for his knowledge. For this earlier date, a final point that needs explaining is the money Lu Xun gave to "a person from a Nanjiang store" on February 16. Zhang suggests that the word in the diary for "gave," *fu* 付, especially when used in connection with "store," means "paid," as in concluding payment, and also that funds were needed for the many expenses after death. This is possible, especially since "Nanjiang store" is a still cryptic code.[59]

Let us now look at the Remembrance poem and see how it can be read against the 1903 poem; how, though an intensely personal poem, Lu Xun treated it quite differently from the early poem; and how when he published it he set it up in a certain way that opened up classical poetry as a resource for himself. The poem was published with a description of the situation and setting in which it was composed. This description serves as the preface that often heads a classical poem, especially an untitled one, and provides its background.

> It was deep into the night. I stood in the courtyard of the inn, surrounded by piles of broken discards. Everyone was asleep, including my wife and child. My heart was heavy with the feeling that I had lost good friends, that China had lost good young people. Gradually I grew calmer in my sorrow and from that calmness old habits emerged and led me to put together these lines.

He then gives the poem.

慣於長夜過春時　挈婦將雛鬢有絲
夢裏依稀慈母淚　城頭變幻大王旗
忍看朋輩成新鬼　怒向刀叢覓小詩
吟罷低眉無寫處　月光如水照緇衣

> Though accustomed to the long nights, now it is spring
> Leading wife and child by the hand, my hair has grown white
> From dreams the lingering sense of a loving mother's tears
> At city's walls the flags of kings change
> I cannot bear to see friends become new ghosts
> Angry I face a thicket of knives to find my poem
> My song chanted, I look down, no place to write it
> The moon's light, like water, shines on my black gown.[60]

This poem was much admired by Lu Xun's contemporaries. The poet Liu Yazi, the recipient of the calligraphy of "Self-Mockery," said, "Measured and filled with anger, sensibility, and profundity—it has each of these elements." The critic Liu Dajie wrote, "It has everything.... On the one hand it reflects a dark world under bloody control and praises the courageous ardor of the revolutionary youth; at the same time it shows the love between mother and son and between husband and wife and parents and child....This poem has deep historical meaning, containing a high degree of patriotic thought and revolutionary fervor, combined into a magnificent artistic achievement." In a tribute to its importance, there are many translations into European languages.[61]

How to read this poem against the silent 1903 poem? Both were composed (or written out) in solitude in the middle of the night at Huayuanzhuang.

As it existed on the night of its composition, this octet is as personal as the quatrain. Like the quatrain, its reference to the dead is oblique, for only line 5, "I cannot bear to see friends become new ghosts," makes a direct reference. It is only with the addition of the essay, with its account of the circumstances of the young people's arrests and the description of his sorrow which heads the poem, that the poem can be appreciated as an elegy. This need for context is also the case with the 1903 poem, and in both cases it is typical of the demands made on readers by classical poems.

Classical poetry is the most private of Lu Xun's many genres in terms of readership. The 1903 poem was written at a time when *shi* poetry was the primary form of self-expression and before any other form was available. In 1931 his reasons for writing in the classical form must differ, if only because he had other forms available. The 1931 poem's genre and solitary composition suggest that it is a personal work, written essentially for himself. As the prefatory words explain: "Old habits emerged," and they "led me to put together these lines." So, to begin with, he wrote it for himself, as with the rewriting of the quatrain.

Unlike the young man's poem, this poem is completely traditional and consistent in terms of language and imagery: the choices in language, focus, and setting mostly stay within the boundaries of lyric poetry (*shi*) convention. Nearly every element that makes up each seven-syllable line is drawn from convention in language and focus. Thus, in the first couplet, the conventional elements in the first line are "long nights," and "spring"; and in the second line, all three elements are conventional, wife, son, and hair growing white. The poem's structure, too, turns conventionally at the halfway point: lines 1–4 describe the setting and circumstances, expanding outward from the poet himself (line 1), to his wife and child (line 2), his mother in Beijing (line 3), and the wars raging outside Shanghai (line 4); and lines 5–8 tell of the topical reason for the poem (the new ghosts) and his responses (lines 6–8). Also typical is the focus on the self as a means of conveying wider meaning—one's aloneness, one's age, one's grief, the moonlight on one's gown. The factualness of the poem is also a convention of tradition. Thus we can assume he *did* write it in the courtyard of Huayuanzhuang, that it *was* a moonlit night, and that his wife and child *were* asleep. Furthermore, all these elements of verisimilitude are also selected according to convention. Line 3, his mother's tears (*cimu lei*) in distant Beijing, can be assumed to be factual. Indeed, his letters show that he knew of his mother's grief when false news of his arrest had reached her. "My old mother's tears" (*laomu yinqi* 老母吟泣), he wrote then.[62] "Tears of the mother" likely additionally refers to Rou Shi's mother, for immediately following this poem Lu Xun notes that she was blind and living in the country, perhaps still thinking her son to be alive, and he described Kollwitz's "Sacrifice," which he gave to the magazine *Big Dipper,* as showing "an agonized mother offering up her son." In sum, in these eight lines, we see a complete list of his responsibilities: his wife, son, mother, country, comrades, and writing, plus his age and time advancing. It is not a young man's poem.

As was the case in 1903, at the time of composition, he wanted to make the poem known. In the quatrain, this is expressed in line 3, "I entrust my thoughts to the star of a cold night, the king does not understand," employing, as is customary, the language of the *Songs of Chu* as political allegory. Thirty years later, the desire is more plainly stated: "My song chanted, I look down, no place to write it" (line 7). The language is not allusive: "no place to write it" 無寫處. The explanation given for this line in the essay is scarcely needed: "In China, there was no outlet, for all was sealed tight as a tin can."

This desire for the Remembrance poem to be made known was carried out in a private way in the next two years before the essay brought it before the reading public. In this slow dispersal, there is nothing hidden or mysterious. It was simply slow. A few days after its writing, he showed it to Feng Xuefeng, as we saw above. Xu Guangping must have read it also. He next made a copy for an intimate. As in 1903, it was for Xu Shoushang. This probably occurred on March 4, a few days after Lu Xun returned to his home, when the diary records a visit.[63] The poem received another reader when, a little more than a year later, in July 1932, he sent it, together with a second, new poem on the Shanghai war of January 1932, to a Japanese acquaintance named Yamamoto Hatsue (1898–1967), who had requested a poem. So both poems associated with the Five Martyrs went to Japanese acquaintants in the year 1932. Yamamoto and her husband had been longtime residents of China, arriving in 1916 and returning to Japan in 1932. She was introduced to Lu Xun in 1930 through Uchiyama and after that appeared scores of times in his diary, nearly always with Mrs. Uchiyama and bringing a present for Lu Xun's son. After her return to Japan, she received more than twenty letters. In this letter of July 1932 the poem on the new January war seems to have been part of the letter, while the Remembrance poem was separately written in a small size format.[64] With the presentation to Yamamoto, this desire for public knowledge was somewhat assuaged, for his diary notes that line 7 was now outdated.

What happened next, on December 9, 1932, is intriguing. In the previous section, we saw that this was the day on which Lu Xun sent to the physician Okamoto the calligraphy of his 1903 quatrain, with one word altered. On the same day, he notes in his diary that he sent to Tai Jingnong in Beijing a "horizontal piece" (*heng fu*).⁶⁵ The identity of this piece was not known until a 2004 book in Hubei published an image—it is this Remembrance poem on a horizontal sheet, which judging from a reproduction in an article, is about three times wider than it is high (no dimensions given).⁶⁶ So the two poems are linked again, in this case with Lu Xun writing them out and sending them off in different directions on the same day. As with Okamoto, it does not seem that the recipient was told the significance of what he had. In a subsequent letter to Tai, Lu Xun merely asked whether he had received a scroll of writing, apologized for its poor quality, and asked that he not have it mounted.⁶⁷

Finally, in 1933, Lu Xun took the final step in releasing the poem when he wrote his essay "Remembrance in Order to Forget." The essay, and the poem along with it, immediately became one of his most widely known works. The author attributes the two-year lapse to circumstances: the one-year anniversary had not been marked because he was forced out of his home by the Shanghai War of 1932. Lu Xun and his family had evacuated on February 6. They first stayed upstairs at Uchiyama's bookstore; later they were taken through the war zone to a branch store in the International Settlement. On their return they found that the district where their home lay had been leveled, although their stretch of road was intact, "not even an umbrella missing."⁶⁸ So it was only in 1933, on the second anniversary, that he was able to write "Remembrance."

The essay brings the poem to a new stage of clarity by setting up essay and poem as equivalents. The essay, in five sections, places the poem near the end of section 4 and states the equivalence in section 5. The first three sections and part of the fourth contain the information on the dead that a eulogy should provide. His account is scrupulous in that he writes only of what he personally knows, so that the most space is given to Rou Shi, next to Bai Mang and Feng Keng, and only a few lines to Li Weisen and Hu Yebin. It is also a restrained account, for we can compare it to the much greater amount of information available and surely known to him. T. A. Hsia, for instance, tells how, by order of the Communist Party, Rou Shi and Feng Keng were living together as man and wife in order to have cover identities.⁶⁹ The essay's last section and a half contain the open mourning and the creation of the equivalence between poem and essay. As we saw earlier, in the fourth section, before quoting the poem, he tells of the conditions under which he came to write the poem, how he stood alone in the courtyard of the inn, and how "everyone was asleep, including my wife and child. My heart was heavy with the feeling that I had lost good friends, that China had lost good young people" and how "gradually I grew calmer in my sorrow and from that calmness old habits emerged and led me to put together these lines." In the same manner, in the final section, he tells of the conditions under which he came to write the essay. What is notable is that the words he uses are identical to those he used for the composition of the poem. The final section begins with an explanation of why the essay would have a date of 1933.

> Two years ago on this day, I was taking refuge in an inn, and they were actually walking on to the execution grounds. Last year on this day, I had fled to the British Concession amid the sound of cannons, and they had long been buried in unknown ground.[70] This year on this day, I am finally sitting in my old home.

Then come the sentences that are identical to those that introduced the poem.

> Everyone was asleep, including my wife and child. Again, my heart was heavy with the feeling that I had lost good friends, that China had lost good young people. Gradually I grew calmer in my sorrow and from that calmness old habits emerged and led me to put together these lines.

As it was two years earlier in Huayuanzhuang, the writer is alone, his family asleep, his thoughts are on the dead, and then, collecting his feelings, he begins to write. Poem and essay are placed on the footing of having the same impulse: "old habits emerged." In the poem, he chafes in line 7 at having "no place to publish." In the essay, "If I were to keep on writing, in the China of today, there would be no place to publish it. All is shut up tight as a tin can." The poem is made accessible by its inclusion in a highly circumstantial essay, while its silent companion remains private.

Such is Lu Xun's power over the interpretation of historical events that his commemorative acts, especially the essay "Remembrance," define for historical memory the bloody contest between the Nationalists and Communists that took its toll on both sides among their civilian fighters. We know much about Rou Shi because of the many projects they undertook together and because of all Lu Xun did to commemorate him. Just as his eulogy for Liu Hezhen made her the face of the forty-seven deaths in the March 18 Incident, so Rou Shi came to represent all five of the Five Martyrs and the Five Martyrs have in turn obscured the total of twenty-four who died that night. They became the symbol and the shorthand of public interpretations of the 1931 deaths. The common view of the Five Martyrs as a clear, unique tragedy persists beyond the Communist Party's contemporary propaganda reach because of the grief so eloquently expressed in this essay and poem. The personal dimensions of the essay, which might otherwise act as a constraint on such an appropriation, instead propel it further.

Implications: The Other Classical Poems

T. S. Eliot observed that when a new important poem appears we have to rearrange the furniture in the room to accommodate it. The 1903 quatrain is clearly such a "new" important poem. It may be that only a slight adjustment is needed to respond to Eliot's insight, but however slight, everything will stand in a different relation than before. In the preceding section, the realignment was made with the other 1931 poem and with the essay in which it was published. In this section, I discuss a rearrangement that involves Lu Xun's classical poems as a whole and conclude with a look at the poem "A Farewell to Mr. O.E." as an instance of a poem whose importance has increased with this rearrangement.

Lu Xun's classical poems are not numerous, and his attitudes toward them must be deduced. He has forty-nine or fifty surviving titles for a total of sixty-five poems (some titles consist of poem sets). Although for some time now every word by Lu Xun has been valued, historically the poems have been variously regarded, not least by himself. They were included only by stages in his collected works, suggesting that as far as the reception of his works is concerned, the classical poems were something of an afterthought. Lu Xun himself omitted them until 1934, when he created a poetry section in the volume *Supplement to the Collected Works*. Into this section went thirteen titles. In a preface, Lu Xun claims that he was not closely involved in the tracking down and inclusion of the poems, classifying them with other out-of-sequence items like the 1903 essay "Sparta." He says that the supplement was put together with the help of one Yang Jiyun, who "startled me . . . with the pile" of early and forgotten pieces.[71] There may be some truth in this disclaimer; for example, the poem "Inscribed in *Hesitation*" is here, separated from its companion "Inscribed in *Call to Arms*," which was written the same evening for the same person.[72] In the next round, twenty-four more titles were gathered in *Second Supplement to the Collected Works,* a collection begun by Lu Xun and completed after his death by Xu Guangping. This group includes the 1903 quatrain. All but two poems were taken from Lu Xun's diary.[73] It was left to the very last volume, the *Third Supplement to the Collected Works* to locate the remaining poems, all very early ones, written in 1900–1902 and collected from the writings of others, chiefly Zhou Zuoren's diaries.[74] Lu Xun was not meticulous about the public poetic record.

His private record-keeping was somewhat different. His many classical poems of the 1930s were all recorded in his diary, which is in turn the main source for *LXQJ*. (The pre-1930 poems were collected from recipients' diaries, publications, etc.) In each case, he recorded the poem or poems, always in their entirety, on the day he wrote them out for others. Curiously, this means the "Remembrance" poem is found in the entry for July 11, 1932, when he gave it to Yamamoto, nearly 18 months after its composition. By recording them in the diary, he shows his intention to have a private record of them. In writing them out for others, he created a circle of people, both acquaintances (nearly all Japanese visitors) and intimates (Xu Shoushang, Yu Dafu, Liu Yazi, Uchiyama), who sought his classical poetry to keep current with his thinking.

This section does not aim to review the classical poems but to sketch from the perspective of the 1903 poem a number of insights into the writer. First, it is possible to see that the "new" poem occupies what has to be considered a significant place in the distribution pattern of Lu Xun's classical poetry. Of his forty-nine or fifty titles, *four-fifths*, or thirty-eight, were written after this time in Huayuanzhuang (ten in 1931, nine in 1932, fourteen in 1933, four in 1934, and one in 1935). Furthermore, of the remaining eleven poems, eight have dates of 1912 or earlier (including of course the quatrain dealt with in this chapter). That is, they belong to a time when only classical-language literature was available, so they fall into a different category. After New Literature came to dominate in 1918 and before 1931, he has only three poems, all of which were written as doggerel (one each in 1925, 1928, and 1930).[75] Thus the three poems of the crisis stand at the beginning of essentially all his classical poems. Moreover, the number of classical poems he wrote once he started, thirty-eight, is fairly large. One might argue that other classical poems have not survived, but it is more likely that any lost poems are from much earlier, 1912 and before. When he burned papers, as he did before going into hiding, they were most likely letters. That Lu Xun wrote many classical poems in the 1930s has often been noted, but the reasoning here suggests that it is the distribution contrast between the plenitude of the 1930s and the dearth before then that should draw our attention, and that this pattern is coincident with the "return of old habits" and the retrieval of a poem that dates from those old habits.

If we think of the Huayuanzhuang weeks as a time when Lu Xun composed a great poem and renewed an early poem in a manner and with a meaning that are of singular significance, and that additionally those days of crisis and grief stand at the head of all his classical poetry, then we must see that *three* poems came into being during these weeks and we must value "A Farewell to Mr. O.E." at least in terms of its role in the revival of classical poetry for Lu Xun. It is, at the least, the first poem he wrote for someone, an important function of traditional poetry.

We look at it now to see how it is a part of the return to classical poetry as a spiritual resource. Written on February 12, this poem dovetails two purposes seamlessly: a farewell to an acquaintance and an expression of grief. They can be joined together because the guest is taking a shipment of orchids back with him, and orchids are a standard political symbol of purity. Like the orchid, the other plants in the poem are from the fourth-century BCE poem "Encountering Sorrow" in *Songs of the South*, and they take their political meaning from that poem, as does "the beauty" of line 1. This is the poem.

"A Farewell to Mr. O.E., Who Is Taking Orchids with Him on His Return to Japan" 送 O.E. 君攜蘭歸國

椒焚桂折佳人老　　獨托幽岩展素心
豈惜芳馨遺遠者　　故鄉如醉有荊榛

The pepper plants are burnt, the cassia broken, the beauty grown old,
Only in refuge in secluded crags can a "pure heart" show itself.
It is a pity that the fragrant scents will leave with the distant person
And home is as though drunk, filled with brambles and thorns.

O. E. is Obara Eijirō, a decades-old friend of Uchiyama who now had a business in Tokyo selling orchids, requiring frequent purchasing trips to China. He often carried out tasks in Tokyo related to Chinese writers at Uchiyama's request.[76] Now, at Uchiyama's prompting, he had called at Huayuanzhuang, a visit of which the poem was a memento. One wonders whether he had a commission that day and, if so, what it was.

The poem begins with expressions of grief, taken from the language of "Encountering Sorrow," which the 1903 poem also uses. In line 1, the pepper plants and cassia are metaphors of political purity, and, given the circumstances, they refer to Rou Shi and the others. The beauty in "Encountering Sorrow" is a scorned beauty symbolizing the exiled poet-official, which is why a beauty can grow old. So line 1 says those who are pure (the pepper plant and the cassia) are killed and injured while the poet himself grows old. In line 2, "pure heart" is another word for orchid, and of course it also has its literal meaning. Orchids grow in the wild; secluded crags are far from court. Thus secluded crags are the haunt of the pure orchid and the beauty. Line 2 may express the general truth that in difficult times those with integrity must go into hiding, or it may have specific reference to his taking refuge in Huayuanzhuang. Line 3 turns courteously to the recipient, his freight, and his departure. The regret in this line, which is standard in farewell poems ("It is a pity that"), turns out to lead, in the next line, to a damning contrast with a disordered home country. With the visitor taking away the orchids, purity will leave the country while brambles and thorns remain. As Lu Xun moves from the high-strung language of "Encountering Sorrow" to the courtesy of a farewell and a bitter reflection on what is left behind when the orchids depart, we see a poem that in a few lines compresses the heightened tension of those days of persecution into the regulated language and form of tradition.

These three poems, positioned at the beginning point of Lu Xun's classical poems, predict the conjunction of nearly all of his classical poems with the political violence of the period. Regarding the poems, one could emphasize the intensely personal level on which Lu Xun uses the traditional *shi* poem. Yes, it *is* traditional to use them as a private meditation on public events, often, as with Lu Xun, coinciding with the impossibility of direct self-expression. But it is evident that he turns to it not only because it is a tradition available to someone of his generation and education, but also because it has come once more to mean something to him. "Old habits emerged," he wrote. "Gradually I grew calmer in my sorrow and from that calmness old habits emerged and led me to put together the following lines."

Although Lu Xun's classical poems could be characterized as another aspect of a multitalented writer, these words suggest something deeper, that they have returned as an essential part of him. Like the prose-poems of *Weeds* in the first half of the 1920s, the poems seem to have supplied the same access to expressiveness in the 1930s, with an important difference. Where many pieces in the published *Weeds* are obscure and thus remain a kind of private language, his classical poems, privately circulated, were not intended to be particularly unfathomable within that circle. It was the genre of classical poetry that ensured this: feelings on dangerous topics could be expressed, but it was not a genre for general transmission. Poetry returned to him and immediately proved useful. After he left Huayuanzhuang, the atmosphere remained tense. The ten months during which Masuda Wataru visited him almost daily were these ten months of 1931, and Masuda remarked that Lu Xun seldom left the house.[77] Under these conditions, the poems were mentally composed and, when the occasion arose, written out. The 1903 quatrain remained private, the Remembrance poem was modernized for readers by providing the context of an essay, and nearly all the other poems remained traditional in all their contexts, that is, they remained handwritten and were shared only by handwritten copy.

The classical poems of a modern prose writer almost by definition constitute an interesting sidebar to his main activities. As it turns out, however, it is their adjunct role that facilitates access to the private dimensions of the writer's thinking, and these were valued by his intimates. They became "a convenient medium by which to express himself . . . later in life," as one critic put it, or, more starkly, "in a time of turbulent civil disorder and darkness, he expressed the deepest grief and sorrow."[78] Lu Xun once said that traditional poems were just an occasional thing for him, but Liu Dajie points out that precisely because he did not write on social occasions or for trivial reasons, when he does write, the results are formidable.[79]

1926 and the Photograph of Self

This section and the next return to a larger time frame stretching before and after 1931. On the strength of the poem's 1931 revival, I propose that we can, by analogy, attach similar significance to the year 1926 and, in the final section, to 1936. In both cases, the poem appears by proxy, in 1926 via the photograph and in 1936 via quatrains by Zhang Binglin published in 1903.

The photograph that was likely the original companion to the poem was made public in 1926 through Lu Xun's agency but without an indication of its short-hair significance. It was included in the first volume of criticism about him, the 1926 *On Lu Xun and His Works*. From there, it entered the public domain and was used in many places, sometimes where an early picture of him made sense, as in a photomontage in a newspaper article about his death, other times printed probably only because it was available. In other words—and this is my point—it circulated without the viewer attaching any meaning to it other than as an available early photograph.

On Lu Xun and His Works is a collection of essays compiled by Tai Jingnong (1902–90) with what must have been Lu Xun's cooperation and advice. We saw Tai in the previous section as the recipient of a horizontal calligraphy of the Remembrance poem. He was one of a dozen youths then in their twenties who worked with Lu Xun in 1925 and 1926, setting up both the magazine *Mangyuan* and the publishing company Unnamed Publishers (Weiming she, which published *On Lu Xun and his Works*). They were frequent visitors to his home and frequent correspondents. In retrospect, 1926 was a good year for such a volume. There was just sufficient criticism to make up such a collection: the very diverse nature of its contents—for example, a high school student writes of Lu Xun's visit to her home—shows that literary criticism was still in its infancy and suggests that nearly every scrap was used. As it turned out, nothing was to be the same after 1926. The volume must have been intended as a major enterprise, for it is a notable specimen of fine publishing, with beautiful typeface and design, generous margins, fine paper, and many pages left blank in the layout to allow articles to start on the recto page. (This 1926 edition can still be found on library shelves.)

In this volume, likenesses of Lu Xun at three points in his life are provided to the reading public. First is a contemporary drawing on the frontispiece, a pencil and charcoal dated 1926 by the artist Tao Yuanqing 陶元慶 (1893–1929), like Tai a frequent visitor in these two years.[80] The 1903 photograph that interests us comes next, while the last one is a photograph from 1909, the year of his return to China.[81] The three likenesses passed into general circulation immediately. For example, the same three were used again, but in chronological order in the 1930 volume *Essays on Lu Xun,* edited by Li Helin, which, unlike this 1926 one, was issued without Lu Xun's participation.[82]

If we think of the 1926 volume as a summing up in which he cooperated, then these portraits are of especial interest since he chose them to mark milestones. Readers, however, only saw a now towering literary figure presented at two points in his youth, without any information on what they were looking at, plus a current drawing. As with the private revival of the poem, in supplying all three images, there was a layer of decision making on Lu Xun's part that was unknown to the reader. There were, for example, other photographs from his early student years in Japan that he did not use. Two surviving ones, very similar to the one chosen, are shown in figures 4.4 and 4.5, each surviving in a print that has a dated inscription on the back.[83] His choice makes it more likely that its identification as the "Hair Cut Short" photograph, which was really made for lack of alternatives, might also be correct. In this 1926 volume, milestones in his life are presented silently in visual form, while the poem that verbalizes one of these visual documents is not revealed at all.

Figure 4.4. Early photograph, from Kōbun Academy period, 1903-04, in light uniform. Courtesy of Beijing Lu Xun Museum.

Figure 4.5. Early photograph, from Kōbun Academy period, in dark uniform, traditionally identified as his graduation photograph. Courtesy of Beijing Lu Xun Museum.

Coda: 1936

In 1936, in the last month of Lu Xun's life, the 1903 poem made a shadowy appearance via an essay on Zhang Binglin (1869–1936), the great revolutionary figure and scholar and his onetime teacher in Japan. Zhang had died that June in Hangzhou, and Lu Xun said that he saw in the papers that the memorial service had been sparsely attended. He wrote a kind of memoir essay entitled "Two or Three Things Regarding Mr. Zhang Taiyan." The next day he began a second essay on "Two or Three Things Brought to Mind by Mr. Zhang Taiyan."[84] (A Zhang Binglin Museum now exists in Hangzhou.) In the event, the second essay, incomplete at the time of his death, became the last work from Lu Xun's hand. It is two poems, in the first essay, that is of interest here. Written by Zhang Binglin and read more than thirty years earlier, the poems form the connection to the 1903 poem I want to bring out in this final section.

The poems are two of four written by Zhang, also a native of Zhejiang, that were published in July 1903 in *Zhejiang Tide*. The first issue of the magazine was published in January of that year by students in Tokyo from Zhejiang province. Xu Shoushang was its editor for a number of issues, and as we saw in chapter 2, Lu Xun published his earliest writings there: "Sparta," "Radium," and "Outline of Chinese Geology." The poems, written while Zhang was himself in prison, all commemorated revolutionary martyrs who had died or later died in Qing dynasty prisons. "To this day I have not forgotten them," Lu Xun writes in 1936. In quoting two of them now, Lu Xun pays tribute, to their two subjects, Zou Rong and Shen Jin, and to Zhang, who, as Lu Xun writes here and elsewhere, had taken immense personal risks throughout the years of his political activism.

Zhang was among the earliest revolutionary activists, his activism beginning in the late 1890s, when reform was still the chief objective.[85] Like the reformers and other revolutionaries, Zhang had several times taken refuge in Japan to escape Qing prosecution. He first went there 1902 (February to July), when, as we saw in chapter 2, he launched the great public relations movement to commemorate the 242nd year of the "loss of the nation" (to the Manchus). Back in Shanghai, he was soon charged with sedition related to articles he wrote for the Shanghai paper *Subao* and imprisoned. This was when *Zhejiang Tide* published his poems from prison. Xu Shoushang remembers that the four poems "drew everyone's notice. Lu Xun especially liked to chant [them]." Xu then quotes two of the poems (not the two that Lu Xun quotes here).[86] On his release in July 1906, a widely celebrated figure, Zhang went to Japan, where he stayed until November 1911. Many students, Lu Xun among them, attracted by his revolutionary stature, attended his lectures on his other deep interest, historical philology. During this time, Lu Xun compiled an anthology of writings by twelve persons. Of the sixty items included, Zhang Taiyan and Zhou Zuoren had the largest number (twenty-five and twelve); he also included six of his own, putting him in third place. All the works had been published between 1903 and 1908 in Chinese periodicals in Japan.[87] Later, in Beijing in 1916, our author, then still known as Zhou Shuren and an official in the Ministry of Education, with others visited Zhang while he was under house arrest. Zhang was not a major character in Lu Xun's life in measurable, visible ways, but he was of recurring importance. In this respect, Zhang's role resembles the 1903 poem.

Here are the two poems Lu Xun quotes in 1936. They may have been quoted from memory because there are a number of (unimportant) variants between this version and the ones published in *Zhejiang Tide*. The first addresses Zou Rong (1885–1905), who later died in prison after a trial for the same sedition case as Zhang. (It was the publication in *Subao* of an article introducing Zou's anti-Manchu *Revolutionary Army* and Zhang's foreword to it that led to their arrests.) Zou received a sentence of two years in prison and Zhang three. The lines as Lu Xun quotes them are:[88]

"From Prison, Presented to Zou Rong" 獄中贈鄒容

獄中吾小弟　被髮下瀛洲　快剪刀除辮　乾牛肉作餱
英雄一入獄　天地亦悲愁　臨命須摻手　乾坤只兩頭

In prison is my younger brother,
With unbound hair he went down to the fabled isles of the east
With swift shears he cut off the queue,
And dried beef was his feed.
When a hero enters prison,
Heaven and earth both lament.
On the edge of death, we should clasp hands
Within the cosmos, just two heads.

The queue of line 3 is surely Zou's.[89] He cut his on board ship on the way to Japan and threw it overboard. Lines 7–8 show that Zhang anticipates death for himself as well.

The second poem is about Shen Jin (Shen Yuxi, 1872–1903), who died of beatings in prison in Beijing. According to Young-tsu Wong, Shen was executed and his death was the reason British authorities did not extradite Zhang and Zou to Qing authorities but tried them in mixed court in Shanghai instead.[90] The poem as Lu Xun quotes it is:

178 : MEMORY, VIOLENCE, QUEUES: LU XUN INTERPRETS CHINA

"From Prison, I Hear that Shen Yuxi Has Been Killed"
獄中聞沈禹希見殺

不見沈生久　　江湖知隱淪　　蕭蕭悲壯士　　今在易京門
螭魅羞爭焰　　文章總斷魂　　中陰當待我　　南北幾新墳

Long had I not seen Master Shen
I knew he was concealed among the rivers and lakes
The soughing winds mourn that valiant man
Who today is at the gate of the capital.
Ghosts and demons do not contend for his flame
His writings overpower me with grief
In the netherworld he must be waiting for me
North and south—how many new graves.

The preparedness for death is emphasized in both poems—as in Lu Xun's quatrain as well. In the poem to Zou, Zhang describes himself and Zou as prepared for death; in the second poem, Shen has already sacrificed his life. Zhang was prepared to die, then and many times later.

Where is Lu Xun's poem in this? Xu recollects his friend's deep admiration for Zhang's poems. They were published in July, and it is tempting to propose a July date for Lu Xun's quatrain. (The militant "Sparta" was published in June.) We can tentatively agree with V. I. Semanov when he writes, "In the newly created journal *Chekiang Tide*, Lu Hsun read poems that Chang Binglin wrote while in prison and under their influence he composed the poem 'Inscription on My Portrait,' promising to give my blood for my native land."[91] We can speculate more confidently about 1936, when we find him looking into his past, selecting elements from it, and putting a narrative frame around the poems of a politically intense time of high ideals and self-sacrifice. In 1936, his 1903 poem is a shadow of the recollections of his earliest years in Japan as they relate to commemorative poems on those who died, Zou Rong at twenty, Shen Yuxi at thirty.

Conclusion

A poem written in 1903 is known to have been of value to its young author by the way he transmitted and preserved it. He also had a photograph whose title of "Photograph with Hair Cut Short" was provided by him. Inscribing the poem on the photograph, he gave the combination to a close friend who, as it turned out, became a lifelong intimate. The poem's attachment to the photograph proves beyond doubt that the act of queue cutting preserved in the photograph, whatever else it might have encompassed, was connected to the poem's ardent political sentiments.

This bundle of patriotism and sentiment might have remained a period piece, an artifact that captures a period of intense feeling and desire for action. Any additional value would have stemmed from readers' awareness that its author became Lu Xun rather than from any information provided by him. As it was, there was no way for someone on the outside to appreciate that the poem and photograph might continue to grow and change in its author's storehouse of memory. The publication in 1926 of the photographic half of the emblem constituted a clue, but only in retrospect could someone guess that if the photograph survived for its subject, so might the poem for its creator.

It took a later incident of political violence to summon forth this old poem, to reveal that after nearly three decades it retained a kind of truth about China and its people that could be revived. The arrests, imprisonment, and executions of Rou Shi and the other writers in 1931 gave an unexpected, terrible pertinence to the poem and to a temperament that was of a remembering kind. The poem's retrieval is magnified by the writing of another poem, one for which Lu Xun took care to provide a major setting, the "Remembrance" essay. If he then talked about the silent quatrain with Qu Qiubai late the next year, we can see that his likely attitude might resemble Qu's reflection on his own youthful poem, "written a lifetime ago." The simultaneous loyalty and distance in this phrase show why the 1903 poem remained private. Qu's light yet serious disclaimer, made to Lu Xun alone, could not be made by Lu Xun to his huge readership, as the history of the poem's use since his death has shown.

In the last month of Lu Xun's life, his memory returned to the original world of the poem's writing, when political activism, or what became the same thing, political violence, was at an early height among Chinese students in Tokyo. He quoted two of Zhang Binglin's poems on those who died in the anti-Qing movements. Zhang was much else, a man of action and physical courage and a philologist who in a venerable tradition studied the classics in a modern light; likewise, Lu Xun's two essays on him were about much else besides the poems. In them, his own poem is present only as a shadow.

The 1903 poem, which has usually been probed for, essentially, its predictive powers about the nascent Lu Xun, turns out to have an ongoing importance. Continuing political violence made the poem continually pertinent. Violence links each of the poem's several surfacings in his life, a fact that can be seen only in retrospect. When Zhang Taiyan's poems that so stirred Lu Xun were published in *Zhejiang Tide* in 1903, Shen was dead, though Zou

Rong was not yet. Lu Xun wrote his quatrain with its acceptance of, indeed desire for, a martyr's death in the final line. Then came Zou's death in 1905. He was twenty. The deaths in Zhang's four poems came at the hands of the Qing authorities. Rou Shi was killed in 1931 under the Republic. By the time he died, there had been many arrests and imprisonments among Lu Xun's circle. Living in Shanghai in the 1930s among activists on the underground Left, there could only be increasing number of victims of official violence against civilians, of violent civilian actions, and of instances of intramural strife.

What Lu Xun did with his grief and his memories was to write. In the case of Rou Shi and the others, he did so with the 1903 quatrain, the Remembrance poem, the poem to Mr. O. E., and then the essay, plus much else. He took action also, trying many paths while they were in prison and doing much after their deaths, but, defined as a writer and with the gifts of a great essayist, writing was both his solace and his weapon. His writings of this time left us with a powerful narrative of innocent suffering that was, as always with him, scrupulously restrained. His scrappy, no-holds-barred fighting style was kept out of elegies. Innocent suffering, however, also fit neatly into the Communist Party's designation of dead as the Five Martyrs. Thus there is a multi-way tension, more traceable here than elsewhere in his life, between what he privately put down on paper, what he was willing to publish, and what the public found in his words, at the time and subsequently.

5

In the Hands of Others, 1934–36: The Visual Materials

The materials of this chapter consist of the visual renditions of Lu Xun's fiction that were made in his lifetime. Portraits of him make up a secondary focus. Compared to the flood that appeared in later decades, these illustrations are few—only forty or so for the fiction plus the work of the highly prolific Liu Xian and a further dozen portraits. Representing an earlier stage than generally seen, they also have an intrinsic interest as early material. Such secondary material may seem to move us away from studying Lu Xun to studying the views of others on him, but this does not have to be the case or is not solely the case. As it happens, with the visual materials we have, unusually, some reactions from him, and this allows a refocus back onto Lu Xun.

Others had been interpreting Lu Xun since the early 1920s, but he had always been a master of silence when it came to his creative writings. The visual materials, however, drew something from him. Many were by young artists committed to social issues in their subject matter, and many worked in the woodblock medium. Neither artist nor medium was something he could pass over. More than that, he acquiesced. What he acquiesced to was the definition—really the redefinition—of his legacy as a belonging on the Left. His criticism of China, which was a profoundly cultural and emotional one, was now recast in specifically political terms. His response and his acquiescence seem to owe something to the importance of the visual medium to him as the carrier of criticism. The materials of this chapter allow us to observe a guarded author as he watched his legacy pass into the hands of others.

In analyzing the multiple connections among the author, the artists, and their subject matter and media, this chapter has two goals relating to Lu Xun.

1. What they add to our knowledge of Lu Xun's attitude toward his writings. That Lu Xun knew relinquishment of control over a work's meanings must occur at publication can be seen in the way he always parried solicitations of his meaning. Adaptations, however, mark a different type of reader control over meaning. They highlight the appropriation of his work as inherited subject matter usable for the adaptors' contemporary purposes. In this chapter, we shall use his responses to understand an aspect of these last years, combining a sense of mortality and the consciousness of legacy. His work, especially salient features of it such as the queue, belonged to the past, known, as he remarked, only to those old enough to have a memory of that past and thus a knowledge of its significance. Yet the adaptations were intended to bring them into the future. Moreover in regard to illustrations, this was a task undertaken, as Lu Xun knew, by young artists who courted arrest and imprisonment by their choice of medium and subject matter. This chapter explores the complex of personal and political considerations as they bear on the depictions of his fiction and his person and reveal how in the final years of his life, which were crowded with events, persons, and activities, can be seen new developments of persistent themes.

2. The role of visual material in the interpretation and transmission of Lu Xun's legacy. In 1934, when the visual portrayals of Lu Xun's creations began to appear, it was some fifteen years and an influential lifetime after the publication of his first work of fiction. The literary-intellectual world had changed a great deal. The personalities and individually derived associations of the first half of the 1920s had regrouped along explicitly stated political lines. This reflected a more polarized political world in which the Nationalists had come to dominate as a national power and had forced underground the activities of its onetime ally, the Communist Party. In the literary world, debate on the nature and goals of literature raged, particularly on the Left. It was on the Left that Lu Xun played a role, in part by his own choice. His very eminence made him a focus of controversy. In Lu Xun's last decade, one debate that was taking place among Communist Party theorists concerned the question of how to reach the masses. Within that important issue, vigorous arguments were devoted to the peculiarly Communist preoccupation with identifying the correct stance and class identity of an author (known as the third-category question), the correct type of protagonist, and more practically, selecting the genres and media that would be comprehensible to the masses. Once the goal became reaching the masses, the focus perforce had to shift, as Marston Anderson put it, from the "literary invention" that preoccupied May Fourth to questions of "literary consumption."[1] The urban elite that created and was created by the New Literature, with its orientation toward Western models and ideas, was no longer the focus of critical interest. Many critics believed that "only a revolution in form could close the gap between the new literature and the masses." By putting the future form of literature in these terms, the debate essentially called into question all the May Fourth cultural enterprises, including Lu Xun's, both in their goals and in their pertinence. Thus the party intellectual Zhou Yang argued that while a character such as Ah Q was common among Chinese peasants before 1911, this was no longer true. Now Ah Q was, in Anderson's elegant paraphrase, "typical only of a former and now fading reality, not of a present or future one." In this new type of search for pertinent form and meaning, it was made clear, a dominant body of works like Lu Xun's was not to serve as a model for the road ahead.

The new, visual materials, which were simultaneously creative and reliant on received subjects, gave evidence that the practice of artists was carried on somewhat separate from the debate among theorists. The illustrations helped change the focus of Lu Xun's fiction from May Fourth iconoclasm to socialist class division, and in this sense they constituted a kind of answer to the debate. The leftist identities of the artists and the links they made between their politics and their art guaranteed this assertion of relevance. To the artists, Lu Xun's fiction was already legacy rather than innovation, so Zhou Yang's criticism was in part irrelevant, but rather than outdated, they saw the fiction as ripe for renewal and reinterpretation. This chapter will trace the multiple factors that politicized the interpretation of Lu Xun's fiction and how its politicization placed it on the Left.

Parallel to the visual materials of this chapter are the verbal materials that use Lu Xun's fiction for further creativity. Zhang Mengyang has gathered and analyzed a dozen works of fiction that allude to "The True Story of Ah Q" in a feature or theme without explicitly naming their model, while Paul Foster has done the same for adaptations onstage and on film, as well as works that announce a filiation in their title (such as "Miss Ah Q").[2] Like the visual materials, however, works that date from before Lu Xun's death are very scarce compared to those of later years.[3]

Although Lu Xun cannot be characterized as willing, the interrelationship of artists, the often violent fates they met, the dominant medium of woodcuts, the subject matter of his own creation, and his own responses all add up to Lilliputian threads that restricted his range of responses to what was happening to his legacy.

The Visual Materials

Surviving illustrations of Lu Xun's fiction begin about 1934, while portraits of him occur a few years earlier. They are not well known in Lu Xun studies or, for these early years, in art history. Some of the artists went on to notable careers either in art or in the art bureaucracy, but their early work, such as is seen in this chapter, has mostly fallen out of sight. They were made in a variety of media. Woodcuts predominate, but there are also line drawings and watercolors. This period also saw the first portraits of the author made by those outside his circle, mostly in woodcuts and sometimes surrounded by vignettes from his fiction, so these will also be included in the materials of this chapter. For many of those artists, "publication" meant that they themselves made the multiple prints and sewed the sheets together. If more conventionally published, they tended to appear in short-lived media such as newspapers, with the originals apparently discarded. The stand-alone sheets sent to publishers also did not survive unless the artist also sent a print to Lu Xun, which often happened when the medium was woodcut, as his active promotion of woodcuts was well known. But perhaps the most important reason for the high percentage of loss was that woodcut art, with its suspect goal of political activism, was often destroyed by Nationalist authorities. Four successive art societies held eight exhibitions between 1931 and 1936, and of these, four were closed down and their art destroyed. In several cases, the artists were arrested. The loss of works of woodcut art was great, and it seems reasonable to suppose that illustrations of Lu Xun's fiction were among them.

The illustrations of 1934–36 constitute a set whose historical circumstances were not to continue beyond 1936. Its endpoint, the year of Lu Xun's death, coincides with far-reaching changes in China's military and political situation. The next year, after more than a decade of increasingly open Japanese aggression, fighting finally broke out between China and Japan, marking the beginning of World War II in Asia. The Japanese, who had occupied Manchuria since 1931, extended their occupation southward and within the year approached as far south as Shanghai. Both existing and developing patterns of cultural production were disrupted. Many artists of all political leanings turned to wartime topics; many artists on the Left in Shanghai departed for the Communist base in Yan'an in the far northwest.[4] There the Communist Party's appropriation of Lu Xun's legacy was institutionally staked out by the 1938 founding of the Lu Xun Academy of Literature and Arts and sealed by several speeches about him delivered by Mao Zedong in 1937, 1940, and twice in 1942. At the Lu Xun Academy in Yan'an and elsewhere, artists took up wartime topics as their mission, as opposed to subject matter from Lu Xun's work.

During the war years, Feng Zikai (1898–1975) and Ding Cong (1915–2009) produced illustrations of Lu Xun's fiction, which they both republished after the war. Unlike the artists of this chapter, both men were already established before the war, Feng since the 1920s. Ding Cong, though very young, was the son of the well-known cartoonist Ding Song and was not struggling to make his name. Feng made three sets of illustrations of "Ah Q" in 1937, 1938, and 1939, but the first set of fifty-four illustrations was lost when the publisher's offices were destroyed in Shanghai. Of the second set, six out of eight sheets were lost in wartime Guangzhou. The two that did survive are said to have been published in *Wencong* in 1938, but I have not found them in those issues.[5] It may be that there are other versions of *Wencong* or the reference may simply be inaccurate. (As we shall see later, Feng also made at least one illustration before 1936, which Lu Xun mentioned but I have not located.) Feng's lost illustrations may resemble his later work—judging from other works, his style was already largely defined by the early 1930s—but there is no way to know for certain. At any rate, in 1949 he published a volume on "Ah Q" and one on several other short stories, so his work predates the official approbation of the 1950s.[6] Figure 5.5 shows a scene from his "Kong Yiji." For his part, Ding Cong had twenty woodcuts published in 1944 in wartime Chongqing, which he republished in 1956 without alteration, and these are widely known.

A major change came after 1949 with a great increase in the role of state control. Illustrations of Lu Xun's work that are familiar from frequent republication nearly all date, at the earliest, to the 1950s, when, as Michael Sullivan remarks, no artist's portfolio would be complete without "the inevitable illustrations for Lu Xun."[7] One example from this period will suffice. This one by Cheng Shifa (1921–2007) shows Ah Q at the moment of his execution (fig. 5.1); it was published in 1961, a year when the eightieth anniversary of Lu Xun's birth resulted in many commemorative works.[8]

All in all, the circumstances that led to the illustrations in this chapter turned out to be exceptional. Moreover, this visual material encapsulated a period in which old and new elements of Lu Xun's influential presence converged. His responses to the illustrations, which make up the other source material for this chapter, are likewise unique in their circumstances. Together

Figure 5.1. Cheng Shifa, Ah Q is executed. From *Yangcheng Evening News*, November 9, 1961.

they constitute an example of the fluidity of the situation, in which many factors came together for a brief period of time within a context of long-term changes in society.

The visual material of this chapter makes up one portion of the larger story of new art in China, which, like literature, turned in the first decades of the twentieth century to Western techniques, materials, and subject matter. The work considered here—nearly all drawings and woodcuts, nearly all black and white—constitutes only two of the many media that attracted artists, each of which has its individual history and major figures. The larger story of this art is, for example, the subject of Sullivan's *Art and Artists of Twentieth-Century China*, one of whose threads, politically committed artworks, is taken up in this chapter. Xiaobing Tang's *Origins of the Chinese Avant-Garde* specifically concerns the medium of the modern art woodcut, "the avant-garde," and within his framework the materials of this study constitute a subfield that takes Lu Xun as its topic. As Tang shows, a full account of the woodcut needs to begin with the history of new art in general, the founding of art schools, their evolution into the art institutes known today, the journals they published, and theories they propounded.[9] For the prewoodcut years, Tang pays particular attention to leftist publications that used black-and-white graphics that emulated woodblock prints. From this he traces the separating out of a stream of artists focused on woodcuts in the late 1920s and Lu Xun's large and varied role in this development. The illustrations analyzed in this chapter coincide with the most active period of woodcuts before the war against Japan, while the emphasis will be on their content, their makers, and their makers' relation to Lu Xun, with their art historical contexts discussed only as necessary.

The material falls into three groups (see appendix B with thumbnail reproductions). The first group consists of fifteen works that were published in 1934 in *Theater* (*Xi*) to accompany the installment publication of a playscript adaptation of Lu Xun's fiction made by Yuan Muzhi, who is a prominent figure in histories of 1930s film as director, stage and later film actor, and scriptwriter. *Theater* was a weekly supplement of *Zhonghua ribao*, the newspaper of Wang Jingwei's reform wing of the Nationalists, and was published in Shanghai from April 1926 to August 1945. The supplement's editors were the playscript's author Yuan Muzhi (1909–78) and Tian Han (1898–1968), a playwright, Communist Party member, and author of the lyrics for "March of the Volunteers." The mottoes printed on the masthead of every issue were *dazhonghua, dazhong yuyan* ("massification, language of the masses"), open declarations of both its goals and its leftist allegiance. The playscript, which has the title "The True Story of Ah Q," began in the first issue of *Theater* on August 19, 1934, and ended before it was complete on December 30, 1934, with the eighteenth installment (twentieth issue), about one-third of the way through Ah Q's saga. It is more than the work "Ah Q," however, for it incorporates the plots and characters of all the other short stories that are set in the locations of Luzhen, S-cheng, and Weizhuang.

Illustrations were solicited with the third installment and began with the fourth. They were published from September 9 to December 30, 1934, fifteen illustrations by thirteen artists, and are reprinted here for the first time. They represent a variety of media—pen and ink, watercolor, oils, woodcuts, line drawings, and drawings with gray washes. As printed, the illustrations vary in size from 2 x 3 to 3 x 4 inches. Eight are of Ah Q, and two are of Kong Yiji, while the remainder consist of one each of Old Master Zhao; the Successful Provincial Candidate; the young nun, also from "Ah Q"; the peasant Runtu from "Hometown"; and the tavern owner from "Storm." The connections of the supplement's artist contributors are with each other, the supplement's editor, and the editor's activities in film and onstage more than with Lu Xun, although connections with Lu Xun exist also. Only five of the thirteen artists had direct contact with Lu Xun: Ma Guoliang; Zhang E; Xu Xingzhi; Ye Lingfeng, who was an antagonist; and Chen Tiegeng whom I list with the second group.

The second group consists of everything else I found relating to the fiction. As more material is discovered, the group will become larger. Among the artists, Liu Xian has by far the largest number of works: 3 fascicles of *lianhuanhua* (serial images) of 3 short stories and a fascicle of the prose poems *Weeds*, for a total of 106 prints. Figures for the remaining artists are of a much smaller order of magnitude: Chen Tiegeng had the next largest number at 10 (7 of which have not survived), then Wei Mengke with 6 (5 of which have not been located), and so on. Nearly everyone has surviving artworks on other subjects than those considered here. For the woodcuts in this second group, a valuable source is the 1991 *Banhua jicheng* (Catalog of Woodcuts). Its five volumes collect and reproduce all the woodblock prints that were in Lu Xun's possession at his death (though not art in other media).[10] They came from purchases and artists who sent their work to Lu Xun. *Catalog of Woodcuts* is incomplete in that it does not have some woodcuts he is known to have once possessed, in some cases because he had sent them on to publishers, and those not published are lost. For example, Lu Xun sent the 10 prints by Chen Tiegeng to *Theater*, and only the 3 that were published survive (the adaptation was never finished). Another example is five cartoons by Wei Mengke that were commissioned and sent to Edgar Snow for his anthology of short fiction, *Living China*, but not used when "Ah Q" was cut for reasons of space. So far,

I have not located the drawings. Other illustrations have been located on a case-by-case basis, and these are noted as they are discussed.

The third group is made up of portraits of the author, many by artists who had not yet met Lu Xun. (*Catalog of Woodcuts* is the source of many of these portraits.) Since many portraits contain little sketches from the fiction in the margins and some illustrators of the fiction also made portraits, there is overlap between the second and third groups. In addition, in these two groups nearly everyone either began with a connection to Lu Xun or created one as a result of his artwork. These categories are open-ended and will grow as more works are discovered. There are illustrations Lu Xun writes about that I have not been able to locate, and conversely, illustrations have been reproduced in publications from China that I have not been able to identify further but belong to this 1934–36 time period.

A word is needed concerning the stylistic level of the illustrations. Earlier I mentioned that the materials of this chapter are a subset of the story of art in the early decades of the twentieth century. With respect to woodcuts, I should additionally note that, as is evident even in the thumbnail reproductions in appendix B, the works here are fairly unskilled, whereas a history of woodcuts in this period would include works that show a much higher level of skill, for example, Li Hua's (1907–94) "Roar, China!" also from 1934 (fig. 5.2). Lu Xun was aware of the great range of skill levels. Writing to Jin Zhaoye, who was organizing the 1935 Coordinated National Woodcut Exhibit, he named Li Hua and together with Luo Qingzhen as "two in China whose skills are high."[11] (He had received woodblock works from both men.) By contrast, Liu Xian, the most prolific among the artists with whom we are concerned and whose work soon was to reach a high level, was now at a much rawer stage. Even though he has four fascicles of woodcuts, and one of them, the *lianhuanhua* "Kong Yiji," was published by the magazine *Intellectual Life* (*Dushu shenghuo*), he was just beginning to learn.

Figure 5.2. Li Hua, *Roar, China!* From *Catalog of Woodcuts*.

According to one biography, he took up woodcut upon witnessing the plight of the many refugees who flooded Beijing following the Japanese invasion of Manchuria (September 18, 1931).[12] He would have been sixteen years old at the time. The implication must be that he was initially self-taught. A typical work by him at this time is given here, a frame from "Kong Yiji" in which the children scamper away from Kong after he gives them some of his aniseed beans (fig. 5.3). Liu left in 1935 to study in Japan and became a well-known established artist. A second example of an artist still learning his craft is Cao Bai, who was newly enrolled in the Hangzhou Art Academy. Figure 5.4 is his "Lu Xun and Xianglin sao," from "New Year's Sacrifice," in which the protagonist (Cao Bai takes him to be Lu Xun) meets a former servant, now a beggar. The austerity of Lu Xun's personality can be seen in his response. In writing to the young Cao Bai about another of his woodcuts, "Lu Xun" (fig. 5.25), he gave a frank opinion in a way that nonetheless was not discouraging.

> Your woodcut arrived today. In terms of skill, it is, of course, not mature. But I want to preserve this woodcut because it is the work of a young person who has experienced hardships.[13]

The "hardships" are Cao Bai's imprisonment and interrogation after a search of his room at Hangzhou Art Academy turned up "incriminating" evidence. Of Cao Bai's friend Liqun, who as Lu Xun knew had also recently been released from prison, he employs the same dispassionate tone, placing their common objective in the goals of art. Writing to Cao Bai, he said of a Liqun print Cao sent, "It comes

Figure 5.3. Liu Xian, a scene from "Kong Yiji," *Intellectual Life*, 1935. Courtesy of Harvard Yenching Library.

Figure 5.4. Cao Bai, a depiction of Lu Xun and Xianglin sao in "New Year's Sacrifice." Source: *Catalog of Woodcuts*.

alive, but there are some faults in the way it looks. This comes from needing to undertake further studies of the human figure."[14] Skill, however, was not Lu Xun's sole interest, nor is it ours. Greater than the question of skill is to see in what manner Lu Xun's works survive into the 1930s. That the distribution of skills in our material is skewed in comparison to other parts of the art world is perhaps a sign of Lu Xun's continued influence on the developing consciousness.

Material by Lu Xun

Directly relevant material by Lu Xun is scattered and in ephemeral genres (letters, diary entries), short pieces (prefaces to collections and exhibition catalogs), and incidental remarks made in the course of essays that primarily concern other topics. Regarding letters, the pertinent ones form a small subset of the many letters that are written to artists. His diary for 1931–36 records a total of 171 letters to young artists (123 survive), of which 73 come in 1934 alone.[15] The letters reply in detail to artists who sought his views, and they give help on many practical points. In other letters, he asks his correspondents to help with purchasing and exchanging European and Soviet woodcuts. Letters concerning illustrations of his fiction are much fewer. The longest items are two open letters he wrote to the editors of *Theater*, both in November 1934. A related item from the pages of *Theater* is a description by someone of a lunch with Lu Xun and others, recounted in extenso on October 28 (installment 10). Also notable are five letters he wrote to Liu Xian, varying in length from several paragraphs to two lines.[16]

In general, the materials on his side show that his relations with the artists did not have the intimacy of those with his literary disciples. Two of the artists in this chapter, Chen Tiegeng and Zhong Buqing, were participants in the 1931 woodcut workshop. Three were among the eight included in the 1934 *Muke jicheng* (Record of Wood Engravings), the only volume of Chinese woodcuts that Lu Xun published. They are Chen Tiegeng again, Liu Xian, and Luo Zhenqing. He knew many only by correspondence (Liqun, Lai Shaoqi) and met others only once (Wang Junchu, Cao Bai), but his sense of connection and responsibility was very deep. He wrote prefaces for exhibitions and individual fascicles, while letters he wrote quickly appeared in print as evidence of his support, as he must have known would happen. His presence was always sought at exhibits of art woodcuts, where it was an encouraging confirmation to the artists in their dangerous endeavors. Careerist motives on the part of the artists might be in the mix, as was also the case with the young writers who approached him, but many of his admirers were young and dedicated, and their chosen type of art had no financial value. In a 1934 letter to Yao Ke on commissioning artwork for Edgar Snow's proposed anthology, he said that few were left from the time of the woodcut workshop, for most had starved, been arrested, or been forced to change their direction.[17]

The story that the visual material tells is a complicated one. The highly politicized nature of literary and artistic activity in Shanghai was increased by the unpredictable violence employed in its suppression. Lu Xun's writings were placed squarely in the path of political pertinence by this situation. With regard to the artists, his responsibility was complex. By the 1930s, Lu Xun's fiction had long been a common intellectual reference point. Now its translation into a visual medium intensified this phenomenon while further complicating it. For some time, the educated public had confidently employed the fiction's characters, settings, and language as intelligible allusions in criticisms of the Chinese character and society. The rendering of this widespread consensus in visual form had the potential to create a wider audience, but it also brought with it issues common to the adaptations of classics, even modern classics. Especially notable are competing ideas of what constituted faithfulness to the original, meaning not only the original literary work but the original world—Weizhuang and other settings—that he had sought to capture. In this changeover in media, Lu Xun was also a participant, so that the process of shaping his legacy contained much that is reflexive.

Lu Xun Responds: Particularity and Universality

The depiction of Lu Xun's writings in visual form raises questions of both particularity and universality, both of which bear on the survivability of his legacy, as Lu Xun was aware. Historically, these contrary qualities have proved to be necessary for both book and illustrations. The questions of how much and in what proportion must be separately addressed by each creator. For illustrations, initially, the new considerations were most obviously about particulars. Many things now needed to be known that did not have to be exactly known about the written work. An important question is what do things look like? What does a wall, the corner of a room, or a table look like in that place, in that time? What about clothing, shoes, hats? Or, on a larger scale, a river village in the south? As for the people, what do the characters look like? Of pertinence to this study, Lu Xun specifically raises the questions of what queues look like. And what does Ah Q look like? Artists needed information on these points, even if they were to ultimately use a highly stylized approach (although none do in our 1930s material except for Zhang E's portrayal of the nun in fig. B.6). In 1934–36, the passage of time and the urbanized life of artists constituted obstacles to knowing the answers from firsthand knowledge, while individual observational ability and artistic judgment also came into play. Lu Xun's response to inaccuracy ranges from tolerance to exactitude. One sees in them, on the one hand, his and Zhou Zuoren's careful attention to accurate detail and, on the other hand, a sensible clarity about adaptations.

There is an infinite number of factual items to be rendered visually, and many gradations of accuracy are likely to be acceptable, although some choices must remain puzzling. Fan Zeng (b.1938), well known for his work in historical, dynastic-period subject matter, brought some of the same aesthetics to his treatment of the determinedly grim settings of Lu Xun's stories. To take one illustration from his portrayal of "Medicine," in a scene in which the poverty-stricken parents are coaxing their son to drink a medicinal broth, the table and cabinet in the room are improbably ornate, there are a great many generously cut lengths of cloth in the room, in the manner of a historical painting.[18] At the opposite end of the spectrum is the disclaimer of Feng Zikai, who declared that, although his hometown in Zhejiang province was no more than two or three hundred *li* from Shaoxing, the scenery, clothing, and customs he knew were not the same as in Ah Q's village, meaning that he laid no claim to accuracy.[19]

This is being a stickler carried to the extreme. It is certainly true that in the countryside many variations are to be found in local cultures over even a small distance, but what seems at stake here is a story of dueling exactitudes between two giants in their respective spheres. It began with some remarks Lu Xun made that were reported in *Theater*. The two men had been introduced in 1927 at Feng's request by the artist Tao Yuanqing a month after Lu Xun's arrival in Shanghai.[20] Earlier I mentioned the several batches of illustrations Feng made in the war years that were mostly lost to battle flames. Judging from the lunch conversation reported in *Theater* (October 28, 1934), Feng had made at least one illustration of Lu Xun's fiction while Lu Xun was alive. Many remarks by Lu Xun were quoted in the newspaper account. The part pertinent to Feng began when Lu Xun said that *Theater*'s adaptation gave the sense of a grander Weizhuang than was true. He brought up, as an example of grandness in general, wineshop signs. "In Shaoxing," he said,

> we do not really have such grand wineshops. The signs would not have such elegant sentiments as "Lingering Evocations of Li Bai" 太白遺風. A sign would more likely say, "Price is Firm" 不二價.

It turns out that his example of "Lingering Evocations of Li Bai" was not plucked from thin air, for he continued:

> The other day I saw Feng Zikai's illustration [or illustrations]—a workman was leaning against the counter drinking and next to him were written the words "Lingering Evocations of Li Bai."

Evidently he was merely speaking as thoughts occurred to him, for these words in turn caused him to wonder whether the saying was standard elsewhere (and therefore Feng was in fact accurate): "Can it be that wineshops in other provinces have this saying?"

But the damage had been done. The question of accuracy in local color had been raised by the great man himself and reported in print. Feng's 1939 comment that customs in his hometown three hundred *li* away were very different, though made after Lu Xun's death, was probably still a response to this. When he illustrated "Kong Yiji" again in 1950 (plus seven other stories), there was a silent change: in a similar scene, where Kong Yiji leans against the counter drinking, the sign that hangs next to him reads "All Elegant People Come Here" (fig. 5.5). One wonders whether this sign, also quite refined, could be more accurate. Lu Xun's remark must have still stung, for in the same preface, Feng noted that back in 1939, before he sent off his wartime "Ah Q," he showed it to two friends who were Shaoxing natives and one of them, "who had some art skills," drew for him a *wupeng* boat presumably more accurate in detail than his own.[21] This almost fetishistic accuracy is fed by remarks from Lu Xun, whose predisposition to exactitude can be found even in our limited sample.

On the other hand, it is not always essential to get the details right. As Lu Xun wrote of one of the illustrations of "Ah Q" he received from Wei Mengke, "The fastenings are on the wrong side, but no matter, it does not need to be corrected."[22] (In fact, this is an interesting oversight in artistic observation, since as far back as Confucius, clothing had been fastened on the right).[23]

Figure 5.5. Feng Zikai, from "Kong Yiji." The vertical placard reading "All Elegant People Come Here" is over his right shoulder. Above the doorway is the name of the wineshop, Xianheng hao, itself rather elegant, and the four words to the right and left make a propitious saying, "May Flowers Bedeck Your Later Years." Source: *Illustrations of Lu Xun's Fiction,* 1950.

One instance where he did mind concerned Ah Q's hat. He said of an illustration in *Theater* that it was all wrong, that Ah Q's would have been a kind called *zhanmao*, made of felt with a turn-up of an inch around the edge. Instead, *Theater* showed a *guapimao* on him.[24] This would have been a reference to Ye Lingfeng's illustration (fig. 5.6). The problem might have been that the inaccuracy was distracting: a *guapimao*, made of satin segments pieced together, as in Ye's drawing, is worn by gentry. The incongruity, of the same kind as for the scene from "Medicine" discussed earlier, says something about the artists' attitude to the connection between observation and rendition.

Some of this exactness is informative about the boundaries Lu Xun set for interpretation. For example, he says of Liu Xian's Ah Q, "As for Ah Q's appearance, to my mind, his thuggish look (*liumangqi*) should be softened a bit."

> Where I come from, if someone is that thuggish looking, he could eat for free, he would not need to work for anyone. Old Master Zhao might be such a one.[25]

This is an interesting distinction in gradations of bullying. Ah Q was alert to chances to take advantage of those weaker than himself, whether the young nun, who was always vulnerable, or Whiskers Wang, who was momentarily vulnerable. Evidently, however, Lu Xun did not think him up to Old Master Zhao's level. By contrast, he is reported to have said of a 1927 cover done for George Leung's translation that Ah Q was "more cunning than this, he was not so honest-looking."[26] What thuggishness Lu Xun saw in Liu's portrayals is worth considering. Here is a frame that seems to fit the description of being too thuggish (fig. 5.7). Then again, the problem may be a question of skill: Ah Q's heft may result from the artist's attempt to show a seated figure, for his Seven-Pounds is seated and almost identically portrayed (fig. 5.8) and he is not a domineering figure.

Figure 5.6. Ye Lingfeng, Ah Q. The white lines make clear the headgear's construction and hence its material. *Theater*, 1934.

It was Lu Xun's custom in general to raise objections on points of factual accuracy, but nearly always it was an entry point to other issues, in this case the question of whether his work would survive to interest a generation for whom the settings and details would be solely historical questions. The primary concern is not with authenticity in depiction, or with ascertaining the amount or type of accuracy needed to achieve authenticity. Rather visual representations highlight issues of universality and thus enable us to use his comments on accuracy and authenticity as a proxy for his thoughts about related issues.

Two opposing issues are involved: particulars and universality. Rather than how much detail must exist to remain connected to the original inspiration, the question is what changes are needed to make it universal for a different time or place? We see from Lu Xun's comments that he was very much alive to the potential for updates and modifications. Several times he suggested equivalents that extended his fiction's relevance to the world outside Shaoxing. For example, he suggests to Yang Muzhi that he be flexible in staging his adaptation, saying that if Luzhen is moved north, then Seven-Pounds could be a carter instead of a boatman. In another case, he gives a pass to a northern feature, a mule cart, in one of Liu Xian's illustrations (fig. 5.9). "We don't have those where I come from," he writes, but then adds: "But that's all right. Anyway, it makes me think that if Kong Yiji had been born in the north, it would have been in such a setting."[27] He does draw the line at motorized transportation, however. Of one of Chen Tiegeng's illustrations, he says, deadpan, "It is far from the truth. How could there be a motorized vehicle for Ah Q at that time?"[28] Unfortunately for us, this is one of the sheets by Chen that has not survived.

Figure 5.7. Liu Xian, Ah Q, possibly a pugnacious look. Source: *Catalog of Woodcuts*.

Figure 5.8. Liu Xian, Seven-Pounds, similarly seated, similar look. Source: *Catalog of Woodcuts*.

Even for Ah Q, who might seem a quintessentially country type, he suggests modern, urban equivalents.

> In Shanghai, one can probably find Ah Q's type among the rickshaw pullers or the cartpullers, but not looking like a thug.[29]

This is especially interesting because the most organized attacks on Lu Xun had taken the form of asserting that Ah Q was a figure of the past, but his two letters to *Theater* show a comprehensive understanding of the limits of both language and visual content.

Figure 5.9. Liu Xian, a scene from "Kong Yiji" with a (Red Cross?) cart in the background. Note also the clothing fastened on the left. Source: *Catalog of Woodcuts.*

Given his temperament, it is all the more important to see that Lu Xun in fact was not a stickler for detailed fidelity. He was willing to transpose the story to a different setting and time. To him, the question was how writing can transcend or escape its fixity in local color in order to retain its symbolic value. It turns out that one feature that was not easily amenable to alteration or updating was the queue and together with it, its most prominent wearer, Ah Q.

"Not a Single Queue Looks Naturally Grown"

Once Lu Xun's writings became subjects for illustration, the inhabitants of Weizhuang, Luzhen, and S—cheng, who populate his best-known stories, all had to be visualized. Since these works are set in the pre-Republican years, queues are inevitably a feature. Even when they are not a thematic point of the story, they constitute a feature of the decayed atmosphere that an illustration needs to capture. In addition to "Storm," "A Story about Hair," and "Ah Q" (the stories of chapter 3), works requiring the queue would additionally include "Kong Yiji," "Medicine," "White Light," "Village Opera," and probably "Tomorrow," as well as the recollections that take up part of "Hometown" and "Upstairs at the Tavern." The characters in these works had become standard symbols in the discourse on China's situation. Yet their queues are the least universal of features. The most salient feature of these characters is one from a bygone era, one that is difficult to substitute for and difficult to update. What happens, then, when they are to be portrayed?

Let us begin with some striking comments from Lu Xun on the portrayals he had seen.

> I also like to look at pictures (*hua*), especially depictions of people. In those by Chinese, whether of long-gowned people, or those in short clothing, I have never, that I can remember, seen a queue. Among drawings by westerners, [I see] stout fellows with skewed features, women with fat legs, but to my memory I have have never seen a queue. Then recently I saw some pen-and-ink drawings and also some woodcuts of Ah Q, and now I can say that I have met with the queue in art. Not a single one looks naturally grown.[30]

A long passage concludes with a damning summation: "Not a single one looks naturally grown." As Lu Xun must have been well aware, the depiction of queues raises questions about the survival and transmission of his work, and in drawing attention to this, he draws attention to the narrowness of his appeal.

What depictions could he have had in mind in making this sweeping remark? This essay was completed on December 17, 1934. By then he would have seen what in the event were all the installments in *Theater* except Zhang Yunhong's portrait of the tavern keeper in "Storm", and he would have received the works of two of the artists from the second group: by then, Liu Xian had sent him all four fascicles, and he had Chen Tiegeng's ten woodcuts.[31] As noted earlier, he would also have seen Feng Zikai's illustration(s). But he would not yet have seen, for example, Lai Shaoqi's or Cao Bai's work. In this passage, he mentions two media, pen-and-ink drawings and woodcuts. Feng's works are in brush and ink, as, presumably, are Wei Mengke's missing works (judging by his surviving one), so neither falls into the group panned by Lu Xun. The ones in *Theater* are mostly pen and ink, while Liu Xian's and Chen Tiegeng's are woodcuts, so these are our possibilities. In *Theater*, if we restrict ourselves to depictions of Ah Q, which is what Lu Xun mentions, then Hong Zhenglun (fig. 5.10) and Ye Lingfeng (fig. 5.6) could be included in his stricture. Both show small vestigial pigtails rather like Kang Youwei's when he was growing his out. From the category of woodcuts, Liu Xian's work offers many examples of improbable queues, in his case because of the way they perch on the head. Figure 5.11 is a detail from a scene late in the novella in which Ah Q is striding through the streets shouting "revolution!" The queue can be seen from several angles: Ah Q from the back and the two gentry from the front, one bareheaded, one beneath a cap. So these are the probable objects of the author's criticism. In a conversation reported in *Theater*, Lu Xun said that some drew the queue too low and it needed to be moved up a bit because the shaved parts went all around the head.[32] This remark certainly applies to the examples discussed above.

What Lu Xun says next is equally interesting. He seems to soften this sweeping dismissal with a speculation, but in doing so he raises more questions.

> Yet when you think about it, it is not so strange. A young person of twenty or so today would have been born when it was already the Republic, and even someone of thirty would have personal knowledge of the period of the queue only up to the age of four or five. Of course, such a person could not know the fine points of the queue to any great degree.

He said much the same thing in the conversation reported in *Theater*. It is true that the ages of many of the artists bear him out. Chen Tiegeng was born 1908, Huang Miaozi in 1913, and Liu Xian in 1915, so Huang and Liu were

Figure 5.10. Hong Zhenglun, *Ah Q. Theater*, 1934.

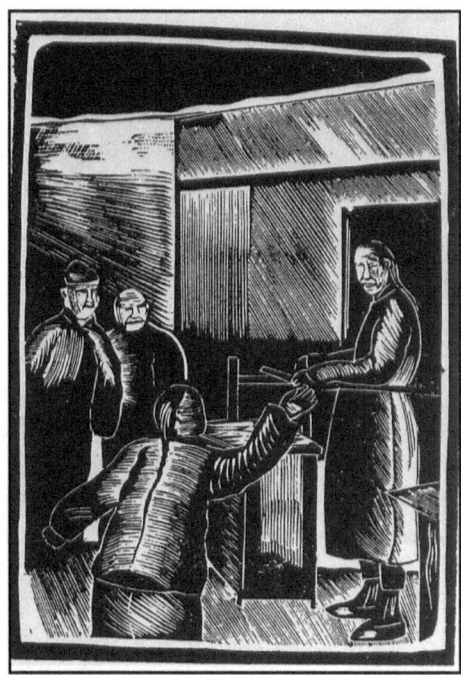

Figure 5.11. Liu Xian, several views of queues in a scene from "Ah Q." Source: *Catalog of Woodcuts*.

born after the Republic's founding, and Chen would have been less than four at the time. But if we accept this reasoning, then many things are condemned to be depicted by people who a priori cannot depict it. After all, the number of people personally acquainted with the look of the queue can only dwindle.

Feng Zikai makes a comment like Lu Xun's in his 1950 preface to his illustrations. As we saw earlier, parts of it seem to be a retrospective reply to Lu Xun on the question of regional accuracy, but in this comment, when he must also have had Lu Xun in mind, he agrees with him.

> In these short stories is seen mostly the world of the end of the Qing dynasty. The men have their queues trailing behind them, the women all have small bound feet. At the time of the Republican revolution, I was fifteen, I had lived as a Qing dynasty person for fourteen or fifteen years, and even now when I close my eyes, I can readily recall the world of the end of the Qing dynasty. So for me to make these illustrations is much more convenient than for those who are less than forty years old.[33]

Feng is correct that his illustrations are convincing, and certainly he can recall the Qing dynasty, but there are many possible replies to the comments of these two men who want to link the two points.

It is clear that, on the one hand, Lu Xun knew that in artistic terms this was not a sensible argument. He was not trying to make a defensible remark. On the other hand, he liked the idea of sounding as though his time had passed, that soon the queue was going to be a total unknown. To take his first point, obviously it is possible for an artist to render things with which he or she has no firsthand experience. Observations Lu Xun made elsewhere show that he was well aware that the problem is not solely a question of knowledge or even skill. He notes, for instance, that in some woodcuts, faces meant to be Chinese are Western looking.[34] That is, faces for which the models are all wholly familiar to the artist turn out to be Western looking. In one clear instance, a work by Xu Shiquan (fig. 5.12), the subject is Lu Xun himself. Xu made it while enrolled in a woodcut class in Germany, so perhaps that is a factor. A later example from 1948 is a mother keeping watch by a sickbed (fig. 5.13). There are many more examples in *Catalog of Woodcuts*. The Western look of these is owing to the opposite kind of problem Lu Xun attributes to the queue: in the adoption of a new visual language, artists were consulting published Western models more than life. As E. H. Gombrich argued in detail, to draw something for which one has no schema is hard: depiction is not a matter of looking at something and rendering it faithfully, for what one depicts is dependent on what one has learned to see.

A particularly telling example Gombrich gave was the rhinoceros, whose depictions were influenced by the armored body Albrecht Dürer gave it long after artists had access to more accurate information.[35] In the case of these Western-looking faces, Western models had a stronger effect on the eye and hand than the faces all around one.

The second point here is that sometimes Lu Xun liked to sound out of date. Apparently by the 1930s, queues were as peculiar in Chinese eyes as they had been a few decades earlier in non-Chinese eyes. Only someone with a long, carefully nourished memory could tell you what it had been like and why there were even pitched battles over it. When we consider aspects of Lu Xun's writings in his final years with this thought in mind, we can see how at this point his long-standing personal inclination to look back shows the limits of his psychological preference for memory. In the preface to *Call to Arms*, memory was a personal trait that was also able to serve the future, for it acted as a weapon to validate the stories' rejection of tradition. Now, by contrast, to have a memory of that long-ago time serves chiefly to emphasize his solitary position. This is not the only time he portrays himself as recalling an era and its queues that no one can remember any longer. Another instance is in a rueful self-portrait in what was his final essay, written days before his death.[36] The essay begins with the arrival of newspapers that morning. When he saw their date, October 10, he realized with surprise, he said, that it was again National Day: "Nationalist China has already survived for a quarter of a century, how quickly time has flown!" Saying so, he touched the back of his head, his

Figure 5.12. Xu Shiquan, Lu Xun. *Shuqin*, 1933.

Figure 5.13. Li Hua, *The Child is Sick*. Source: *Liu Xian muke xuanji*.

customary gesture, he said, when surprised or thinking. Why so? This was the gesture, he explained, of someone of his generation, and a gesture only his generation could understand, for he was feeling the place where his queue had been, feeling the strange freedom from the queue. In other words, he was an out-of-date man with out-of-date habits. And in case this is not clear enough, he follows up with another fuddy-duddy habit: instead of the more current phrase "twenty-five years," he still uses "quarter of a century," excusing himself by saying it seems to bring out more clearly the largeness of the number.

For people of Lu Xun's age and disposition, the queue was a reality by its absence. Ah Q was intended to transcend his Weizhuang setting so as to discomfit the reader with identification.[37] But adaptations that require depiction of a feature whose meaning has been lost may quickly point up the limits of his universality from another direction. This was a question Lu Xun addressed in his second letter to *Theater*.[38]

"What Does Ah Q Look Like?"

What does Ah Q look like? When he existed solely in words, this question did not have to be answered in a detailed way. The idea of Ah Q was more vivid than the specifics. He is not explicitly described, but some information does come up incidentally, as when he "takes a break from his labors," presenting "a bare torso, and scrawny, lazy" figure. The reader gathers that he is an unimpressive specimen. His queue is part of this general lack of stature even though logically speaking every male had a queue then. In undertaking an illustration, however, the visual reality of the verbally described character must be conceived beyond these few words. What *does* an Everyman such as Ah Q look like? What *should* he look like?

Artistically speaking, this answer is an interpretative decision to be made by the individual illustrator, perhaps based to some degree on historical knowledge if he is inclined. But it is also of special interest when raised by the author and, as we shall see, it is partially answered by the author. In his letter, Lu Xun begins with a specific criticism about the appearance of Ah Q in *Theater*. He says that the various Ah Q depicted were *tai tebie* 太特別 and *guliguguai* 古里古怪. Both adjectives are interesting: *tai tebie* means too unusual; and *guliguguai* means odd, too idiosyncratically conceived. He did not specify which of the portrayals of Ah Q he thought "too unusual," but four depictions of Ah Q were published in *Theater* before this letter was written on November 18. The four are by Hong Zhenglun, Lu Shaofei, Ye Lingfeng, and Xu Xingzhi. We saw Hong's and Ye's earlier. Here are Lu's (fig. 5.14) and Xu's (fig. 5.15). As to which of these four seem "too idiosyncratic," perhaps it is the power of suggestion, but only Lu Shaofei's (with the long pipe) seems possibly exempt from this charge. Earlier, we saw Hong's and Ye's as possible examples of unlikely looking queues, and we further saw that the headgear Ye gave Ah Q was criticized as being not the right kind. As for Xu's, certainly everything about it looks too idiosyncratic.

In the same passage, Lu Xun offers some thoughts about Ah Q that are somewhat perplexing. Ah Q, he wrote, is "in my view, about thirty, very ordinary in appearance, the look of a farmer, slow-witted, but also with some of the cunning of a drifter." What is one to make of this information? On the one hand, an author's views are of inestimable interest. And in general it is easy to see his meaning: "very ordinary in appearance" and "the look of a farmer" are archetypal traits, while "the cunning of a drifter" supplies the element that differentiates Ah Q sufficiently from the others for him to be Ah Q. On the other hand, the suggestion that Ah Q is "about thirty," even from the author, seems overly specific, not "ordinary" enough. Yet Lu Xun offered this even though he was not being cornered into a physical description of Ah Q. Perhaps in the China of the 1910s and 1920s, "about thirty" was an age that was not *tai tebie*.

To continue with the two letters to *Theater*, in rejecting *too unusual, too odd*, Lu Xun shows to what degree he conceives of Ah Q in universal terms. Indeed, besides this comment on Ah Q's appearance, he has more to say that pertains to the issue of universality. In particular, he asks the question of

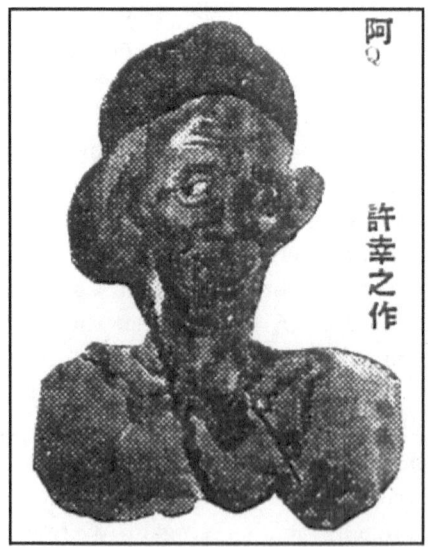

Figure 5.14. Lu Shaofei, *Ah Q*. From *Theater*, 1934.   Figure 5.15. Xu Xingzhi, *Ah Q*. From *Theater*, 1934.

what language Ah Q speaks in a stage adaptation. His concern about finding a workable oral form of communication here has parallels with his interest in finding usable visual communication in his letter to Liu Xian, an abstract question but also one that bears on the future of his work. With neither language nor depiction does he assume that adaptation into an oral (or visual) form automatically equals comprehensibility. The orality of staging did not in itself remove the problem of accessibility that is posed by a written text in an overwhelmingly illiterate society. What is accessible about spoken language? he asked. In fact, spoken language is not universal at all. The language of Shaoxing, he pointed out, would be scarcely comprehensible by any audience beyond Shaoxing, and furthermore, in a given region, there were also more language distinctions up and down the social scale. His suggested solution was to use traditional resources. He understood that the highly stylized repertory of the traditional genres of opera or sung drama, with their easily recognized character types, was more easily updated than the seemingly approachable, realistic-seeming "spoken drama" of Western provenance. The language that is more readily comprehensible on the stage, Lu Xun suggests, is the stylized speech of traditional sung drama in which each repertory role is assigned a level of language.

> In Shaoxing plays, the upper classes speak *guanhua* [Mandarin] and the lower classes, *tuhua* [local dialect], which is to say, the hero, heroine, and male supporting character speak Mandarin and the comic speaks the local dialect. The reason is not just class distinction: satire [the province of the comic] must be in the local dialect so that local audience can understand it. If you are performing this play in Shaoxing, all the characters can use Shaoxinghua because their speech can be [further] distinguished by style, complexity, etc. But if it is performed for audiences elsewhere, then this playscript is weak or even completely useless.[39]

Another possibility, Lu Xun suggests, is for the basic script to be in *baihua* (standard vernacular) and then variations on the adaptation can be made, so that when "one goes to a particular county or village, then this script would just be a basis, and its standard vernacular can all be changed into that locale's regional dialect." He makes the further suggestion that it is "not just the language, even the setting, the names, all can be changed, so that the audience feels it is more true to life."

These suggestions on making major changes show Lu Xun's readiness to relinquish the issues of verisimilitude that had fascinated him at the time of writing "Ah Q." At that time, in 1921–22, he had a great interest in capturing the Shaoxing nuances of the setting. As Chuandao, a Shaoxing student at Beijing University recalled, he used to come into the offices of *New Tide* to talk over with the Shaoxing students there the various hometown ways of saying something so as to use exactly the authentic phrase.[40]

What was true of language was true of visual depictions. Instinct might argue that popularization is aided by the elimination of written words and the substitution of images. But in fact, the reading of two-dimensional visual representations must be learned by the observer. Lu Xun describes his experience on this point to Lai Shaoqi.

> One needs to be taught to look at drawings.... I've shown drawings of even the most common plants to villagers who had never seen drawings before, and they could not understand it. For a solid thing to become flat—they just could not imagine that there could be such a thing.

The experience of showing drawings of plants to villagers probably dates from his pre-Republican years, when he first returned to China and botanized in the countryside around Shaoxing while teaching secondary school.[41] His experience fits nicely into Gombrich's exploration in *Art and Illusion* into how any reading of visual information is conditioned by the viewer's cultural expectations. The drawings to be found in, say, the standard plant reference work *Bencao gangmu* are as unreadable to the visually uninitiated as its words are to the unlettered. A remarkable thing about Lu Xun is that he noticed this and drew lessons from it. In the same vein, his letters to woodcut artists often caution that the reception for their work will be small for some time or suggest topics such as local color that might help them increase their viewership.

Lu Xun saw that one practical solution is to try many approaches. Thus his letter to Lai Shaoqi continues, "This is why I propose that in making *lianhuanhua*, one should use many different drawing styles." Another solution is to see that two-dimensional renditions might be understandable if they are derived from conventions already familiar to the intended viewer. To this end, as with drama, Lu Xun suggests a move toward the stylizations of tradition rather than the seeming naturalness of verisimilitude. In the case of visual material, he proposes a drawing style that is taken from the familiar images of *nianhua* or from the traditional prints of door gods. Liu Xian sent him some, to which he responded: "These are found in Shaoxing also. I feel their technique should be used as much as possible."[42]

Whatever the container, the content, that is, the plots in Lu Xun's fiction that were so new to Chinese literature when he began to write, still proved to be a prohibitive barrier beyond the urban elite. The thinking that gave his fiction its force is not so easily sneaked in under the guise of familiar styles, visual or otherwise. Being able to read a story from visual material required prior knowledge not only of visual rules but of the story's content.

> The difference is that traditional stories are already known before people see the depictions, whereas now one sees the depictions and through them learn the story, so its construction will be more complicated.

To the audience targeted by "massification" and "language of the masses," Lu Xun's works would not have been among those "already known." They would have had to be "learned" before their illustrations could be comprehensible. The unfamiliar content and models that were the definition of the literature of the new elite in the May Fourth Movement, and that had proved conceptually difficult to accept in the early years, made it visually unreadable to many, including the group the woodcuts sought to reach. Depictions, rather than propagating his legacy, made clear that its essence was less universal, less suited to translation into other media.

In the Hands of Others: Lu Xun Acquiesces in the Redefinition

The illustrations of Lu Xun's fiction and person in the 1930s constitute early examples of the political definition that came to be imposed on his legacy. They helped to redefine it from the May Fourth iconoclasm of fifteen years earlier to leftist exposé literature and its vocabulary of class oppression. This development, which began in Lu Xun's lifetime, anticipated the politicization that developed more fully after his death and then became the party policy of the next half century. In examining this, my focus is on what he thought and felt on seeing his work in the hands of others. I am not attempting a history of Lu Xun's reputation in the 1930s but will be concerned with what we can learn about him when we look at in this process. We know that by early 1930, when he took a part in the founding of the League of Left-Wing Writers, the Communist Party could definitely count him among their allies. As the dominant literary figure of his time, Lu Xun's activities, opinions, and visibility were all of great value to the Communist Party. The adaptations or proposed adaptations of individual works constituted one mechanism of renewal within larger changes in context and direction. Xiaobing Tang has interpreted this appropriation with an emphasis on "reclaiming of the cultural agenda." Writing about the "many woodcuts" of the 1930s that were titled "Nahan," he felt that "together [all the "Nahan" woodcuts] amounted to a determined reclaiming of the cultural agenda and spiritual heritage of the May Fourth era."[43] One could also see it as a claiming rather than a reclaiming—that the visual material retroactively enrolled his fiction in the cause, an example of how his later career hijacked the meaning of his earlier one.

In the 1930s, Lu Xun's criticism of China was retrospectively resituated as specifically political, as opposed to the deep cultural criticisms he also intended. The visual evidence shows this very clearly: it is not just the content but the producers that are on the left. Circumstances moved the fiction and its author from being the common property of the readers of the new elite (as in the days of *Call to Arms*) to being politicized as representing class oppression. His fiction moved from being works that, in the manner of the May Fourth young people in Ba Jin's fictional *Family*, constituted the common language of all who were against the Confucian status quo to being works that were against a status quo in the sense of being anti-Nationalist and pro-Communist.

The visual material politicizes his legacy in multiple ways: by (1) the style of the work, (2) the subject matter, (3) the choice of woodblock and cartoon media, and (4) the background of the artist. On the issue of style, in our material, only Chen Tiegeng employs a style that in itself compels a political interpretation, although as a group the illustrations entitled "Nahan" (figs. B.25–28) do so as well. On the second point, subject matter, in our material, in contrast to the socialist realism that was to come, the content of the art is generally identifiable as political only because the individual works are associated with Lu Xun, not by their choice of elements. The exceptions are Wang Junchu and Wei Mengke, who use content to convey a clearly leftist interpretation. All the portraits of Lu Xun also belong to this category of pictorial content as message. The third point, choice of media, is more of an identifying feature with these examples, for woodblocks were begun with a political purpose and cartoons became political when a contingent of cartoonists organized themselves to align art with politics. Finally, the background of the artist is probably the universal characteristic. Every artist in this chapter has some allegiance to the Left. As artists organized around a set of developing beliefs about the role of art in China, the projects they undertook, including illustrations of

Figure 5.16. Hu Yichuan, *To the Front*. Source: *Catalog of Woodcuts*.

Lu Xun's fiction, were of constant relevance to their political activism. Thus illustrations that are visually nonideological have a context of ideology in terms of the creator. Taken together these four points ensure that the leftward interpretation of Lu Xun's interpretation of China is overdetermined. As each of the traits is examined below, we shall see that Lu Xun's support and responsiveness add up to an acquiescence in the redefinition of his legacy.

Style

Style, in theory the core of artistic work, is in fact the least commonly deployed feature in the materials of this chapter. The skill or the intention to depict political viewpoint through pictorial means existed at this time, but it is not among the illustrations in this chapter. By contrast, in Hu Yichuan's 1932 print "To the Front" (fig. 5.16), a copy of which Lu Xun owned, the energy of the print is completely focused on its political point. This was an early indication of what was to be the achievement of the 1950s artists.

In our examples, only Chen Tiegeng conveyed his political interpretation of a particular work of fiction through style and structural language. His three published prints on Ah Q employ an internally consistent style in their use of close cropping, low perspective, and heavy, closely set lines that render in visual terms the oppressive atmosphere he perceives in "Ah Q." The scene of Ah Q being struck in the face (fig. 5.17) shares with Käthe Kollwitz's

Figure 5.17. Chen Tiegeng, rectangle of white in background against low, dark foreground in a scene from "Ah Q." Caption reads: "Ah Q kept his mouth shut. He was thinking of retreating, when Old Master Zhao took a quick step forward and slapped him across the face." *Theater*, 1934.

Figure 5.18. Käthe Kollwitz, *Misery*. Rectangle of white in background. © 2010 Artists Rights Society (ARS), New York / VG Bild-Kunst, Bonn.

"Misery" (fig. 5.18), the low ceiling and dark scene set against a stark rectangle of white light in the back. The scene in which Ah Q cries, "A gentleman uses his words, not his hands" (fig 5.19) is like Edvard Munch's "Smell of Death" (fig. 5.20), with the picture surface divided into sections defined by deeply scored parallel lines. Chen's use of a range of contemporary techniques is consistent with what we know of his other surviving pieces from this time. The inspiration that his series "Meshes of Law" drew from Frans Masereel's "Die Passion eines Menschen" is the most well documented, but each of his other surviving prints demonstrates his close study of radical European artists who depicted the dispossessed and the suffering.[44] (Kollwitz and Masereel were among the models studied in the August 1931 workshop on woodcuts.)

The other example of works that convey their point through style is a category of woodprints, all entitled "Nahan." This is not surprising as the portrayal of the word *nahan* demands energetic lines. As Xiaobing Tang notes, this "was far from a coincidence," and he draws attention also to the aural dimension of such works.[45] The four that were in Lu Xun's hands are in figures B.25–28. The people in them are posed in abstract energized stances and are visual renditions of the aural summons to arms issued by the influential anthology.

Figure 5.19. Chen Tiegeng, heavily scored parallel lines in a scene from "Ah Q." Caption reads: "'A gentleman uses his words, not his hands!', cried Ah Q with his head at wedged at an angle." *Theater*, 1934.

Figure 5.20. Edvard Munch, *Smell of Death*. © 2010 The Munch Museum / The Munch-Ellingsen Group / Artists Rights Society (ARS), New York.

Subject Matter

Examples of politicized subject matter are works by two artists, Wang Junchu and Wei Mengke, and the entire category of portraits of Lu Xun. Both Wang and Wei are represented by works that are political in content but not in style.

Wang Junchu. Wang's 1935 oil, entitled "Reading *Call to Arms*" (fig. 5.21), so attractive to look at and stylistically neutral, actually has an ideological content: the readers who are gathered around to read the same copy of *Call to Arms*, shown in its iconic vermillion cover, are not a random group of three but a student, a soldier, and a worker. They represent the essential classes in the leftist struggle, and their shared activity demonstrates their solidarity. The presentation is not aggressive, but the three classes are identifiable, and the political point is inescapable. (This trio provides insight into Communist policy in 1935, since the alliance in the demonstrations of the May Fourth era had been among an urban trio of students, workers, and merchants.)[46]

Wang gave this oil to Lu Xun in 1935 on the eve of his departure from the country. He had been living in Beijing, and when arrest seemed imminent a passage was arranged for him to the Soviet Union, where he was to study art. In Shanghai on his way out of the country, he was introduced to Lu Xun. The painting still hangs in Lu Xun's home, now a museum site.[47] Although "Reading *Call to Arms*" makes its point in a mild manner, many of Wang's drawings from 1937, even while using a similar gentle rounded surface, are more explicitly political both in their choice of subject matter (e.g., "The Carriages of Chinese Labor," fig. 5.22) and in the dramatic nature of the worker's pose, signaling the creation of a new category of man for the viewer to appreciate.[48]

The socialist realism that took over in the 1950s used the same selectivity of details

Figure 5.21. Wang Junchu, *Reading "Call to Arms,"* 1935. Student *center*, soldier *left*, and worker. Courtesy of Shanghai Lu Xun Museum.

210 : MEMORY, VIOLENCE, QUEUES: LU XUN INTERPRETS CHINA

in a much more aggressive way. For example, in Cheng Shifa's portrayal of Ah Q's execution, which we saw earlier (fig. 5.1), the people standing around make up a gallery of the enemies of the people, just as the student-soldier-worker trio expresses solidarity. In Cheng, among those looking on, with differing expressions, all discreditable to them, are several military men, one of them corpulent and one with a weapon (behind the executioner); a man with a bowtie, in a frockcoat, and carrying a cane (perhaps a westerner since he is bald and has a moustache); a rich man, also fat; and behind them an intellectual wearing glasses. This is not the crowd that watched the execution in "The True Story of Ah Q." That scene draws power from a crowd that is both representative and faceless until just at the end, when they become only wolf eyes. The despicable class enemies arrayed in Cheng's illustration blunt the satisfaction sought by the hungry onlookers in the novella and the complex moral that the author draws from it. Cheng's illustration enables the viewer, who is not a member of any of these groups, to condemn such class enemies.

Pairings. Wei Mengke (1911–84) was, like Feng Zikai, a cartoonist with a gentle style who worked in brush and ink. As with Wang Junchu, the interpretation is in the content not the style. This is achieved by pairing Lu Xun with Maksim Gorky (1868–1936), a heroic figure in China on the Left, known in tsarist times for novels that depicted the oppressed and in Bolshevik times as a pioneer of socialist realism (fig. 5.23).

Wei is unusual in our material in that he took a sarcastic tone with the great man, at least initially. In this 1933 brush-and-ink drawing (a little

Figure 5.22. Wang Junchu, *The Carriages of Chinese Laborers*. Nym Wales Collection, Hoover Institution Archives, Stanford University Library.

ahead of this chapter's dates of 1934–36), republished here from *Lunyu* for the first time, we see a very tall, stalky Gorky next to a very short, wide Lu Xun. Gorky was indeed tall and Lu Xun short, although he was not wide. The drawing resembles a recent group photograph in which the tall Bernard Shaw, on his hugely publicized visit to Shanghai in February of that year, stood next to the short Lu Xun, wide in his winter padded clothes but not *that* wide. A detail from the group shot of five persons shows the similarities (fig. 5.24). The critic Chen Haowang says the likeness was not an accident, that Wei had earlier written a satire of the visit, which he published in a little magazine he had founded.[49]

At any rate, some backpedaling soon seemed prudent. Wei sought Lu Xun's acquaintance by letter, protesting that he had nothing to do with the phrase *yanran* ("Dignified Indeed!") on the upper left, and after a few rounds of hurt feelings on Wei's part, Lu Xun was able to soothe him enough to produce a correspondence and eventually a friendship. This was well done, since presumably Lu Xun is the one who should have been miffed.

Figure 5.23. Wei Mengke, Lu Xun and Gorky. *Lunyu*, June 1, 1933.

Figure 5.24. Lu Xun and Shaw – a detail of photograph. Source: Chen Shuyu, et al., eds. *Pictorial Biography of Lu Xun*.

Lu Xun's judgment was not impaired by Wei's lèse majesté. He suggested Wei as the illustrator for stories that were to be included in Edgar Snow's planned volume of contemporary short stories from China, *Living China*. Snow was a journalist whose glowing account of Mao Zedong in Yan'an, *Red Star over China*, published the following year, was to be highly influential in the United States. We know that Lu Xun received five drawings from Wei but they are not in *Living China*, for, although "Ah Q" was indeed translated, it was not included for reasons of space. I am still trying to track them down.[50]

Sometimes the pairings of political subjects is not made in the same work but across the total output of an artist. For instance, Cao Bai made a portrait of Anatoly Lunacharsky and then one of Lu Xun: they were the same kind of heroes to him. The portrait of Lunacharsky, the Soviet literary critic and minister of education first under Lenin and then under Stalin (until 1929), was made when Cao was a student and became a point in his prison interrogation. He was also questioned about letters found in his room whose language borrowed from "Diary of a Madman": "The world is a feast of cannibalism. Your mother was eaten and so will countless other mothers in this world be eaten."[51] Then after his prison term, he made a portrait of Lu Xun.

Portraits. Portraits of Lu Xun constitute a special case in this category of political intent expressed through subject matter, for in the 1930s they were

Figure 5.25. Cao Bai, Lu Xun, 1936. Source: *Catalog of Woodcuts*.

Figure 5.26. Chen Guangzong, Lu Xun, 1932. Source: *Catalog of Woodcuts*.

uniformly suspect to censors. The little vignettes surrounding several of the portraits make it clear that the criticism of China that drove the fiction had been found applicable to criticism of the current authorities. Furthermore, the difficulty the artists had in exhibiting or publishing the portraits indicates that Lu Xun as subject matter was in itself politically charged. A woodcut portrait done by Cao Bai (fig. 5.25) was removed by censors before the Second Coordinated National Woodcut Exhibit. Lu Xun's response implies that it was removed simply because of the subject matter. On the print Cao sent him, he wrote, "When works [submitted for the exhibition] were first examined by the city's Nationalist unit, 'the old man' singled out this woodcut and said, 'This will not do!' and so cut it out." From this began their correspondence. Chen Guangzong's portrait (fig. 5.26) was sent to four editorial offices, which were all prevented by censors from publishing it. A third example is Lai Shaoqi, who could be said to emphasize works and author equally (fig. 5.27). His work was published in *Literature* (*Wenxue*), where Lu Xun sent it, but Lu Xun notes "If the censors do not recognize me, it will probably be published," so the presence of Lu Xun was the subversive element.[52] (Indeed, the face on the ink bottle, supposed to be Lu Xun's, is not very like him.)

Figure 5.27. Lai Shaoqi. Two titles have been used of this image, *The True Story of Ah Q* and *Portrait of Lu Xun*. Wenxue, 1935.

Choice of Media: Woodcuts and Cartoons

To different degrees, woodcuts and cartoons were both identified with political and social criticism. In the case of woodcuts, from their inception, they were ipso facto political and closely identified with Lu Xun. Cartoons' longer history dates to the nineteenth century; like their Western models, their mode was social and political satire. In the 1920s, the first societies were formed, including three artists in *Theater* (Lu Shaofei, Ye Qianyu and Zhang Zhengyu), and by the 1930s, many cartoonists belonged to the League of Left-Wing Artists.

The intensely political character of the woodcut movement determined its short but violent history and accounts for both why so little of the work survives and why the woodcut's use of Lu Xun as subject matter politicized his earlier fiction. Its history began with the formation of the Eighteen Society in 1929 (named after the year of its founding, the eighteenth year of the Republic) at the Hangzhou Art Academy and ended in 1936–37, after which Japan's occupation of northern and central China redirected the artists' work almost exclusively to the war effort. Its course is marked by the formation of successive woodcut societies, each disbanded and reformed under persecution; the exhibits they held; and the censorship, confiscations, and often arrests and imprisonment that accompanied the exhibits. The history of the Eighteen Society intersected with Lu Xun when its members visited Shanghai and saw his and Rou Shi's Zhaohuashe publications. They met with Lu Xun, who suggested woodcuts as a medium. This society chose the participants for Lu Xun's 1931 workshop, sending six from their own membership. Lu Xun wrote the preface for an exhibit in summer 1931, organized by the Shanghai branch of the Eighteen Society (Hu Yichuan brought 180 works from Hangzhou). The authorities tried to remove the preface, then tried to confiscate all copies of the catalog, and Hangzhou Art Academy expelled the remaining student members of the Eighteen Society (Cao Bai and his two fellow student prisoners were among them). The society then changed its name to the Spring Field Art Society (Chundi huahui) and under this name organized an exhibit June 1932 at the Shanghai YMCA, which was closed down, the art destroyed, and the members arrested. This exhibit included European prints from Lu Xun's own collection. At about the same time the Wooden Bell Society (Muling muke yanjiushe) mounted two exhibits. At the first one, its entire print run of 120 catalogs sold out in two hours. At the second exhibit, held jointly with White Willow for three days beginning on June 15, 1932, there were 200-plus items brought from Hangzhou, including 60 woodcuts. All the participants were arrested on October 10, 1932. Finally the M.K. Society (M.K. for *muke*), founded in 1932, mounted four exhibitions, each marked by arrests and confiscation of materials; by the end, the society was in effect dissolved. The next landmark events were two nationwide traveling exhibitions. The first began in Beijing on January 1, 1935, went to Tianjin, and then went to Shanghai. It consisted entirely of woodcuts and most—like Hu Yichuan's "To the Front!"—called for resistance to Japanese military aggression. An educational component introduced the tools, materials, and techniques of wood engraving. The second national exhibit was organized from Canton by Li Hua and Lai Shaoqi and eventually went to twenty-eight cities. This is the one that Lu Xun visited in Shanghai in October, a few days before his death.

The next year the war with Japan altered the connections among the artists, and their subject matter was redirected to the war.

The medium's history was perforce short. Furthermore, Michael Sullivan points out that within this short spa of time, only a small percentage of art students were radicals (though all chose the woodcut medium).[53] Only two or three years after it began, the woodcut artists had been nearly wiped out by persecution. Writing in 1934, Lu Xun said, "There are no longer any woodcut groups in Shanghai. . . . Some have been imprisoned, some have returned home or scattered. There is one more point, which is that ultimately, oppression scattered everyone." The same year, in his preface to *Muke jicheng*, he listed four woodcut societies that used to publish and did not survive the arrests and confiscation of materials and added, "From what I can tell, there is not one society left dedicated to studying woodcuts. . . . In truth, among the young people in Shanghai who loved woodcuts, many are radical and so now to say 'woodcut' is often tantamount to saying 'revolutionary' and will immediately arouse suspicion."[54]

To Lu Xun, woodcuts were an important form because of the simplicity and availability of their materials and tools. "That with a few cutting knives, a piece of wood, one could create a great many works of art and propagate them among the masses—this is the modern woodcut." In the short history of the art woodcut, a landmark event was the workshop that Lu Xun organized in August 1931 to teach techniques of woodcut carving and printing. The immediate cause was the presence in Shanghai of Uchiyama's brother Kakichi, an elementary school teacher who was trained in woodcut techniques. Lu Xun purchased the tools, convened the workshop, translated for Kakichi, and paid him with six of his twelve Kollwitz prints.[55] He also provided the woodcut models studied: ukiyo-e; works by Kollwitz, Carl Meffert (1903–88), and Vladmir Favorsky (1886–1964); and works by Russian constructivists. The strong lines and stark imagery in these models and their uncompromising depiction of suffering, loss, and brutal authority are to be seen in many of the prewar woodcuts in China. A photograph taken on the workshop's last day (August 22) shows thirteen participants plus Lu Xun and Uchiyama Kakichi (fig. 5.28). Chen Tiegeng and Zhong Buqing are among them.

The genre of cartoons (*manhua*) was more commercially oriented and less self-consciously ambitious in artistic terms, and consequently it had a greater range of subject matter and tone and was able to support artists of more varied goals. Satire was always an element, but the satire had more of a social than a political bent. Mentioning only the cartoonists whose works are in this chapter, on the light side was the long-running "Mr. Wang" series in *Shanghai manhua* (Shanghai sketch) by Ye Qianyu, "the most famous comic serial of 1930s

216 : MEMORY, VIOLENCE, QUEUES: LU XUN INTERPRETS CHINA

Figure 5.28. Participants in the woodcut workshop held August, 1931. Source: Chen Shuyu, et al., eds. *Pictorial Biography of Lu Xun*.

Shanghai" and "a true portrayal of . . . everyday life of the middle and lower classes."[56] Within this broader stream, cartoonists emerged in the 1930s who were committed to using their art to fight for political ends. As Geremie Barmé observes, "by the mid-1930s, the manhua artist and calligrapher Huang Miaozi could confidently claim that 'manhua are produced to incite people, to stimulate them.'"[57] He quotes similarly emphatic words from Zhang E: "Manhua artists in China today should turn every fountain pen, brush, and eraser into a tool for struggle and share in the common responsibility of all those who paint.'" Such declarations meant that cartoons came under the same pressures from authorities as woodcuts did. Huang Miaozi's *Xiaoshuo banyue kan* (Fiction semimonthly) was closed down by censors after fourteen issues (1934–35). *Manhua shenghuo* (Cartoon life) was closed down by censors after one year (September 1934–September 1935). As Sullivan notes, cartoonists went "hand-in-hand with the woodcut movement and suffered the same restraints."[58]

The Background of the Artists

The background of the artists is the most decisive factor in the politicization of Lu Xun's fiction, for as we saw above, despite the choice of suspect media and content, the politicized intent often cannot be discerned in the features of the art itself. By contrast, in the artists' background there can be found an unmistakable commitment to the Left. Every artist can be identified with some group or organization that took part in leftist underground activities in the cultural sphere. These activities began early and were multiple. (I consider only the pre-1936 period as the artists' later careers varied widely.) Their associations expressed the ideology of their artistic ideals, in which illustration of Lu Xun's person or fiction had a part. The information concerning the art societies they formed and their political activities is so thoroughly consistent as to seem overmuch by way of demonstrating my point. In part they constitute evidence of the effective permeation of the Communist Party's cultural work.

We take first the artists published in *Theater*. Together with the editor, Yang Muzhi, they formed a loose network connected by two other areas of the Shanghai communications world: cartoons and film. Six of the contributors were cartoonists who drew for the (somewhat) commercially viable pictorials that found a ready market in 1930s Shanghai. A seventh from our materials in this network was Feng Zikai. Three other artists plus the editor Yang Muzhi were connected through left-wing film companies. Despite their leftist connections, at this time not every artist was wholly political in his work, but starting in 1937 all became active in propaganda work in the war effort.

The contributors to the "Ah Q" installments in *Theater* are but a small fraction of the many artists who were active in the 1930s, but their relations give a sense of the interconnections among Shanghai's artists, as the same names turn up in each other's magazines. Taking first those who were cartoonists, three of the artists here, Lu Shaofei, Ye Qianyu, and Zhang Zhengyu., were among the organizers of the earliest *manhua* group, Shanghai manhua hui, in 1927.[59] This association published *Shanghai Sketch*, whose content helped create an image of Shanghai as a metropolis and which ran, we saw above, Lu's social satire series, "Mr. Wang." This pictorial lasted for three years, longer than most, perhaps because it was not primarily political and often featured (artistically rendered) male or female nudes on its covers. The war changed this situation, and these three artists were among the many notable organizers of the war effort to reach the masses. Two more artists in *Theater*, Ma Guoliang and Zhang E are connected through *Manhua shenghuo* (Cartoon life). Ma Guoliang was also the editor of the long-running (1926–46) pictorial *The Companion* (*Liang you*), which had a pretty face on the cover of every single issue and whose pages, much enhanced by photographs and other visuals, conveyed essential general knowledge to its readership, a goal that can be seen as continuing the broad outlines of the May Fourth project. Ma also succeeded in getting an interview and photo session with Lu Xun, which he happily ran in *The Companion*.[60] Another notable figure in this list is Huang Miaozi whose militant words were quoted earlier. His *Fiction Semimonthly* published cartoons by Lu Shaofei and Ye

Qianyu and illustrations of fiction by Li Xudan, Ma Guoliang, and Zhang E. It also published two of Lu Xun's essays, "On Face" and "Ah Jin," both substantial ones, likely a sign of his desire to support the magazine.

Zhang Yunqiao and Xu Xingzhi are two of the contributors connected through film with the editor and actor Yuan Muzhi. In this year, Zhang was art director of the movie *Tao Li qie* (Plunder of Peach and Plum) in which Yuan took the role of the male lead. Today this story of the exploitation and destruction of a husband (surnamed Li) and wife (surnamed Tao) by the owner of the factory where they both work is a part of every course in Chinese film history. It was from the film company Diantong, which had underground Communist connections. The second figure connected to Yuan was Xu Xingzhi, who was set designer for another leftist film company, Tianyi. The next year, at Diantong, he directed the film *Children of Wartime* (Fengyun ernü) that featured what became the anthem of the People's Republic, "March of the Volunteers" (*Yiyongjun jinxingqu*) (and starred Yuan Muzhi).[61] The year after Lu Xun's death, he created a stage adaptation also called *The True Story of Ah Q*.

Turning to the artists in groups II and III of appendix B, we note that nearly all began with enrollment in art academies. The academies typically took students at a young age. Liu Xian was fifteen and Cao Bai sixteen when they enrolled in Beijing and Hangzhou respectively. Not surprisingly, there the young people found others of like mind and formed societies to carry out their goals and express their philosophies through art. The most politically active centers were in Hangzhou, Shanghai, Beijing, and Guangzhou. All the artists treated here belonged to or founded associations that published woodcuts or organized exhibits of them or both. Liu Xian cofounded the Unnamed Woodcut Society (Weiming muke she) in 1933, which published woodcuts, his and others, including illustrations of political novels like Mao Dun's *Midnight*. He was still only eighteen. Chen Tiegeng, from Guangzhou, was a member of, among many other groups, the Eighteen Society and Muling Woodcut Society at Hangzhou Art Academy. The former was the earliest of the art groups, founded at Hangzhou Art Academy. This was the group charged with selecting the participants of the 1931 workshop. It sent six from the group, including Chen, and allocated the other seven places among three other associations.[62] Zhong Buqing was another participant in the workshop, interestingly one of *five* participants from the same county of Xingning in Guangzhou. Luo Qingzhen, though not in the workshop, was also from Xingning and was a friend of Chen Tiegeng. Lai Shaoqi was based in Guangzhou. With his teacher, Li Hua, he organized the Research Society on the Modern Woodcut among his classmates in 1932, and the group mounted frequent exhibits, produced the monthly *Contemporary Woodcuts* (*Xiandai banhua*), and, its largest project, organized the national traveling exhibition of 1936. Wei Mengke, then twenty-two, joined the League of Left-Wing Writers in 1933 (he was also a writer) and later joined the Tokyo branch. Cao Bai, then age sixteen, and Liqun, age nineteen, were the founders of Muling Woodcut Society at Hangzhou Art Academy. Its existence, he later learned, triggered his and Liqun's arrest, together with that of a third student. Wang Junchu, based in Beijing, was among the organizers of the Anti-feudalist Anti-imperialist Art Exhibition in 1925 (at the age of twenty). He helped found the Society of Proletarian Painters in 1931, for which he was arrested, and Beijing's League of Left-Wing Artists in 1932.[63]

The four characteristics of the visual material that have been detailed in this section—the style of the work, the subject matter, the choice of the medium of cartoon or woodblock and the background of the artist—have the combined effect of realigning Lu Xun's work with the social purposes of literature and other media as those purposes evolved in Communist Party policies in the early 1930s. In this manner, his work, whose many merits might well have enabled it to survive beyond the time of its creation without this assistance, was made pertinent to the new conditions, definitively so once Mao Zedong added his voice. Communist activists saw the need to reach the masses with the same urgency that the founders of May Fourth periodicals did regarding the creation and nurturing of a new class with a knowledge of the world outside Confucianism and outside China. This step, which could be considered a historical development out of the original May Fourth goals, was instead expressed as a repudiation of them. The work of Lu Xun, Mao Dun, and some other major writers was brought into the new era after some fiddling with ideology. The adaptations of these works, by contrast, was not ideologically contentious on the Left, and once illustrations, films, stage adaptations, ballets, and more streamed in with state support, the underlying questions of interpretation and pertinence were subsumed by issues related to the adaptations. Certainly this has been the case with the visual materials of this chapter.

Conclusion: New Art Woodcut and New Literature

From the viewpoint of literary biography, the last decade of Lu Xun's life lacks clear features even though the decade has unusually neat boundaries in other respects. He was exactly ten years in Shanghai (October 1927–October 1936). His activities and associations in Shanghai, which increased significantly in range and quantity, were nearly all unified by his new alliance with the Communist Party. Unlike the first decade of his literary life, 1918–26, however, it has proved difficult to specify clear literary features in the Shanghai years. The decade 1918–26 had seen his essays occupy a groundbreaking position in both style and thought, and just a recitation of the collections and their dates would quickly produce an outline of his life in that decade. By contrast, the Shanghai decade seems to have been dominated by events and people rather than writing.

The materials of this chapter suggest that Lu Xun continued to search for a meaningful, feasible way to make incisive criticisms of China through works of the imagination and that this time he sought to do so in a visual medium. The decade, which might seem like mostly reaction and response to rapidly moving events, also shows a steady growth in his involvement with the visual arts. His multifaceted activities in woodcuts (and in art in general) can be seen as a return in visual form of his labors in the verbal realm with New Literature. With some isolated exceptions, he did not produce art himself, and this is a great difference from the writing, but the other similarities are there. When he turned to woodcuts, he devoted as much energy to establishing and promulgating them as he had to literature, and he did so with the same approach and the same principles. As he had done with literature in 1906–9 in Japan, and again in the years of the May Fourth movement, likewise he now searched for models from abroad and actively undertook their promulgation. Whereas in literature his roles gradually multiplied, in woodcuts his roles were diverse from the beginning—he was introducer, promulgator, promoter, sponsor, printer, collector, publisher, and critic. Another change is that in the early years of the New Literature era he took on each new role reluctantly, whereas he now actively undertook different kinds of actions.

Lu Xun began to feel his way toward this new direction the year after he gave up both *xiaoshuo* fiction and the freedom to not make political commitments. In October 1927 he arrived in Shanghai. By 1928 he had identified the art woodcut as an interest and begun to collect woodcut examples from Europe of the social criticism he had in mind. The year 1929 saw concrete results with the founding of Zhaohuashe for publishing prints from the volumes that he had bought to serve as information and example. The rest of his activities followed from there: to students from Hangzhou who sought his advice, he suggested the medium of woodcuts; he organized the August 1931 workshop in woodcut methods; and in 1934 he published a first volume of works by Chinese woodcut artists in *Record of the Wood Engravings (Muke jicheng)*.[64] These were meticulous, small-scale acts: there were 120 copies, and after 40 were set aside for the artists and others concerned, 80 remained for sale through Uchiyama's bookstore.[65] Through all these years, he tirelessly gave advice and encouragement in many letters, prefaces, and gatherings.

These parallels suggest that, biographically speaking, he gave up on creative writing in some way but was still looking forward, this time proposing a serious visual culture for everyone versus, previously, creating a serious literature of the new elite. He remained embroiled in literary matters, for this was inescapable for him. There were new contentions over "the purposes of literature." Even here, despite his own achievements, he was willing to start from basic questions of what that literature might be, what it would do. (Not that there were any answers.) During this time, his work from the past was being continually reissued in new printings.

His past and the future met when adaptations appeared. Time would have brought about adaptations of his work in any case, but that it happened in his lifetime in a medium he nurtured (as well as in other media) presented a conundrum for Lu Xun. On the one side, given the fiction's serious social goals when he took up the path of writing in 1918, he must have wanted his fiction to be universal in its lessons, rooted though it is in the provincial city and character types of his youth. We saw that he guarded against easy, ad hominem readings of his fiction, which would have essentially sidestepped its wider applicability. On the other hand, logically speaking, it was not his design that his work would last, for he looked to the day when the world depicted in it would no longer be recognizable. He was not an optimist, but he had not thought that the conditions he exposed through fiction and essays would still be grimly relevant in the 1930s. This paradox was always implicit in his situation, but adaptations brought them to the fore. At the same time, he—and many like-minded figures in the cultural world—had been initiated into the outside world by the adaptations and translations of their immediate forebears, and their own first actions were to continue this legacy.

His fiction was, unfortunately, still pertinent, but was it still universal? Could it still be understood? These questions could be phrased today in the present tense as well. He only lived to see adaptations made within the confines of realism. Besides the visual works of this chapter, there was a handful of proposed adaptations for the stage and several proposals for films that did not materialize in his lifetime.[66] In the eight decades since then, large numbers of adaptations have been made in diverse media such as dance and opera and in countries outside China, many of them accompanied by online information. Perhaps metaphorical substitutes for the queue will seize the general imagination. One cannot say that this will not happen if Lu Xun and the China of his writings continue to be seen as having pertinence.

Conclusion

The name of Lu Xun is inseparable from the emergence of China into the interconnected world of nations that formed at the turn of the previous century. His education and memories of his youth placed him in the last generation in a China that could conceive of itself as a state that could unilaterally establish its own world position and assume that in its economic and political relations other nations would make adjustments to that ideology. The defeat of this traditional China in military, diplomatic, and economic spheres by Western nations and then Japan in the nineteenth and early twentieth centuries gradually forced on it an enlarged frame of reference. Against this background, the founders of *New Youth* and others put forward the view that everything that had been believed, done, thought, and planned needed to be overthrown. A more moderate version was that other nations had their own, often more effective systems of knowledge and identity. At that moment in history, the writings of Lu Xun were its epitome. "Call to arms" was its summons. To think about Lu Xun today is to gauge his portrait of China and, more self-consciously, our understanding of that portrait and our predecessors' reception of it.

His life spanned China from the late nineteenth century to the eve of World War II in Asia. This is the China that haunted his writings. By the time he came to write in 1918, there was much to interpret and a great need for interpretation. He experienced much, for his life began in the backwaters of Shaoxing and the countryside that surrounded it and ended in Shanghai, the largest and most international of the Chinese cities. Once he left Shaoxing, with a few brief exceptions, he lived successively in political capitals: Tokyo, Nanjing when it was the capital in 1912, Beijing when it was the capital in 1912–26, and Shanghai when it was within the political reach of nearby Nanjing, now once again the capital. His life and writings reflected the vast material and mental changes that China underwent in a half century, in part because urban changes were greater.

Although Lu Xun's life encompassed many transformations and his influence was great, this study does not present an overarching hypothesis about them but examines some consistent themes in them. It is true that a subtitle like "Lu Xun Interprets China" can imply synthesizing, but these chapters examined intervals and components of his lifelong engagement with China in order to refine our knowledge of its nature. The steadiness of his task does not mean that its content did not change. I used the metaphor of a core sample in the introduction, and, as with core samples, it is possible for the resulting cross-sectional information to go in many directions. The points of access named in this study's title are three among many possibilities, but the chosen examples will naturally magnify the role of these factors as stimuli for the writings.

Of these, quantitatively the smallest role is taken by the queue. In the beginning of the fifteen or twenty years during which it was under contention, the queue was a freighted thing both for those who changed their views and for those who held fast. It could not be anything else given the external pressures of general scorn and the internal resistance at many levels. It was everything to those who wanted to keep it and to those who wanted to get rid of it.

Yet on the decision as Lu Xun made it only a general kind of light can be shed. As far as insight into the young student is concerned, the strongest clue—and also what was valid for the briefest time—is the poem *as it existed at that time*, when its significance was augmented by the author's inscription of it on the back of a photograph whose name also had him as the source. In this context, yes, there was a component to this action that was principled in motivation, but the actual cutting of the queue remained in the background, refracted only in the friendly scene in Xu Shoushang's study room. His refusal to make known, much less to elaborate on, two such solid early artifacts was typical. The silent revivals of the poem and the photograph that are discussed in chapter 4, the former perhaps shared with Qu Qiubai, allow us to know that these early artifacts were significant then and remained so later.

The public function that he did assign to the queue was as an instrument of moral division in the history he lived through. There was heroism for a few men; convenience and other such offhand considerations for himself and many others; and a third, less classifiable kind of test in the complexity of fiction. For the few, he stated that cutting the queue constituted a principle. Found mostly in essays, this judgement was reserved as a shorthand for those whom he admired. For Zhang Binglin and Zou Rong, defiance was a political gesture that was followed by action, in their cases, verbal incendiary action that led to jail for both, and for Zou Rong, death at age twenty (chapter 2). Zhang's death in 1936 drew from Lu Xun an essay in which Zhang's old fights were refought and explained to a new age and his poems that honored those who died were quoted. For himself and for many others, in contrast to men like Zhang, the Republican Revolution was merely the chance to get rid of an awkward encumbrance or, if that was done already, to live in a world where that was now the right style of hair.

In his fiction, the presence or absence of a queue is also a moral division but, as befitting Lu Xun's kind of complex fiction writing, there is no single way in which this division is applied and the picture of China is accordingly complicated. For the villagers of "Storm," it is not the presence or absence of a queue that puts them on one side or the other of a moral divide. Seven-Pounds has no queue while the other villagers in this countryside do, and, although the latter briefly have the advantage of him, the sharper line is drawn against the versatility of the tavern keeper, who has it both ways. So there is an unprincipled person, but there are no principled persons. In "A Story about Hair," the dead revolutionaries that N remembers do not need to have their style of hair mentioned, for their valor has made them the victims both of their murderers, as with those Zhang Binglin's poems commemorated, and of the short memories of those on their own side. The ones who do have their queues mentioned are the students, who want to cut their queue because they want to be revolutionaries, and N, who cut his queue and then purchased a false one, left it off, and then hit with a cane the passersby who heckled him. These were widely employed strategems, but are invested by Lu Xun with such barbs as to make them impossible to associate with the author. For N and the students, having or not having a queue is a division, but what does it divide? Interestingly, no clear answer is given. In "The True Story of Ah Q," the division made by the possession of a queue is most subtle at the end, when the absence of a queue marks one as principled, as might be expected from his writings on Zhang Binglin and others, but in an unexpected way. Near the end, Ah Q coils up his queue, which is almost the same as cutting it, and soon he is executed, in almost the way the revolutionary had been earlier in the story. It is the culmination of a series of steps by means of which he is somehow no longer the painful figure of fun he had been at the novella's start but is still a painful figure to contemplate.

For more than a decade before the Republican revolution, the queue was a ready symbol of many things in many situations. Afterward, it could still be a symbol for those who could, as Lu Xun pointed out, remember what it was like a quarter century earlier in 1911, or indeed thirty-five years from his own queue cutting. By this time, the last diehards had died, the queue was a curiosity, like bound feet or crinolines, and, as he observed, only his generation knew the lingering everyday habits that marked their freedom from it.[1] Like the fight for using punctuation and the fight for the third person singular to have "she" and "it" forms, that for abolishing the queue seemed simple once it had been won, but there had been serious consequences for its advocates.[2] In the last two years of his life, the woodblocks that illustrated his fiction caused him to feel its final passage. In using the queue to give an interpretation of

China, the question is not whether it will work, for it worked for Lu Xun, but whether anyone will understand it in later years. Its meaning of political rebellion was a simple one; it is only when personal and cultural elements are factored in, something Lu Xun was so skilled at, that things become interesting. If it has only a residue of political meaning, can it still be used to make subtle differentiations? One possible outlet is that today's media, with their vast appetite for visual materials in video games and virtual worlds, will raid the visual past (and present) of all world cultures in a kind of Rorschach test of lightning recognition. Perhaps the queue has already found its place in that kind of human memory. A deeper possibility is historical fiction, where it would be interesting to see it with a rich role in a work concerned with those decades.

Given how the queue was intertwined in Chinese culture and its abolition was drawn out over many years and different for each person, its capacity to function as a symbol was limited only by the user's imagination. The various characters concerned with the queue that Lu Xun supplied in the fiction and the ambiguous and offhand tone he employed in the essays suggest how rich the cultural history of the queue's last, eventful decades would be. The increasing academic studies of hair and dress in other literatures provide a sense of how rich such studies would be for the Chinese situation.

The second element of this study, political violence, is a constant in the history of Lu Xun's lifetime and an increasingly important topic in literary studies, as was discussed in chapter 1. The subsequent chapters aimed to further examine, as precisely as possible, these connections, for they exist on both readily evident and hidden levels, and both are productive in further analysis.

Overall, compared to the amount of violence he witnessed and knew of, he wrote relatively little, yet when he wrote, the results were influential.[3] The record of his participation in the meetings and demonstrations common to his day is a slim one. How it is then that a subtitle like this study's, "Lu Xun Interprets China," raises no eyebrows? That it even seems commonplace shows how thoroughly his political thinking is diffused through the writing. Two essays mentioned often in this study are examples of this. For the March 18 Incident, he remained home that day, kept Xu Guangping from joining the demonstrations by giving her copying tasks, did not go to any of the numerous commemorative events in Beijing, and attended only the first of two memorial services at Beijing Women's Normal College for its students Liu Hezhen and Yang Dequn. Yet his was the elegy that defined it in the public memory and resonates to this day on dissenters' blogs. (Although he did not participate, he wrote more than a dozen other essays in the next weeks on the students' deaths.) To a lesser extent, this was also the situation during the time Rou Shi and the others were imprisoned. He was again on the sidelines, although there was nothing much that could be done by anyone during the crisis. After their deaths, he wrote many more commemorative pieces and helped publish many commemorative works in the teeth of censorship, as recounted in chapter 4. And again he wrote the essay that established the emblematic image of youth cut short (and, in an unintended consequence, diverted attention from the other eighteen who had been killed but were not writers).

What if anything should we make of this discrepancy between a small amount of political participation and a large amount of influence? The small amount of political participation was an outcome of temperament rather than of lack of interest. There is no doubt that he was keenly aware of and had strong views about political developments. Li Anbao's *Lu Xun and Modern Chinese History* reviews active political engagement, so the result is a slender record but very useful because narrowly defined.[4] The title of Ni Moyan's *Lu Xun's Societal Activities* shows that he casts a wider net (and indeed his book comes in at 436 pages versus 188 for Li Anbao's), and, pertinent to the argument here, the end result is that he did not write that much when compared to others in Ni's study. Harriet C. Mills has suggested that he needed something personal as a point of connection and, as regards the fiction, "he could not use [it] to depict the reality of something external to him or his experience."[5]

This study also approached the connection between violence and the writing through the personal dimension, in particular to increase the recognition of when personal aspects of political events led Lu Xun to write. The main factor employed here is his tendency to let some time lapse before writing of it, sometimes a lapse of years. Two of the chapters are concerned with examples of this delayed manner of writing. The three works of fiction analyzed in chapter 3 suggest that the process by which certain events came back to his mind and into writing was the personal experience of Beijing in battles between rival armies. The queue-cut-short poem in chapter 4 illustrates the same dynamics. The poem's longer-term validation was retrieved at a time when political violence touched the author personally through the betrayal, arrests, and secret executions of Rou Shi and the other writers. Leaving behind its queue-related life on the back of a photograph, it entered his life in the 1930s in multiple ways. Many other instances of delayed responses to political violence were mentioned in passing in this study. This is related to memory. and memory, as we shall see next, is the thread that ties much together for Lu Xun. Two essays from 1925 were quoted ("Various Memories" and "'Fair Play' Should be Postponed"), which reviewed some of the vengeance that he saw in 1911 in Shaoxing and later in the Second Revolution. The 1933 preface discussed in chapter 3 names the *fengbo* between 1911 and 1918.

There are two major exceptions to this pattern of delayed expression of violence. One is the 1903 quatrain "Inscribed by the Author on a Small Likeness," whose connection to violence he soon ceased to advocate. The other is the whole category of his classical poems of the 1930s. Most of them allude to battles and deaths as they occurred, not delayed by time. The classical poetry, likely initiated by the poems he wrote following the deaths of Rou Shi and others, remained nearly all topical. The genre of lyric poetry, traditionally a vehicle for personal sorrow and frustration in a political context, came back as a personal resource.

The comments on violence in this section can be gathered together with a concluding look at an essay Lu Xun wrote in 1926, "The Great Sight of Chopping Down Communists."[6] The essay responds to an account in Shanghai's *Shenbao* of an extraordinary day in Changsha during which an endless sea of people had surged back and forth from one end of the city to the other to get a look at the bodies and heads of executed Communists that were on display. Thirty-plus Communist Party leaders had been captured and condemned to death, and "eight were executed on the anniversary of Huanghuagang" (March 29, an important Republican revolutionary date). *Shenbao* published it as a "Letter from Changsha." I translate here the entire passage that Lu Xun quotes from Shenbao and follow with some of his comments. Here is the quotation from the letter.

> After the executions, because three of the criminals were female [the names and ages, sixteen, fourteen, and twenty-four, were given here], everyone in the city, men and women, came to look, mountains and oceans of people all day long jam-packed together. In addition, the ringleader Guo Liang's head was suspended before government headquarters for all to see, so even more people went to see that. Traffic was at a standstill at the eight-sided pavilion by the court. After the people by South Gate had seen Guo Liang's head, they would go to the Board of Education to look at the women's corpses. And after the people at North Gate had seen the women's corpses by the Board of Education, they would go to government headquarters to see Guo's head. The entire city was on the move, the atmosphere around chopping down the Communists had totally aroused them. It was not until late at night that the crowd that came to see the sights eased a bit from the daytime.

This is a vivid piece of reporting. Its brevity and force impressed Lu Xun: "In this article, there are only 156 characters and yet see how effective it is" (he passes over the writer's hostility toward Communists). Two things are interesting in his next comments. The first is an astonishing paraphrase he makes of the letter's picture of how a mania for bloody sights had seized the populace of Changsha that day, for his paraphrase employs a manner as vivid as the original while adding two details of his own supposition.

> When I read it, it seemed as though I could see the head suspended before government headquarters, and could see the three headless female corpses before the Board of Education. Furthermore, most likely they were naked. . . . And the large numbers of "the people," one group went from north to south, another from south to north, crowding, shouting. . . . And I will add the extra detail that in their faces one could see some who were elated and some who have been satisfied.

Despite the correspondent's vivid account, Lu Xun evidently feels there are other elements that can explain the near mob. His paraphrase adds two factors that he imagines to be the case: that the girls' bodies had been stripped and that the crowd looked elated and satisfied. He adds true fictional details that locate the cause of the teeming crowd and its excited state in the sight of the headless, naked female bodies. In a way, he proves that fiction—the added details—can be acute in diagnosis, can get to the reason for the mass excitement that lasted into the evening.

The second interesting thing about this passage is that though he has just speculated, as a work of the imagination would, about the fevered scene in Changsha, he goes on to aver that no work of fiction has proved equal to this news report, and then repeats his sense of how its brevity adds to its effectiveness.

> In "revolutionary literature" and "realistic literature" I have not seen any writing that is as strong and forceful as this. . . . In little more than a hundred plus characters, it far surpassed any number of fiction works, and moreover, this is the truth, it happened.

It is true that the Changsha news item is the "strong and forceful" writing that he feels is required by the violent times, but it is also true that his quotation of it and commentary on it alter it from a report on a "ringleader" and his associates to a horrifying portrayal of every person's complicity. But this is not his view of the adequacy of writing in the face of violence.

In later years, he ascribes more personal reasons to the impossibility of matching reality with words. After the January 1932 Shanghai war, as we saw in chapter 3, he says that he witnessed the enormous damage but could not begin to write of it, for he "would not know where to begin." He had come to see the limits of what his kind of literary temperament could accomplish in fiction. The following year, he again writes of how the fact of violence defeats his ability to write fiction. Observing that "I have not written short stories in a long while," he follows up in what initially seems a disconnected way. He writes "Today people are suffering even more, my views have changed since former times, and furthermore I see the trends in the new literature. In these circumstances, I cannot write something new and am unwilling to write anything old."[7] He seems to give three reasons why he is not writing fiction. The first, "today people are suffering even more," seems illogical. If anything, more suffering should point to more need for attention. But as it happens, "my views have changed since former times." For him, the increase in suffering is connected to his sense that literature, from his hand at any rate, is no longer sufficient. A third factor, "trends in the new literature," likely refers to the proletariat literature that he now advocates, a trend that does indeed logically rule out his participation. He cannot write as he thinks the times demand and he will not write as he used to. Here is an unsettling judgment on his own life.

One more element of the present volume's title, memory, is also much studied in literary criticism. Of the title's three elements, it most directly concerns a person's psychological makeup. For this reason and because it is frequently mentioned by Lu Xun as a force that helped shape his personality and his writings, it was surveyed most extensively in chapter 1.

For Lu Xun, memory encompasses both personal and national matters, highlighted differently in the 1923 and 1933 prefaces and constant throughout his writings. Significantly, his sole work of fiction that predates the vernacular writing of New Literature, from 1911, is already entitled "Remembering the Past," and contains both types of memory. Here the child narrator one day experiences a pleasant break from his lessons caused by a rumor of rebels approaching, and that evening he listens as his amah and the old manservant regale each other with tales of the bloody events that occurred when the Taiping rebels came to the house "more than forty years earlier." The instinct in Lu Xun's first work of fiction is to extend his child narrator's short memory by borrowing from his elders,[8] and it already contains memory that is both personal (a boy in the countryside suffering through lessons and enjoying his unexpected free time) and national (political unrest as it plays out for individuals caught in it).

Here early on is his ability to quickly capture the adventures and interests of childhood that were to "beguile" him his whole life. This is the personal, affectionate aspect of memory that readers have always responded to. Here is also memory of national events, which in this story makes a twofold commentary on the present of 1911. What their forebears had done to survive the Taiping rebellion was imitated forty years later by the tutor and neighbors on either side. Some thought to flee and save themselves; others, to stay and placate the new powers with banquets and gifts. Forty-plus years would place the anxious self-preservation of the gentry at about 1905, a time when there was indeed widespread local unrest in the run-up to the successful Republican Revolution. This story, written in 1911, used 1905 as a facade. "Ah Q" and many other writings have given us sardonic portraits of the uncertainties introduced as the 1911 revolution approached Shaoxing that are not unlike these events. The satire is as much about the previous year's revolution shorn of its republican ideals as it is about its ostensible time.

A more problematic feature of memory became deeply troublesome for Lu Xun over the years. If memory is history on the level of individual consciousness, then from this flows his great fear, expressed by N in "A Story about Hair" and repeated in many essays, that suffering and sacrifice will be forgotten because individuals are unreliable. He became a stickler about what memory and whose memory. He protected his version of things by means of precision. Especially in tense times and regarding people, he wrote only of what he knew directly (although he also left much out), so his eulogies avoided the emotionalism of a writer's ego. The facts themselves became the eloquence of the essay. Indeed, the details are not always complimentary to the dead, but somehow the total effect is more human and memorable. This is one reason his eulogies are so remarkable across a range of people, types of relationships, and time periods.[9] Who is to do the remembering also became an issue. Lu Xun feared that Liu Hezhen's memory was being trivialized as gossip and even that form of trivialized memory was short In this respect, Lu Xun did, as his critics accused him, live in the past. Another word for *memory* might be *experience*, and as experience accumulated without being lost along the way, he became more pessimistic.

Lu Xun's writings, which came at a timely moment, were instrumental in demonstrating to his emerging readership that when given an alternative the old had to be rejected. They gave readers the understanding and thus the directions for breaking away. In the earliest essays and a handful of vernacular language poems, he offered new visions—how to be a father (essays), how to love (poems). In other words, he wrote about how to be a person without Confucianism, how to be a father, a husband, and citizen without Confucian structures. Through translations, he and others provided instead the models of Dostoyevsky and Ibsen, Chekhov and Gogol. At the same time, the fiction offered the strong medicine of grim analyses. These writings, which had components of wishfulness and even hope, fit with the total iconoclasm advocated by New Culture Movement and its New Literature.

Today, nearly a century after the publication of his first writings, the watchwords are no longer *modern* and its variations but words like *market economy* and *globalization*. Lu Xun is still everywhere in contemporary Chinese society, but to a large extent, to use a new watchword, his presence is as a *brand* in the heritage industry. This is not the individual entrepreneurial spirit that causes someone, say, to open a Kong Yiji wineshop in Shaoxing (which does exist) but the organized, commercial-bureaucratic exploitation of a high-recognition name through projects such as theme parks with Lu Xun–related items that can be purchased (there is one outside Shaoxing). Not unlike Mozart chocolates, Lu Xun brand cigarettes and Lu Xun liquor have been proposed, perhaps even produced. A search of the Internet in Chinese in any given week produces news releases of plans for more Lu Xun–related tourist destinations, often partly government sponsored. One intriguing plan that did not come to pass is a high-tech park outside Beijing named after Lu Xun that was preemptively described as being ready for the city's 2008 Olympics.

The vast and rapid changes of recent years in China test the relationship of the past to the present, including the early modern past that is represented by Lu Xun. The government retains a stake in the status of Lu Xun as the country's most important modern writer if only because it has made him the literary centerpiece of its account of the rise and eventual victory of communism during the stages of early modern history, though that account is undergoing change. This support is concretely expressed in his selections in textbooks and in the continued development of acceptable commentaries in them for the use of students and teachers. However much such processes are recognized as the inculcation of ideology, the overall outcome tends to be, from a governmental point of view, the desired narrowing of ways to read a highly original author. However, such is the complex capacities of Lu Xun's writings that any promotion of them can come back to bite the promoters, as dissenting blogs in China continually demonstrate. The situation on the individual level is different: the magnetism of his writings has always created their own field of attraction, as the critics drawn on in this study have amply proved. A different stake in Lu Xun is held by the educated elite, especially those who have convincingly established a claim on the international stage in contemporary art, whether film, writing, or the visual arts. Here we see a general acknowledgment of a lineage that can be traced back to phenomena of the May Fourth era, including Lu Xun. As for the arts of traditional China, they likewise have an undisputed claim to international attention. It is the early modern past that is still in flux.

A fundamental challenge is that the prospects for serious literature are not clear, especially in terms of its size and its relation to the literate public. For millennia, literature, carefully, "naturally," defined in a certain way, has been the province of an elite, which has adjudicated matters of value and retention in a protracted time frame of its own. Once the readership was deliberately expanded, a direction successfully initiated during the May Fourth Movement and in step with worldwide postindustrial developments, the factors affecting literature's survivability were considerably changed. In China's case, this was initially obscured by a half century of controlled economics. Now, however, the survival of any serious author, much less a serious author from the 1920s and 1930s—the survival, not the pertinence of the author—is continually being tested by market forces in an arena where the dynamics are far from clarifying themselves. The segments of society that traditionally valued the goals of serious literature still thrive, as both scholarship and popular writing attest, but their relation to the commercial urban population is, quantitatively speaking, getting smaller. In such a world, adaptations and translations, or translation with adaptation, can represent ways to reach new audiences. These are avenues to which Lu Xun was very open, as his responses to the visual depictions of his work showed. Although he was cooler toward some of the proposed performances, other factors might have been at work, for many instances suggest a congenital sympathy on his part for new territory. He remarked once about "moving images" (*huodong dianying*) that teaching with them would most likely work better than lectures from a teacher and that one day perhaps all teaching would be in that form. He made this comment in passing, he said, and before he finished he was drowned out in laughter.[10] Of the future of "Ah Q" in translation, he said that "since life differs according to the author who looks at it and a work differs according to the reader of it, then the eyes of a [non-Chinese] reader, who has not the slightest sense of 'our traditional way of thought,' will perhaps see reflected in this work yet another kind of narrative. This seems very appealing to me."[11] Here is a writer ready to meet new worlds. The present study belongs to a more conventionally faithful genre of exploration than do adaptations, but the goal is similarly to convey the strong claim that is to be made upon our contemporary attention by Lu Xun's unique creations.

Appendix A

"Inscribed by the Author on a Small Likeness": Dating the Evidence; the Meaning of *shenshi* in Line 1

Dating the Evidence

There are three related questions: the date of the photograph, the date of the poem, and the date when the two were combined. These all have a bearing on their traditional association with Lu Xun's act of cutting his queue. Some repetition of chapter 2 is needed to make a clear exposition here.

The endpoint for dating the "Photograph with Hair Cut Short" (*duanfa xiang*) is clear enough, as is its association with queue cutting. Zhou Zuoren, then at Jiangnan Naval Academy in Nanjing, records the photograph's receipt in his diary on the twelfth day of the third month (April 10, 1903). There he gives it the name we know, presumably on the basis of the accompanying letter, dated April 2. As we saw in chapter 2, it was one of two photographs among a large number of books and other items carried by a friend from Japan. The diary entry, however, does not mention a poem on the back of the photograph. Since Zuoren did record the receipt of a 1902 photograph and did copy the poem inscribed on its back into his diary, it is reasonable to suppose that he did *not* receive the 1903 poem in its iconic form, on the back of the photograph. The careful conclusion would be that Xu Shoushang (see below) was the sole recipient of the photograph-cum-poem.

This leaves the date of the poem still open. The most common basis for dating the poem is based on Lu Xun's postscript when he wrote it out again in 1931, in which he says, "Composed at age 21, written out at age 51." This seemingly plain statement is unsatisfactory in a number of ways. Since he was then fifty-one by Chinese count, if we take twenty-one also to be the Chinese age, subtraction would give a date of 1901, when he was still in Nanjing. This would produce no association with the photograph or the queue-cutting. It is possible to get a later, and satisfactory, date of 1903 by arguing that while fifty-one is the Chinese count, twenty-one could be the Western count, and support this with evidence that there are other places where he uses two different systems in the same statement (a photograph of himself "at fifty" with his son "at one" uses both systems). Twenty-one also reflects the age he gave in numerous official documents of the time, for registration in Japan required the Western system and twenty-one in the Western system would give us 1903, which is highly satisfactory. Ni Moyan further shows that at other times Lu Xun got his dates of composition wrong, for example, for some of his stories.[1] A separate suggestion for 1903 is that he is rounding off, so fifty-one and twenty-one have a nice gap between them. He was definitely inclined to round off, for when he wrote out the poem again the next year (see chapter 4), he was still using thirty years' difference: his colophon read "first written 30 years ago."

Approaching the date of the poem from another angle, we might ask when Lu Xun paired the poem with the photograph. This also turns out not to be simple, although here the choices go in the other direction, between 1903 and 1904. Xu Shoushang is the source for both dates, providing 1903 twice and 1904 once. The first time is eight days after Lu Xun's death, when he writes, "In 1903, when we were students in Tokyo, he gave me a small photograph and later added a poem to it which read [and he quotes the poem]."[2] In this account, the photograph came first, in 1903, but the words "later added" have the sense of "soon after" so the two items are nearly coincident and the poem can still be from 1903. Two months later Xu gives an account in which he describes poem and photograph as sent to him as a unit in 1903: "In 1903 when he was 23, there was a poem 'Inscribed by the Author on a Small Likeness' which he gave me."[3] The same reference to Lu Xun's age as twenty-three when he sent the poem is made again in 1942, so we might count this as a third mention of 1903.[4]

Unfortunately, when Xu tells the story again, in October of 1947, though poem and photograph are again a unit, he gives 1904 as a date. And it is not a case of being off by a year. The circumstances he describes for 1904 could only have occurred in that year, for he writes, "After he had left for Sendai [in June 1904], he sent me a photograph on the back of which was a quatrain that read [and he quotes the poem]."[5] This is a hard memory to explain away. Indeed, he goes on to refer to one of his earlier accounts, saying, "I have already published about this in my essay 'Remembering the Past,'" without noting either the discrepancy, or the fact that there were two earlier accounts. The critic Yang Yanli takes it that both accounts are accurate, that Lu Xun sent the poem to Xu twice, although she does not wonder why he would do that.[6] To most critics, however, accepting 1904 means having to explain away 1903. For 1904, we would also need go to the content and suggest why the poem would be meaningful in Sendai when it presented a much different situation for Lu Xun than Tokyo had. Under these conditions, 1903 is both easier to justify and more desirable.

Finally, 1902 is another suggestion, but this one we can suppose is thrown into the mix because some critics want so much to reject 1901 but find Lu Xun's own words too hard to discount, and 1902 is the closest date to 1901 that would give us Japan as the location. But 1902 still predates the queue cutting and is unsatisfactory for that vested interest. Its existence only shows that once a suggestion is made, everyone has to chase it down if only to disprove it.

The Meaning of *shenshi* in Line 1

We know the overall topic of the poem is political because its vocabulary draws on standard political language as used in lyric poetry. Here I consider only the meaning of *shenshi* in line 1, "My mind has no wish to avoid the arrows of the god," for *shenshi* is interesting beyond its occurrence in this line: its unknown meaning presents a different kind of problem from the those of the other lines, which are only missing their topical references. The various attempts to gloss *shenshi* sheds an interesting light on vocabulary in a time of vast cultural transition; on the protectors of Lu Xun's legacy, chiefly Xu Guangping and Xu Shoushang; and on our assumptions as critics.

One solution was suggested in chapter 2, which is that lines 1 and 4 allude to a well-known poem of Liang Qichao's at a time when his ascendancy as a revolutionary was at its height. Liang's line is "I willingly offer my person as the target of ten thousand arrows." His willing self-sacrifice is in Lu Xun's line 4, and the arrows are in his line 1. *Shenshi* would then be the arrows in the political world that he would willingly endure, indeed steels himself to endure (steeling himself in that *lingtai*, the Taoist seat of one's being, is a strong term for "I"). The question remains, however, why add *shen* to *arrows*, why not just use *arrows*? The mature Lu Xun himself suggested a reason. Writing in 1934 about "Sparta," also from 1903, he told of his love for novelty in vocabulary at the time and gave an example of another instance of a coinage that is "something probably understood only by me now."[7] Using new words at a time when thought was all excitingly new—*shenshi* of the same year fits into this category.

There are other interpretations of the word *shenshi*.[8] One asks which god has arrows. The answer is Cupid, and both Xu Guangping and Xu Shoushang take the "arrows of god" to be the arrows of Cupid, though to different ends. Xu Shoushang says this twice, both times when writing about Lu Xun's classical poems. Listing some characteristics of the classical poems, he says that one favorite feature is the use of Greek and Roman allusions (which is actually not the case). Both times he gives the same example: "With *shenshi*, he is alluding to Cupid in Roman mythology" (using *Cupid* in English), and "he is using the love god of Roman mythology."⁹ Elsewhere he says that among the books on Lu Xun's desk in Tokyo (before Sendai) were volumes on Greek and Roman mythology.¹⁰ One would think that Xu, as a contemporary recipient, would know the meaning, but after glossing *shenshi* he does not then explain the line.

Xu Guangping also interprets the arrows as Cupid's, but she suggests, perhaps not unnaturally, that the young author is warding off the marriage that had been arranged for him at home to Zhu An or—the opposite suggestion—that he refers to going through with his arranged marriage to her.¹¹ Apparently Cupid would be a reference to his own love (actually loveless) situation. There is a logical problem here. The critic Li Yunjing recognizes that if line 1 is about the unwilling marriage and the photograph is about cutting the queue, the marriage and photograph have to be connected somehow. So he gives the following reconstruction. After Lu Xun learns of the marriage arranged for him, he tries to refuse but gets no answer from his mother: "It was in this period of conflict that, with a heavy rebellious heart, he cut off that queue hanging in the back of his head, that symbol of ethnic oppression, and furthermore had a photograph taken."¹²

In a larger context, the puzzle of *shenshi* brings up interesting issues about language in this time of cultural expansion. New words are very problematical. The fact that they are put together using common characters does not remove this difficulty of assigning them a meaning. Furthermore, although newly coined words came to be routine in vernacular poetry (and do occur in Lu Xun's few vernacular poems), new words are a rarity in classical lyric (*shi*) poetry, and new metaphors are also rare. Every new word is a major problem, as commentaries show. Its sense is comparatively certain when it has a direct Western-language equivalent, as was the case from the 1890s onward when many words were being invented or borrowed from Japanese inventions. In advocating "Cupid's arrows," both Xu Guangping and Xu Shoushang are placing *shenshi* into this category of new words with exact Western equivalents. Thus, although the comprehensive dictionary of modern Chinese, *Hanyu da cidian*, does include this word, it gives this poem as the example and Xu Shoushang's gloss of it as "a divine arrow" as the definition.

In appearance Cupid evolved into a chubby, naked little fellow with arrows at least as far back as the Renaissance. Botticelli's putto centered over the main figure in "Primavera" is so recognizable that he needs no explanation in popular culture, as his late-twentieth-century appearance a *New Yorker* cartoon shows (fig. A.1). When this figure appears in an utterly serious Chinese quatrain in 1903, we must ask whether a god with arrows ever meant anything other than love.

I have come across one serious use of, not exactly Cupid—no arrows—but winged putti that do not refer to love at the turn of the previous century and in quite a visible place, suggesting that although the example is from 1904 rather than 1903, modifications to Cupid may have been quite commonplace at one point. It is the identifying graphic for the magazine *Alarm Bell* (*Jingzhong*), which seeks to "awaken" the reader. The winged putto is on the cover of this progressive magazine (fig. A.2), striking the bell to awaken China's citizens to new knowledge, new views. The magazine contains progressive content: introductions to scientific information, famous historical figures, current events, and so on. The illustration in figure A.2 is a cover from 1904. (Later, only the bell was used.)

In the same period, a common use for a winged putto is the more familiar one of Cupid. These are advertisements for "renzao zilai xue" (man-made circulating blood?) evidently a nostrum that, according to the advertisement, strengthens the blood, cures symptoms of fatigue, and so on. The product had a long life: figure A.3 is from 1903 and figure A.4, a sleeker design with straight black hair, is from 1910. The latter, in *Shibao*, ran every day and came with testimonials from named people. While *Alarm Bell* shows that putti do not have to be about love, this advertisement must be about love, or at any rate a virilizing nostrum.

Figure A.1. Bernard Schoenbaum, "Come Back, Young Man. He Needs a Booster Shot." ©*The New Yorker*, February 11, 2002.

Figure A.2. A putto strikes the alarm bell that illustrates the magazine's name. The characters *jingzhong* are incised on the bell. 1904.

Finally there is an example in which Lu Xun does use a baby god with arrows in a poem, and he *is* Cupid. The clarity of this reference shows that the mysterious *shenshi* is probably not about love's arrows. In 1918 Lu Xun writes a poem, a vernacular poem, in which he invokes Cupid and explicitly identifies him. The god of love is in the title, *ai zhi shen* 愛之神; he is described in the first line, *xiaowazi* 小娃子 (baby); and he "spreads his wings in the air / An arrow (*jian* 箭, not *shi* 矢) in one hand, a bow in the other" (lines 1–2). He shoots it, and it strikes the poet in the breast (line 3), whereupon an exchange ensues about love, whom to love, and how to love.[13] Of course the time and language are very different in 1918 than in 1903, but still there is something to think about here. The poem is among a batch of writings Lu Xun sent to *New Youth* that were published in the May 1918 issue, the most famous of them being "Diary of a Madman." "Diary" was published under the pen name Lu Xun, and this poem, one of three, was published under the pen name Tang Si. It is interesting that in the first batch of pieces he wrote for *New Youth*, love is one topic. (The other two poems are intriguing too.) At any rate, those who want to find something personal on the question of love in Lu Xun's utterances might look there.

Figure A.3. A putto, European in hair and features, possibly Cupid, in an advertisement for a nostrum from *Eastern Miscellany*, 1903.

Figure A.4. His successor advertises the same item every day in *Shibao* in 1909.

Appendix B

Illustrators and Illustrations of Lu Xun's Fiction and His Person, 1934–36

This appendix lists the illustrations of Lu Xun's fiction and person made in his lifetime that I have located so far. They are grouped in three sections: (I) illustrations of the fiction published in *Theater* (September–December 1934), (II) all other illustrations of the fiction, and (III) portrayals of the author. Thumbnails are given of all available illustrations with the exception of those of Liu Xian (II.1), whose large volume of work is only sampled here.

I. Illustrations Published in *Theater*

Fifteen illustrations. The date of publication in *Theater* is given.

1. *Zhang Yunqiao* 張雲喬 (1910–2006). Kong Yiji. September 9, 1934. The writing behind Kong is the text of the adaptation running into the picture frame. Scrawny, holding a wine cup. An actor at this time, in this year Zhang was the cinematographer for the movie "Plunder of Peach and Plum" (*Tao Li jie*), which starred *Theater*'s editor and "Ah Q" adaptor Yuan Muzhi, who also wrote the film's script. The production was from the film company Diantong, which had underground Communist connections.[1]

Figure B.1. Zhang Yunqiao, *Kong Yiji*.

2. *Hong Zhenglun* 洪正倫. Head of Ah Q. September 15, 1934. Scrawny, very short queue, just to the nape of the neck. Hong is identified as one of the founders of the Chinese Drama Association (Zhongguo xiju xuehui), whose first production was a Cao Yu play produced on January 1, 1937.[2]

Figure B.2. Hong Zhenglun, *Ah Q*.

3. *Ma Guoliang* 馬國亮 (1908–2001). Runtu, the peasant from "Hometown." September 23, 1934. Almost half length, full-faced, sturdy, with a hat pulled down. Ma was a longtime editor at the Shanghai pictorial magazine *The Companion*. His memoirs, published 2002, describe how while editor he was able to arrange a photography session with Lu Xun through an introduction by the artist Situ Qiao but was not able to repeat that feat when he tried again.³ For his portrait of Lu Xun, see figure B.36.

Figure B.3. Ma Guoliang, *Runtu*.

4. *Lu Shaofei* 魯少飛 (1903–95). Ah Q. September 30, 1934. Half length, scrawny, holding a pipe. A cartoonist active in Shanghai in the 1920s and 1930s. Editor of *Modern Sketch (Shidai manhua)* at this time. One of founders in 1928 of the weekly entertainment illustrated paper *Shanghai Sketch* (with Ye Qianyu), for which he drew, in Sullivan's phrase, "vulgar covers."⁴ His activism in the use of art for political purposes came later, in the war against Japan. In February 1934, Lu did an imagined group portrait of Shanghai literary notables that included Lu Xun (see fig. B.42).

Figure B.4. Lu Shaofei. *Ah Q*.

5. *Ye Qianyu* 葉淺予 (1907–95). Old Master Zhao. October 7, 1934. Full length, tilted, thin and bulgy face, mandarin cap. Old Master Zhao is the head of one of two gentry families in Weizhuang village in "Ah Q." He is the one who slaps Ah Q in the scene depicted by Chen Tiegeng in figure B.16. The style is like other examples of Ye's work. A self-taught painter and cofounder of *Shanghai Sketch*, for which he drew, again in Sullivan's phrase, "lurid covers," Ye created the long-running social satire series "Mr. Wang" (Wang xiansheng). He, Lu Shaofei (I.4), and Zhang Zhengyu (I.7) are three of the six founders of the Shanghai Cartoon Society (Shanghai manhuahui).

Figure B.5. Ye Qianyu, *Old Master Zhao*.

6. *Zhang E* 張諤 (1910–95). The young nun in "Ah Q." October 14, 1934. Highly stylized in use of clothing, moxa marks contributing to the stylization. She is the one Ah Q pats on the head and pinches on the cheek, the

touch leaving his hand with a strange sensation for days. Zhang was a graduate of art academies in Hangzhou and Shanghai; joined the League of Left-Wing Artists on its inception in 1930; was art editor at *Zhonghua ribao*, the paper for which *Theater* is a supplement; and was editor at *Manhua yu shenghuo* (Cartoons and life), which published several Lu Xun essays. In the debates in the mid-1930s over the mission of *manhua*, Zhang E "issue[d] a call-to-arms to his fellows: 'Manhua artists in China today should turn every fountain pen, brush, and eraser into a tool for struggle and share in the common responsibility of those who paint.'"⁵

Figure B.6. Zhang E, *The Young Nun of Jingxiu Convent*.

7. *Zhang Zhengyu* 張正宇 (1900–76). Successful Provincial Candidate from "Ah Q." October 28, 1934. Full length, stout, glasses, long gown, jacket, mandarin cap, reading. This person lives in town and agilely secures a position in the new government when the revolution arrives. Zhang was a native of Jiangsu and a decorative painter and stage designer, as well as cartoonist. He was the twin brother of Zhang Guangyu 張光宇, also a cartoonist (though not in this set). Both were founding members of the Shanghai Cartoon Society and were active in the societies founded during the war effort against the Japanese beginning in 1937.

Figure B.7. Zhang Zhengyu, *Successful Provincial Candidate*.

8. *Ye Lingfeng* 葉靈鳳 (1904–75). Ah Q, head. November 4, 1934. Shown with very short queue and a cap made of pieces of satin pieced together. Comment on right reads, "if he were living today, Ah Q would surely not look like this." Here Ye probably allies himself with Lu Xun's critics from the Creation Society, the new radicals who called him (and Ah Q) figures of the past. Signed "LF" at lower left. A printmaker and active in artistic periodicals, Ye is probably most familiar for his Aubrey Beardsley-like prints. He was a founding member of the Creation Society, a group with which Lu Xun had a contentious relationship even after they and he had both moved over to the Left. The two men have a history of mutual antagonism in which Lu Xun imputes plagiarism to Ye, taking the trouble to publish

Figure B.8. Ye Lingfeng, *Ah Q*.

volumes on two artists to demonstrate the close similarity between their work and Ye's. In turn, Ye has a character in a work of fiction say that he is going to use *Call to Arms* as toilet paper.⁶ Yet in an introduction to an important woodcut supplement to *Les Contemporains* (*Xiandai*), Ye singled out Lu Xun's discerning support of woodcuts.⁷

9. *Xu Xingzhi* 許幸之 (1904–91). Ah Q, head. November 11, 1934. This is a strange depiction: Ah Q, his hair (or his ear?) bulging out on the left, from which a thin queue descends. The editor notes that Xu had rushed out this work for the supplement and adds that "this is a watercolor. It is a pity we cannot show you the colors but it will be gathered into 'Illustrations of Ah Q' (*Ah Q huaji*)," a plan evidently never realized. The watercolor medium probably accounts for why the newsprint version is so murky.

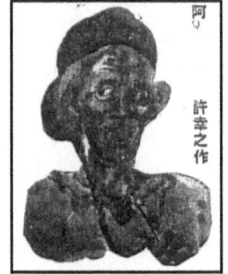

Figure B.9. Xu Xingzhi, *Ah Q*.

Xu initially studied art in Shanghai, then in Japan from 1924 to 1930. When he returned to Shanghai, he was appointed chair of painting at China Art College (where the League of Left-Wing Writers held its founding meeting), took a major part in the debates on the Left on the goals of visual arts that paralleled the debates on the literary side, and helped found the League of Left-Wing Artists. He was connected to both film and Lu Xun. His work in film was hugely popular during the war against Japan, one film featuring what became the national song of the People's Republic.⁷ He made a death portrait of Lu Xun. The following year he published a stage adaptation, called "The True Story of Ah Q," in six acts, which he revised many times in its publication history.⁸

10. *Huang Miaozi* 黃苗子 (1913–). Kong Yiji. November 18, 1934. Full length, long gown, cap, wispy beard, gaunt. Huang was a *manhua* artist, calligrapher, art critic, and friend of Feng Zikai.⁹ Like several others listed here, he drew cartoons for *Shanghai Sketch* through Ye Qianyu's (I.5) introduction. As a twenty-one-year old he was made art editor of *Fiction Semimonthly* from the third, overhauled issue to the final, nineteenth issue. It became a large-format, lavishly produced literary magazine that published many of the artists listed here: Feng Zikai, Ma Guoliang, Li Xudan, Lu Shaofei, Ye Qianyu, and Zhang E. Mao Dun soon decided that the

Figure B.10. Huang Miaozi, *Kong Yiji*.

magazine was "petits fours for the bourgeoisie," but Lu Xun sent two essays and appeared in several of its sections.[10] In 1935, Huang laid out a credo in "My Theory of Manhua" stating that social themes must be treated in fresh ways based on observation.[11] His portrait of Lu Xun is at figure B.40.

11. Li Xudan 李旭丹. Ah Q, head. November 25, 1934. Wearing a small cap and looking completely shaven, head thrust out of a window. Character "Dan" on lower left. Although I have found little about Li, he must have been an integral member of the art and literary scene, for a great many of his illustrations of the works of well-known writers were published in Huang Miaozi's *Fiction Semimonthly*.

Figure B.11. Li Xudan, *Ah Q*.

12. Chen Tiegeng. "And Slapped Him." December 2, 1934. See figure B.16.

13. Zhang Yunhong 張雲鴻. Tavern owner in "Storm." December 23, 1934. Wearing a cap, his queue not visible, front of head shaven, holding a long pipe. The tavern owner brought the news of the emperor's restoration and gloated while Seven-Pounds worried about his suddenly wrong short hair. I have found no information on Zhang.

Figure B.12. Zhang Yunhong, *The Tavern Owner*.

14. Chen Tiegeng. Uncaptioned. December 16, 1934. See figure B.17.

15. Chen Tiegeng. "Words not Hands." December 30, 1934. See figure B.18.

II. Other Illustrations of Lu Xun's Fiction

Artists are listed in order of the quantity of their work on Lu Xun's fiction before 1936, including works that are known to have existed but have not been located. Nearly all are woodcuts.

1. *Liu Xian* 劉峴 (1915–90). 106 woodcuts in four volumes of *lianhuanhua*, plus others. This is by far the largest number of illustrations of Lu Xun's work in his lifetime. Liu was the recipient of five long letters from Lu Xun on woodcuts, which he published as a postface to his "Ah Q." Initially self-trained in woodcuts, Liu became a well-established woodcut artist after his return from study in Japan (1934–37). It is informative about the woodcut scene in the 1930s to see the energy with which the very young Liu Xian approached his calling. He may be typical of the world in which he was immersed, but in his case, we are fortunate to have a great deal of surviving evidence as far as his Lu Xun-related subject matter is concerned. In 1934–36, he illustrated *Weeds* and made *lianhuanhua* of four works of fiction, three of which comprise volume 2 of *Catalog of Woodcuts* (the fourth, "White Light," presumably did not survive). From Lu Xun's letters, we know that Liu Xian also sent him a number of other single-sheet works.[12] In chronological order, Liu's works are as follows.

Weeds (35, 1 per page), dated 1934. The first "publication" of the Unnamed Woodcut Society, 未名木刻社, of which Lin was a cofounder, and evidently the only copy made. This is a good example of the improvised nature of the publication of woodcuts.

"Storm" (20, 2 per page), dated 1934, sent to Lu Xun but not subsequently published.

"Ah Q" (20, 1 per page), published in June 1935 by the Unnamed Woodcut Society.

"Kong Yiji" (31, 2 per page plus one last page), published serially in the periodical *Intellectual Life* 2, nos. 3–12 (June–October, 1935).[13]

According to Liu Xian, he also illustrated "White Light," which does not survive. Another work, a cover that is a collage of the main characters, does not survive.[14]

Three illustrations are given here. The first (fig. B.13) is a scene from "Storm" in which Seven-Pounds and his family watch the tavern owner approach. The second (fig. B.14) is the execution scene in "Ah Q," the same moment as in Cheng Shifa's (fig. 5.1). The last (fig. B.15) illustrates "Kong Yiji" at the same moment in the story when Kong is hesitating over his handful of aniseed peas, having already given too many to the children.

Figure B.13. Liu Xian, from "Storm."

Figure B.14. Liu Xian, from "Ah Q."

Figure B.15. Liu Xian, from "Kong Yiji."

2. *Chen Tiegeng* 陳鐵耕 (1908–70). Ten woodcuts of "Ah Q," three known. Chen was a participant in the 1931 woodcut workshop organized by Lu Xun, one of five from Xingning, Guangzhou. Lu Xun had the illustrations. Three survive because they were published in *Theater* (December 2, 16, 30). The others were presumably discarded or lost when the adaptation ceased. We know that one has a motorized vehicle (*motoche*) in it.[15] The three are published here for the first time since *Theater*. A fascicle of Chen's other work is in *Catalog of Woodcuts*, vol. 2.

B.16. A scene from "Ah Q." The caption reads "Ah Q kept his mouth shut. He was thinking of retreating, when Old Master Zhao took a quick step forward and slapped him across the face." This occurs in chapter 1, when Ah Q claims that his family name is also Zhao, though, if you count carefully, he is in fact three generations older than the Zhao family's Successful County Candidate. The illustration shows Old Master Zhao's response.

B.17. No caption. A man faces front with his right hand raised. It is not clear which moment in "Ah Q" is illustrated. The caption simply says "second 'Ah Q' illustration."

B.18. Caption. "'A gentleman uses his words, not his hands!' cried Ah Q, with his head wedged at an angle." Ah Q has just picked a fight with Whiskers Wang, and when Wang grabs his queue and twists, he quotes this proverb hopefully.

Figure B.16. Chen Tiegeng, "*and Slapped Him*."

Figure B.17. Chen Tiegeng, uncaptioned.

Figure B.18. Chen Tiegeng, "*Words, Not Hands!*"

3. *Wei Mengke* 魏猛克 (1911–84). Five drawings of "Ah Q." Not located. They were commissioned from Wei at Lu Xun's suggestion (*Letters* 340306)[16] for Edgar Snow's proposed publication of "Ah Q" in English translation in his *Living China*. He received five and sent them on. This information on the commission is frequently repeated, but in fact, as Snow notes in his preface, for reasons of space the anthology did not include "Ah Q" and the illustrations were not used. They are not in the two British editions I have seen (1936 and 1937) nor in the 2 U.S. editions of 1936 and 1937. They seem not to be in Snow's papers at the University of Missouri nor with the papers of Nym Wales, then Snow's wife, at Stanford's Hoover Institution. For Wei's rendering of Lu Xun, see figure B.37.

4. *Qu Qiubai* (1899–1935). Two drawings (or perhaps one if fig. B.20 is not correctly attributed), both of Ah Q. In this drawing, a doodle really, 4 cm square, done with a calligraphy brush, Ah Q is a composite of ten *Q*s. Initially he is an odd-looking figure, but soon the balance becomes apparent: the right leg is bent at the knee against the left arm akimbo at the elbow, and the whole is alive and balanced against the thin line of the lash, which is formed by extending the tail of one *Q*. The words "Steel lash in hand I will thrash you" are on the right. This is a stirring line sung by a derring-do fellow in a sung drama. The drawing was found in 1982 in central government archives among Qu Qiubai's manuscripts and is described as using the same type of paper as Lu Xun's manuscripts.[17] Hence the suggested date is 1933, when Qu and his wife took refuge in Lu Xun's home.

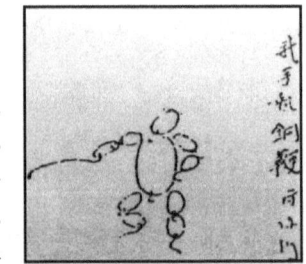

Figure B.19. Qu Qiubai, "*Steel Lash in Hand.*"

The second drawing is printed here from its publication in *Seventy Years of Ah Q*, where its previous attributions are visible: on the upper left of this republication are the characters "Ah Q" and on the lower right, the characters "by Qu Qiubai." It is a very different drawing from figure B.19. Gao Xin finds it practiced, but with a force and style that is more typical of professional illustrators. Moreover, he could not find the publication and issue sourced by *Seventy Years of Ah Q* for this.[18]

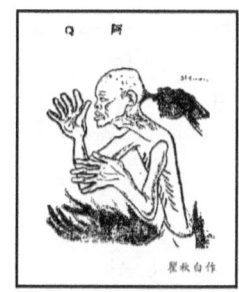

Figure B.20. Qu Qiubai (attrib.), *Ah Q*.

5. *Cao Bai* 曹白 (b. 1917). One woodcut. "Lu Xun and Xianglin sao." *Catalog of Woodcuts*, 5:1598. The narrator and Xianglin sao meet in the opening scene of "New Year's Sacrifice." The narrator is taken to be Lu Xun; Xianglin sao, formerly a servant in his uncle's household, is now clearly a beggar. The two figures are surrounded by vignettes from the story. Above them to the right, lightly incised, is Xianglin sao being pulled two ways in the afterworld by her two husbands, as she believes will happen. Below them, also lightly cut, is a wolf, which in the story had killed her son when they lived in the mountains. Other elements are puzzling. Why are sharp lines emerging from around his head? Why is there a white block (of light?) around the two figures? Cao also did a portrait of Lu Xun (fig. B.41), and two other woodcuts by him are preserved in *Catalog of Woodcuts*.

Figure B.21. Cao Bai, Lu Xun and Xianglin sao.

6. *Lai Shaoqi* 赖少麒 (1915–2000). "Portrait of Ah Q" (Ah Q xiang). This was the title when it was published in *Wenxue* 5, no. 1 (July 1935), and this is how Lu Xun refers to it as well. Lai, however, titles it "Mr. Lu Xun" in his *Poetry and Woodcuts* 詩與版畫. Lu Xun sent it and another woodcut to *Wenxue*, of which he was an editor.[19]

Figure B.22. Lai Shaoqi. *Portrait of Ah Q*.

Lai's design is not easy to read. It takes a while to work out why some of the items are so large, but after a while one sees that the depicted objects come in two sizes. In the large size are a book on whose open pages sit a quill pen (!) and bottle of ink; other items in this size are a stopper (on the lower left) and a lit candle (!). The small-scale items are vignettes from the fiction, indicating the purpose of the large objects. A notable element is Lu Xun's face on the label of an ink bottle. It is not quite recognizable, which Lu Xun says allowed it to pass the censors, thus seeming to suggest that poor resemblance was intentional. In the lower left corner is the character *qi* for Lai Shaoqi.

7. *Wang Junchu* 王鈞初 (1905–86). One oil painting, dated summer 1935, and titled "Reading *Call to Arms*." It shows a student, a soldier, and a worker together reading a copy of the anthology in its iconic vermillion cover. It was given to Lu Xun by the artist at their first meeting and was in Lu Xun's living room at his death, where it remains today. Wang was in Shanghai for about two months on his way from Beijing to study in the Soviet Union. There are many records of drawings by Wang in the Nym Wales archives at the Hoover Institution.

Figure B.23. Wang Junchu. *Reading "Call to Arms."*

8. *Feng Zikai* 豐子凱 (1898–1975). I list Feng conservatively as having one illustration, the one referred to in Lu Xun's conversation as reported in *Theater* on October 28, 1934. There it is described as an illustration of a laborer leaning against a counter, drinking, and behind him a placard in the wineshop that reads 太白遺風, "Lingering Evocations of Li Bai." I have not located the cartoon in question, but a 1950 illustration of Kong Yiji leaning against a counter, with a different placard behind him, is used here as a placeholder.[20]

Figure B.24. Feng Zikai, from "Kong Yiji".

9. *Artist unknown.* Illustration for the wrapper of George K. Leung's translation of Ah Q (Lu Xun, *True Story of Ah Q* [Shanghai:Commercial Press in Shanghai, 1926]. Ni Moyan must have seen this, for he describes it in detail:

> It is a watercolor that extends to the back of the wrapper. Ah Q sits by the side of the road on a large stone. All around him are fields, and in the fields are work buffaloes. In the near distance are trees, some homes, a river; further on are mountain peaks, and behind him is a mud shrine. This is a typical farming village of the Jiangnan area. Ah Q trails a long queue behind him

APPENDIX B : 249

and wears a black top and blue pants. He is barefoot and smoking a pipe. This is consistent with farming people in Jiangnan, although the clothing is too tidy and does not reflect Ah Q's poverty. This is also true of his face, which is somewhat refined for what he is.

From Zhang Yiping (1902-46), we also learn that upon seeing it, Lu Xun "commented, 'Ah Q was more cunning than this, he was not so honest-looking'."[21] Zhang was one of the young people who worked with Lu Xun on the periodical *Yusi* and became a member of the League of Left-Wing Writers. He had heard that the illustration was by a German. The copies I was able to see did not have wrappers, nor did the ones I could find for sale on line.

10. *Woodcuts entitled "Nahan," diverse hands.* Four woodcuts from this period in *Catalog of Woodcuts* bear the title "Call to Arms" (Nahan). (1) Chen Zhonggang 陳仲鋼 (active 1930s). Published in *Xiandai banhua*, 1934. *Catalog of Woodcuts*, 1:227. One man, half length, with arms lifted, shouting. (2) Tang Yingwei 唐英偉 (b.1915). Published in *Xiandai banhua*, 1934. *Catalog of Woodcuts*, 1:265. Three men, half-length, one in front, all shouting. (3) Tang Yingwei (again). Published in *Muke jie*, 1936. *Catalog of Woodcuts*, 5:1523. Five figures, full length. One man in front, four smaller ones behind him, all arms raised in some fashion, shouting. Tang did the cover for *Muke jie*, a similar print entitled "Forward!" See http://kaladarshan.arts.ohio-state.edu/exhib/gug/indxs/mod/modgraphdes.html (4). Xu Lian 徐濂. Published in *Zhonghua muke ji*, 1936. *Catalog of Woodcuts*, 4:1200. Four men, half figures, raising their arms and fists up to the sky, clearly based on the well-known 1924 Olympic poster.

Figure B.25. Chen Zhonggang, *Nahan*.

Figure B.26. Tang Yingwei, *Nahan*.

Figure B.27. Tang Yingwei, *Nahan*.

Figure B.28. Xu Lian, *Nahan*.

III. Portrayals of Lu Xun

Surviving portraits of Lu Xun predate surviving illustrations of the fiction. The list here begins in 1930. Omitted are portraits done by artists in his circle, that is, portraits resulting from frequent personal contact such as Tao Yuanqing's. Most of those listed here are not from life; in most cases, the artists did not know Lu Xun personally at the time of the drawing, but nearly all came to have an association with him. Several portraits are decorated with figures and scenes from his fiction, an indication of how much the person and the work were identical in the artists' minds. As to sources, some are reproduced here from their initial publication. Four were woodcuts and in Lu Xun's possession at the time of his death (Xu Shiquan, fig. B.30; Chen Guangzong, fig. B.35; Cao Bai, fig. B.41; and Zhong Buqing, fig. B.43), and hence are in *Catalog of Woodcuts*. Finally, Ye Shusui and Yang Yanli's chapter on likenesses of Lu Xun contains a number of works from the Beijing Lu Xun Museum that I have not seen published elsewhere.[22] The listing is by date.

1. *Artist unknown*. Cover of Li Helin, ed., *Essays on Lu Xun*, the 1930 collection of criticism published without Lu Xun's cooperation. Figure B.29 is not a recognizable likeness except for the moustache. It does bear some resemblance to Ma Guoliang's sketch, figure B.36.

2. *Xu Shiquan* 徐詩荃 (b. 1909). 1931. *Catalog of Woodcuts*, 5:1467. Very large at 29.2 x 19.4 cm. A sheet at Shanghai Lu Xun Museum shows that on the bottom left, outside the print area, are the words "respectfully made by Fengli" 風笠謹制 and the date 1931.1. Almost a half-length portrait, the face is Western in appearance. The Chinese gown is fastened with noticeable frogs and a patterned collar and yoke.

Primarily a writer, Xu met Lu Xun in 1928. The next year he went to study in Germany, where he purchased many books, magazines and woodcuts for Lu Xun. Xu made this portrait in Germany, for while a student at Heidelberg University, he also enrolled in a woodcut class at an art school.[23] The image here is the cover of *A Day's Work* (*Yitian de gongzuo*), an anthology of Russian short stories translated by Lu Xun and published 1936. The advertisement used here ran in *Harp* (*Shuqin*) (see also figure B.36).

Figure B.29. Artist unknown. Cover of *Lu Xun lun*.

Figure B.30. Xu Shiquan, portrait of Lu Xun as cropped for cover of *A Day's Work*.

3. *Liu Xian.* Four portraits. 1932–33. The prolific Liu Xian produced more portraits than the others listed here. Except for figure B.31 (*Catalog of Woodcuts* 3:829), the others exist only in photographic records at the Beijing Lu Xun Musuem.[24] Figure B.32 shows Lu Xun in a black scholar's gown and square-cut hair, familiar from formal photographs from the mid-1920s onwards. Figures B.33 and B.34 are based on newspaper photographs: Lu Xun lecturing on his return to Beijing in 1932, when he stood on a table above the crowd that had gathered to hear him; and George Bernard Shaw's visit to Shanghai in 1933. In figure B.37, Wei Mengke makes use of the same Bernard Shaw visit and photograph.

Figure B.31. Liu Xian, Lu Xun, from *Yecao*.

Figure B.32. Liu Xian, Lu Xun, portrait.

Figure B.33. Liu Xian, Lu Xun lecturing out of doors, after news photograph.

Figure B.34. Liu Xian, Lu Xun and Bernard Shaw, after news photograph.

4. *Chen Guangzong* 陳光宗 (1915–91). 1932 and 1934. Portrait from 1932 a woodcut (*Catalog of Woodcuts*, 5:1469). In three-quarter profile, smiling(?), messy hair. On the right are the words "Portrait of Lu Xun by Chen Guangzong"; on the left, "Presented by Dongtang Literature and Art Society." A note on the back, addressed to a fellow Wenzhou native, reads, "Please print in *Lunyu* or transmit to Mr. Lu Xun. He likes woodcuts, so this may be a specimen." Lu Xun noted its receipt in his diary on August 1, 1933. A web site on Wenzhou artists and Lu Xun dates this to just before Chen's 1932 graduation from high school.[25]

Figure B.35. Chen Guangzong. *Portrait of Lu Xun*.

Lu Xun mentions a second portrait in a 1935 letter, referring to it as a drawing (*manhua*), now lost. It had gone the rounds of four magazines: three feared being closed down by censors, while one ceased publication before it could publish the work. Lu Xun asked that it be forwarded to him, for he thought perhaps when he next made up a collection of essays, he might be able to publish it there.[26] It is described by Ye Shusui and Yang Yanli as a full-length portrayal, casually posed.[27]

5. *Ma Guoliang.* January 1933. Cover of a 1933 volume of translated Russian short fiction *Harp* (*Shuqin*), edited by Lu Xun, in a series published by Liangyou. (As noted in B.3, Ma was the editor of Liangyou's pictorial magazine *Companion*). Figure B.36 is from the advertisement for *Harp* (an advertisement which appeared in that work!). Liangyou publishers issued both *Harp* and *A Day's Work* (see fig. B.31). The identification of the artist is made by Ye Shusui and Yang Yanli.[28]

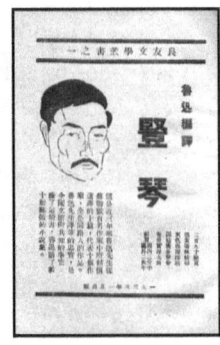

Figure B.36. Ma Guoliang, Lu Xun on cover of *Harp*.

6. *Wei Mengke.* "Lu Xun and Gorky," published in *Lunyu*, June 1, 1933. Brush and ink. An extremely tall, stalky Maksim Gorky is next to an extremely short, wide Lu Xun. The characters *yanran* (Dignified Indeed!) are on the upper left. Published here for the first time since *Lunyu.* See II.3 for an account of Wei's "Ah Q" drawings.

7. *Liang Yiqiu* 梁以俅 (1906–). September 1933. Chalk, after the photograph taken for Edgar Snow's *Living China*. Received by Lu Xun via Snow's English secretary Yao Ke, September 24, 1933. Figure B.38 is now in the Beijing Lu Xun Museum.[29]

Figure B.37. Wei Mengke, *Lu Xun and Gorky*.

8. *Luo Qingzhen* 羅清楨 (1905–42). 1933. "Portrait of Mr. Lu Xun." *Catalog of Woodcuts*, 2:889. Dimensions 32.3 x 23 cm. It is Luo, together with Li Hua, who was commended by name by Lu Xun for his skill. From 1933 on, Lu Xun's diary records numerous exchanges of letters and woodcuts, and in the summer of 1934 Luo made Lu Xun's acquaintance at Uchiyama's Bookstore. This portrait, however, came before their meeting and is based on a photograph that Lu Xun had sent him "taken this year, too serious in appearance." He wrote a few weeks later to say that if Luo had not started yet, to hold off a bit and he would find one or two that might better serve as the basis for a portrait. Two days later, however,

Figure B.38. Liang Yiqiu, Lu Xun.

two prints arrived. Lu Xun praised them and said that several of his friends would like one, so he was sending Luo some paper for, if possible, four or five further prints. These Luo sent on the twenty-fourth, together with prints on other subjects. Many at Luo's middle school in Guangdong also had asked for prints, so there must be many extant.[30] Figure B.39 was also published in 1934 in Qingzhen Woodcuts 清楨木刻畫, second collection.

Figure B.39. Luo Qingzhen, Lu Xun, *Qingzhen muke hua*.

9. *Huang Miaozi* 黃苗子. 1934. Figure B.40 is one of four in a projected series of portraits, "Writers and Artists," published in his *Fiction Semimonthly*. For more information about the magazine and for his drawing of Kong Yiji, see figure B.10 and accompanying text.

10. *Cao Bai*. 1935. *Catalog of Woodcuts*, 5:1599. The head of Lu Xun is surrounded by ten or twelve vignettes, some of which I cannot identify. Both this and "Lu Xun and Xianglin-sao" (fig. B.21) were made after his release from prison in spring 1935. Cao sent this woodcut to the Second Coordinated National Woodcut Exhibit where it was rejected by the censors because of the subject matter. He then sent it to Lu Xun, who wrote an explanation of this history in the left margin (not shown).

Figure B.40. Huang Miaozi, *Lu Xun*.

11. *Lu Shaofei*, 1936. "Portrait of a Literary Tea," done for the inaugural issue of *The Six Arts* (*Liu yi*) in this year. The gathering is an imagined one, many personalities gathered in one room, each given a brief characteristic in the witty identifying commentary below the illustration. Lu Xun is standing in the back, second from the left. Lu has him talking to the famous novelist Ba Jin about a publishing project. Lu's portrait of Ah Q is at figure B.4.[31]

Figure B.41. Cao Bai, *Lu Xun*.

Figure B.42. Lu Shaofei, *Portrait of a Literary Tea*.

12. Zhong Buqing 鍾步清 (b. 1910). 1936. "Portrait of Lu Xun," *Catalog of Woodcuts*, 5:1706. Lu Xun's diary records his receipt of a letter and woodcut on May 28, 1936. Zhong was from the county of Xingning, Guangzhou, and a student at Shanghai Art Acadamy, He was a participant in the August 1931 woodcut workshop and helped found the MK Society in 1933. This portrait has a handwritten paragraph underneath, addressed to Lu Xun. It says, among other things, "This portrait is not a good resemblance because it is based on a group shot taken at the 1930 [*sic*] woodcut workshop. . . . If you have a more recent photograph, could you please send me a copy and I will make another one. It is sure to be an improvement on this."

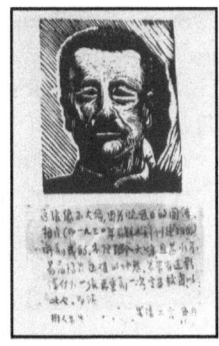

Figure B.43. Zhong Buqing, *Lu Xun*.

13. Liqun 力群. (b. 1912). 1936. *Catalog of Woodcuts* 5:1384. On the upper right are two shelves of books; to the left, a comb (?); and to the lower left a hand grasping a pen with a kind with nib and a dog looking up at it. The woodcut reached Lu Xun through Cao Bai, and he thanked Liqun through Cao. Earlier in the year, Lu Xun had chosen a woodcut of Liqun's for Mao Dun's project "A Day in China" (中國的一日). Liqun met his subject only days before Lu Xun's death, at his last public event, the Second Coordinated National Woodcut Exhibit's Shanghai venue. He was one of the pallbearers at the funeral, and figure B.44 was one of three portraits used in the funeral procession. This woodcut by Liqun is frequently incorporated as an element in the design of book covers.

Figure B.44. Liqun, Lu Xun.

List of Characters

A Ying 阿英
Ah Q huaji 阿Q畫集
Ah Q zhengzhuan: wenxue juben
    阿Q正傳: 文學劇本
Ah Q zhi di 阿Q之弟
Ai Qing 艾青
Anhui suhua bao 安徽俗話報

Baren 巴人
Bai Mang 白莽
baihua 白話
beiai 悲哀
Beidou 北斗
Beijing ribao 北京日報
beizhuang 悲壯
Bencao gangmu 本草綱目
bilei yixin 壁壘一新
bianzi jiangjun 辮子將軍
bianzi jun 辮子軍
Buzhou mountain 不周山

Cai E 蔡鍔
Cai Yuanpei 蔡元培
Cao Juren 曹聚仁
Caoyan jiyong 操演技勇
Cao Yu 曹禺
Chen Duxiu 陳獨秀
Chenbao fukan 晨報副刊
Chenbao wenxue xunkan
    晨報文學旬刊
Chenlun 沉淪
Cheng Shifa 程十髮
chiren 吃人
chiren yu lijiao 吃人與禮教

Chuci 楚辭
Chuangxia suibi 窗下隨筆
Chuangzao she 創造社
chuangzuo tan 創作壇
Chundi huahui 春地畫會

dayoushi 打油詩
daode 道德
dazhonghua 大眾化
dazhong yuyan 大眾語言
Diantong 電通
dianying 電影
Ding Ling 丁玲
Ding Song 丁悚
Dongcheng 東城
Dushu shenghuo 讀書生活
duanfa xiang 斷髮相
Duan Ganqing 段干青
Duan Qirui 段祺瑞

Fan Ainong 范愛農
Fan Zeng 范曾
Feng Keng 馮鏗
Feng Sheng 風聲
Feng Wenbing 馮文炳
Feng Xuefeng 馮雪峰
Feng Ziyou 馮自由
fengbo 風波
Fengyun ernü 風雲兒女

geyan 格言
Gong Zhuxin 宮竹心
guapimao 瓜皮帽
guanhua 官話

Guo Shiqi 郭士琦
Guomin gongbao 國民公報

Han Qiangshi 韓強士
Hanyu da cidian 漢語大詞典
Hanzu 漢族
hao 號
hengfu 橫幅
Hu Gongshou 胡公壽
Hu Yebin 胡也瀕
Hu Yichuan 胡一川
hua diao wannian 花雕晚年
Huayuanzhuang 花園莊
Huang Houhui 黃后繪
Huang Jinxiang 黃金祥
Huang Su 黃素
Huang Xing 黃興
huodong dianying 活動電影

jimo 寂寞
Jian cai qiyi 見財起意
Jiang Feng 江豐
Jiang Jingsan 蔣徑三
Jing Meijiu 景梅九
Jing Yinyu 敬隱漁
Jingzhong 警鍾
ju E yiyongjun 據俄義勇團
juyi 局易
Juewu 覺悟
junzi 君子

Kang Youwei 康有為
Kōbun Academy 弘文學院

Li Dazhao 李大釗
Li Hua 李樺
Li Lisan 李立三
Li sao 離騷
Li Weisen 李偉森
Li Yuanhong 黎元洪
Liangyou 良友

lianhuanhua 連環畫
Liang Qichao 梁啓超
Liangjiang 兩江
Lin Shu 林紓
Lingshi zhuo du 領事捉賭
Liu Bannong 劉半農
Liu Feiqi 柳非杞
Liu Jian'an 劉建庵
Liulichang 琉璃廠
Liu Yazi 柳亞子
Liu yi 六藝
liumangqi 流氓氣
Lunyu 論語
Luzhen 魯鎮

MK Society MK 木刻研究會
manhua 漫畫
Manhua shenghuo 漫畫生活
Manhua yu shenghuo 漫畫與生活
Mangyuan 莽原
Mao Dun 矛盾
Masuda Wataru 增田涉
Minzu bao 民族報
Minzu de guomin 民族的國民
minzu hun 民族魂
ming 名
motoche 摩托車
Muke jicheng 木刻紀程
Muling muke yanjiushe 木鈴木刻研究社

Nagao Kagekazu 長尾景和
nu hu ba, Zhongguo! 怒哮吧, 中國!

Obara Eijirō 小原榮次郎
Okamoto Shigeru 岡本繁
Oya Takeo 大家武夫
Ou Mei mingjia duanpian xiaoshuo congkan 歐美名家短篇小說叢刊

pifa 披髮
Puyi 溥儀

Qi Shoushan 齊壽山
qiyan lüshi 七言律詩
Qian Xingcun 錢杏邨
Qian Xuantong 錢玄同
Qianshao 前哨
Qiu Jin 秋瑾
Qiu Sha 裘沙

Ren Yi 任頤
renyi 仁義
renzao zilai xue 人造自來血
Rou Shi 柔石
Runshui 閏水
Runtu 閏土

Seijō Academy 成城學院
shangdeng xiaoshuo 上等小說
Shanghai manhua 上海漫畫
Shanghai manhua hui 上海漫畫會
Shanghai shenghuo 上海生活
Shen Congwen 沈從文
Shen Fei 神飛
Shen Jin 沈藎
Shenbao 申報
shenshi 神矢
shenzu 神鏃
shi 詩
shi xiang shi buxiang 十降十不降
shilian 失戀
Shinozaki Hospital 篠崎醫院
shiyou 柿油
shou zhi gangbian jiang ni da 手執鋼鞭將你打
Shuqin 豎琴
shui zhong 水腫
si 死
Si Tang 俟堂
Situ Qiao 司徒喬

Subao 蘇報

Tang Si 唐俟
Tang Song shichun yu Lu Xun jiushi 唐宋詩醇與魯迅舊詩
tanzaku 短冊
Tao Li qie 桃李劫
Tao Yuanqing 陶元慶
Tian Han 田漢
Tianyi 天一
tongku 痛苦
tuhua 土話
tui wenyi 推文藝

Uchiyama Kakichi 內山喜吉
Uchiyama Kanzō 內山完造

Wang Huazhu 王華祝
Wang Jingwei 汪精衛
Wang Weijun 王偉君
Weiming she 未名社
Weiming muke she 未名木刻社
Wei Suyuan 韋素園
Wencong 文叢
wenxue he meishu 文學和美術
wenxuejie 文學界
Wenyi xinwen 文藝新聞
wenyi yundong 文藝運動
Wu Youru 吳友如
Wu Yu 吳虞
wuliao 無聊
Wuming mukeshe 無名木刻社
wupeng 烏篷

Xi 戲
Xiren chengxiong 西人逞兇
xiadeng xiaoshuo 下等小說
Xiandai 現代
Xianheng hao 咸亨號
xiao bian'er 小辮兒
xiaofu 小幅

xiaoshuo 小說
Xiaoshuo banyuekan 小說半月刊
Xiaoshuo yuebao 小說月報
Xinchao 新潮
Xinjing bao 新京報
Xinmiao 新苗
Xinmin congbao 新民叢報
Xinqingnian 新青年
Xinsheng 新生
xinwei 辛未
Xu Guangping 許廣平
Xu Jishang 許季上
Xuedeng 學燈

Y Sheng Y生
Yamamoto Hatsue 山本初枝
Yan Fu 嚴復
yanran 儼然
yanyi 演義
Yang Cunbin 楊村彬
Yang Dequn 楊德群
Yang Jiqun 楊霽雲
Yang Keyang 楊可揚
Yang Quan 楊銓
yangwu 洋物
Yao Ke 姚克
Yao Wenfu 姚文甫
Yige ren de shounan 一個人的受難
yiran 怡然
Yitian de gongzuo 一天的工作
Yiyongjun jinxingqu 義勇軍進行曲
Yin Fu 殷夫
Yu Cheng 俞成
Yu Dafu 郁達夫
Yu Kunshan 余坤珊
Yulun shishibao 輿論時事報
Yuwai xiaoshuo ji 域外小說集
Yuan Muzhi 袁牧之
Yuan Shikai 袁世凱

zagan 雜感
zawen 雜文
Zhang Binglin 章炳麟
Zhang Shizhao 章士釗
Zhang Xianzhong 張獻忠
Zhang Xun 張勳
zhanmao 氈帽
Zhang Yiping 章衣萍
Zhao Yannian 趙延年
Zhaohuashe 朝花社
Zhejiang chao 浙江潮
Zhixinbao 知新報
Zhonghua ribao 中華日報
Zhongguo xiju xuehui 中國戲劇學會
ZhongXia wangguo erbai sishiernian jinian 中夏亡國二百四十二年紀念
Zhou Haiying 周海嬰
Zhou Yang 周揚
Zhou Zhangshou 周樟壽
Zhu An 朱安
Zhuoren wei nu 捉人為奴
zi 字
ziyou 自由
Zou Rong 鄒容
zujie 租界
Zui an 罪案

Finding List for Lu Xun's Writings

Again on the Collapse of Leifeng Pagoda 再論雷峰塔的倒掉 *LXQJ* 1:201-05

Ah Zhang and *Classic of Mountains and Seas* 阿長與山海經 *LXQJ* 2:250-55

Announcement concerning *Record of Wood Engravings* 木刻紀程告白 *LXQJ* 8:512

Author's preface to the English translation of *Anthology of Short Stories* 英譯本短篇小說選集自序 *LXQJ* 7:411-12.

Biographical Note on Rou Shi 柔石小傳 *LXQJ* 3:285-86

Call to Arms 吶喊 *LXQJ* vol. 1

Celebrating the Victories in Shanghai and Nanjing 慶祝滬寧克服的那一邊 *LXQJ* 8:196-98

Chinese Revolutionary Proletariat Literature and the Blood of Its Vanguard 中國無產階級革命文學和前驅的血 *LXQJ* 4:289-90

Confucius in Today's China 在現在中國的孔夫子 *LXQJ* 6:324-30

Dairy of a Madman 狂人日記 *LXQJ* 1:444-55

Dawn Blossoms Gathered at Dusk 朝花夕拾 *LXQJ* vol. 2

Excursions in the Year 1911 辛亥遊錄 *LXQJ* 8:45-46

"Fair Play" Should be Postponed 論<費危潑賴>應該緩刑 *LXQJ* 1:286-93

Fan Ainong 范愛農 *LXQJ* 2:321-328

Flight to the Moon 奔月 *LXQJ* 2:370-81

Foreword to *Collected Works of Shouchang* 守常全集題記 *LXQJ* 4:538-40

Further Thoughts after an Illness 病後雜談之餘 *LXQJ* 6:185-97

Grave 墳 *LXQJ* vol. 1

The Great Sight of Chopping Down Communists 鏟共大觀 *LXQJ* 4:106-107

Hesitation 徬徨 *LXQJ* vol. 2

A History of Chinese Vernacular Fiction 中國小說史略 *LXQJ* vol. 9

History of Humankind 人之歷史 *LXQJ* 1:8-17

Hot Air 熱風 *LXQJ* vol. 1

Hometown 故鄉 *LXQJ* 1:501-10

Huagai ji 華蓋集 *LXQJ* vol. 3

Kong Yiji 孔乙己 *LXQJ* 1:457-61

In Defense of *lianhuanhua* 連環圖畫辯護 *LXQJ* 4:457-61

In Memory of Liu Hezhen 記念劉和珍君 *LXQJ* 3:289-294

Letter in Reply to the Editors of *Theater* 答戲週刊編者信 *LXQJ* 6:148-52

Letter Sent to the Editors of *Theater* 寄戲周刊編者信 *LXQJ* 6:154-55

The Loner 孤獨者 *LXQJ* 2:88-110

Medicine 藥 *LXQJ* 1:463-72

Mending Heaven 補天 *LXQJ* 2:357-366

Mr. Fujino 藤野先生 *LXQJ* 2:313-19

My Views on Chastity 我之節烈觀 *LXQJ* 1:121-30

Names 名字 *LXQJ* 8:122-24

New Year's Sacrifice 祝福 *LXQJ* 2:5-21

Old Tales Retold 故事新編 *LXQJ* vol. 2

On "Adopting the Conventions of Tradition" 論<舊形式的採用> *LXQJ* 6:23-24

On Minding Other People's Business, Etc" 雜論管閒事作學問灰色等 *LXQJ* 3:197-203

On Radium 說鐳 *LXQJ* 7:21-26

Outline of Chinese Geology 中國地質略論 *LXQJ* 8:5-20

Outline of Science 科學史教篇 *LXQJ* 1:25-35

Piecemeal Memories 瑣記 *LXQJ* 2:301-07

Postface to *Grave* 寫在<墳>後面 *LXQJ* 1:298-303

The Power of Mara Poetry 摩羅詩力說 *LXQJ* 1:65-103

Preface [to *Call to Arms*] 自序 *LXQJ* 1:437-442

Preface to *Collection of the Unnamed Woodcut Society* 無名木刻集序 *LXQJ* 8:406

Preface [to *Dawn Flowers Gathered at Dusk*] 小引 *LXQJ* 2:235-36

Preface [to *Grave*] 題記 *LXQJ* 1:3-5

Preface to *The New Literature of China: A Comprehensive Anthology, Short Stories, Volume 2* 中國新文學大系> 小說二集序 *LXQJ* 6:246-64

Preface to the Russian Translation of "The True Story of Ah Q," with an Autobiographical Notice by the Author 俄文譯本阿Q正傳序及著者自敘傳略 *LXQJ* 7:83-86

Preface to *Self-Selected Anthology* 自選集自序 *LXQJ* 4:469-71
Preface [to *Supplement to the Collected Works*] 序言 *LXQJ* 7:3-5
The Present State of Literature and Art in Darkest China 黑暗中國的文藝界的現狀 *LXQJ* 4:292-95
A Public Example 示眾 *LXQJ* 2:70-75
Random Thoughts, unnumbered 隨感錄 *LXQJ* 8:94-95
Random Thoughts 25 隨感錄 *LXQJ* 1:311-12
Random Thoughts 35 隨感錄 *LXQJ* 1:321-22
Regret for the Past 傷逝 *LXQJ* 2:113-33
Remembering Mr. Liu Bannong 憶劉半農君 *LXQJ* 6:73-75
Remembering Mr. Wei Suyuan 憶韋素園君 *LXQJ* 6: 65-70
Remembering the Past 懷舊 *LXQJ* 7:225-232
Remembrance in Order to Forget 為了忘卻的記念 *LXQJ* 4:493-502
Roses without Flowers (2) 無花的薔薇之二 *LXQJ* 3:277-80
Ruminating to Myself 自言自語 *LXQJ* 8:114-20
Second Supplement to the Collected Works 集外集拾遺 *LXQJ* vol. 7
Semi-concession Anthologies 且界亭雜文 *LXQJ* vol. 3
Soap 肥皂 *LXQJ* 2:45-56
Some Dissent from "The Wrong People Were Killed" <殺錯了人>異議 *LXQJ* 5:100-03
Some Notes on Hong Kong 略談香港 *LXQJ* 1:446-53
Soul of Sparta 斯巴達之魂 *LXQJ* 7:9-16
Storm 風波 *LXQJ* 1:491-99
A Story about Hair 頭髮的故事 *LXQJ* 1:484-88
Supplement to the Collected Works 集外集 *LXQJ* vol. 7
"Surrendering in Life but not in Death" <生降死不降> *LXQJ* 8:121
Third Supplement to the Collected Works 集外集拾遺補編 *LXQJ* vol. 8
"This Too is Life" <這也是生活> *LXQJ* 6:622-26
Tomorrow 明天 *LXQJ* 1:473-79
The True Story of Ah Q 阿Q正傳 *LXQJ* 1:512-52
Two or Three Things Regarding Mr. Zhang Taiyan 關於太炎先生二三事 *LXQJ* 6:565-67
Two or Three Things Brought to Mind by Mr. Zhang Taiyan 因太炎先生而想起的二三事 *LXQJ* 6:576-79

Upstairs at the Tavern 在酒樓上 *LXQJ* 2:24-34

The Uneven Development of Culture 文化偏至論 *LXQJ* 1:45-58

Various Memories 雜憶 *LXQJ* 1:233-39

Village Opera 社戲 *LXQJ* 1:587-97

Waking 覺 *LXQJ* 2:228-230

What Happens after Nora Leaves Home? 娜拉走後怎樣 *LXQJ* 1:165-71

White Light 白光 *LXQJ* 1:570-75

Weeds 野草 *LXQJ* vol. 2

The Writing of "The True Story of Ah Q" <阿Q正傳>的成因 *LXQJ* 3:394-400

Written in Deep Night 寫於深夜裡 *LXQJ* 6:517-28

Poems

After the January 28 War 一二八戰後 *LXQJ* 7:458

Dream 夢 *LXQJ* 7:31

Elegy for Fan Ainong, Three Poems 哀范君三章 *LXQJ* 7:448

A Farewell to Mr. O. E., Who is Taking Orchids with Him on His Return to Japan 送 O.E. 君攜蘭歸國 *LXQJ* 7:147

[For My Middle Brother, Inscribed on a Photograph] 題照贈仲弟 *LXQJ* 8:542

God of Love 愛之神 *LXQJ* 7:32

[Inscribed by the Author on a Small Likeness] 自題小像 *LXQJ* 7:447

Inscribed in *Call to Arms* 題吶喊 *LXQJ* 7:466

Inscribed in *Hesitation* 題徬徨 *LXQJ* 7:156

Peach Blossoms 桃花 *LXQJ* 7:33

Self-Mockery 自嘲 *LXQJ* 7:151

Song of the Xiang River Goddess 湘靈歌 *LXQJ* 7:150

To Detain Ding Yaoqing, a Couplet 挽丁耀卿聯 *LXQJ* 8:541

Untitled {"The countryside is filled with brambles"] 大野多鉤棘 *LXQJ* 7:148

Untitled {"Though accustomed to"] 慣於長夜 *LXQJ* 4:500-01

Illustration Credits

2.1-2.3, 2.9-2.13, 3.3, 3.5, 3.6, 4.1, 4.3-4.5, B.19, B.32-34, B.38 Courtesy of Beijing Lu Xun Museum.

2.4, 3.4, 5.24, 5.28 Ouyang Wenli, ed., *Pictorial Biography of Lu Xun*.

2.5 Courtesy of the New York Public Library.

2.6 Gift of Professor and Mrs. Theodore Herman, Picker Art Gallery, Colgate University.

2.7, 2.8, 2.15-17, 2.20-22 Courtesy of Library of Congress.

2.14, 2.18 Courtesy of Yale Center for British Art, Paul Mellon Collection.

2.19 Courtesy of Winterthur Museum.

2.23 *Yulun shishi bao tuhua*, 1904.

2.24 *Anhui suhua bao*, 1904.

2.25, 2.26, 3.2, 5.3, 5.9, 5.27, A.4, B.15, B.22, B.29, B.37, B.40 Courtesy of Harvard Yenching Library.

3.1 Courtesy of Yale University Library.

4.2 *Lu Xun Research Monthly*, September, 2007.

5.1 *Yangcheng Evening News*, November 9, 1961.

5.2, 5.4, 5.7, 5.8, 5.11, 5.13, 5.16, 5.25, 5.26, B.13, B.14, B.21, B.25-28, B.31, B.35, B.39, B.41, B.43 *Catalog of Woodcuts*.

5.5, B.24 Feng Zikai, *Illustrations of Lu Xun's Fiction*.

5.6, 5.10, 5.14, 5.15, 5.17, 5.19, B.1-B.12, B.16-18. Courtesy of Library of the Institute for Sinology, Heidelberg University.

5.12, B.30, B.36, B.44 Courtesy of Cornell University Library.

5.18 Käthe Kollwitz, *Misery*. © 2010 Artists Rights Society (ARS), New York / VG Bild-Kunst, Bonn.

5.20 Edvard Munch, *Smell of Death*. © 2010 The Munch Museum / The Munch-Ellingsen Group / Artists Rights Society (ARS), New York

5.21, B.23 Courtesy of Shanghai Lu Xun Museum.

5.22. Nym Wales Collection, envelope mAB, Hoover Institution Archives, Stanford University Library.

A.1 © *The New Yorker*, February 11, 2002.

A.2, A.3, B.42 Courtesy of Stanford East Asia Library.

B.20 Peng Xiaojie and Han Geli, eds., *Seventy Years of Ah Q*.

Notes

Introduction

[1] Yan Fu's goals in his essays and translation projects and his identification of the necessary knowledge as lying outside China are named in the title and subtitle, respectively, of Benjamin Schwartz's study, *In Search of Wealth and Power: Yen Fu and the West*. For Lin Shu's goals, see Wang-chi Wong, "Translation of Western Fiction," in *The Literary Field of Twentieth-Century China*, ed. Michel Hockx, 32–34. For Liang Qichao's "inflated and contradictory expectations for the novel," see Theodore Huters, *Bringing the World Home*, 112–20.

[2] Christopher A. Reed, *Gutenberg in Shanghai*, provides in chapter 5 a vivid history of Commercial Press and the other two, slightly later, publishing giants, Zhonghua and World, and their foundation in the lucrative textbook market. They were already the "second-generation of new-style ... print capitalists" (204).

[3] "Preface to *The New Literature of China: A Comprehensive Anthology. Short Stories, Volume 2*," dated 1935. In Lu Xun, *Lu Xun quanji* (Complete works of Lu Xun, hereafter *LXQJ*), 6:246.

[4] Pierre Bourdieu, *The Field of Cultural Production*.

[5] *Short Story Monthly* (*Xiaoshuo yuebao*), 12, no. 8 (August 1921).

[6] Bonnie S. McDougall and Kam Louie, *The Literature of China in the Twentieth Century*, 2, 6.

[7] Authors and publications reported by students at teachers' schools in 1930–37, primarily leftist according to their biographies and autobiographies, are tabulated in Xiaoping Cong, *Teachers' Schools and the Making of the Modern Chinese Nation-State, 1897–1937*, 175–78.

[8] Gao Xudong, *Lu Xun for the Twenty-first Century*, 82.

[9] Paul Debreczeny, *Social Functions of Literature*, 223–46; Stephanie Sandler, *Commemorating Pushkin*, 85–135.

[10] "On New Democracy," in Mao Zedong, *Mao's Road to Power: Revolutionary Writings, 1912–1940*, 1:360–61.

[11] An illustration of this view is in the introduction by Feng Xuefeng to Lu Xun, *Lu Xun: Selected Works*, trans. Yang Xianyi and Gladys Yang, 1:9–31. This introduction

was also used for many years in the one-volume Lu Xun, *Lu Hsun: Selected Stories*, published by W. W. Norton, until the Chinese-American novelist Ha Jin provided a new introduction in 2003.

[12] Works of this type cited in this study include Hangzhou Lu Xun jinian guan, ed., *In the Footsteps of Lu Xun in Shaoxing*; and Zhou Guowei and Peng Xiao, *In Search of Lu Xun's Steps in Shanghai*, both newer entries in a venerable category.

[13] Jing Wendong, *Symbol of Defeat*, 4.

[14] Wang Xiaoming, *A Life that Cannot be Directly Faced*, 3–4.

[15] Jing Wendong, *Symbol of Defeat*, 3–6.

[16] See Leo Ou-fan Lee, *Voices from an Iron House*; and his edited volume, *Lu Xun and His Legacy*.

[17] Wang Furen, *The Shadow of Predecessors*, 13–14.

[18] Beijing Lu Xun Museum, *Lu Xun Chronology*, 4: 503, postscript. Chen was remarking on the changes in political conditions since the work's first edition in 1981, which marked the centenary of Lu Xun's birth.

[19] Wang Xiaoming, *A Life that Cannot be Directly Faced*; Wang Dehou, *Personal Readings of Lu Xun*; Wang Hui, *Resisting Despair*.

[20] Gao Xudong, ed., *Controversies about Lu Xun at the End of the Century*, provides good synopses and copious quotations. See also Lin Qingxin, "Reloading the Canon," 181–92; Liu Yukai, *Misconstruing Lu Xun*; Chen Shuyu, ed., *Storms over Lu Xun*; and Chen Shuyu, ed., *Who Is Challenging Lu Xun*.

[21] This is David E. Pollard's term in his "The Life of Lu Xun as Told in China," 242.

[22] Hu Yinqiang, *In Hope of Destroying the Iron House*, 424–25.

[23] Bourdieu, *The Field of Cultural Production*.

[24] Michel Hockx, *Questions of Style*.

[25] Ibid., 5.

[26] Hu Shi, *Chinese Literature of the Past Fifty Years*. The publication date is 1924; the text is dated 1922.

[27] Zhao Jiabi, ed., *The New Literature of China: A Comprehensive Anthology*, 10 vols., 1935–36. Lu Xun made the selection for the second of its three volumes of short stories, for which he also provided the preface (*LXQJ*, 6:246–64). See note 3.

[28] Lydia Liu, *Translingual Practice*, 228.

[29] Milena Doleželová-Velingerová and Oldřich Král, eds., *The Appropriation of Cultural Capital in China's May Fourth Project*, 2001.

[30] Denise Gimpel, *Lost Voices of Modernity*.

³¹ Susan Daruvala, *Zhou Zuoren and an Alternative Chinese Response to Modernity*, 11.

³² Ni Moyan, *Lu Xun's Societal Activities*, 3–42. For dates and coverage of the five reports, see 3-4.

³³ Wu Haiyong, *Lu Xun as a Civil Servant;* on income, Chen Mingyuan, *Cultural Figures and Money*, 140–67, gives a high figure. Wang Xirong rebuts Chen and provides far lower figures in *Continuing Controversies Regarding Lu Xun's Life*, 244–78.

³⁴ Bonnie S. McDougall, *Love-Letters and Privacy in Modern China*; other works on his personal life include Li Yunjing, *Lu Xun's Emotional World* and Cai Dengshan, *Those whom Lu Xun Had Loved*. In Haiyan Lee, *Revolution of the Heart*, Lu Xun is instructively one example among many.

³⁵ Eva Shan Chou, "The Political Martyr in Lu Xun's Writings," 155–58.

³⁶ Phillip Pan, "Chinese Evade Censors to Discuss Police Assault," *Washington Post*, December 5, 2005, A1.

³⁷ Detailed in Kirk A. Denton, "Museums, Memorial Sites, and Exhibitionary Culture in the People's Republic of China," 578–80.

³⁸ The news of impending changes fired up many parties. An early source in English is Arthur Waldron, "So long, Lu Xun," August 19, 2007—see www.commentarymagazine.com/2007/08/28/so-long-lu-xun—which drew attention to their close connection to official suppression of the memory of the Tian'anmen massacre. In the event, the scale of changes was larger than Lu Xun alone. A brief news item on new textbooks that names some of the new entries and is followed by many online comments can be found at Sina.com (September 9, 2010), http://news.sins.com.cn/c/sd/2010-09-08/050621059400.shtml.

³⁹ Chen Shuyu, ed., *Who Is Challenging Lu Xun*; Wang Furen and Zhao Zhuo, *Breaking through Blind Spots*; Yi Tu, ed., *The Twenty-first Century*; Qiu Cunping, *"Call to Arms" for People Today*.

⁴⁰ This was the third "anniversary of the political lie" organized by the Peter Weiss Foundation for Art and Politics in Berlin. The second anniversary commemorated the slain Russian journalist Anna Politkovskaya. This information was kindly sent to me by Wolfgang Kubin, together with the names of the poets involved.

⁴¹ Alfred Nobel's meaning is not fully clear. According to his will, the prize is to be awarded to "the person who shall have produced in the field of literature the most outstanding work of an ideal direction." This translation can be found at http://nobelprize.org/alfred_nobel/will/will-full.html.

⁴² Quoted from Foster, *Ah Q Archaeology*, 253. Much is unclear about the evidence for Rolland's words. They are quoted as Jing Yingyu relayed them in a letter to Lu Xun (summarized *LXQJ* 15:611, n.6). A letter from Rolland to be conveyed to Lu Xun was, according to Jing, in his charge, but the letter is lost to history, as is Rolland's letter to *Europe*. Wang Xirong reports that the latter surfaced in 1986 in France

(*Continuing Controversies*, 103-04), but gives no further information. Direct evidence of Rolland's praise of "Ah Q" seems to exist: Foster quotes a longer, similar passage from "a letter" found "among his posthumous manuscripts" (253).

[43] Julia Lovell, *The Politics of Cultural Capital*, 3, 6.

[44] Letter to Tai Jingnong, 270925 (1), *LXQJ* 12:73–74. It is also reproduced in Lovell, *The Politics of Cultural Capital*, 82. In 2000, an attempt was made by a Chinese historian to clarify directly with the Swedish Academy whether this had happened or not, but the answer was inconclusive (84–85).

[45] This muddled situation is detailed in Paul Foster, *Ah Q Archaeology*, 250–72.

[46] An exception was George Kin Leung, a Christian who translated Lu Xun in 1926.

[47] Irene Eber, "The Reception of Lu Xun in Europe and America," 255–56, 245.

[48] Maruyama Noboru, "Lu Xun in Japan," 218–24. Letter 331105, to Yao Ke, lists translations up to 1933 (*LXQJ* 12:480).

[49] David Damrosch, *What Is World Literature?* Quotations and opinions are from pages 1 (Goethe), 117 (entry points), 3 ("less a . . . network"), 5 ("mode of circulation"), 4 ("all literary works"), and 24 ("works of literature").

[50] Milan Kundera, "Die Weltliteratur," 29.

[51] Mark Gamsa, *The Chinese Translation of Russian Literature*, 47. See also, Raoul David Findeisen, "Does the East Asian-European Interliterary Communication in the Late Qing–Late Meiji Periods Offer a Model for a Globalized Literature?" 562.

[52] His comments are collected in Fujian shifan daxue zhongwen xi, ed., *Lu Xun on Foreign Literatures*.

[53] Lu Xun, preface to *Call to Arms*, *LXQJ*, 1:439.

[54] See Lu Xun, "The Power of Mara Poetry" (*LXQJ* 1:65–100), where these writers are mentioned on pages 87, 88, 92, and 97. Rizal is the subject of an unpublished, unnumbered "Random Thoughts" essay dated by the editors of *LXQJ* to some time in his first year of writing in the vernacular (*LXQJ* 8:94–95); Byron, Mickiewicz, Petőfi, and Rizal are named again in a similar context in the 1925 "Various Memories" (*LXQJ* 1:234-35).

Chapter One: Renewing a Seminal Literary Figure

[1] Y Sheng (identity not known) and Feng Wenbing (1901–67), quoted in *On Lu Xun and His Works*, ed. Tai Jingnong, 69, 86.

[2] Lu Xun, *Ah Q and Others: Selected Stories of Lusin*, trans. Chi-chen Wang, dedication page.

[3] Leo Ou-fan Lee, *Voices from an Iron House*; David E. Pollard, *The True Story of Lu Xun*.

⁴ Michel Hockx has drawn attention to a short story in the vernacular that predates by one month the May 1918 publication of "Diary of a Madman." Written by one of the first women to attend college in the United States with government sponsorship and published in a Chinese student magazine in the United States, the story depicts a day in the life of American college girls and the questions they have for their Chinese classmate (*Questions of Style*, 145–47). This example demonstrates that historical phenomena have multiple strands, some of which do not develop further (the author did not publish any more fiction), and that the elite among Chinese overseas students published many magazines. (Among the students in Tokyo, the magazines tended to be province based.) It is also interesting that the story deals with the immigrant topos of the outsider in a host country and in this sense fits well into the genre of Asian American literature written in the immigrant's native language.

⁵ Preface to the 1920 reissue of Lu Xun and Zhou Zuoren's 1909 *Anthology of Literature from Foreign Lands*, *LXQJ* 10:178. Although it is signed by Zhou Zuoren, the preface was written by Lu Xun (*LXQJ* 10:178, n. 1).

⁶ Mao Dun, "Reading *Call to Arms*," 1923, in *On Lu Xun and His Works*, ed. Tai Jingnong, 54.

⁷ "My Views on Chastity," "Random Thoughts 24," and "Random Thoughts 35" (*LXQJ* 1:121–30; 1:311–12; 1:321–22, all from 1918).

⁸ *LXQJ* 7:31, 32, 33.

⁹ Sun Fuyuan, *Two or Three Things about Mr. Lu Xun*, 24.

¹⁰ *Short Story Monthly* 13, no. 2 (February 10, 1922): 5.

¹¹ *Morning Post Supplement* (*Chenbao fukan*), March 1922.

¹² Wu Yu, Essay in *New Youth* 6, no. 6 (November 1, 1919); Eva Shan Chou, "Learning to Read Lu Xun," 1050–52.

¹³ Ba Jin, *Family*, 42–47, 11, 31; Ba Jin, *The Family*, trans. Sidney Shapiro, 38–43, 8, 27.

¹⁴ In its twelfth printing, in 1930, Lu Xun removed "Buzhou Mountain" from *Call to Arms*. In 1935, when he compiled *Old Tales Retold*, he placed the story there, retitled as "Mending Heaven" (*LXQJ* 1:436, editorial note).

¹⁵ *Short Story Monthly* 12, no. 8 (August 10, 1921): 5.

¹⁶ *Awakening* (*Juewu*), August 31, 1923.

¹⁷ The expanded sense of the category is used by Julia Lovell in her 2010 translation of "the complete fiction" (Lu Xun, *The Real Story of Ah Q and Other Tales of China: The Complete Fiction of Lu Xun*), whereas Yang Xianyi and Gladys Yang's earlier, 1981 translation in Lu Xun, *The Complete Stories of Lu Xun* does not. The timing in scholarship is similarly in transition. We have the "thirdness" of the collection and an increasing number of studies of *Old Tales Retold*, but we do not yet have analyses that

treat all three collections in an integrated manner as fiction.

[18] Preface to *Self-Selected Anthology,* 1932, *LXQJ* 4:469.

[19] This is how he dated an essay written that day, "Roses without Flowers (2)," *LXQJ* 3:280. The essay, the second with that title, concerned other matters, but when news of the killings came, he broke off to write of it, and the break in subject matter became a stark metaphor of how the event burst upon the nation.

[20] "In Memory of Liu Hezhen," *LXQJ* 3:289–94.

[21] Preface to *Grave, LXQJ* 1:4.

[22] See the surveys and analyses in David E. Pollard, "Lu Xun's Zawen," 54–89; and Leo Ou-fan Lee, *Voices from the Iron House,* 110–29.

[23] Chang Hui, "Recollections of Mr. Lu Xun's Lectures at Beijing University," 89, cited in Raoul Findeisen, *Lu Xun,* 155–59. A coterie of students who founded *New Tide,* many of them from Shaoxing, did know his identity.

[24] The letter in which he laid the false trail is 210905, *LXQJ* 11:418–19. Gong Zhuxin had first sought advice from Zhou Zuoren, but Zuoren was convalescing at Western Hills and Lu Xun undertook the correspondence. Gong was not known to them, but Lu Xun thought his letter was "probably not a fraud" and could be answered (letter to Zuoren, 210727, *LXQJ* 11:398). His caution in disclaiming any identity with "Lu Xun" was wise: in the event, Gong seemed to have become importunate, and Lu Xun was able to say, in the final letter of their correspondence, apparently regarding a request, that someone in the education world, as he was, had very little clout (220206, *LXQJ* 11:427–28).

[25] The preface was published at about the same time as the anthology's issuance in a Beijing literary supplement, the *Morning Post Literary Trimonthly* (*Chenbao wenxue xunkan*), August 21, 1923 (*LXQJ* 1:442, n. 1).

[26] Marston Anderson, *The Limits of Realism,* 77.

[27] His better-known name, Zhou Shuren, was given to him by a clan uncle to mark the beginning of his education in Nanjing.

[28] *LXQJ* 1:437.

[29] "Piecemeal Memories," *LXQJ* 2:302–3.

[30] See Andrew Morris, "To Make the 400 Million Move," 876–82. On pages 881–82, he quotes Cai E, later a military hero, who was in Tokyo the same years as Lu Xun, who advocated physical training and gave many examples of the victory of brawn over civilization from Sparta onward.

[31] Preface to *Call to Arms, LXQJ* 1:415–16.

[32] Zhou Zuoren, *Lu Xun's Family,* part 3, item 24. A fourth person, who left for England, on whom Lu Xun had counted for correspondent materials from that country, did not come through.

[33] This discussion relies on Wang Xirong, *Continuing Controversies Regarding Lu Xun's Life*, 16–41, whose examination of the issue draws on contemporary Sendai newspapers and magazines.

[34] The second account, the briefest, is in "Preface to the Russian Translation of 'The True Story of Ah Q,' with an Autobiographical Notice by the Author," 1925, *LXQJ* 7:85; the third is in "Mr. Fujino," 1926, *LXQJ* 2:317. See Lu Xun, *Selected Works*, 1:409.

[35] This is according to Dong Bingyue, "Behind the Myth of Sendai," 55. Lu Xun says that he was the only one ("Mr. Fujino," *LXQJ* 2:313–14).

[36] Wang says it could be tracked down, but he had not done so yet (*Continuing Controversies*, 40). Lydia Liu, *Translingual Practice*, contains a photograph of such a scene (62); another photograph can be found at the Beijing Lu Xun Museum.

[37] Lin Qingxin, "Reloading the Canon," 188.

[38] Leo Ou-fan Lee, *Iron House*, 17–19; the quotations are from page 18.

[39] Wang Xirong, *Continuing Controversies*, 38–41.

[40] Dong Bingyue, "Behind the Myth of Sendai," 54–59. There is a photograph of Lu Xun with one Shi Lin, identified as "the other Chinese student at Sendai Medical College" (*Lu Xun's Life*, ed. Xue Suizhi, vol. 2, photograph [36]; 2:7).

[41] Wang Xirong, *Continuing Controversies*, 23, 30.

[42] This college for women underwent several name changes from its founding in 1908 until its merger with Beijing Normal University. The translation here, *Beijing Women's Normal College*, aims to be informative rather than to reproduce every element of its contemporary name.

[43] See McDougall, *Love-Letters and Privacy in Modern China*, 43–57.

[44] Leo Ou-fan Lee tracks the author's gradual arrival at this view through his use of Marxist language (*Voices from the Iron House*, 136–43).

[45] These negative comparisons were made by Ge Hongbin and quoted in Lin Qingxin, "Reloading the Canon," 187.

[46] Anderson, *The Limits of Realism*, 76–92.

[47] Frederic Wakeman, *Policing Shanghai*, 132–61.

[48] This is Ian Brunskill's fine phrase in "Günter Grass," 3.

[49] A Ying (pen name of Qian Xingcun), "Ah Q's Age Is Dead and Gone," in *Lu Xun lun*, ed. Li Helin, 71.

[50] *LXQJ* 1:4.

[51] Ibid., 1:303.

[52] Ibid., 2:235–36.

53 "Waking," *LXQJ* 2:228–30.

54 Ibid., 2:230, n. 2.

55 "'This Too Is Life'," dated August, 23, 1936, *LXQJ* 6:625–26.

Chapter 2: Cutting His Queue: Nationalism, Identity, and Other Unknowns

1 The certificate is reproduced in *Lu Xun Chronology*, 1:88.

2 Ibid., 1:85–87.

3 Lu Xun gathered and republished the 1903 writings in 1934; the 1907 writings had been republished earlier, in 1925. For 1903, see "Soul of Sparta," *LXQJ* 7:9–16; "On Radium," *LXQJ* 7:21–26; and "Outline of Chinese Geology," *LXQJ* 8:5–20.

4 "Confucius in Today's China," *LXQJ* 6:326.

5 The four essays are "History of Humankind," *LXQJ* 1:1:8–17; "Outline of Science," *LXQJ* 1:25–35; "The Uneven Development of Culture," *LXQJ* 1:45–58; and "The Power of Mara Poetry," *LXQJ* 1:65–103.

6 The translations are not collected in *LXQJ*. The postface to Verne is in *LXQJ* 10:163.

7 The dates of 1903–1924 are used in Wang Hui's analysis of the concept of self and individuality (*Resisting Despair*, 53-111).

8 Kitaoka Masako, in "Historical Materials Relating to the Period of Lu Xun's Study in Japan," gathers the official materials pertaining to Kōbun Academy: its quasi-official founding, the regulations governing it, its academic and student regulations, and so on.

9 The registrar's records, weekly syllabus, and certificate are reproduced in *Lu Xun Chronology*, 1:84, 1:126. The syllabus is also reproduced in Kitaoka Masako, "Historical Materials," 31.

10 On Lu Xun's presence at meetings, see Shen Diemin, "Some Recollections of Lu Xun in the Early Years at Kōbun Academy."; for the connections Lu Xun formed at the academy, see Shen Diemin, "Some Memories of Lu Xun's Activities in the Early Years."

11 Li Suizhi recollects that his classmate said at the time, "Such humiliating words should be put into our folk songs to spur us on to strengthen ourselves" ("A Classmate of Fifty Years Ago—Mr. Lu Xun").

12 Zhang Xiehe, "Remembering Lu Xun at Nanjing's School of Mines and Railways."

13 Ni Moyan, *Lu Xun's Societal Activities*, 20–42. On "Sparta," see pages 33–36; on "Geology," see pages 39–42.

14 See Li Anbao's *Lu Xun and Modern Chinese History*, which in effect shows that Lu Xun's direct participation in political activities was, with a few exceptions, meager throughout his life.

15 "Mr. Fujino," 2:313; "On Minding Other People's Business, Etc.," *LXQJ* 3:199–200.

16 I convert back to British measures from the metric dimensions of 10 x 7.1 cm provided by Beijing Lu Xun Museum, ed., *Lu Xun (1881–1936)* (1976), unpaginated. The resulting whole dimensions suggest that British units of measure were used at the photographer's studio.

17 *LXQJ* 7:447.

18 There is little scholarship on the photograph but a great deal on the poem. The major studies for the poem are summarized in Jon Eugene von Kowallis, *The Lyrical Lu Xun*, 100–107, which includes a translation (100–101). Other translations may be found in Wang Shiqin, *Lu Xun*, trans. Bonnie S. McDougall, 54; Lu Xun, *Poèmes*, trans. Michelle Loi, unpaginated; Lu Xun, *Lu Hsun*, trans. David Y. Ch'en, 65; Lu Xun, *Werke in sechs Banden*, trans. Wolfgang Kubin, 6:19. An example of a unified interpretation is in Ni Moyan, *Lu Xun's Traditional Poetry*, 33–36.

19 Xu gives three accounts of how the poem and photograph came together, for two significantly different versions. See appendix A.

20 *Dairy*, 1:384, twelfth day of third month (April 10).

21 See chapter 4.

22 Zhou Zuoren, *Diary*, 1:384, where the date of April 2 is given for Lu Xun's letter.

23 In Xu Shoushang, *Memories of My Late Friend*, 4.

24 Zhou Zuoren, *Lu Xun's Youth*, 33; Xu, *Memories of My Late Friend*, 3.

25 Lin Zhihao, *Lu Xun Biography* (1991), 28. Other accounts include the following. "In the last part of March 1903, he was the first in his Jiangnan class at Kōbun Academy vehemently to cut off that queue that symbolized 'the obedient subject of the Qing empire' and make a formal, definitive break with the corrupt and reactionary Manchu government" (Cheng Ma, *Lu Xun's Student Years in Japan*, 22). "Thus spurred by the anti-Qing movement, he vehemently cut off his queue" (*Lu Xun Chronology*, 1:105). "Unhappy with the supervisor threatening to stop their stipend, he vehemently cut off his queue to express his break from the Qing" (Wang Dongfang, *Striding into Modernity*, 50). "It was at this time . . . that Lu Xun vehemently cut off his queue" (Ni Moyan, *Lu Xun's Societal Activities*, 27). "[He was] the first in his Jiangnan group to cut his queue . . . to express his resistance to ethnic oppression and his resolve to participate in anti-Qing revolution" (Ma Li, "Lu Xun at Kōbun Academy," 2:16–17).

26 These statements occur, respectively, in "A Story about Hair," *LXQJ* 1:486; "Further Thoughts after an Illness," *LXQJ* 6:194; and "Two or Three Things Brought to Mind by Mr. Zhang Taiyan," *LXQJ* 6:579.

[27] Preface to *Supplement to the Collected Works* (Jiwaiji), *LXQJ* 7:4. For the poem's poetic diction derived from tradition, see Ni Moyan, *Lu Xun's Traditional Poetry*, 30–33.

[28] Both prints are reproduced in many publications. Yang Keyang, "Pawn Shop and Chemist," in Chen Shuyu et al., eds., *A Pictorial Biography of Lu Xun*, 19, in black and white; the original is a color print, one copy in Beijing Lu Xun Museum. Zhao Yannian, "Leaving Home for Nanjing," in Chen Shuyu et al., eds., *A Pictorial Biography of Lu Xun*, 19. In addition, Ouyang Wenli, ed., *Pictorial Biography of Lu Xun*, 37, publishes a photograph of the exterior of the family compound that is the setting of this farewell, and charcoal drawing by Zhao of this perspective. One sees the iconography taking shape.

[29] Watercolor, young Lu Xun on way to Nanjing, no artist given; in the collection of Beijing Lu Xun Museum. Oil, arriving Nanjing, no artist given; in Ouyang Wenli, ed., *Pictorial Biography of Lu Xun*, 61. Hair already cut short before embarking for Japan, in Zheng Hui and Xu Shan, eds., *Pictorial Biography of Lu Xun*, 22.

[30] Young Lu Xun and Runtu, Han Heping, illus. *Hometown*. Liu Jian'an's image of Ah Q is a single sheet, courtesy of Colgate University. Other images of Ah Q by Liu Jian'an can be found in *Seventy Years of Ah Q*, eds., Peng Xiaojie and Han Geli, gathered at the front of the volume.

[31] Xu, *Memories of My Late Friend*, 2.

[32] Sun Fuyuan, *Two or Three Things about Mr. Lu Xun*, 62.

[33] For the poem, *LXQJ* 8:542, where the editors have supplied the title "For My Middle Brother, Inscribed on a Photograph"; recorded in Zhou Zuoren, *Diary*, 1:335 (eleventh day of fifth month, 1902).

[34] This poem is quoted in whole by two critics without any comment. See Cheng Ma, *Lu Xun's Student Years in Japan*, 23, and Hu Bing, next note.

[35] Hu Bing mentions the 1902 set, saying that Lu Xun had "frequently" put poem and photograph together, but he proceeds to emphasize the 1903 set (*Researches on Lu Xun*, 106).

[36] *Lu Xun Chronology*, under March 21, 1898, 1:51. Date known from Zhou Zuoren's diary.

[37] "To Detain Ding Yaoqing, a Couplet," *LXQJ* 8:541. Each half of the couplet contains three segments. Part of line 1 is quoted here.

[38] Recorded in Zhou Zuoren, *Diary*, 1:321, eleventh day of second month (March 24, 1902).

[39] Zhou Zuoren, *Lu Xun's Youth*, 33, emphasis added.

[40] Ibid.

[41] H. Y. Lowe, *The Adventures of Wu*, 5, reference from Edward Rhoads, *Manchus and Han*, where the figure is reproduced facing page 182.

42 "Mr. Fujino," *LXQJ* 2:313; Lu Xun, *Selected Works*, 1:404.

43 Marius Jansen, "Japan and the Chinese Revolution of 1911," 352.

44 The manuscript essay is entitled *"Great Poems of Tang and Song* and Lu Xun's Classical Poems" *(Tang Song shichun yu Lu Xun jiushi)*. I have not seen it. It is quoted in *Lu Xun Chronology*, 1:119–20, without date or source.

45 The question from Hu Bing and Zuoren's reply are in Hu Bing, *Researches on Lu Xun*, 111. The reference is from *Lu Xun Chronology*, 1:119.

46 Huang Qiaosheng, *Together for the Ages*, 121, 125.

47 *Lu Xun Chronology*, 1:105. Note the use of *yiran* again.

48 "Two or Three Things Brought to Mind," *LXQJ* 6:579. These comments are also noted in Shi Yuhua and Beijing Lu Xun Museum, eds., *Lu Xun Documents and Visual Materials*, 31, but are not linked to the author's scathing remarks about others. For the inconvenience of the queue (worn in the regular manner) in the early years of Western-style physical education, see Andrew Morris, "To Make the 400 Million Move," 899.

49 *Dianshizhai Pictorial* 14 (1884): 14–15.

50 He is so identified in Beijing Lu Xun Museum, ed., *Lu Xun, 1881–1936*, photograph 2, and in the museum's file photograph. It is an odd way to count: fifteenth from the left makes third from the right.

51 The three photographs are reproduced from Cai Jian'guo, ed., *Pictorial Biography of Cai Yuanpei*, 25–27.

52 David E. Pollard, *The True Story of Lu Xun*, 22.

53 Ni Moyan, *Lu Xun's Societal Activities*, 17.

54 Zhou Zuoren, *Diary* 1:327, ninth day of third month, 1902.

55 Ni Moyan, *Lu Xun's Societal Activities*, 12.

56 Shen Deimin, "Lu Xun at Kōbun Academy." Critics are about evenly divided on whether to accept Shen's memory that Lu Xun is the author of this triangle-shaped poem.

57 "What Happens after Nora Leaves Home?" *LXQJ* 1:170; Lu Xun, *Selected Works*, 2:91.

58 Chou, "Literary Martyrs in Lu Xun's Writings," 145, 157–58.

59 Wang Dehou, *Personal Readings of Lu Xun*, 282–85.

60 Qiu Cunping, *"Call to Arms" for People Today*, 1–25.

61 Preface, *Call to Arms*, *LXQJ* 1:438.

62 Masuda Wataru, "Lu Xun and Guangfu hui," 340.

63 The critic Ge Hongbin vigorously pursues this point. See Lin Qingxin, "Reloading the Canon," 189.

64 Dikötter, *The Discourse of Race in Modern China*, 65–66.

65 Pollard, *The True Story of Lu Xun*, 23.

66 *Lu Xun Chronology*, 1:104.

67 No account is contemporary. The closest in time is Zhang Binglin's in his 1905 elegy of Zou Rong. Four much later ones are by men who were in Tokyo at the time (Lu Xun, Xu Shoushang, Zhang Shizao, and Feng Ziyou). They vary in detail, but clearly the incident itself did occur. Zhu Zheng quotes the five, plus a sixth, highly embellished account by the son of someone who was a student at the time ("A Story of Queue-cutting," 95–96).

68 Xu, *My Late Friend*, 2; Zhou Zuoren, *Diary*.

69 Xu, *My Late Friend*, 3; "A Story about Hair," *LXQJ* 1:486.

70 Edmund Leach, "Magical Hair," 159–50; C. R. Hallpike, "Social Hair," 257–28. The differing viewpoints of these authors are announced by their titles.

71 Xu, *My Late Friend*, 3.

72 "Further Thoughts after an Illness," *LXQJ* 6:187–88.

73 *LXQJ* 6:576; Lu Xun, *Selected Works*, 4:327.

74 See also Zhang Shiying, "Queue-Cutting Movements in the Late Qing, Early Republican Era," 30–33.

75 Confucius, *The Analects* 14.18.

76 The Taiping rebels, known as "Longhairs," quickly became the stuff of folklore and also figured in Lu Xun's first short fiction, "Remembering the Past" (*Huai jiu*), a 1911 classical-language work (*LXQJ* 7:225–32).

77 Hallpike, "Social Hair," 260; the next quotation from page 261.

78 For the imposition of the queue and several examples of resistance, see Weikun Cheng, "Politics of the Queue," 125–26; and Wang Dongfang, *Striding into Modernity*, 11–13.

79 Weiikun Cheng, "Politics of the Queue," 126.

80 Philip A. Kuhn, *Soulstealers*, 12, 22.

81 Reference from Richard Vinograd, *Boundaries of the Self*, 141. Ren's career as a successful commercial artist is examined in Tang Li, "Art for the Market: Commercialism in Ren Yi's Figure Painting," from which we can surmise the cultural invisibility of the queue.

82 Edward Rhoads, *Manchus and Han*, 252–54.

83 This and next two quotations are from "Further Thoughts after an Illness," *LXQJ* 6:192, 185, 193. The "Ah Q" quotation is from *LXQJ* 1:543.

84 Reed, *Gutenberg in Shanghai*, 95.

85 "The Sight of Riches Spawns a Plan" (*Jian cai qiyi*), *Dianshizhai Pictorial* 3 (1884): 21; "Officials Capture Gamblers" (*Lingshi zhuo du*), *Dianshizhai Pictorial* 23 (1885): 85.

86 Dikötter, *The Discourse of Race in Modern China*, 14–18.

87 "A Young Chinese Scholar," also in *Image of China*, 58. The wallpaper is from the Winterthur Museum and is a typical motif of wallpaper.

88 "History Repeats Itself," in Neville Edwards, *The Story of China*, 36; "The Most Unkindest Cut of All," *New York Herald*, November 6, 1911, 3.

89 Sun Yat-sen, *Kidnapped in London*. J. Y. Wong, in *The Origins of an Heroic Image: Sun Yat-sen in London, 1896–97*, analyzes the crucial role of the detention in Sun's world image. He also persuasively argues that Dr. Cantlie, who negotiated Sun's release, was the actual author of *Kidnapped*. Both arguments suggest the importance of this photograph's presentation of Sun.

90 The European beating a Chinese (*Xiren cheng xiong*) is from *Yulun shishi bao tuhua*, in Guojia tushuguan fenguan, ed. *Compendium of Illustrations*, 9. (The editors go on to point out a moral about standing up for oneself: the servant went to the concession police, and the head of police reported the incident to the consular office.) The illustration from *Anhui suhua bao* (*Zhuoren wei nu*) is one of seven published during the paper's short life, all teaching about aspects of European imperialism in China. The reference is from Zheng Xuejia, *Biography of Chen Duxiu*, vol. 1, unpaginated before text proper.

91 *Shibao* April 13 and 15, 1910. The illustrations are reproduced in Edward J. M Rhoads, *Manchus and Han*, following page 182.

92 Joan Judge, *Print and Politics*, 35.

93 Weili Ye, *Seeking Modernity in China's Name*, 1–2. For other proposals on the eve of 1911, especially that of Wu Tingfang (1842–1922) on his return from an ambassadorship to the United States, see Rhoads, *Manchus and Han*, 163–66.

94 Descriptions of the mass queue cutting may be found in, among others, Harrison, *The Making of the Republican Citizen*, 20–21, 33–36; and Rhoads, *Manchus and Han*, 163–66.

95 Harrison, *The Man Awakened from Dreams*, 94.

96 For the villagers, see *LXQJ* 1:497; for the tavern owner, see 1:494.

97 See, for example, Wang Dongfang, *Striding towards Modernity*, 45–46; and Zhang Shiying, "Queue-cutting Movements in the Late Qing, Early Republican Era," 14–19.

⁹⁸ Zhang Binglin, in Young-tsu Wong, *Search for Modern Nationalism*, 24–27, quoted at 26; Zou Rong, in Zhang Binglin, "Life of Zou Rong"; Sun Yat-sen, in Feng Ziyou, *Geming yishi*, quoted in Wang Dongfang, *Striding towards Modernity*, 52, and in *Biographical Dictionary of Republican China*, ed. Howard Boorman; Chiang Kai-shek, in *Biographical Dictionary*; ed. Howard Boorman; Huang Xing, in Wang Dongfang, *Striding towards Modernity*, 70. Wang Dongfang gives about a dozen other examples, including those of Chen Duxiu and Zhang Ji (47–89).

⁹⁹ The historian Wang Xiangrong, quoted in Douglas Reynolds, *China, 1898–1912*, 42.

¹⁰⁰ Reynolds provides a comparative table of three scholars' estimates of these numbers in ibid., 48. Where the numbers differ, I use Sanetō Keishū's figures, also in ibid. Marius Jansen describes Sanetō's figures as "conservative contemporary estimates," in *The Cambridge History of China*, vol. 11, pt. 2, 350.

¹⁰¹ Jing Meijiu, *Zui an* 罪案, quoted in Jansen, *The Cambridge History of China*, 354–55, together with information on other memoirists (352, n. 19); *New Fiction* (Xin xiaoshuo), no. 1 (1902), tenth month, referenced in Cheng Ma, *Lu Xun's Student Years in Japan*, 19; Zou Rong, *Revolutionary Army*, preface; Liu Dajie, "Lu Xun's Traditional Poetry."

¹⁰² "Further Thoughts after an Illness," *LXQJ* 6:193.

¹⁰³ Kai-wing Chow, "Imagining Boundaries of Blood," 36, 52.

¹⁰⁴ Ni Moyan, *Lu Xun's Societal Activities*, 21. A photograph of the student center is reproduced on page 6.

¹⁰⁵ "Two or Three Things Brought to Mind," *LXQJ* 6:578.

¹⁰⁶ This and other accounts of Zhang here draw on Young-tsu Wong, *Search for Modern Nationalism,* and Laitinen, *Chinese Nationalism in Late Qing Dynasty.*

¹⁰⁷ Huang Fuqing, *Chinese Students in Japan*, 178; Wong, *Search for Modern Nationalism*, 35.

¹⁰⁸ Ni Moyan, *Lu Xun's Societal Activities*, 22.

¹⁰⁹ Zou Rong, *Revolutionary Army*, preface; Xu, *My Late Friend*, 13.

¹¹⁰ The following account draws chiefly from Huang Fuqing, *Chinese Students in Japan*, 201–8; and Ni Moyan, *Lu Xun's Societal Activities*, 34–36.

¹¹¹ Ni Moyan, *Lu Xun's Societal Activities*, 36.

¹¹² Letter 311110, *LXQJ* 12:282.

¹¹³ *LXQJ* 7:9. For Xu's editorial comment, see *Zhejiang Tide* 5 (June 1903): 1.

¹¹⁴ Dikötter, *Discourses of Race*, 116; Chow, "Imagining Boundaries of Blood," 46.

[115] Liang's influence on this quatrain is also noted by Wu Haifa in "Lu Xun's 'Inscribed by the Author'," 65–66. Wu notes that Liang's poem was published in *Qing yi bao* in 1901, and shows that the Tokyo-based periodical was seen in China by the young Lu Xun. Since it was also published in 1902 in Japan, it is possible that Lu Xun saw this one. For other interpretations of line 1, see appendix A.

[116] "Various Memories," *LXQJ* 1:234; "Some Notes on Hong Kong," *LXQJ* 2:451–52; "Various Memories," *LXQJ*. 1:233.

[117] Preface to *Grave*, *LXQJ* 1:3.

[118] Preface to *Supplement to the Collected Works*, *LXQJ* 7:4.

[119] "Various Memories," *LXQJ* 1:234.

[120] "Two or Three Things Regarding Mr. Zhang Taiyan," *LXQJ* 6:567; "Two or Three Things Brought to Mind," *LXQJ* 6:579.

[121] "Fan Ainong," *LXQJ* 2:324.

Chapter 3: The Literary Afterlife of the Queue: A Closer Look at the Years 1920–22

[1] I use Julia Lovell's apt translation of the names in "A Passing Storm," in Lu Xun, *The Real Story of Ah Q*, 61–69.

[2] *LXQJ* 1:491–99. The translation most often used for the title is Yang Xianyi and Gladys Yang's "Storm in a Teacup" (Lu Xun, *Selected Works*, 1:79). Their title wittily captures both the *fengbo* ("wind and waves" or "storm") of the title and, with "in a Teacup," the story's satiric content of a revolution writ small. I use "Storm" alone so that, as with the original, the sarcasm is not apparent until you know the storyline.

[3] *LXQJ* 1:484–88. In *Call to Arms*, "A Story about Hair" is placed before "Storm," but that is not the order in which the stories were written or published. It has been translated by Jacques Seigner in "Une histoire de nattes," *France-Asie* (December 1953): 51–55, cited in Irene Eber, "The Reception of Lu Xun in Europe and America," 278. It is also among the translations of the complete stories by Yang Xianyi and Gladys Yang, William Lyell, and Julia Lovell.

[4] "Surrendering," *LXQJ* 8:121; "Names," *LXQJ* 8:127. Both were written on May 5. The former was published on May 6 and the latter on May 7.

[5] *LXQJ* 1:512–52. Compilations of analyses include Peng Xiaojie and Han Geli, eds., *70 Years of Ah Q*; Zhang Mengyang, *New Criticism on "Ah Q"*; and Chen Shuyu, ed., *The Inexhaustible Topic of Ah Q*.

[6] "Hometown" (*LXQJ* 1:501–10) was published in *New Youth*. It is a fictionalized version of an experience of December, 1919, when Lu Xun had taken a month's leave to move the Shaoxing household to Beijing.

[7] *LXQJ* 1:307.

[8] "Lu Xun's Zawen," 62.

[9] Wu Haiyong gives the number of hours Lu Xun spent at the ministry and their gradual reduction, which began with the government's inability to meet its payroll and the need for ministry workers to hold other jobs (*Lu Xun as a Civil Servant*, 60–61). For Lu Xun's half-day hours in 1921, see his letter to a young writer on how best to catch him in (Letter 210816, *LXQJ* 11:407).

[10] See the prefaces in *LXQJ* 10:176–228. My count uses strictly the eighteen-month limit of the five works under consideration in this chapter.

[11] "The Birth of "Ah Q," in *The Inexhaustible Topic of Ah Q*, ed. Chen Shuyu, 210.

[12] "The Writing of 'The True Story of Ah Q,'" *LXQJ* 3:398.

[13] Patrick Hanan, "The Technique of Lu Hsun's Fiction," 72.

[14] Instead we can see Seven-Pounds's role at home as related to the domestic comedy found in stories such as "Soap" and "Flight to the Moon," where despite being the man of the family, the protagonist has no position with his strong wife nor, additionally for Seven-Pounds, with his complaining mother.

[15] "A Reply to the Editors of *Theater*," *LXQJ* 6:151.

[16] "Preface to the Russian Translation of 'The True Story of Ah Q,'". *LXQJ* 7:77.

[17] Ziang Tianyi ("On 'The True Story of Ah Q'"), 1941; in *70 Years of Ah Q*, eds. Peng Xiaojie and Han Geli, 122, 125.

[18] This work is analyzed in my article "'A Story about Hair': A Curious Mirror of Lu Xun's Pre-Republican Years," and some parts of the discussion here draw on it.

[29] See ibid., 434–41.

[20] Lu Xun, *Selected Works*, 1:116 , with slight changes.

[21] *LXQJ* 8:123, n. 2. The inaugural issue was October, 1905.

[22] This likely refers to the posthumous titles that the Qing imperial household continued to bestow after abdication, even though these actions contravened the 1912 abdication agreement and were expressly forbidden in 1914 and again in 1925 (Edward J. M. Rhoads, *Manchus and Han*, 237, 248).

[23] Zhou Zuoren, *People and Things in Lu Xun's Fiction*, item 30.

[24] Chuandao, *In the Days When I Knew Lu Xun*, 13.

[25] Zhou Zuoren, *People and Things*, item 41. Next quotation is also from item 41.

[26] See further description in appendix B, fig. B.19.

[27] Gathered before text in *70 Years of Ah Q*.

28 The cover of *The True Story of Ah Q: a Literary Playscript* (*Ah Q zhengzhuan: wenxue juben*). From Ouyang Wenli, ed., *Pictorial Biography of Lu Xun*, 414. Illustrator and playwright not identified; date not provided; work not locatable through WorldCat.

29 Playscript, Chen Baichen, *The True Story of Ah Q*. Chen also did a filmscript in this year (1981) published by Zhongguo dianying chubanshe.

30 Foster, *Ah Q Archaeology*, 6, 17, n. 28. Pen names may be found in Xu Naixiang and Qin Hong, eds. *The Pen Names of Modern Chinese Writers*, 853, 181, 552. The reference is from Foster, *Ah Q Archaeology*, 286.

31 "'Fair Play' Should be Postponed" *LXQJ* 1:288.

32 Interestingly, the general and the army are always referred to in English as Pigtail General and Pigtail Army, but everything else gets the more dignified translation of "queue." I follow custom, since "The Queue General" and "The Queue Army" will not meet with recognition in English.

33 This sketch forms the first section, the "Preface," of a running feature called "Thinking to Myself" (Ziyan ziyu), published in the column "New Literature" (Xin wenyi), August 19, 1919, under the pen name Shen Fei.

34 *Lu Xun Chronology* has a contrasting suggestion for the genesis of "Storm." The editors cite a newly discovered letter from Chen Duxiu to Zhou Zuoren in which Chen says that *New Youth* would really like to have another work of fiction from his brother (2:26). The editors of *Lu Xun Chronology* say, and Chen Shuyu seems to agree (4:499), that it was in response to this letter that "Storm" was written. The trouble is that, although it is nice to have this newly found letter drawn to our attention, it was written in March, rather far from August. This story may seem to be a response to the relayed request only because it is the first story since the letter was written.

35 Zhou Zuoren, *People and Things*, item 27.

36 Lu Xun, *Diary*, *LXQJ* 15:287-95 and 15:405-07; Zhou Zuoren, *Diary*, 1:678-84 and 2:124-37; Zhou Zuoren, *Zhitang Memoirs* 1:319-29; *Lu Xun Chronology*, 1:362-64 and 2:22-24.

37 Zhou Zuoren, *Zhitang Memoirs*, 1:324.

38 Quoted in *Lu Xun Chronology*, 1:363.

39 The next day's *Beijing Daily* (*Beijing ribao*), quoted in *Lu Xun Chronology*, 1:363.

40 *New Capital Paper* (*Xin jing bao*), quoted in *Lu Xun Chronology*, 2:24.

41 *LXQJ* 4:468. The preface was actually written in December 1932, but it is more convenient to use the 1933 year of the anthology.

42 Mao Dun, "Reading *Call to Arms*," in *On Lu Xun and His Works*, ed. Tai Jingnong, 57.

[43] *Lu Xun Chronology*, under the year 1916; Wu Haiyong, *Lu Xun as a Civil Servant*, 52–54. For the fiction awards and comments on high-quality fiction, see *Lu Xun Chronology*, 1:343. For the review and anthology, see 1:366–67.

[44] "Some Dissent from 'The Wrong People Were Killed,'" *LXQJ* 5:100–01. Lu Xun is dissenting from an essay by Cao Juren, "The Wrong People Were Killed," whose title imitates his deadly tone.

[45] "Further Thoughts after an Illness," *LXQJ* 6:185. In "Again on the Collapse of Leifeng Pagoda," Lu Xun lists Zhang Xianzhong among the mass murderers of history (1:203).

[46] Zhou Zuoren, *Zhitang Memoirs*, 1:200; Lu Xun, 1923 Preface; *Lu Xun Chronology*, 1:345.

[47] "Two or Three Things Regarding Mr. Zhang Taiyan," *LXQJ* 6:569; Lu Xun, *Selected Works*, 4:325.

[48] Zhou Zuoren, *Zhitang Memoirs*, under "Si Tang and Chen Shizeng."

[49] On the National Day stamp, see Lu Xun, *Diary*, October 10, 1913; on Yuan's birthday, see the entry for September 16, 1914. Both are cited in Wu Haiyong, *Lu Xun as a Civil Servant*, 106.

[50] On the audience with Yuan, see *Diary*, December 12, 1912; on the burial, see the entries for June 15 and June 28, 1916; on Lu Xun as a ministry representative, see *Lu Xun Chronology*, 1:348, which quotes from newspaper and official documents.

[51] *Lu Xun Chronology*, 1:412.

[52] Preface to *Anthology*, *LXQJ* 10:176.

[53] Anderson, *The Limits of Realism*, 77, 86.

[54] T. A. Hsia, "The Power of Darkness in Lu Hsun," in *The Gate of Darkness*, 146–62; Huters, *Bringing the World Home*, 261–63.

[55] "Further Thoughts after an Illness," *LXQJ* 6:195–96.

[56] The congratulatory essay, "Celebrating the Victories in Shanghai and Nanjing," *LXQJ* 8:196. This was written April 10, 1927, a few days before the next violent event, the sudden purging of Communist members by the Nationalists. For traveling north in 1913, Lu Xun, *Diary*, June 20, 1913, *LXQJ* 15:20.

[57] Zhou Zuoren, *Zhitang Memoirs*, 1: 320-29, this quotation p. 320; for the effect on *New Youth*, see also Michel Hockx, *Questions of Style*, 173, and Timothy B. Weston, *The Power of Position*, 128-30.

[58] "Further Thoughts after an Illness," *LXQJ* 6:196.

[59] See the discussion in Patrick Hanan, "The Technique of Lu Hsun's Fiction," especially pages 5–9.

[60] Jordan, *China's Trial by Fire*, 46–48.

⁶¹ Letter 320605, *LXQJ* 12:308.

⁶² These figures are from Fogel, "Shanghai-Japan: The Japanese Residents' Association of Shanghai," 936; and the chapter "Cost of the Shanghai War," in Jordan, *China's Trial by Fire*, 186–204, especially pages 192–93 and 199.

⁶³ Letter 350629, *LXQJ* 13:492–94. Optimists, including the recipient Lai Shaoqi, prefer to quote the next sentence: "A large building is built up timber by timber, stone by stone, so why should we not try to fashion such a block of timber or block of stone?"

⁶⁴ This last, on their passing Qiu Jin's execution ground everyday is from a 1934 essay on the same incident, in a nonfiction context ("Further Thoughts After an Illness," *LXQJ* 6:195), not from N's words in the fiction.

⁶⁵ "Preface to the Russian Translation of 'The True Story of Ah Q'," *LXQJ* 7:83.

⁶⁶ "Written in Deep Night," *LXQJ* 6:519; Lu Xun, *Selected Works*, 4:265–66.

⁶⁷ "Written in Deep Night," *LXQJ* 6:520; Lu Xun, *Selected Works*, 4:266.

⁶⁸ Qu Qiubai, in *Biographical Dictionary of Republican China*, ed. Howard Boorman.

⁶⁹ "The Writing of 'The True Story of Ah Q,'" *LXQJ* 3:397.

⁷⁰ Ibid., 398-99. Lu Xun uses the German word *grotesk*.

⁷¹ "Preface to the Russian Translation," *LXQJ* 7:84.

Chapter 4: The Life of a Poem, 1903–36

¹ *LXQJ* 7:447.

² Xu Shoushang, *The Lu Xun I Knew*, 75.

³ "Tradition and Modernity in the Writings of Lu Xun," in Leo Ou-fan Lee, ed., *Lu Xun and His Legacy*, 21–23. For "Self-Mockery," see *LXQJ* 7:151.

⁴ A 1943 letter from Xu Shoushang to one Liu Feiqi queries Liu's dating it to 1912 in a collection Liu made. Quoted in Ah Yuan, "'Inscribed by the Author on a Small Likeness' Was Not First Published in 'Memories,'" 84.

⁵ It was collected from "Memories" (Huaijiu), which is dated December 19, 1936, and published in *New Sprouts* (*Xin miao*) in January 1937. See Xu Shoushang, *The Lu Xun I Knew*, 24. Xu mentioned his priority in publication more than once. Ah Yuan points out that in fact another essay of Xu's, named "The Lu Xun I Knew" like the volume that contains it, also quotes the quatrain in its entirety and predates "Memories" by two months (dateline of October 27, 1936). See Ah Yuan, "'Inscribed by the Author on a Small Likeness' Was Not First Published in 'Memories,'" 84.

⁶ The dimensions are given in Shi Yuhua and Beijing Lu Xun Museum, eds., *Lu Xun Documents and Visual Materials*. I convert from the museum's metric dimensions

of 61 x 32.8 cm because the resulting whole numbers, 24 x 13 inches, suggest that the original sheet of paper was cut on British measures.

[7] The modern-day souvenir is metric, as one would expect: 15 x 10 cm.

[8] According to Xu, this was from memory, *The Lu Xun I Knew*, 26.

[9] There are different opinions about who among the Communists might have betrayed the meeting, but scholars agree that there was a betrayal. Analyses generally begin with deductions about the agenda and status of the meeting (and hence who might have been their enemy), and these in turn are connected to the power struggle that had consumed the party since September 1930. See Wang-chi Wong, *Politics and Literature in Shanghai*, 100–106; and "Enigma of the Five Martyrs," in T. A. Hsia, *Gate of Darkness*, 227–33.

[10] Lu Xun gives both twenty-three and twenty-four for the number executed; other texts place the number at twenty-four or twenty-five. In 1952, twenty-three bodies were located (T. A. Hsia, *Gate of Darkness*, 165, quoting Feng Xuefeng).

[11] For the phrase "my student," see Letter 310204, *LXQJ* 12:255.

[12] "Remembrance in Order to Forget," *LXQJ* 4:500–501.

[13] Frederick Wakeman, *The Policing of Shanghai*, 132–61.

[14] Contemporary suspicions are described in Wong, *Politics and Literature in Shanghai*, 104–5; and Hsia, *Gate of Darkness*, 230–31.

[15] T. A. Hsia, *Gate of Darkness*, 166.

[16] Letter 310224, *LXQJ* 12:259.

[17] For a description of the birthday party, see Wong, *Politics and Literature in Shanghai*, 99; for the ban on and arrests of league members, see 99–100.

[18] Hsia, *Gate of Darkness*, 191–92.

[19] Wakeman, *Policing Shanghai*, 134.

[20] Ruth Price, *The Lives of Agnes Smedley*, 216.

[21] This information is drawn from Lu Xun, Letter 310121, *LXQJ* 12:251 and Letter 310123, *LXQJ* 12:251–52, editorial notes to them, and his account in "Remembrance in Order to Forget."

[22] Letter 310224, *LXQJ* 12:259.

[23] Letter 310123, *LXQJ* 12:251–52 and editorial notes.

[24] Letter 310121, *LXQJ* 12:251; punctuation added by editors.

[25] Letter 310123 and 310202 and editorial notes, *LXQJ* 12:251–54.

[26] Letter 310204 and editorial notes *LXQJ* 12:254.

27 Letter 310205, *LXQJ* 12:257.

28 Wang-chi Wong, *Politics and Literature in Shanghai*, 106.

29 Lu Xun used code names in his diary at other times. For example, letters sent from prison by the artists Jiang Feng and Ai Qing in 1932 were noted as received from "Jie Fu" and "Jia" (Julia F. Andrews, *Painters and Politics in the People's Republic of China, 1949–1979*, 420, n. 31).

30 *LXQJ* 17:210.

31 Lu Xun, *Diary*, February 16, 1931. The editors of the 1981 edition of *LXQJ* say that the matter is "awaiting research" (14:842, n. 4). The editors of the 2005 edition identify the phrase as referring to "Rou Shi and others" without explanation, *LXQJ* 16:244, n.4.

32 Lin Zhihao, *Lu Xun Biography*, 416–24; *Lu Xun Chronology*, entries for February 15 and 18, 3:249; Miu Junqi and Shanghai Lu Xun jinianguan, eds., *Illustrated Biography of Lu Xun*, 133; Lin Xianzhi, *Lu Xun among Mortals*, 704–10.

33 Nagao Kagekazu, "Getting to Know Lu Xun in Shanghai at Huayuanzhuang," in *Lu Xun Remembered: Articles*, ed. Beijing Lu Xun bowuguan, 3:1524–25. Nagao did not know the reason for Lu Xun's being at Huayuanzhuang, only that there was reason to fear suspicious-looking individuals.

34 Some comments include (1) "On Feb 16, the eve of the New Year, he wrote out again a poem 'written at the age of 21 and written out again at 51.' With the reality of struggle before him, Lu Xun once again gave voice to his determination to 'offer my blood up for the descendants of the Yellow Emperor'" (Zhou Guowei and Peng Xiao, *In Search of Lu Xun's Steps in Shanghai*, 14); (2) "When he recopied the poem in February of 1931, Lu Xun must have attached a new value to its concluding couplet, perhaps a reaffirmation of his determination to dedicate his life to the recovery of his nation from the hands of its benighted rulers" (Kowallis, *The Lyrical Lu Xun*, 106); (3) "'I would offer my blood for the descendants of the Yellow Emperor' became his lifelong motto, and in February, 1931, he once again wrote out this poem, with the postscript 'written at the age of 21 and written out again at 51'" (Zhou Zhenfu, *Notes on Lu Xun's Poetry*, 28); and (4) "Under the pressure of the White Terror, Lu Xun, in hiding, wrote out again this poem, and noted upon it the generation that separates the year of writing and the year of rewriting.... Does this not indicate that in the year of writing he vowed to sacrifice himself for the old democratic revolution and later he vowed to sacrifice himself for the new democratic revolution?" (*Lu Xun Chronology*, 1:116 [under 1903]).

35 The ellipses are Zhang's, *Annotations on the Poetry of Mr. Lu Xun*, 88.

36 *LXQJ* 3:285–88, 3:289–91.

37 Ruth Price, in *The Lives of Agnes Smedley*, 217, says the letter was published in *New Masses* and *New Republic*.

38 *LXQJ* 4:292–95. The translation of the essay title is by Pollard in *The True Story of Lu Xun*, 154.

39 On Ding Ling, see Jun-mei Chang, *Ting Ling*, 56.

40 "Written in Deep Night," *LXQJ* 6:517–18.

41 Wang Shijia, "Why Did Lu Xun Discard a Copy of the Poem 'Inscribed by the Author on a Small Likeness'?" 58.

42 Ye Shusui and Yang Yanli, *Learning about Lu Xun through Physical Artifacts*, 69, quoting Zhou Haiying; Wang Shijia, "Why Did Lu Xun Discard a Copy of the Poem?" 59–60.

43 The dimensions are given in Shanghai Lu Xun Museum. ed., *Lu Xun shigao*, 1.

44 These poems are "A Farewell to Mr. O.E. Who Is Taking Orchids with Him on His Return to Japan," *LXQJ* 7:48; "Untitled" ("The countryside is filled with brambles"), *LXQJ* 7:148; and "Song of the Xiang River Goddess," *LXQJ* 7:150. They were published in *Literature and Art News* (*Wenyi xinwen*) on August 10, 1931, with editorial remarks that seem to have Lu Xun as their source.

45 *The Lu Xun I Knew*, 24.

46 Shi Yuhua and Beijing Lu Xun Museum, ed., *Lu Xun Documents and Visual Materials*, 30. The caption says it was written out on December 9, 1931, but this cannot be the correct year, for the *Diary* entry that corresponds to it is in 1932.

47 These are awkward, fractional numbers whether in metric or British measures.

48 Zhang, *Annotations*, 88–91.

49 A photo reproduction of Qu's poem and its postscript is found in *Lu Xun Chronology*, 3:361.

50 The poems are reproduced in facsimile and discussed in Ye Shusui and Yang Yanli, *Learning about Lu Xun through Physical Artifacts*, 122–26. The quotation of Xu Guangping is on page 124. Qu's letter with the jesting poem is featured on Beijing Lu Xun Museum's website, http://www.luxunmuseum.com.cn/tabid/135/InfoID/294/Default.aspx

51 *LXQJ* 4:501-02.

52 The essay is at *LXQJ* 4:493-504. Its title contains a paradox that is hard to translate. The Yangs translate the title as "Written for the Sake of Forgetting" (Lu Xun, *Selected Works*, 3: 234-46), Pollard as "To Remember in Order to Forget" (*The True Story of Lu Xun*, 225-37). My translation keeps "Remembrance" as a noun. The other two poems widely quoted today are the 1903 quatrain of this chapter, which as noted, came to the fore only in the 1950s; and the poem "Self-Mockery" (see n. 3) in part because Mao Zedong praised it. Mao wrote out a couplet from "Self-Mockery" for a pair of scrolls, also in the 1950s, and for a while it was duplicated everywhere.

⁵³ *LXQJ* 7:147.

⁵⁴ Ni Moyan, *Lu Xun's Traditional Poetry*, 74; Wang Shijia, "The Seven Copies of Lu Xun's 'Untitled [Though accustomed to the long nights, now it is spring],'" 89–90.

⁵⁵ Zhang, *Annotations*, 166–71.

⁵⁶ Ibid., 166, 87–88.

⁵⁷ Zhang Ziqiang, *Annotations*, 167-68. Ding Ling, "The Life of a Sincere Person," 102-07. Shen Congwen, *Remembering Ding Ling*, 38-107; this 1936 volume was first published in serialized form in 1933, when she had been arrested and was thought dead; hence "remembering." For her three-year house arrest, see Jun-mei Chang, *Ting Ling*, 60-65.

⁵⁸ Shen's three trips to Nanjing, *Remembering Ding Ling*, 55-57, 58, 87-95. His actions are summarized in Jeffrey Kinkley, *The Odyssey of Shen Congwen*, 203; 342-43, n. 52. The receipt of the letter, Shen, *Remembering Ding Ling*, 93-95.

⁵⁹ Zhang has a suggestion for the code (ibid., 170–71). Some of the other arguments he makes are not particularly conclusive. For instance, he has the clever idea of looking to see which night would have had moonlight (per line 8) by checking the notations about the weather in Lu Xun's diary. But February 10, which he favors, is as far in time from the new moon of the sixteenth as is the traditional date of the twenty-third, and the weather on the tenth, as recorded in Lu Xun's diary (partly cloudy), is not really more favorable to moonlight than the twenty-third (cloudy), although Zhang says it is (169). Zhang radically redates quite a few other poems besides this one, and this is probably one reason to be wary in an overall way, although extrapolating from Ding Ling's and Feng Xuefeng's experiences certainly is a reliable procedure.

⁶⁰ There are many variants of this poem because Lu Xun wrote it out several times after its first composition and changed a word or two each time or changed one back. The version here is from its publication in "Remembrance."

⁶¹ Liu Dajie, "Lu Xun's Traditional Poetry," *Wenyi yuebao* October 1956, 64-65. Translations of the poem only are in Kowallis, *The Lyrical Lu Xun*, 149; Wang Shiqing, *Lu Xun*, fronticepiece, trans. W. J. F. Jenner; Lu Xun, *Lu Hsun*, trans. David Ch'en, 75; Lu Xun, *Poèmes*, trans. Michelle Loi, second poem; and Lu Xun, *Werke in sechs Banden*, trans. Wolfgang Kubin, 6:29. Two works translate the essay and in this way include the poem: Lu Xun, *Selected Works*, 3:243; and Pollard, *The True Story of Lu Xun*, 235.

⁶² Letter 310204, *LXQJ* 12:255.

⁶³ There is some difficulty with the date because the colophon reads "written in spring of wu-year" (that is, *gengwu* year). The problem is that *gengwu* largely corresponds to 1930, and so "spring of wu-year" would be the lunar New Year of early 1930, which is clearly not possible. "Spring" for the next year begins on February 16, 1931. Ni Moyan concludes that the year is off (*Lu Xun's Traditional Poetry Explained*, 75).

Wang Shijia dates it quite differently, to the lunar New Year of 1933 (January 26), in "The Seven Copies of Lu Xun's 'Untitled [Though accustomed to],'" 88–89, 91. The calligraphy is reproduced in Ouyang Wenli, ed., *Pictorial Biography of Lu Xun*, 212.

[64] For Yamamoto, see Zhou Guowei, *Lu Xun and Japanese Friends*, 152-57. According to the unusually long diary entry for July 11, 1932, Lu Xun wrote Yamamoto a letter that included a newly composed poem, "After the January 28 War" (*LXQJ* 7:458). Additionally he wrote out on a separate sheet of paper (*xiaofu*) "an old composition," and here followed the complete text of this Remembrance poem. He said that he would "ask Uchiyama Bookstore to forward" both letter and calligraphy. Neither letter nor calligraphy has surfaced. This dairy entry provides the text for the "January 28" poem and variant characters for the Remembrance poem.

[65] Tai Jingnong (1902–90) worked on many publishing projects with Lu Xun, especially at Unnamed Society (Weiming she). As will be seen in the next section, he was the editor of the first collection of Lu Xun criticism, the 1926 *On Lu Xun and His Writings*. He remained in the north, and their correspondence was frequent. According to the editors of the 1981 *LXQJ*, this "horizontal piece" was one of three pieces of calligraphy Lu Xun gave to Tai (*LXQJ* 17:46).

[66] Reproduced in Wang Shijia, "The Seven Copies of Lu Xun's 'Untitled [Though accustomed to],'" with a citation for the 2004 publication (88). The current owner is not identified.

[67] Letter 321213, *LXQJ* 12:352.

[68] Letter 320320, *LQXJ* 12:292.

[69] T. A. Hsia, *The Gate of Darkness*, 197–205. See also Wakeman's account of the elaborate covers created by the Communist Party for its operatives in Shanghai, with safe houses complete with servants and instant relatives spanning several generations, as well as real estate agencies and all manner of shops to supply their needs (*The Policing of Shanghai*, 139–40).

[70] Lu Xun used the older name British Concession rather than International Settlement.

[71] *LXQJ* 7:3. The poems are in *LXQJ* 7:145–62.

[72] "Inscribed in *Hesitation*," *LXQJ* 7:156; "Inscribed in *Call to Arms*," *LXQJ* 7:466.

[73] The two exceptions are this quatrain, whose text was based on his 1931 calligraphy, and "Elegy for Fan Ainong, Three Poems." A single poem of the latter was printed in *Supplement to the Collected Works*. So this collection adds twenty-two rather than twenty-three titles to Lu Xun's total of forty-nine. The added poems are in *LXQJ* 7:400 and 7:447–75.

[74] They are gathered in *LXQJ* 8:531–42.

[75] The 1925 poem is in *LXQJ* 3:57; a 1928 poem is taken from the end of an essay at *LXQJ* 4:93; and a 1930 poem was discovered in the notebook of a female medical

student (a cousin of Xu Guangping) in 1976 (*LXQJ* 8:345). See Ni Moyan, *Lu Xun's Traditional Poetry*, 55–57, 58–62, 63–66; and Kowallis, *The Lyrical Lu Xun*, 121–25, 126–30; 131–33.

[76] Zhou Guowei, *Lu Xun and His Japanese Friends*, 182.

[77] Masuda Wataru, "Lu Xun and Guangfu hui," 334.

[78] David Ch'en, *Lu Hsun*, 16; Liu Dajie, "Lu Xun's Traditional Poetry," 65.

[79] Liu Dajie, "Lu Xun's Traditional Poetry," 65.

[80] Tao designed the covers for three of Lu Xun's first four collections, *Grave, Hesitation, Dawn Blossoms Gathered at Dusk*, and for many translations. (Lu Xun designed the cover of *Call to Arms* himself.) Tao died in 1929 at the age of thirty-six.

[81] They are on the frontispiece, facing page 70, and facing page 104.

[82] Evidently Lu Xun wanted nothing to do with it, writing, "Many of us are attacked in the papers, with attacks on me especially numerous, so that [works about me] would make up a small volume if collected together. It does no harm to me, and Beixin Publishers is now able to advertise, like 'wanted posters,' the sale of *Essays on Lu Xun*. It has been ten years, it hasn't harmed me any, and to accrue profits to others is after all not a bad thing" (Letter 300524) *LXQJ* 12:235. *Essays on Lu Xun* must have just come out.

[83] There is conflicting date information for the photographs, but for this chapter it is only important that both possibilities are early, 1903 and 1904. On the back of the photograph in figure 4.4 with the light uniform, Xu Shoushang wrote the information "Photograph of Lu Xun age 24 in Tokyo in 1904" when he gave it to one Yu Kunshan (in what year is not known). It has been identified as a detail from a group shot of Shaoxing students (Ye Shusui and Yang Yanli, *Learning about Lu Xun through Physical Artifacts*, 451, 453). I have not seen the group photograph. Another print of it has been published in a very narrow, cropped form with the corners still held down with stickers (Ouyang Wenli, ed., *Pictorial Biography of Lu Xun*, where it is dated 1903). As for figure 4.5 (dark uniform), one print that surfaced in 1978 has an inscription by Lu Xun on the back that is dated "in spring of *guimou* written in Tokyo, Japan, that is, in the 36th year of Meiji" (both dates are 1903) (Ye Shusui and Yang Yanli, *Learning about Lu Xun through Physical Artifacts*, 451, from 1978 Japanese publication). As Ye and Yang point out, it is more usually identified as taken for his 1904 graduation from Kōbun Academy.

[84] *LXQJ* 6:565–67 and *LXQJ* 6:576–79. In this section, all quotations are from the first essay unless otherwise noted.

[85] Young-tsu Wong, *Search for Modern Nationalism*, 48.

[86] Xu Shoushang's comment in *My Late Friend*, 13; the poems quoted in Xu, *My Late Friend*, 13 and 14.

[87] See Yang Yanli, "Essays Collected and Edited by Lu Xun," where two handwritten pages of its contents are reproduced. The reference is from *Lu Xun Chronology*, 1:405.

[88] In *Zhejiang Tide*, line 1 reads 鄒容吾小弟, and line 6 has 悲秋 instead of 悲愁, the latter likely a typo. Translation also in Lu Xun, *Selected Works*, 4:323.

[89] The paraphrase by Wang Dongfang differs on several points: "The first 4 lines give an overview of Zou going to Japan and [in line 3] his revolutionary act in cutting off Yao Wenfu's queue, and the brevity of the revolutionary activities into which he plunged. The last four lines celebrate the great heroic example of his sacrificing himself to revolution" (*Striding into Modernity*, 69).

[90] Wong, *Search for Modern Nationalism*, 42, 43.

[91] Semanov, *Lu Xun and His Predecessors*, 9.

Chapter 5: In the Hands of Others, 1934–36: The Visual Materials

[1] Anderson, *The Limits of Realism*, 60. The section entitled "The Search for a New Audience" (60–76) provides both overview and analysis of this extended controversy and its participants and arguments, including the differing views of Qu Qiubai and Lu Xun. The next two quotations are also Anderson, pages 70 and 62–63.

[2] Zhang Mengyang, "The Literary Descendants of 'Ah Q,'" 215–30; Paul Foster, *Ah Q Archaeology*, 273–338.

[3] Zhang Mengyang, "The Literary Descendants of 'Ah Q,'" 215–18, for works before Lu Xun's death; Foster, *Ah Q Archaeology*, 3, 205, 224, 273. Three stage adaptations of "Ah Q" appeared as tributes the year after his death, although only Tian Han's was performed (224–30).

[4] In the short interval after Lu Xun's death and before the outbreak of war, many works of art were published, some stimulated by his death, others probably already gestating in 1936. But Lu Xun has died, so I am not counting them. Mentioning only the figures in this chapter, these include Ye Qianyu, who published illustrations of "Ah Q" in 1937 (for an adaptation by Tian Han) and Xu Xingzhi who wrote a playscript.

[5] Chen Xing provides information on the two sets lost to the advance of war, the first to Japan's capture of Shanghai and the second to its capture of Guangzhou ("Two Topics Concerning Feng Zikai and Lu Xun," 32–33). It is Chen who states that two illustrations were published in *Wencong* in 1938 (32). They were commissioned by Kaiming Publishers (Geremie Barmé, *An Artistic Exile*, 285).

[6] Both works have 1949 editions.

[7] Michael Sullivan, *Art and Artists of Twentieth-Century China*, 172.

[8] In the end, Cheng made 108 illustrations.

[9] Xiaobing Tang, *Origins of the Chinese Avant-Garde*, 10–40 (early history), 86 (graphics).

¹⁰ Shanghai Lu Xun Museum, *Catalog of Woodcuts*. The editors of this large project include two artists associated with Lu Xun, Li Hua and his student Lai Shaoqi.

¹¹ For the synergy that caused many works in other media and languages in these year to use the title "Roar, China!" (*nu hu ba, Zhongguo!*), see Xiaobing Tang, "Echoes of 'Roar, China!'," 483-91. This image is likely based on one by Frans Masereel, reprinted *Holzschnitte gegen den krieg* (Leipzig: Insel-Verlag, 1989), 11 (with thanks to Amira Goehr). For Lu Xun's evaluation of Li Hua and Luo Zhenqing, see Letter 350214, *LXQJ* 13:388. Li Hua has no Lu Xun-related works in this period; Luo Zhenqing has a portrait (fig. B.40).

¹² Ren Yin, "The Famous Woodcut Artist Liu Xian."

¹³ Ironically, Cao later also fell afoul of the Communist powers—after he became a reporter during the war against Japan—and was in the "rightist" camp in the 1950s. As a result, information on him in *LXQJ* stops at 1936, even in the 2005 edition.

¹⁴ Letter to Cao Bai, 360605, *LXQJ* 14:61. For Liqun's portrayal of Lu Xun, made before they met, see figure B.44.

¹⁵ These figures are from Lai Shaoqi, "A Block of Timber, a Block of Stone," 106–10.

¹⁶ Letters to Liu Xian, *LXQJ* 14:405–08. These five letters were collected from the postface of Liu Xian's *Ah Q*, published 1935 by the Unnamed Woodcut Society, which he cofounded in 1933. There are two additional notes from Lu Xun of one line each.

¹⁷ Letter 340306, *LXQJ* 13:39.

¹⁸ This image from "Medicine" can be found at http://www.china.org.cn/culture/2006-04/07/content_1164936.htm.

¹⁹ Feng Zikai, preface to *Cartoons of "The True Story of Ah Q."*

²⁰ Chen Xing, "Feng Zikai and Lu Xun," 31.

²¹ Feng, preface to *Illustrations of Lu Xun's Fiction*. *Wupeng* was a kind of covered boat, peculiar to Shaoxing and in many of Feng's drawings. It is what the children took to see the "Village Opera"; it is also how the Successful Provincial Candidate in "Ah Q" conveyed his goods to Weizhuang for safekeeping in advance of the revolution.

²² Letter to Yao Wei, 340403, *LXQJ* 13:60. To Wei Mengke, on the same day, he wrote only in general terms: "Although there are some minor inaccuracies, they do not affect the overall impression, so I have sent them out already" (Letter 340403, *LXQJ* 13:60. The work has not been located.

²³ *Analects* 14.18.

²⁴ "Letter Sent to the Editors of *Theater*," *LXQJ* 6:154.

²⁵ *LXQJ* 14:406.

²⁶ Quoted in Xiong Rong, "Some Comments by Lu Xun on Depictions of Ah Q," *Yangcheng Evening News* November 9, 1961. See Appendix B, entry at II.9.

[27] Letter to Liu Xian, *LXQJ* 14:406.

[28] "Letter Sent to the Editors of *Theater*," *LXQJ* 6:154.

[29] Ibid.

[30] "Further Thoughts after an Illness," *LXQJ* 6:197. This essay was written on December 17, 1934, after his two letters to *Theater*.

[31] Lu Xun also had thirteen other works by Chen in loose sheets (*Catalog of Woodcuts*, 2:547–59).

[32] *Zhonghua ribao,* October 28, 1934.

[33] Feng Zikai, Preface, *Illustrations of Lu Xun's Fiction*

[34] Letter to Li Hua 350909, *LXQJ* 13.539. I provide substitute examples.

[35] E. H. Gombrich, *Art and Illusion*, 81–82.

[36] "Two or Three Things Brought to Mind," *LXQJ* 6:576.

[37] "At that time I thought, if I wrote a novel of exposure and specified that it occurred in a certain place, then people from that place would do anything to get out of being identified with it, whereas people from somewhere else would respond as if watching the fire from the other shore. So neither side would examine themselves" ("Letter in Reply to the Editors of *Theater*," *LXQJ* 6:149).

[38] "Letter Sent to the Editors of *Theater*," *LXQJ* 6:154-55.

[39] *LXQJ* 6.150.

[40] Chuan Dao, *In the Days When I Knew Lu Xun*, 13-14.

[41] Letter to Lai Shaoqi, *LXQJ* 13:493. At the time, Lu Xun did not record this gap in comprehension regarding drawings of common plants shown to villagers, but he did note that botanizing without a practical purpose, such as a medicinal one, did not make sense to country people. This he recorded in "Excursions in the Year 1911," *LXQJ* 8:45-46.

[42] This and the next quotation are from *LXQJ* 14:405-06. As with anything he said, this proved to be a two-edged sword. In the 1940s, for the purposes of propaganda, the Communists briefly designated *nianhua* as the appropriate style, and because of this comment of Lu Xun's, the Communist Party promotion of *nianhua* style sailed under his flag.

[43] Xiaobing Tang, "Echoes of 'Roar, China!'"497.

[44] The Chinese title of Masereel's series was "Yige ren de shounan" 一個人的受難 (One man's suffering). Michael Sullivan notes that Chen's work followed immediately after Lu Xun published Masereel's series (*Art and Artists*, 84–85 and fig. 8.4). Sheets from Chen and Masareel are juxtaposed in Ellen Johnston Laing, *The Winking Owl*, figs. 9, 10.

⁴⁵ Xiaobing Tang, "Echoes of 'Roar, China!'," 497.

⁴⁶ This classic trio was invoked again in the aftermath of the Tian'anmen Square Incident of 1989. The concrete aid that workers gave to the student demonstrators had been much noted at the time. Afterwards, one of the students, Wang Binzhang, and his co-author Chong-Pin Lin, wrote regretfully of the absence of the third element, the soldiers, in "Student Movement, Workers' Movement, Soldiers' Movement: Overthrow Dictatorship Soon," 152.

⁴⁷ Robert Farnsworth, *Edgar Snow in Asia, 1928–41,* 186–89. Lu Xun *Diary*, August 3, 1935. A photograph of it in the living room after Lu Xun's death is in Kong Haizhu, *A Sorrowful Parting from Lu Xun*, 23.

⁴⁸ "Laborers," Nym Wales Collection, box 58002-10, folder ID mAB, Hoover Institution Archives, Stanford University. Title supplied by a handwritten notation.

⁴⁹ Chen Haowang, "An Age-Bridging Friendship between Lu Xun and Wei Mengke," http://www.renwu.com.cn.

⁵⁰ Lu Xun acknowledges receipt, Letter 340403, *LXQJ* 13:60. For archives searched, see appendix B, Wei Mengke III. 3.

⁵¹ "Written in Deep Night," *LXQJ* 6:522.

⁵² For Cao Bai, "Written in Deep Night," *LXQJ* 6:522; for Chen Guangzong, Letter 350410, *LXQJ* 13:436 and 13:435, n. 5; for Lai Shaoqi, Letter 350629, *LXQJ* 13:493.

⁵³ Sullivan, *Art and Artists of Twentieth-century China*, 83, 88.

⁵⁴ The quotations are from Letter 340306, *LXQJ* 13:39, and "Preface to *Record of Wood Engravings*," *LXQJ* 6:49.

⁵⁵ "Preface to *Collection from the Unnamed Woodcut Society*," *LXQJ* 8:406. Julia Andrews, *Painters and Politics*, 13–15.

⁵⁶ Kuiyi Shen, "Lianhuanhua and Manhua," 106, 114.

⁵⁷ This and the next quotation are from Geremie Barmé, *An Artistic Exile*, 95.

⁵⁸ Michael Sullivan, *Art and Artists*, 190.

⁵⁹ Kuiyi Shen, "Lianhuanhua and Manhua," 111.

⁶⁰ Ma Guoliang, *Reminiscences of "The Companion,"* 39–41.

⁶¹ Pang, *Building a New Chinese Cinema*, 95-98.

⁶² Julia Andrews, *Painters and Politics*, 14–15.

⁶³ Michael Sullivan, *Modern Chinese Artists*.

⁶⁴ There was no sequel to this collection, but then Lu Xun had made that possibility clear too, writing, "This volume is not a periodical. There may be two in a year, or one over several years, or this may be the only one" ("Announcement concerning *Record of Wood Engravings*"), *LXQJ* 8:512.

65 Ibid.

66 Paul Foster, *Ah Q Archaeology*, 3–4.

Conclusion

1 Edward Rhoads estimates that by mid-1920s the queue was no longer an issue widespread enough to require further government action (*Manchus and Han*, 24).

2 The fight over punctuation was waged by Liu Bannong. See "Remembering Mr. Liu Bannong," *LXQJ* 6:73–75.

3 Psychological violence is a different matter. The violence of social relations inflicted among neighbors and within the family is found in nearly every story and memoir essay.

4 Li Anbao, *Lu Xun and Modern Chinese History*, provides an overview of the major writings and many incidental mentions and lists notably few meetings and such.

5 Harriet C. Mills, "Literature and Revolution," 196–97.

6 *LXQJ* 4:106–7. This essay is also discussed in David Der-wei Wang, *The Monster That is History*, 22.

7 "Author's Preface to the English translation of *Anthology of Short Stories*," *LXQJ*, 7:412. This anthology, proposed by Edgar Snow, was never published (*LXQJ* 7:412, n. 1).

8 As it turns out, this was borrowed from his amah's memory, for he tells her story in the 1926 "Ah Zhang and *Classics of Mountains and Seas*," *LXQJ* 2:254. In this 1926 recollection, the Zhous are the gentry family that flees the Taiping rebels and the old gatekeeper and a woman stay behind, with a similarly gruesome outcome for him.

9 Besides those already mentioned in this study, precise formulations characterize the elegies for Li Dazhao, a colleague at Beijing University and one of the founders of the Communist Party, killed in 1927 ("Foreword to *Collected Works of Shouchang*," *LXQJ* 4:538-40); Liu Bannong, never a close colleague and later an estranged one yet movingly commemorated ("Remembering Mr. Liu Bannong," *LXQJ* 6:73-75); and, in a younger generation, Wei Suyuan, an idealistic editor and translator at Unnamed Society ("Remembering Mr. Wei Suyuan," *LXQJ* 6: 65-70).

10 "In Defense of *lianhuanhua*," *LXQJ* 4:457.

11 "Preface to the Russian Translation of 'The True Story of Ah Q,'" *LXQJ* 7:84.

Appendix A: "Inscribed by the Author on a Small Likeness": Dating the Evidence; the Meaning of *shenshi* in Line 1

[1] For two systems used in a photograph with Haiying, see Cheng Ma, *Lu Xun's Student Years in Japan*, 27. For the official documents in Japan, see *Lu Xun Chronology*, 1:119. For the required use of Western dating in Japan and for other times when Lu Xun's dates erred, see Ni Moyan, *Lu Xun's Traditional Poetry*, 17.

[2] "The Lu Xun I Knew," in Xu Shoushang, *The Lu Xun I Knew*, 4.

[3] "Remembering the Past," in Xu Shoushang, *The Lu Xun I Knew*, 24.

[4] "Preface to *Lu Xun's Traditional Poems*," in Xu Shoushang, *The Lu Xun I Knew*, 83.

[5] "Studying Medicine in Sendai," in Xu Shoushang, *My Late Friend*, 18.

[6] Ye Shusui and Yang Yanli, *Learning about Lu Xun through Physical Artifacts*, 65–67, 452–53.

[7] *LXQJ* 7:4.

[8] Kowallis gives a thorough account in *The Lyrical Lu Xun*, 100–107.

[9] Xu Shoushang, *The Lu Xun I Knew*, 82, 83.

[10] Xu Shoushang, *My Late Friend*, 5.

[11] Xu Guangping to the critic Xi Jin, quoted in Kowallis, *The Lyrical Lu Xun*, 103, n. 3.

[12] Li Yunjing, *Lu Xun's Emotional World*, 19.

[13] "God of Live," *LXQJ* 7:32.

Appendix B: Illustrators and Illustrations of Lu Xun's Fiction and His Person, 1934–36

[1] Begun as a film equipment company, Diantong made three other highly regarded leftist movies in the two years of its existence, 1934–35. Laikwan Pang, *Building a New China in Cinema*, 53–55.

[2] *Shanghai xiju*, no. 5 (2008), two pages.

[3] Ma Guoliang, *Reminiscences of "The Companion,"* 39–41.

[4] Sullivan, *Modern Chinese Artists*.

[5] Information on the editors of *Zhonghua ribao* is from *LXQJ* 17:119. The quotation is from Barmé, *An Artistic Exile*, 95.

[6] *LXQJ* 6:50, n. 3. Ye Lingfeng was expelled from the League of Left-Wing Writers in April 1931 for apostasy. Wang-chi Wong, *Politics and Literature in Shanghai*, 111.

[7] Xiaobing Tang, *Origins of the Chinese Avant-Garde*, 127.

⁸ For the death portrait, see Kong Haizi, *A Sorrowful Parting*, 39. For the stage adaptation, see Foster, *Ah Q Archaeology*, 224–30.

⁹ Huang Miaozi's memoirs were published as *Friends and Teachers in the Art Scene*, 1998.

¹⁰ Xie Qizhang gives a brief description of the notable features of this magazine in "Liang Desuo and His 'Magazine World.'" Other information, including the quotation from Mao Dun, is from Xie Qizhang, "Huang Miaozi and *Fiction Semimonthly*."

¹¹ Huang Miaozi, "My Theory of Manhua," in *The Essay and the Cartoon*, ed. Chen Wangdao, 60–61.

¹² *LXQJ*, 14:406.

¹³ The surviving copy of "Kong Yiji" gives a date of May 17, 1934, on the cover; there is no indication that it was ever separately published than in Intellectual Life. Lu Xun likely owned the "prepublication" leaves of this work.

¹⁴ Its existence is known from *LXQJ* 14:406, 14:408, n. 2.

¹⁵ See chapter 5, n. 28.

¹⁶ Letter to Yao Ke, 340306, *LXQJ* 13:39.

¹⁷ Gao Xin, "Qu Qiubai's Drawing of Ah Q," 63.

¹⁸ The drawing, evidently a pen-and-ink, is included in *Seventy Years of Ah Q*, eds. Peng Xiaojie and Han Geli, illustrations gathered at front, unpaginated. On Gao Xin's frustrated search for its original publication, see "Qu Qiubai's Drawing of Ah Q," 64.

¹⁹ The title of "Portrait of Ah Q" used in letter to Lai Shaoqi, 350629, *LXQJ* 13:493. The other woodcut is entitled "Lost Love" (*shilian*), showing a mother with a dead child.

²⁰ Feng Zikai, *Illustrations of Lu Xun's Fiction*, 57.

²¹ For Ni Moyan's description, see "Lu Xun on depictions of Ah Q," 73. Zhang Yiping is quoted in Xiong Rong as "a certain Zhang," "Some Comments by Lu Xun on Depictions of Ah Q," *Yangcheng Evening News*, November 9, 1961. The comment is identified by an online bookseller as being from his *Chuangxia suibi* (Notes by the Window) (http://blog.sina.com.cn/s/blog_593b2b72010013zs.html).

²² Ye Shusui and Yang Yanli, *Learning about Lu Xun through Physical Artifacts*, 451–53.

²³ Ye Shusui and Yang Yanli, *Learning about Lu Xun through Physical Artifacts*, 363.

²⁴ They are reproduced from Ye Shusui and Yang Yanli, *Learning about Lu Xun through Physical Artifacts*, 364.

²⁵ "Portraits of Lu Xun by Natives of Wenzhou," http://www.pep.com.cn/xiaoyu/jiaoshi/tbjxzy/tupian/xy6s/200707/t20070731_405657.htm.

²⁶ Letter 350410, *LXQJ* 13:436. (1). The editors of *LXQJ* date it to the previous autumn and say that the four magazines are *Wenxue*, *Taibai*, *Manhua yu shenghuo*, and *Mangzhong* (n. 3).

²⁷ Ye Shusui and Yang Yanli, *Learning about Lu Xun through Physical Artifacts*, 368. They date the portrait 1935.

²⁸ Ye Shusui and Yang Yanli, *Learning about Lu Xun through Physical Artifacts*, 365.

²⁹ Letter to Yao Ke, 330924, *LXQJ* 12:447. In Beijing Lu Xun Museum, see Ye Shusui and Yang Yanli, *Learning about Lu Xun through Physical Artifacts*, 367.

³⁰ The too-serious photograph, Letter 331026, *LXQJ* 12:467; will send some other ones, Letter 331205, *LXQJ* 12:509-60l; more prints requested, Letter 331207, *LXQJ* 12:514-15; requests from artist's school, Ye Shusui and Yang Yanli, *Learning about Lu Xun*, 367.

³¹ *Liu yi* (The Six Arts), February 15, 1936, 8–9. Under the double-page drawing is Lu Shaofei's amusing identification of each of the figures. The drawing alone may be found in Jonathan Hutt, "La Maison d'Or," 112.

Works Cited

Ah Yuan 阿袁. "'Ziti xiaoxiang' bing fei zai 'huaijiu' zhong shouxian fabiao de" 自題小像並非在懷舊中首先發表的 ("Inscribed by the Author on a Small Likeness" was not first published in "Memories"). *Lu Xun yanjiu yuekan* 魯迅研究月刊 (hereafter *Lu Xun Research Monthly*) 7 (2009): 84.

Anderson, Marston. *The Limits of Realism: Chinese Fiction in the Revolutionary Period.* Berkeley: University of California Press, 1990.

Andrews, Julia F. *Painters and Politics in the People's Republic of China, 1949–1979.* Berkeley: University of California Press, 1994.

Ba Jin 巴金. *Jia* 家 (Family). 1933. Reprint, Beijing: Renmin wenxue chubanshe, 1953.

———. *The Family.* Trans. Sidney Shapiro. Beijing: Foreign Languages Press, 1964.

Barmé, Geremie. *An Artistic Exile: A Life of Feng Zikai (1898–1975).* Berkeley: University of California Press, 2002.

Banhua jicheng 版畫紀程 (Catalog of woodcuts). See Shanghai Lu Xun jinianguan.

Beijing Lu Xun bowuguan (Beijing Lu Xun Museum), ed. *Lu Xun: 1881–1936.* Beijing: Wenwu chubanshe, 1976.

———. *Lu Xun huiyi lu: zhuanzhu* 魯迅回憶錄 專著 (Lu Xun remembered: Books). 3 vols. Beijing: Beijing Lu Xun Museum, 1997.

———. *Lu Xun huiyi lu, san pian* 魯迅回憶錄 散篇 (Lu Xun remembered: Articles). 3 vols. Beijing: Beijing Lu Xun Museum, 1999.

———. *Lu Xun nianpu* 魯迅年譜 (Lu Xun chronology). Rev. ed. 4 vols. Beijing: Renmin wenxue chubanshe, 2000.

———. *Beijing Lu Xun bowuguan* 北京魯迅博物館 (Beijing Lu Xun Museum). Dai ni zoujin bowuguan series. Beijing: Wenwu chubanshe, 2005.

Boorman, Howard L., ed. *Biographical Dictionary of Republican China.* 4 vols. New York: Columbia University Press, 1967–79.

Bourdieu, Pierre. *The Field of Cultural Production: Essays on Art and Literature.* Edited and introduced by Randal Johnson. New York: Columbia University Press, 1993.

Brunskill, Ian. "Günter Grass." *Times Literary Supplement*, September 29, 2006, 3.

Cai Dengshan 蔡登山. *Lu Xun aiguo de ren* 魯迅愛過的人 (Those who Lu Xun loved). Shanghai: Wenhui chubanshe, 2008.

Cai Jian'guo 蔡建國, ed. *Cai Yuanpei huazhuan, 1868–1940* 蔡元培畫傳 (Pictorial biography of Cai Yuanpei). Shanghai: Shanghai renmin meishu chubanshe, 1988.

Chang Hui 常惠. "Lu Xun xiansheng zai Beida jiangshou Zhongguo xiaoshuo shi de huiyi" 魯迅先生在北大講授中國小說史的回憶 (Recollections of Mr. Lu Xun's lectures at Beijing University on the history of Chinese fiction). In *Lu Xun yanjiu luncong*. Changchun: Jilin renmin wenxue chubanshe, 1980.

Chang, Jun-mei. *Ting Ling: Her Life and Her Work*. Taipei: Institute of International Relations, National Cheng-chih University, 1978.

Chen Baichen 陳白尘. *Ah Q zhengzhuan: qimu huaju* 阿Q正傳: 七幕話劇 (The true story of Ah Q: A play in seven acts). Beijing: Zhongguo xiju chubanshe, 1981.

Chen Haowang 陳浩望. "Lu Xun yu Wei Mengke de wangnian jiao" 魯迅與魏猛克的忘年交 (An age-bridging friendship between Lu Xun and Wei Mengke). *Wenwu* 人物, no. 1 (2001). Also at http://www.renwu.com.cn/UserFiles/magazine/article/RW0143_200102211630001831.asp

Chen Mingshu 陳鳴樹. *Baowei Lu Xun di zhandou chuantong* 保衛魯迅的戰鬥傳統 (Preserving Lu Xun's fighting spirit). Tianjin: Tianjin baihua wenyi chubanshe, 1959.

Chen Mingyuan 陳明遠. *Wenhua ren yu qian* 文化人與錢 (Cultural figures and money). Tianjin: Tianjin baihua wenyi chubanshe, 2001.

Chen Shuyu 陳漱渝. *Lu Xun shishi qiuzhen lu* 魯迅事實求真錄 (Ascertaining facts relating to Lu Xun). Changsha: Hunan wenyi chubanshe, 1987.

Chen Shuyu, ed. *Shuobujin de Ah Q: Wuchu buzai de hunling* 說不盡的阿Q: 無處不在的魂靈 (The inexhaustible topic of Ah Q: A spirit that is everywhere). Beijing: Zhongguo wenlian chubangongsi, 1997.

———. *Lu Xun fengbo* 魯迅風波 (Storms over Lu Xun). Beijing: Dazhong wenyi chubanshe, 2001.

———. *Shei tiaozhan Lu Xun: Xin shiqi guanyu Lu Xun de lunzheng* 誰挑戰魯迅: 新時期關於魯迅的論爭 (Who is challenging Lu Xun: Controversies on Lu Xun in a new era). Chengdu: Sichuan wenyi chubanshe, 2002.

Chen Shuyu et al., eds. *A Pictorial Biography of Lu Xun*. Beijing: People's Fine Arts Publishing House, [1981].

Chen Wangdao 陳望道, ed. *Xiaopinwen he manhua* 小品文和漫畫 (The essay and the cartoon). Shanghai: Shenghuo shudian, 1935.

Chen Xing 陳星. "Feng Zikai yu Lu Xun er ti" 豐子凱與魯迅二題 (Two items concerning Feng Zikai and Lu Xun). *Lu Xun Research Monthly* 4 (1990): 31–33.

Cheng Ma 程麻. *Lu Xun liuxue Riben shi* 魯迅留學日本時 (Lu Xun's student years in Japan). Shanxi: Renmin chubanshe, 1985.

Cheng, Weikun. "Politics of the Queue." In *Hair: Its Power and Meaning in Asian Cultures*, ed. Alf Hiltebeitel and B. D. Miller. Albany: State University of New York Press, 1998, 123–42.

Chou, Eva Shan. "The Literary Martyr in Lu Xun's Writings." *Asia Major*, 3d ser., 12, no. 2 (1999): 139–62.

———. "Learning to Read Lu Xun, 1918–23: The Emergence of a Readership." *China Quarterly* 172 (December 2003): 1043–64.

———. "'A Story about Hair': A Curious Mirror of Lu Xun's Pre-Republican Years." *Journal of Asian Studies* 66, no. 2 (May 2007): 421–59.

Chow, Kai-wing. "Imagining Boundaries of Blood: Zhang Binglin and the Invention of the Han 'Race' in Modern China." In *The Construction of Racial Identities in China and Japan*, ed. Frank Dikötter, 34–52.

Chuandao 川岛. *He Lu Xun xiangchu de rizi* 和魯迅相處的日子 (In the days when I knew Lu Xun). Beijing: Zhonghua renmin chubanshe, 1961.

Confucius. *The Analects*. Trans. D. C. Lau. New York: Penguin, 1979.

Cong, Xiaoping. *Teachers' Schools and the Making of the Modern Chinese Nation-State, 1897-1937*. Vancouver: University of British Columbia Press, 2007.

Damrosch, David. *What Is World Literature?* Princeton: Princeton University Press, 2003.

Daruvala, Susan. *Zhou Zuoren and an Alternative Chinese Response to Modernity*. Cambridge: Asia Center, Harvard University, 2000.

Debreczeny, Paul. *Social Functions of Literature: Alexander Pushkin and Russian Culture*. Stanford: Stanford University Press, 1997.

Denton, Kirk A. "Museums, Memorial Sites, and Exhibitionary Culture in the People's Republic of China." *China Quarterly* 183 (2005): 565–86.

Dianshizhai huabao 點石齋畫報 (Dianshizhai pictorial). An insert in Shanghai's *Shenbao* 1895–1908. Reprint. 2 vols. Yangzhou: Jiangsu guangling guji keyin chuban, 1990.

Dikötter, Frank. *The Discourse of Race in Modern China*. Stanford: Stanford University Press, 1992.

Dikötter, Frank, ed. *The Construction of Racial Identities in China and Japan*. Honolulu: University of Hawai'i Press, 1997.

Ding Cong 丁聰. *Ah Q zhengzhuan de chatu* 阿Q正傳的插圖 (Illustrations of "The True Story of Ah Q") 1944. Reprint, Beijing: Chaohua meishu chubanshe, 1956. 20 plates.

———. *Lu Xun xiaoshuo chatu* 魯迅小說插圖 (Illustrations of Lu Xun's fiction). Beijing: Renmin meishu, 1978.

Ding Ling, "Yige zhenshi ren de yisheng: ji Hu Yebin" 一個真實人的一生：記胡也瀕 (The life of a sincere person: remembering Hu Yebin), 1950. Rpt in *Ding Ling sanwen xuanji* (Selected essays of Ding Ling), ed. Wu Zaiping. Tianjin: Baihua wenyi chubanshe, 1991, 87-109.

Ding Shouhe 丁守和, ed. *Xinhai geming shiqi qikan jieshao* 辛亥革命時期期刊介紹 (Introduction to periodicals of the 1911 Revolution era). 4 vols. Peking: Renmin chubanshe, 1982.

Doleželová-Velingerová, Milena, and Oldřich Král, eds. *The Appropriation of Cultural Capital in China's May Fourth Project*. Cambridge: Asia Center, Harvard University, 2001.

Dong Bingyue 董炳月. "Xiantai shenhua de beimian" 仙台神話的背面 (Behind the myth of Sendai). *Lu Xun Research Monthly* 10 (2002): 54–59.

Du Yibai 杜一白. *Lu Xun yanjiu shi gao* 魯迅研究史稿 (Toward a history of Lu Xun studies). Shenyang: Liaoning daxue chubanshe, 2000.

Eber, Irene. "The Reception of Lu Xun in Europe and America: The Politics of Popularization and Scholarship." In *Lu Xun and His Legacy*, ed. Leo Ou-fan Lee, 242–85.

Edwards, Neville P. *The Story of China: With a Description of the Events Relating to the Present Struggle*. London: Hutchinson, 1900.

Fan Zeng 范曾. *Lu Xun xiaoshuo chatu ji* 魯迅小說插圖集 (Illustrations of Lu Xun's fiction). Beijing: Xinhua shudian, 1978.

Farnsworth, Robert M. *From Vagabond to Journalist: Edgar Snow in Asia, 1928–1941*. Columbia: University of Missouri Press, 1996.

Feng, Jin. *The New Woman in Early Twentieth-Century Literature*. West Lafayette, IN: Purdue University Press, 2004.

Feng Zikai 豐子凱. *Manhua "Ah Q zhengzhuan"* 漫畫阿Q正傳 (Cartoons of "The True Story of Ah Q"). Shanghai: Kaiming shudian, 1949.

———. *Huihua Lu Xun xiaoshuo* 繪畫魯迅小說 (Illustrations of Lu Xun's fiction). Shanghai: Wanye shudian, 1950.

Findeisen, Raoul David. *Lu Xun: Texte, Chronik, Bilder, Dokumente*. Basel: Stroemfeld, 2001.

———. "Does the East Asian-European Interliterary Communication in the Late Qing–Late Meiji Periods Offer a Model for a Globalized Literature?" *Canadian Review of Comparative Literature* 30, nos. 3–4 (2003): 555–64.

Fogel, Joshua. "Shanghai-Japan: The Japanese Residents' Association of Shanghai." *Journal of Asian Studies* 59, no. 4 (2000): 927–50.

Foster, Paul B. *Ah Q Archaeology: Lu Xun, Ah Q, Ah Q Progeny, and the National Character Discourse in Twentieth Century China.* Lanham, MD: Lexington Books, 2006.

Fujian shifan daxue zhongwen xi, ed. *Lu Xun lun waiguo wenxue* 魯迅論外國文學 (Lu Xun on foreign literatures). Beijing: Waiguo wenxue chubanshe, 1982.

Gamsa, Mark. *The Chinese Translation of Russian Literature: Three Studies.* Leiden: Brill, 2008.

Gao Xin 高信. "Qu Qiubai hua de Ah Q xiang" 瞿秋白畫的阿Q像 (Qu Qiubai's drawing of Ah Q). *Lu Xun Research Monthly* 12 (1994): 63–64.

Gao Xudong 高旭東, ed. *Shiji mo de Lu Xun zhenglun* 世紀末的魯迅爭論 (Controversies over Lu Xun at the end of the century). Beijing: Dongfang chubanshe, 2001.

———. *Zouxiang ershiyi shiji de Lu Xun* 走向二十一世紀的魯迅 (Lu Xun for the twenty-first century). Beijing: Zhongguo wenlian chubanshe, 2001.

Gimpel, Denise. *Lost Voices of Modernity: A Chinese Popular Fiction Magazine in Context.* Honolulu: University of Hawai'i Press, 2001.

Godley, Michael. "The End of the Queue: Hair as Symbol in Chinese History." *East Asian History* 8 (1994): 53–72.

Goldman, Merle, ed. *Modern Chinese Literature in the May 4th Era.* Cambridge: Harvard University Press, 1977.

Gombrich, E. H. *Art and Illusion: A Study in the Psychology of Pictorial Representation.* Bollingen series, no. 35. New York: Pantheon, 1960

Guojia tushuguan fenguan (National Library, branch library), ed. *Qing mo Min chu baokan tuhua jicheng* 清末民初報刊圖畫集成 (Compendium of illustrations from newspapers and magazines at the end of Qing and the beginning of the Republic). 20 vols. Beijing: Quanguo tushuguan wenxian weisuo fuzhi zhongxin, 2003.

Ha Jin. "Foreword." In Lu Xun, *Lu Hsun: Selected Stories.* New York: Norton, 2003.

Hallpike, C. R. "Social Hair." *Man,* new series, 4, no. 2 (1969): 256–64.

Han Heping 韓和平, illus. *Guxiang* 故鄉 (Hometown). Shanghai: Shanghai renmin meishu chubanshe, 1979.

Hanan, Patrick. "The Technique of Lu Hsun's Fiction." *Harvard Journal of Asiatic Studies* 34 (1974): 53–96.

Hangzhou Lu Xun jinian guan, ed. *Lu Xun zai Shao zongji duoshi* 魯迅在紹踪迹掇拾 (In the footsteps of Lu Xun in Shaoxing). Hangzhou: Hangzhou daxue chubanshe, 1991.

Harbsmeier, Christoph. *The Cartoonist Feng Zikai: Socialist Realism with a Buddhist Face*. Oslo: Universitetsforlaget, 1984.

Harrell, Paula. *Sowing the Seeds of Change: Chinese Students, Japanese Teachers, 1895–1905*. Stanford: Stanford University Press, 1992.

Harrison, Henrietta. *The Making of the Republican Citizen: Political Ceremonies and Symbols in China, 1911–1929*. Oxford: Oxford University Press, 2000.

———. *The Man Awakened from Dreams: One Man's Life in a North China Village, 1857–1942*. Stanford: Stanford University Press, 2005.

Hockx, Michel, ed. *The Literary Field of Twentieth-Century China*. Honolulu: University of Hawai'i Press, 1999.

———. *Questions of Style: Literary Societies and Literary Journals in Modern China, 1911–1937*. Leiden: Brill, 2003.

Hsia, T. A. *The Gate of Darkness: Studies on the Leftist Literary Movement in China*. Seattle: University of Washington Press, 1968.

Hu Bing 胡冰. *Lu Xun yanjiu zhaji* 魯迅研究札記 (Researches on Lu Xun). Shanghai: Xin wenyi chubanshe, 1958.

Hu Shi 胡適. *Wushi nian lai Zhongguo zhi wenxue* 五十年來中國之文學 (Chinese literature of the past fifty years). 1924. Reprint, Taipei: Yuanliu chubanshe, 1984.

———. *Sishi zishu* 四十自述 (Memoirs at forty). Shanghai: Yadong tushuguan, 1939.

Hu Yinqiang 胡尹強. *Pohui tie wuzi de xiwang: "Nahan" "Panghuang" xinlun* 破毀鐵屋子的希望 — 吶喊徬徨新論 (In hope of destroying the iron house: New essays on *Call to Arms* and *Hesitation*). Beijing: Renmin wenxue chubanshe, 2001.

Huang Fuqing 黃福慶. *Qing mo liu-Ri xuesheng* 清末留日學生 (Chinese students in Japan at the end of the Qing dynasty). Taipei: Academia Sinica, 1975.

Huang Mengtian 黃蒙田. *Lu Xun yu meishu erji* 魯迅與美術二集 (Lu Xun and art, second collection). Hong Kong: Daguang chubanshe, 1977.

Huang Miaozi 黃苗子. *Huatan shiyou lu* 畫壇師友錄 (Friends and teachers in the art scene). Taibei: Dongta tushugongsi, 1998.

Huang Qiaosheng 黃喬生. *Dujin jiebo: Zhoushi san xiongdi* 度盡劫波：周氏三兄弟 (Together for the ages: The three Zhou brothers). Peking: Qunzhong chubanshe, 1998.

Huiyi Lu Xun de meishu huodong 回憶魯迅的美術活動 (Remembering Lu Xun's fine arts activities). Beijing: Renmin meishu chubanshe, 1979.

Huiyi Lu Xun ziliao jilu 回憶魯迅資料輯錄 (Recollections of Lu Xun: Collected materials). 6 vols. Tianjin: Tianjin renmin chubanshe, 1980.

Hung, Chang-tai. "Two Images of Socialism: Woodcuts in Chinese Communist Politics." *Comparative Studies in Society and History* 39, no. 1 (1997): 34–60.

Huters, Theodore. *Bringing the World Home: Appropriating the West in Late Qing and Early Republican China*. Honolulu: University of Hawai'i Press, 2005.

Hutt, Jonathan. "La Maison d'Or: The Sumptuous World of Shao Xunmei." *East Asian History* 21 (June 2001): 111–42.

Imamura Yoshio 今村與志雄. *Ro Jin to 1930 nendai* 魯迅と1930年代 (Lu Xun in the 1930s). Tokyo: Kenbun shuppan, 1982.

Jansen, Marius. "Japan and the Chinese Revolution of 1911." In *The Cambridge History of China*. Vol. 11, pt. 2: *Late Ch'ing, 1800–1911*, ed. John K. Fairbank and Kwang-ching Liu, 339–74. Cambridge: Cambridge University Press, 1980.

Jenner, W. J. F. "Lu Xun's Last Days and After." *China Quarterly* 91 (September 1982): 424–45.

Jiang Weipu 姜維朴, ed. *Lu Xun lun lianhuanhua* 魯迅論連環畫 (Lu Xun on serial picture books). Beijing: Zhongguo lianhuanhua chubanshe, 1992.

Jiang Yasha 姜亞沙 et al., eds. *Minguo manhua qikan ji cui* 民國漫畫期刊集粹 (Best of the pictorials of the Republican era). 10 vols. Beijing: Zhongguo tushuguan wenxian weisuo fuzhi zhongxin, 2004.

Jing Meijiu 景梅九. *Zui an* 罪案 (Criminal Cases). In *Xinhai geming ziliao leibian* 辛亥革命資料類編 (Source materials for the 1911 revolution). Vol. 34. Beijing: Zhongguo shehui kexue chubanshe, 1981.

Jing Wendong 敬文東. *Shibai de ouxiang: chong du Lu Xun* 失敗的偶像：重讀魯迅 (Symbol of defeat: A new reading of Lu Xun). Guangzhou: Huacheng chubanshe, 2003.

Jordan, Donald. *China's Trial by Fire: The Shanghai War of 1932*. Ann Arbor: University of Michigan Press, 2001.

Judge, Joan. *Print and Politics: "Shibao" and the Culture of Reform in Late Qing China*. Stanford: Stanford University Press, 1996.

Kinkley, Jeffrey. *The Odyssey of Shen Congwen*. Stanford: Stanford University Press, 1987.

Kitaoka Masako 北冈正子. "Ryūgakuki Rojin kanren shiryō tansō" 魯迅留日時期關聯史料探索 (Historical materials relating to the period of Lu Xun's study in Japan). *Chūgoku bungei kenkyūkai kaihō* 68–110 (July 1987–December 1990). Trans. He Naiying 何乃英. In *Lu Xun Research Monthly* 2 (1988); 11 (1989): 46–51, 42; 12 (1989): 45–48; 2 (1990): 30–36; 3 (1990): 49–55; 4 (1990): 25–31.

Kong Haizhu 孔海珠. *Tongbie Lu Xun* 痛別魯迅 (A sorrowful parting from Lu Xun). Shanghai: Shanghai shehui kexueyuan chubanshe, 2004.

Kowallis, Jon Eugene von. *The Lyrical Lu Xun: A Study of His Classical-Style Verse.* Honolulu: University of Hawai'i Press, 1996.

———. "Lu Xun: The Sexier Story—a Review Article." *CLEAR* 27 (2005): 151–66.

———. "Lu Xun and Terrorism: A Reading of Revenge and Violence in Mara and Beyond." In *Creating Chinese Modernity: Knowledge and Everyday Life, 1900–1940*, ed. Peter Zarrow, 83–98. New York: Peter Lang, 2006.

Kuhn, Philip A. *Soulstealers: The Chinese Sorcery Scare of 1768.* Cambridge: Harvard University Press, 1990.

Kundera, Milan. "Die Weltliteratur: How We Read One Another." Trans. Linda Asher. *New Yorker*, January 8, 2007, 28–35.

Lai Shaoqi 賴少麒. "Yi mu yi shi" 一木一石 (A block of timber, a block of stone). In *Huiyi Lu Xun de meishu huodong*, 106–10.

Laing, Ellen Johnston. *The Winking Owl: Art in the People's Republic of China.* Berkeley: University of California Press, 1988.

Laitinen, Kauko. *Chinese Nationalism in Late Qing Dynasty: Zhang Binglin as an Anti-Manchu Propagandist.* London: Curzon, 1990.

Leach, Edmund. "Magical Hair." *Journal of the Royal Anthropological Institute of Great Britain and Ireland* 88, no. 2 (1958): 147–64.

Lee, Haiyan. *Revolution of the Heart: A Genealogy of Love in China, 1900-1950.* Stanford: Stanford University Press, 2007.

Lee, Leo Ou-fan. *Romantic Generation of Modern Chinese Writers.* Cambridge: Harvard University Press, 1973.

———. *Voices from an Iron House: A Study of Lu Xun.* Bloomington: Indiana University Press, 1987.

Lee, Leo Ou-fan, ed. *Lu Xun and His Legacy.* Berkeley: University of California Press, 1985.

Legouix, Susan. *Image of China: William Alexander.* London: Jupiter, 1980.

Li Anbao 李安保. *Lu Xun yu xiandai Zhongguo shi* 魯迅與現代中國史 (Lu Xun and modern Chinese history). Harbin: Heilongjiang renmin chubanshe, 1991.

Li Helin 李何林, ed. *Lu Xun lun* 魯迅論 (Essays on Lu Xun). Beijing: Beixin shuju, 1930.

Liqun 力群, Li Hua 李樺, Li Shusheng 李樹聲, and Ma Ke 馬克. *Zhongguo xinxing banhua yundong wushi nian 1931–1981* 中國新興版畫運動五十年 (Fifty years of the rebirth of woodcuts in China). Shenyang: Liaoning meishu chubanshe, 1981.

Li Suizhi 厲綏之. "Wushi nian qian de xueyou—Lu Xun xiansheng" 五十年前的学友－魯迅先生 (A classmate of fifty years ago: Mr. Lu Xun). 1961. Reprinted in Beijing Lu Xun Bowuguan, ed., *Lu Xun Remembered: Articles,* 1:40–41.

Li, Tang. "Art for the Market: Commercialism in Ren Yi's Figure Painting." MA thesis, University of Maryland, 2004.

Li Yunjing 李允經. *Lu Xun de qinggan shijie* 魯迅的情感世界 (Lu Xu's emotional world). Beijing: Beijing gongye daxue chubanshe, 1996.

Lin Qingxin. "Reloading the Canon: The Fin-de-Siècle Controversies over Lu Xun." In *Critical Zone 2: A Forum of Western and Chinese Knowledge*, ed. Q. S. Tong et al., 181–92. Hong Kong: Hong Kong University Press, 2005.

Lin Xianzhi 林賢治. *Ren jian Lu Xun* 人間魯迅 (Lu Xun among mortals). 2 vols. Hefei: Anhui jiaoyu chubanshe, 2004.

———. *Lu Xun huazhuan: fankang zhe ji qi yingzi* 魯迅畫傳: 反抗者及其影子 (Lu Xun illustrated biography: A resister and his images). Beijing: Tuanjie chubanshe, 2004.

Lin Zhihao 林志浩. *Lu Xun zhuan* 魯迅傳 (Lu Xun biography). Rev. ed. Beijing: Beijing chubanshe, 1991.

Link, Perry. *Mandarin Ducks and Butterflies: Popular Fiction in Early Twentieth Century Chinese Cities*. Berkeley: University of California Press, 1981.

Liu Dajie 劉大杰. "Lu Xun de jiushi" 魯迅的舊詩 (Lu Xun's traditional poetry). *Wenyi yuebao* 文藝月報, October 1956, 64–65.

Liu, Lydia. *Translingual Practice: Literature, National Culture, and Translated Modernity—China, 1900–1937*. Stanford: Stanford University Press, 1995.

Liu Xian 劉峴. "Yi Lu Xun xiansheng" 憶魯迅先生 (Remembering Mr. Lu Xun). 1956. Reprinted in *Huiyi Lu Xun de meishu huodong*, 66–70.

———. "Huiyi xuoji" 回憶瑣記 (Miscellaneous recollections). 1961. Reprinted in *Huiyi Lu Xun meishu huodong*, 63–65.

———. *Liu Xian muke xuanji* 劉峴木刻選集 (Liu Xian's selected woodcuts).

Liu Yukai 劉玉凱. *Pojie Lu Xun* 破解魯迅 (Misconstruing Lu Xun). Baoding: Hebei daxue chubanshe, 2008.

Liu Zhongshu. *Nahan Panghuang yishu lun* 吶喊徬徨藝術論 (The artistry of *Call to Arms* and *Hesitation*). Changchun: Jilin daxue chubanshe, 1999.

Lovell, Julia. *The Politics of Cultural Capital: China's Quest for a Nobel Prize in Literature*. Honolulu: University of Hawai'i Press, 2006.

Lu Jin 廬今. *Nahan lun* 吶喊論 (On *Call to Arms*). Shaanxi: Shaanxi renmin jiaoyu chubanshe, 1996.

Lu Xun. *True Story of Ah Q, by Lu-hsün*. Trans. George Kin Leung 梁社乾. Shanghai: Commercial Press, 1926.

———. *Ah Q and Others: Selected Stories of Lusin*. Trans. Chi-chen Wang. New York: Columbia University Press, 1941.

———. *Lu Xun: Selected Works*. Trans. Yang Xianyi and Gladys Yang. 4 vols. Beijing: Foreign Languages Press, 1959.

———. *The Complete Stories of Lu Xun*. Trans. Yang Xianyi and Gladys Yang. Bloomington: Indiana University Press, 1981.

———. *Lu Xun quanji* 魯迅全集 (The complete works of Lu Xun). 16 vols. Beijing: Renmin wenxue chubanshe, 1981.

———. *Lu Xun: Selected Poems*. Trans. W. J. F. Jenner. Beijing: Beijing Foreign Languages Press, 1982.

———. *Poèmes*. Trans. Michelle Loi. Paris: Arfuyen, 1985. Unpaginated.

———. *Lu Hsun: Complete Poems*. Trans. David Y. Chen. Tempe: Center for Asian Studies, Arizona State University, 1988.

———. *Lu Xun: Werke in sechs Bänden*. Trans. Wolfgang Kubin. Zurich: Uniuonsverlag, 1994.

———. *Lu Hsun: Selected Stories*. Trans. Yang Xianyi and Gladys Yang. New York: Norton, 2003.

———. *Lu Xun quanji* 魯迅全集. *The Complete Works of Lu Xun*. 18 vols. Beijing: Renmin wenxue chubanshe, 2005.

———. *The Real Story of Ah Q and Other Tales of China: The Complete Fiction of Lu Xun*. Trans. Julia Lovell. Harmondsworth: Penguin, 2010.

Lu Xun bianyin huaji jicun 魯迅編印畫集積存 (Collections of illustrations edited by Lu Xun). 4 vols. Shanghai: Shanghai renmin meishu, 1981.

Lu Xun yu dianying: ziliao huibian 魯迅與電影: 資料彙編 (Lu Xun and film: Collected materials). Beijing: Zhongguo dianying, 1981.

Lyell, William A., Jr. *Lu Xun's Vision of Reality*. Berkeley: University of California Press, 1976.

Ma Guoliang 馬國亮. "*Liang you*" *yijiu: yige huabao yu yige shidai* 良友意舊: 一個畫報與一個時代 (Reminiscences of *The Companion*: A pictorial and an era). Beijing: Sanlian shudian, 2002.

Ma Li 馬㻌. "Lu Xun zai Hongwen xueyuan" 魯迅在弘文學院 (Lu Xun at Kōbun Academy). In *Lu Xun shengping shiliao huibian*, ed. Xue Suizhi, 2:16.

Mao Zedong. *Mao's Road to Power: Revolutionary Writings, 1912–1940*. Ed. Stuart R. Schram and Nancy Jane Hodes. Vol. 1. Armonk, NY: M. E. Sharpe, 1992.

Maruyama Noboru. "Lu Xun in Japan." In *Lu Xun and His Legacy*, ed. Leo Ou-fan Lee, 216–41.

Masuda Wataru 増田渉. "Lu Xun yu guangfu hui" 魯迅與光復會 (Lu Xun and Guangfu hui). 1976. Excerpted and trans. Bian Liqiang. In *Lu Xun yanjiu ziliao*, 2 (November 1977): 325–40.

McDougall, Bonnie S. "Brotherly Love: Lu Xun, Zhou Zuoren, and Zhou Jianren." In *China in seinen biographischen Dimensionen: Gedenkschrift für Helmut Martin*, ed. Christina Neder, Heiner Roetz, and Ines Susanne Shilling, 259–76.

———. *Love-Letters and Privacy in Modern China: The Intimate Lives of Lu Xun and Xu Guangping*. Oxford: Oxford University Press, 2002.

McDougall, Bonnie S., and Kam Louie. *The Literature of China in the Twentieth Century*. New York: Columbia University Press, 1998.

Mills, Harriet C. "Lu Xun: Literature and Revolution—From Mara to Marx." In *Modern Chinese Literature in the May Fourth Era*, ed. Merle Goldman, 189–220.

Mittler, Barbara. *A Newspaper for China? Power, Identity, and Change in Shanghai's News Media, 1872–1912*. Cambridge: Harvard University Press, 2004.

Miu Junqi 繆君奇, and Shanghai Lu Xun Jinianguan, eds. *Lu Xun huazhuan* 魯迅畫傳 (Illustrated biography of Lu Xun). Shanghai: Shanghai shudian chubanshe, 2001.

Morris, Andrew. "To Make the 400 Million Move: The Late Qing Dynasty Origins of Modern Chinese Sport and Physical Culture." *Comparative Studies in Society and History* 42, no. 4 (2000): 876–906.

Nagao Kagekazu 長尾景和. "Zai Shanghai Huayuanzhuang wo renshi le Lu Xun" 在上海 '花園庄' 我認識了魯迅 (Getting to know Lu Xun in Shanghai at Huayuanzhuang). Trans. Mei Dao 梅稻 and Zhang Baoshen 张葆莘. 1956. Reprinted in Beijing Lu Xun Bowuguan, ed., *Lu Xun Remembered: Articles*, 3:1520–29.

Neder, Christina, Heiner Roetz, and Ines Susanne Shilling, eds. *China in seinen biographischen Dimensionen: Gedenkschrift für Helmut Martin*. Wiesbaden: Harrassowitz, 2001.

Ni Moyan 倪墨炎. "Lu Xun tan Ah Q huaxiang" 魯迅談阿Q畫像 (Lu Xun on depictions of Ah Q). In his *Xiandai wentan oushi* 現代文壇偶拾 (Occasional essays on the contemporary literary scene), 73–75. Shanghai: Xuelin chubanshe, 1985.

———. *Lu Xun jiushi tanjie* 魯迅舊詩探解 (Lu Xun's traditional poetry explained). Shanghai: Shanghai shudian chubanshe, 2002.

———. *Lu Xun de shehui huodong* 魯迅的社會活動 (Lu Xun's societal activities). Shanghai: Renmin chubanshe, 2006.

Ouyang Wenli 歐陽文利, ed. *Lu Xun huazhuan* 魯迅畫傳(Pictorial biography of Lu Xun). Series Lu Xun yanjiu ziliao xuanbian, bing zhong. Shenzhou: Shenzhou tushu gongsi, 1975.

Owen, Stephen. "What Is World Poetry? The Anxiety of Global Influence." *New Republic*, November 19, 1990, 28–30.

Pan, Phillip. "Chinese Evade Censors to Discuss Police Assault." *Washington Post*, December 5, 2005.

Pang, Laikwan. *Building a New China in Cinema: The Chinese Left-Wing Cinema Movement, 1932–37*. Lanham, MD: Rowman and Littlefield, 2002.

Peng Bo 彭博. *Lu Xun xiaoshuo juewang yu xiwang de duibi jiegou* 魯迅小說絕望與希望的對比結構 (A structural comparison of hopelessness and hope in the stories of Lu Xun). Shanghai: Xuelin chubanshe, 2001.

Peng Xiaojie 彭小節 and Han Geli 韓葛麗, eds. *Ah Q – 70 nian* 阿Q – 七十年 (Seventy years of Ah Q). Beijing: Shiyue wenyi chubanshe, 1993.

Pollard, David E. "Lu Xun's Zawen." In *Lu Xun and His Legacy*, ed. Leo Ou-fan Lee, 34–89.

———. "The Life of Lu Xun as Told in China." In *China in seinen biographischen Dimensionen: Gedenkschrift für Helmut Martin*, ed. Christina Neder, Heiner Roetz, and Ines Susanne Shilling, 239–44.

———. *The True Story of Lu Xun*. Hong Kong: Chinese University Press, 2002.

Price, Ruth. *The Lives of Agnes Smedley*. New York: Oxford University Press, 2005.

Pusey, James. *Lu Xun and Evolution*. Albany: State University of New York Press, 1998.

Qian Xingcun 錢杏邨 [Ah Ying]. "Siqu le de Ah Q shidai" 死去了的阿Q時代 (Ah Q's time is dead and gone). 1928. In *Lu Xun lun*, ed. Li Helin, 71–116.

Qiu Cunping 邱存平. *Xiandai ren de 'Nahan': Lu Xun de rensheng tanqiu* 現代人的吶喊: 魯迅的人生探求 (*Call to Arms* for people today: Lu Xun's explorations of life). Beijing: Jiefangjun chubanshe, 2000.

Qiu Sha 裘沙 and Wang Weijun 王偉君. *Lu Xun zhi shijie quanji* 魯迅之世界全集 (Lu Xun's world: Complete [illustrated] works). 3 vols. Guangzhou: Guangdong jiaoyu, 1996.

Reed, Christopher A. *Gutenberg in Shanghai: Chinese Print Capitalism, 1876–1937*. Honolulu: University of Hawai'i Press, 2004.

Ren Yin 任殷. "Zhuming banhuajia Liu Xian" 著名版畫家劉峴 (The famous woodcut artist Liu Xian). Futian mingren zhuan 福田名人傳, second series, in its online edition 福田叢書网络片 www.futiancemetery.com.cn/ftcs/ftcs2/ftcs2-22-3.htm. 8 pp.

Reynolds, Douglas. *China, 1898–1912: The Xinzheng Revolution and Japan*. Cambridge: Harvard University Press, 1993.

Rhoads, Edward J. M. *Manchus and Han: Ethnic Relations and Political Power in Late Qing and Early Republican China, 1861–1928*. Seattle: University of Washington Press, 2000.

Sandler, Stephanie. *Commemorating Pushkin: Russia's Myth of a National Poet.* Stanford: Stanford University Press, 2004.

Schwartz, Benjamin. *In Search of Wealth and Power: Yen Fu and the West.* Cambridge: Harvard University Press, 1964.

Seigner, Jacques, trans. "Une Histoire de Nattes." *France-Asie,* December 1953, 51–55.

Semanov, V. I. *Lu Hsun and His Predecessors.* Trans. Charles J. Alber. White Plains, NY: M. E. Sharpe, 1980.

Shanghai Lu Xun jinianguan (Shanghai Lu Xun Museum), ed. *Lu Xun shigao* 魯迅詩稿 (Manuscripts of Lu Xun's poems). Shanghai: Shanghai renmin meishu chubanshe, 1983.

———. ed. *Banhua jicheng: Lu Xun cang Zhongguo xiandai muke quanji* 版畫紀程：魯迅藏中國現代木刻全集 (Catalog of woodcuts: The complete modern Chinese woodcuts in Lu Xun's collection). 5 vols. Nanjing: Jiangsu guji chubanshe and Shanghai Lu Xun Museum, 1991.

———. ed. *Shanghai Lu Xun jinianguan cang wenwu zhenpin ji* 上海魯迅紀念館藏文物珍品集 (Fine objects and manuscripts from the Shanghai Lu Xun Museum). Shanghai: Shanghai guji chubanshe, 1996.

Shaoxing Lu Xun bowuguan (Shaoxing Lu Xun Museum), ed. *Lu Xun zai Shao zongji duoshi* 魯迅在绍踪迹掇拾 (In the footsteps of Lu Xun in Shaoxing). Hangzhou: Hangzhou daxue chubanshe, 1991.

Shen Congwen. 沈從文. *Ji Ding Ling xuji* 記丁玲續集 (Remembering Ding Ling, further essays). Shanghai : Liangyou fuxing tushu yinshua gongsi, [1939].

Shen Diemin 沈瓞民. "Huiyi Lu Xun zaonian zai Hongwen shuyuan de pianduan" 回憶魯迅早年在弘文書院的片斷 (Some recollections of Lu Xun in the early years at Kōbun Academy). 1961. Reprinted in *Lu Xun Remembered: Articles,* ed. Beijing Lu Xun Bowuguan, 1:42–50.

———. "Lu Xun zaonian de huodong diandi" 魯迅早年的活動點滴 (Some memories of Lu Xun's activities in the early years). 1961. Reprinted in *Lu Xun Remembered: Articles,* ed. Beijing Lu Xun Bowuguan, 1:51–53.

Shen, Kuiyi. "Lianhuanhua and Manhua: Picture Books and Comics in Old Shanghai." In *Illustrating Asia: Comics, Humor Magazines, and Picture Books,* ed. John A. Lent, 100–120. Honolulu: University of Hawai'i Press, 2001.

Shen, Vivian. *The Origins of the Left-Wing Cinema in China, 1932–37.* New York and London: Routledge, 2005.

Shi Yuhua 時煜華 and [Beijing] Lu Xun bowuguan, eds. *Lu Xun wen xian tu chuan* 魯迅文獻圖傳 (Lu Xun documents and visual materials). Zhengzhou: Dazhong chubanshe, 1998.

Shu, Yunzhong. *Buglers on the Home Front: The Wartime Practice of the Qiyue School*. Albany: State University of New York Press, 2000.

Situ Qiao 司徒喬. "Remembering Mr. Lu Xun" 憶魯迅先生. 1956. Reprinted in *Huiyi Lu Xun de meishu huodong*, 115–20.

Snow, Edgar. *Red Star over China*. London: V. Gollancz, 1937.

Snow, Edgar, ed. *Living China: Modern Chinese Short Stories*. New York: Reynal & Hitchcock, 1936.

Sullivan, Michael. *Art and Artists of Twentieth-Century China*. Berkeley: University of California Press, 1996.

———. *Modern Chinese Artists: A Biographical Dictionary*. Berkeley: University of California Press, 2006.

Sun Fuyuan 孫伏園. *Lu Xun xiansheng ersan shi* 魯迅先生二三事 (Two or three things about Mr. Lu Xun). 1942. Reprint, Shanghai: Zuojia shushi, 1999.

Sun, Shirley Hsiao-ling. "Lu Hsün and the Chinese Woodcut Movement, 1929–1936." PhD diss., Stanford University, 1974.

Sun Yat-sen. *Kidnapped in London: Being the Story of My Capture by, Detention at, and Release from the Legation*. Bristol: J. W. Arrowsmith, 1897.

Sun Ying 孫瑛. *Lu Xun zai jiaoyubu* 魯迅在教育部 (Lu Xun at the Ministry of Education). Tianjin: Tianjin renmin chubanshe, 1979.

Tai Jingnong 臺靜農, ed. *Guanyu Lu Xun ji qi zhuzuo* 關於魯迅及其著作 (On Lu Xun and his works). Peking: Weiming she, 1926.

Takeuchi Yoshimi. *What Is Modernity? Writings of Takeuchi Yoshimi*. Trans. Richard Calichman. New York: Columbia University Press, 2005.

Tambling, Jeremy. *Madmen and Other Survivors: Reading Lu Xun's Fiction*. Hong Kong: Hong Kong University Press, 2007.

Tang, Xiaobing. *Origins of the Chinese Avant-Garde: The Modern Woodcut Movement*. Berkeley: University of California Press, 2007.

———. "Echoes of 'Roar, China!': On Vision and Voice in Modern Chinese Art." *positions: an east asian cultures critique*, 14, no. 2 (Fall 2006): 467-94.

Tsu, Jing. *Failure, Nationalism, and Literature: The Making of Modern Chinese Identity, 1895-1937*. Stanford: Stanford University Press, 2006.

Vinograd, Richard. *Boundaries of the Self: Chinese Portraits, 1600–1900*. Cambridge: Cambridge University Press, 1992.

Wakeman, Frederick, Jr. *The Policing of Shanghai, 1927–1937*. Berkeley: University of California Press, 1995.

Waldron, Arthur. "So Long, Lu Xun." August 18, 2007. www.commentarymagazine.com/blogs/index.php/waldron/843

Wang Binzheng, and Chong-Pin Lin. "Student Movement, Workers' Movement, Soldiers' Movement: Overthrow Dictatorship Soon." *World Affairs*, 152:3 (1989–90), 180–81.

Wang, David Der-wei. *Fin de Siècle Splendor: Repressed Modernities of Late Qing Fiction, 1948–1911*. Stanford: Stanford University Press, 1997,

———. *The Monster That Is History: History, Violence, and Fictional Writing in Twentieth-Century China*. Berkeley and Los Angeles: University of California Press, 2004.

Wang Dehou 王得后. *Lu Xun xin jie* 鲁迅心解 (Personal readings of Lu Xun). Hangzhou: Zhejiang wenyi chubanshe, 1996.

Wang Dongfang 王冬芳. *Maixiang jindai: jianbian yu fangzu* 邁向近代: 剪辮與放足 (Striding into modernity: Cutting queues and unbinding feet). Liaoning: Liaohai chubanshe, 1997.

Wang Furen 王富仁. *Xianquzhe de xingxiang: Lun Lu Xun ji qita Zhongguo xiandai zuojia* 先驅者的形象: 論魯迅及其他中國現代作家 (The shadow of predecessors: On Lu Xun and other modern Chinese writers). Hangzhou: Zhejiang wenyi chubanshe, 1987.

Wang Furen and Zhao Zhuo 趙卓. *Tupo mangdian: shiji mo shehui sichao yu Lu Xun* 突破盲點:世紀末社會思潮與魯迅 (Breaking through blind spots: Intellectual trends in society at the end of the century and Lu Xun). Beijing: Zhongguo wenlian chubanshe, 2001.

Wang Hui 汪暉. *Wudi panghuang: wusi ji qi huisheng* 無地徬徨: 五四及其回聲 (No room for hesitation: May Fourth and its echo). Hangzhou: Zhejiang wenyi chubanshe, 1994.

———. *Fankang juewang: Lu Xun ji qi Nahan Panghuang yanjiu* 反抗絕望: 魯迅及其"呐喊" "徬徨" 研究 (Resisting despair: Researches on Lu Xun and his *Call to Arms* and *Hesitation*). 2nd ed. Shanghai: Shanghai renmin chubanshe, 2000.

Wang Shijia 王世家. "Lu Xun weisheme diuqu le yifu <Zi ti xiaoxiang> shigao" 魯迅為甚麼丟去了一幅<自題小像>詩稿? (Why did Lu Xun discard a copy of the poem "Inscribed by the Author on a Small Likeness"?). *Lu Xun Research Monthly* 9 (2007): 58–60.

———. "Lu Xun 'Wu ti <guan yu chang ye guo chun shi>' de qijian shigao" 魯迅無題<慣於長夜過春時>的七件詩稿 (The seven copies of Lu Xun's "Untitled [Though accustomed to the long nights, now it is spring]"). *Lu Xun Research Monthly* 11 (2007): 87–91.

Wang Shiqing. *Lu Xun: A Biography*. Trans. and ed. Bonnie S. McDougall. Beijing: Foreign Languages Press, 1984.

Wang Xiaoming 王曉明. *Wufa zhimian de rensheng: Lu Xun zhuan* 無法直面的人生：魯迅傳 (A life that cannot be directly faced: A biography of Lu Xun). Taipei: Yeqiang chubanshe, 1992.

Wang Xirong 王錫榮. "Nahan ge ban guoyan lu" 吶喊各版過眼錄 (Editions of *Call to Arms* I have seen). In *Lu Xun zhuzuo ben congtan* 魯迅著作本叢談 (Essays on editions and printings of Lu Xun's works), ed. Tang Tao 唐弢, 49–60. Beijing: Xinhua, 1983.

———. *Lu Xun shengping yi'an* 魯迅生平疑案 (Continuing controversies regarding Lu Xun's life). Shanghai: Shanghai cishu chubanshe, 2002.

Wang Yeqiu 王冶秋. *Minyuan qian de Lu Xun xiansheng* 民元前的魯迅先生 (Mr. Lu Xun before the Republican era). Shanghai: Emei chubanshe, 1947.

Wang Yongpei 王永培 and Wu Xiuguang 吳岫光. *Lu Xun jiushi huishi* 魯迅舊詩汇釋 (Collected commentaries on Lu Xun's traditional poems). 2 vols. Xi'an: Shaanxi renmin chubanshe, 1985.

Weston, Timothy. *The Power of Position: Beijing University, Intellectuals and Chinese Political Culture, 1898–1929*. Berkeley: University of California Press, 2004.

Wong, J. Y. *The Origins of an Heroic Image: Sun Yatsen in London, 1896–97*. Oxford: Oxford University Press, 1987.

Wong, Wang-chi. *Politics and Literature in Shanghai: The Chinese League of Left-Wing Writers, 1930–36*. Manchester: Manchester University Press, 1991.

———. "An Act of Violence: Translation of Western Fiction in the Late Qing and Early Republican Period." In *The Literary Field of Twentieth-Century China*, ed. Michel Hockx, 21–39.

Wong, Yoon Wah. *Essays on Chinese Literature: A Comparative Approach*. Singapore: Singapore University Press, 1988.

Wong, Young-tsu. *Search for Modern Nationalism: Zhang Binglin and Revolutionary China, 1869–1936*. Stanford: Stanford University Press, 1992.

Wu Chuanjiu 吳傳玖. *Lu Xun shi shidu* 魯迅詩釋讀 (Explications of Lu Xun's poetry). Beijing: Kunlun chubanshe, 2005.

Wu Haifa 吳海發. "Lu Xun 'Ziti xiao xiang' yu Liang Qichao de 'Zi li'" 魯迅 自題小像'與梁啟超的 自勵 (Lu Xun's "Inscribed by the author on a small likeness" and Liang Qichao's "Encouraging myself"). *Lu Xun Research Monthly* 6 (2002): 65–66, 75.

Wu Haiyong 吳海勇. *Shi wei gongwuyuan de Lu Xun* 時為公務員的魯迅 (Lu Xun as a civil servant). Guilin: Kuangxi shifan daxue chubanshe, 2005.

Wu He 吳禾, ed. *Zhi shang jingling: ershi shiji sanshi niandai de manhua mingxing* 紙上精靈：20世紀30年代的漫畫明星 (Essence on paper: Luminaries of 1930s cartoons). Beijing: Sanlian shudian, 2003.

Wu Zhongjie 吳中杰. *Lu Xun huazhuan* 魯迅畫傳 (Illustrated biography of Lu Xun). Shanghai: Fudan daxue chubanshe, 2005.

Xie Qizhang 謝其章. Liang Desuo yu ta de "Zazhi shehui" 梁得所與他的《雜誌社會》(Li Desuo and his "magazine world"). September 20, 2004. http://www.pubhistory.com/img/text/2/212.htm.

———. "Huang Miaozi yu 'Xiaoshuo' banyuekan" 黃苗子與小說半月刊 (Huang Miaozi and *Short Story Biweekly*). September 3, 2003. http://www.people.com.cn/GB/14738/28490/29605/29606/2069368.html

Xiong Rong 熊融. "Lu Xun tan Ah Q huaxiang de jiduan hua" 魯迅談阿Q畫像的幾段話 (Some comments by Lu Xun on depictions of Ah Q). *Yangcheng wanbao* 羊城晚報, November 9, 1961.

Xu Naixiang 徐迺翔 and Qin Hong 欽鴻, eds. *Zhongguo xiandai wenxue zuoshe biming lu* 中國現代文學作者筆名錄 (The pen names of modern Chinese writers). Changsha: Hunan weming 1988.

Xu Shoushang 許壽裳. *Wangyu Lu Xun yinxiangji* 亡友魯迅印象記 (Memories of my late friend Lu Xun). Shanghai: Emei chubanshe, 1947.

———. *Wo suo renshi de Lu Xun* 我所認識的魯迅 (The Lu Xun I knew). Peking: Renmin wenxue chubanshe, 1952.

Xue Suizhi 薛绥之, ed. *Lu Xun shengping shiliao huibian* 魯迅生平史料汇编 (Lu Xun's life: Historical documents). 5 vols. Tianjin: Tianjin renmin chubanshe, 198—86.

Yang Tianshi 楊天石 and Liu Yancheng 劉彥成. *Nanshe* 南社 (The Southern Society). Beijing: Zhonghua shuju, 1980.

Yang Yanli 楊燕麗. "Lu Xun shouji zhengli de wenzhang huibian" 魯迅收集整理的文章汇編 (Essays collected and edited by Lu Xun). *Lu Xun Research Monthly* 4 (1990): 23–24.

Ye, Shusui 葉淑穗 and Yang Yanli 楊燕麗. *Cong Lu Xun yiwu renshi Lu Xun* 從魯迅遺物認識魯迅 (Learning about Lu Xun through physical artifacts). Beijing: Zhongguo renmin daxue chubanshe, 1999.

Ye Weili. *Seeking Modernity in China's Name: Chinese Students in the United States, 1900–1927*. Stanford: Stanford University Press, 2001.

Yi Tu 一土, ed. *Ershiyi shiji: Lu Xun he women* 二十一世紀：魯迅和我們 (The twenty-first century: Lu Xun and us). Beijing: Renmin wenxue chubanshe, 2001.

Zhang Mengyang 張夢陽. *Ah Q xin lun: Ah Q yu shijie wenxue zhong de jingshen dianxing wenti* 阿Q新論：阿Q與世界文學中的精神典型問題 (New criticism on "Ah Q": Ah Q and the question of spiritual archetypes in world literature). Xi'an: Shaanxi renmin jiaoyu chubanshe, 1996.

———. "'A Q zhengzhuan' de wenxue houyi" 阿Q正傳的文學後裔 (The literary descendants of "The True Story of Ah Q"). In *The Inexhaustible Topic of Ah Q*, ed. Chen Shuyu, 215–30.

Zhang Shiying 張世瑛. "Qingmo michu de jianbian fengchao ji qi suo fanyang de shehui xintai" 清末民初的剪辮風潮及其所反映的社會心態 (Queue-cutting movements in the late Qing, early Republican era, and the social attitudes they reflect). *Guoshi guan guankan* 國史館館刊 22 (December 2009): 1–56.

Zhang Xiehe 張協和. "Yi Lu Xun zai Nanjing Kuang Lu xuetang" 憶魯迅在南京礦路學堂 (Remembering Lu Xun at Nanjing's School of Mines and Railways). 1956. In *Lu Xun Remembered: Articles*, ed. Beijing Lu Xun Bowuguan, 1:37–39.

Zhang Ziqiang 張自強. *Lu Xun xiansheng shi shuzheng* 魯迅先生詩疏證 (Annotations on the poetry of Mr. Lu Xun). Chengdu: Sichuan wenyi chubanshe, 1992.

Zhao Bingbo 趙冰波. *Lu Xun shi shuo* 魯迅詩說 (Explanations of Lu Xun's poetry). Zhengzhou: Henan renmin chubanshe, 2003.

Zhao Jiabi 趙家壁, ed. *Zhongguo xin wenxue daxi* 中國新文學大係 (The New Literature of China: A comprehensive anthology). 10 vols. 1935–36. Reprint, Shanghai: Shanghai wenyi chubanshe, 2003.

Zheng Hui 正慧 and Xu Shan 胥山, eds., and Wen Xi 文西 and Yi Meng 一蒙, illus. *Lu Xun huazhuan* 魯迅畫轉 (Pictorial biography of Lu Xun). Shanghai: Quanqiu shuju, 1953. Not paginated.

Zheng Xuejia 鄭學稼. *Chen Duxiu zhuan* 陳獨秀傳 (Biography of Chen Duxiu). 2 vols. Taibei: Shibao wenhua chuban qiye gongsi, 1989.

Zhongguo xin wenxue daxi, 1935–36. See Zhao Jiabi.

Zhou Guowei 周國偉. *Lu Xun yu Riben youren* 魯迅與日本友人 (Lu Xun and his Japanese friends). Shanghai: Shanghai shudian chubanshe, 2006.

Zhou Guowei 周國偉, and Peng Xiao 彭曉. *Xunfang Lu Xun zai Shanghai de zuji* 尋訪魯迅在上海的足跡 (In search of Lu Xun's steps in Shanghai). Shanghai: Shanghai shudian chubanshe, 2003.

Zhou Jianren 周建人. "Shaoxing guangfu qian Lu Xun de yi xiao duan shiqing" 紹興光復前魯迅的一小段事情 (Some minor incidents concerning Lu Xun before the revolution in Shaoxing). *Remin wenxue* 7, no. 8 (1961).

———. *Lu Xun gujia de bailuo* 魯迅故家的敗落 (The decline of Lu Xun's old home). Told to Zhou Yeh. Changsha: Hunan renmin chubanshe, 1984.

Zhou Zhenfu 周振甫. *Lu Xun shige zhu* 魯迅詩歌注 (Notes on Lu Xun's poetry). Nanjing: Jiangsu jiaoyu chubanshe, 2006.

Zhou Zuoren 周作人. *Lu Xun de gujia* 魯迅的故家 (Lu Xun's family) 1953. Reprint, Yishi jia zhuang: Hebei jiaoyu chubanshe, 2001.

———. *Lu Xun xiaoshuoli de renwu* 魯迅小說裏的人物 (People and things in Lu Xun's fiction). 1954. Reprint, Yishi jia zhuang: Hebei jiaoyu chubanshe, 2001.

———. *Lu Xun de qingnian shidai* 魯迅的青年時代 (Lu Xun's youth). 1957. Reprint, Yishi jia zhuang: Hebei jiaoyu chubanshe, 2001.

———. *Zhitang huixiang lu* 知堂回想錄 (Zhitang memoirs). 2 vols. Hong Kong: Sanyou tushu wenju gongsi, 1970.

———. *Zhou Zuoren riji* 周作人日記 (Zhou Zuoren diary). 3 vols. Zhengzhou: Da xiang chubanshe, 1996.

Zhu Min 朱忞. *Lu Xun zai Shaoxing* 魯迅在紹興 (Lu Xun in Shaoxing). Hangzhou: Zhejiang renmin wenxue chubanshe, 1981.

Zhu Zheng 朱正. *Lu Xun huiyi lu zhengwu* 魯迅回憶錄正誤 (Correction of errors in [Xu Guangping's] *Lu Xun huiyi lu*). Beijing: Renmin wenxue chubanshe, 1986.

———. "Jian bianzi de gushi" 剪辮子的故事 (A story of queue cutting). *Lu Xun Research Monthly* 8 (2009): 95–96.

Index

A Ying (Qian Xingcun), 45, 271n49
Achebe, Chinua, 18
"After the January 28 War" (poem; Lu Xun), 288n64
"Again on the Collapse of Leifeng Pagoda" (essay; Lu Xun), 282n45
"Ah Jin" (essay; Lu Xun), 218
Ah Q (character; "The True Story of Ah Q"), 19, 24, 32, 183; death of, 103–4, 135, 136, 140, 142–43; images of, 63, 119, 187, 191, 194–98, 201–5, 210, 239–43, 245–49; name of, 115–17; queue of, 41, 99, 119–20, 135, 224
Ah Q-ism, 24, 100, 106, 114–15, 120, 141
"Ah Q's Age Is Dead and Gone" (A Ying), 45
"Ah Zhang and *Classics of Mountains and Seas*" (essay; Lu Xun), 294n8
Ai Qing, 285n29
Alarm Bell (*Jingzhong*; magazine), 237
Alexander, William, 78, 82, 83
Anderson, Marston, 28, 40, 134, 182, 183
Anfu Club, 128
Anthology of Fiction from Foreign Lands (Lu Xun, Zhou Zuoren), 17, 54, 133
The Appropriation of Cultural Capital in China's May Fourth Project, 8
Art, visual, 181–221; accuracy of, 191–96; and culture, 204, 292n41; destruction of, 184–85; examples of, 239–54; and Lu Xun, 39, 185, 189, 190–205, 220; in May Fourth Movement, 17, 217; media used for, 187, 197, 206, 213–16, 219; and politics, 61, 184–86, 191, 206–7, 209, 210, 213–19; queue in, 42, 50, 84, 85, 191, 196–201, 202, 225; and redefinition of Lu Xun's legacy, 205–19; skill levels of, 188–90, 194, 207; style of, 206, 207–8, 219; subjects of, 206, 209–13, 219; surviving, 183–90; Western models of, 17, 186, 199–200, 213, 214, 220. *See also* cartoons; woodcuts
Art and Artists of Twentieth-Century China (Sullivan), 186
Art and Illusion (Gombrich), 204
Art schools, 186, 218
Association of Qing Empire Students (Japan), 9

Ba Jin, 20, 24, 206, 253
Bai Mang, 150, 154–55, 161, 168
Baren (Lu Xun), 24
Barmé, Geremie, 216
Beidou (Big Dipper; magazine), 156, 167
Beijing: arts in, 218; battles near, 123–24, 126–29, 137, 226; Lu Xun in, 30, 34, 37, 45, 47, 48, 131, 222
Beiyang Army, 93, 124, 128, 129, 131
"Biographical Note on Rou Shi" (essay; Lu Xun), 156
Botticelli, Sandro, 236
Bourdieu, Pierre, 2, 7
Boxer Rebellion (1900), 88, 89
Bringing the World Home (Huters), 16

Britain, 65, 150, 177
Buruma, Ian, 13
Byron, Lord, 18, 268n54

Cai E, 132, 270n30
Cai Yuanpei, 30, 38, 70–71, 126–27, 128, 152
Call to Arms (*Nahan*; fiction collection; Lu Xun), 25–26, 73, 222, 242; contents of, 103, 117, 133; cover for, 289n80; and Nahan woodcuts, 205, 206, 208, 249; in painting, 209, 248; preface to, 27, 29, 31, 44, 45, 129, 200, 229
Cao Bai, 190, 197, 214, 218; illustrations by, 189, 247, 253; and politics, 141, 219, 291n13; portraits by, 189, 212, 213, 250, 253, 254
Cao Juren, 282n44
Cao Yu, 239
"Captured to be Slaves" (*zhuoren wei nu*; lithograph), 85
"The Carriages of Chinese Labor" (drawing; Wang Junchu), 209, 210
Cartoon life (*Manhua shenghuo*; magazine), 216, 217
Cartoons and life (*Manhua yu shenghuo*; magazine), 241
Cartoons (*manhua*), 184, 210–17, 241; of Ah Q, 187, 240, 243; of Cupid, 236, 237; and politics, 50, 206, 213, 216, 217, 219; queues in, 84, 85; Western models for, 213
Catalog of Woodcuts (*Banhua jicheng*), 187–88, 199, 250–54
"Celebrating the Victories in Shanghai and Nanjing" (essay; Lu Xun), 282n56
Censorship, 4–5, 10, 149, 226; of art, 50, 214, 216; and portraits of Lu Xun, 61, 213, 248, 251, 253
Chekhov, Anton, 16, 230

Chen Baichen, 118, 281n29
Chen Duxiu, 75, 85, 124, 281n34
Chen Guangzong, 212, 213, 250, 251
Chen Haowang, 211
Chen Leng, 85
Chen Shuyu, 6, 7, 102, 281n34
Chen Tiegeng, 187, 195, 197; and art societies, 218; illustrations by, 240, 243, 245, 246; and queues, 198–99; style of, 206, 207–8; in workshop, 190, 215
Chen Zhonggang, 249
Cheng Shifa, 185, 210, 245
Cheng Weikun, 79
Chiang Kai-shek, 48, 89
Children of Wartime (*Fengyun ernü*; film), 218
China: in "Ah Q" vs. "Storm," 108–9; Lu Xun on, 10–11, 21, 23, 24, 27, 40, 56, 82, 145, 181, 206, 213, 220, 222–23, 224; and Lu Xun's life, 28, 222; and queue, 79, 83–86, 114, 224–25; Western imperialism in, 65, 83–86, 149
China, People's Republic of (PRC), 10; and Lu Xun's legacy, 3–6, 12, 15, 182, 205, 206, 231. *See also* Chinese Communist Party
Chinese Beggar (painting; Alexander), 78
Chinese Communist Party (CCP), 291n13; and arts, 185, 209, 217, 219, 292n42; censorship by, 4–5; and Comintern, 151, 152; and Five Martyrs, 150, 152, 164, 168, 169, 180; founding of, 75; and Lu Xun, 3–6, 12, 15, 36, 38, 45, 52, 61, 144, 182, 184, 205–19, 231; *vs.* Nationalists, 3, 43, 46, 47, 150, 169, 182, 227–28, 282n56, 284n9; in Shanghai, 149, 150–51, 288n69
Chinese language: modernization of, 224; neologisms in, 60, 159, 236; romanizations of, 116–17

Chinese language, classical: Lu Xun's use of, 11, 12, 19, 46, 125, 133; vs. vernacular, 2, 8, 17, 157. *See also* poetry, classical

Chinese language, vernacular, 37, 203, 229; *vs.* classical, 2, 8, 17, 157; Lu Xun's use of, 2, 19, 22–23, 28, 134, 157, 230, 236, 238, 268n54, 269n4; poetry in, 22–23, 157, 230, 236, 238

"Chinese Revolutionary Proletariat Literature and the Blood of Its Vanguard" (essay; Lu Xun), 156

Chow Kai-wing, 91, 94

Chuandao, 116–17, 203

Chuci (Songs of the South), 57, 167, 172–73

Cixi empress, 88

Class, social, 5, 203, 206, 209, 210

"A Comedy of Ducks" (fiction; Lu Xun), 134

Comintern, 151, 152

Commercial Press, 1, 265n2

The Companion (*Liang you*; magazine), 217, 240, 252

Confucianism, 19, 60, 79, 206, 219, 230

Confucius, 78, 133

Constructivism, Russian, 215

Contemporary Woodcuts (*Xiandai banhua*; periodical), 218–19

"Contests of Skill and Courage" (*Caoyan jiyong*; lithograph), 69

Coordinated National Woodcut exhibits, 188, 213, 219, 253, 254

"The countryside is filled with brambles" (poem; Lu Xun), 286n44

Creation Society (Chuangzao she), 45, 241

Crouching Tiger, Sleeping Dragon (film), 78

Cultural Revolution (1966–76), 5, 6, 7

Cultural studies, 7–8, 39

Culture, 7; new, 1–2, 8, 15–16, 25, 60, 230; and queue, 52, 56, 76, 77–79, 83–86, 114, 224–25; visual, 204, 292n41; world, 16, 225

Cupid, 235–38

Damrosch, David, 15, 17

Daoism, 60, 78

Daravula, Susan, 8

Dawn Blossoms Gathered at Dusk (*Zhaohua xishi*; essay collection; Lu Xun), 32, 130, 289n80; memoir in, 27, 29, 34; preface to, 45, 46–47

"A Day in China" (project; Mao Dun), 254

A Day's Work (anthology), 250, 252

Death, 133–43, 178, 208; of Ah Q, 103–4, 135, 136, 140, 142–43; in 1903 poem, 156, 180

Demonstrations, 10, 26. *See also* March 18th Incident; Tian'anmen Square Incident

Dianshizhai Pictorial, 69, 81, 84

Diantong (film company), 218, 239, 295n1b

"Diary of a Madman" (fiction; Lu Xun), 1–2, 9, 21–22, 44, 109, 212

Dikötter, Frank, 74, 82, 94

Ding Cong, 119, 120, 184–85

Ding Ling, 150, 156, 163–64, 287n57, 287n59

Ding Song, 184

"Divorce" (fiction; Lu Xun), 144

Dong Bingyue, 36, 271n35

Dostoyevsky, Fyodor, 16, 230

Drama, 186, 204, 219, 239; "Ah Q" in, 118, 120, 121, 203, 218, 242, 281n29, 290n3

Duan Qirui, 12, 26, 43, 123–24, 127–29

Dumas, Alexandre, 22

Dürer, Albrecht, 200

Eastern Europe, 17, 22, 53–54

Eber, Irene, 15
Eighteen Society, 214, 218
"Elegy for Fan Ainong, Three Poems" (Lu Xun), 288n73
Eliot, T. S., 170
Elite: and Lu Xun, 20, 39, 101, 108, 110, 125, 204, 206, 221, 231; and May Fourth Movement, 12, 205; new, 1–2, 12, 20, 24–25, 39, 101, 110, 205, 206, 221, 231–32; and queue, 85, 87, 110, 122; traditional, 2, 108, 125; urban, 85, 87, 93, 182, 204
"Encountering Sorrow" (poem; *Songs of the South*), 172–73
"Encouraging Myself" (poem; Liang Qichao), 95
English language, 13, 15, 116, 121
Essays on Lu Xun (ed. Li Helin), 175, 250
Evolution and Ethics (Huxley), 53, 60
Examinations, civil service, 23, 30, 32, 87

"'Fair Play' Should be Postponed" (essay; Lu Xun), 122, 226
Family (Ba Jin), 20, 24–25, 206
Fan Ainong, 29, 148
Fan Zeng, 192
"A Farewell to Mr. O. E., Who is Taking Orchids with Him on His Return to Japan" (poem; Lu Xun), 162, 163, 170, 171–73, 180, 286n44
Faulkner, William, 39
Favorsky, Vladmir, 215
Feng Keng, 150, 152, 168
Feng Sheng (Lu Xun), 113
Feng Wenbing, 268n1
Feng Xuefeng, 4, 149, 151, 156, 164, 167, 287n59
Feng Yuxiang, 48
Feng Zikai, 197, 210, 217, 242; on accuracy, 192–93, 199; illustrations by, 119, 120, 184–85, 197, 248
Feng Ziyou, 88, 276n67
Fiction semimonthly (*Xiaoshuo banyue kan*), 216, 217, 242, 243, 253
Film, 13, 78, 186, 187, 231, 232, 239; "Ah Q" in, 183, 281n29; Lu Xun's work in, 219, 221; and New Literature, 8, 9; and politics, 217, 218, 242
Findeisen, Raoul, 16
Five Martyrs, 12, 39, 49, 73, 172; arrest of, 150–52; executions of, 162–64; and 1903 poem, 147–61, 179, 180; and "Remembrance" poem, 161–69
"Flight to the Moon" (*yanyi*; Lu Xun), 280n14
Foster, Paul, 121, 183, 267n42, 268n45
Foucault, Michel, 36
France, 55, 65, 83, 84, 150
French language, 14, 15
"From Prison, I Hear that Shen Yuxi Has Been Killed" (poem; Zhang Binglin), 178
"From Prison, Presented to Zou Rong" (poem; Zhang Binglin), 177
"Further Thoughts after an Illness" (essay; Lu Xun), 292n30

Gamsa, Mark, 16
Gao Xin, 247
Gao Xudong, 4, 7
Gao Yongzhi, 79, 80
García Márquez, Gabriel, 39
Ge Hongbin, 271n45
German language, 121
Germany, 65
Gimpel, Denise, 8
GMD. *See* Nationalist Party
Goethe, Johan Wolfgang von, 15
Gogol, Nikolai, 18, 230
Gombrich, E. H., 199–200, 204
Gong Zhuxin, 270n24

Gorky, Maksim, 210, 211, 252
Gramsci, Antonio, 7
Grave (*Fen*; essay collection; Lu Xun), 27, 45–46, 289n80
"The Great Sight of Chopping Down Communists" (essay; Lu Xun), 227–28
Guan Zhong, 78
Guangxu Emperor, 87
Guangzhou, 43, 47–48, 129, 218
Guo Liang, 227
Guomin gongbao (newspaper), 125
Guomindang. *See* Nationalist Party

Ha Jin, 13, 266n11
Haggard, H. Rider, 53
Hair, 75–76, 78. *See also* queue; queue cutting; "Story about Hair"
Hallpike, C. R., 76, 78
Han Chinese, 90–91, 92, 94–95
Han Heping, 63, 274n30
Han Qiangshi, 63–64
Hanan, Patrick, 105
Hangzhou, 30, 32, 65, 176, 218, 241
Hangzhou Art Academy, 189, 214, 218, 219, 220
Harp (*Shuqin*; magazine), 250, 252
Harrison, Henrietta, 87
Hesitation (*Panghuang*; fiction collection; Lu Xun), 25–26, 144, 289n80
History of Chinese Vernacular Fiction (Lu Xun), 37, 101
"History of Humankind" (essay; Lu Xun), 272n5
"History Repeats Itself" (cartoon), 83
Hockx, Michel, 7, 8, 269n4
"Hometown" (fiction; Lu Xun), 23, 100–101, 102, 116, 279n6; illustrations for, 63, 187, 196, 240; and memory, 44, 45
Hong Zhenglun, 197, 198, 201–2, 239
Hot Air (*Refeng*; essay collection; Lu Xun), 27, 101

Hsia, T. A., 134, 151, 168
Hu Bing, 68
Hu Gongshou, 79, 80
Hu Shi, 8, 37, 86
Hu Yebin, 150, 153, 163–64, 168
Hu Yichuan, 206, 214
Hu Yinqiang, 7
Huang Houhui (Huang Su), 153
Huang Miaozi, 198, 216, 217, 242, 253
Huang Xing, 89, 97, 130
Hugo, Victor, 53
Hundred Days Reform (1898), 53, 87–88, 95
Huters, Theodore, 16, 134
Huxley, Thomas, 53, 60

Ibsen, Henrik, 16, 230
Imitation Foreigner (character; "Ah Q"), 99, 110, 111–12, 121, 122, 142
"In Memory of Liu Hezhen" (essay; Lu Xun), 26, 46, 230; in Tian'anmen Square Incident, 9–10
"Inscribed by the Author on a Small Likeness" (1903; poem; Lu Xun), 57–71, 97, 145–80, 223, 226, 227; *vs.* 1902 poem, 64–68, 70; additions to copies of, 148, 159, 160; changes in, 160–61; and classical poetry, 50, 60, 147, 170–74; dating of, 75, 233–35; discarded copy of, 156–57; dual meanings of, 154, 163; and Five Martyrs, 147–61, 179, 180; neologisms in, 60, 159; and "Photograph with Hair Cut Short," 57–71, 75, 145–46, 174–75, 234; politics of, 72, 73, 74, 94–96, 146, 153, 178–79, 235; and Qu Qiubai, 159–60, 161, 179; recopying of, 147–49, 153, 155, 156–61; and "Remembrance" poem, 164–67; *shenshi* in, 148, 149, 154, 158, 159, 160, 235–38; and Zhang Binglin,

147, 176, 178, 179
"Inscribed in *Call to Arms*" (poem; Lu Xun), 170
"Inscribed in *Hesitation*" (poem; Lu Xun), 170
Intellectual Life (*Dushu shenghuo*; magazine), 188
Italy, 55, 56

Jansen, Marius, 67, 90
Japan: and China, 12, 65, 138–39, 150, 184, 214, 215, 222; Chinese students in, 9, 49, 53, 54, 55, 89–94; Lu Xun in, 9, 11, 15, 17, 27–33, 39, 42, 46, 48–56, 220, 222; and Manchuria, 43, 93, 184, 189; and 1903 poem, 145, 146; political activism in, 55, 89–94; resistance to, 214, 217. *See also* Russo-Japanese War; Sendai Medical School; Sino-Japanese War
Japanese language, 15, 54, 91
Jiang Feng, 285n29
Jiang Jingsan, 153
Jin Zhaoye, 188
Jing Meijiu, 90
Jing Wendong, 5, 6
Jing Yingyu, 267n42
Jing Yinyu, 14
Journey to the Moon (Verne), 53

Kang Youwei, 87–88, 89, 197
Kawabata Yasunari, 14
Kidnapped in London (Sun Yat-sen), 84, 277n89
Knowledge of the New (*Zhixin bao*; newspaper), 65
Kōbun Academy (Japan), 54, 55, 72; uniform of, 64, 66, 68, 175
Kokoro (Natsume Sōseki), 37
Kollwitz, Käthe, 156, 167, 207–8, 215
Kong Yiji (character), 231; images of, 187, 195, 239, 242, 248

"Kong Yiji" (fiction; Lu Xun), 23, 44, 296n13; illustrations for, 185, 188, 189, 193, 196, 244, 245
Kuhn, Philip A., 79
Kundera, Milan, 15, 16

Lai Shaoqi, 139, 190, 197, 204, 214, 218, 283n63, 291n10; portrait of Lu Xun by, 213, 247–48
Lang, Andrew, 53
Leach, Edward, 75–76
League of Left-Wing Artists, 213, 219, 241, 242
League of Left-Wing Dramatists, 153
League of Left-Wing Writers, 43, 219, 242, 249, 295n6b; and Five Martyrs, 151, 152; and Lu Xun, 144, 149, 205
Lee, Leo Ou-fan, 6, 21, 36, 146
Lee Haiyan, 9
"Letter from Changsha" (*Shenbao*), 227–28
Leung, George, 194, 248, 268n46
Li Anbao, 226
Li Dazhao, 294n9
Li Helin, 175, 250
Li Hua, 188, 200, 214, 218, 252, 291n10
Li Lisan, 151
Li Suizhi, 272n11
Li Weisen, 150, 168
Li Xudan, 218, 242, 243
Li Yuanhong, 126
Li Yunjing, 236
Li Zicheng, 92
Liang Qichao, 1, 89, 94, 95, 160, 235
Liang Yiqiu, 252
The Limits of Realism (Anderson), 134
Lin Chong-Pin, 293n46
Lin Qingxin, 7, 36
Lin Shu, 1
Link, Perry, 8
Liqun, 189, 190, 219, 254

Literary Research Association (Wenxue yanjiu hui), 101
Literature: death in, 133–43; Eastern European, 17, 22, 53–54; elite, 231–32; Lu Xun's place in, 12–18, 17, 220–21; massification (*dazhonghua*) of, 8, 144, 186, 205; and politics, 182–83, 292n42; popular, 8–9; proletarian, 38, 229; style in, 2, 19, 292n42; survival of, 231–32; traditional, 1, 37; vernacular, 2, 8, 19, 22–23, 28, 37, 134, 157, 230, 236, 238, 268n54, 269n4; and violence, 138–39, 143–44; Western, 17, 22, 124, 133, 230; world, 12–18. *See also* drama; New Literature; poetry
Literature (*Wenxue*; periodical), 213
Literature of China in the Twentieth Century (McDougall and Louie), 3
Liu, Lydia, 8
Liu Bannong, 294n2, 294n9
Liu Dajie, 90, 165, 174
Liu Dapeng, 87
Liu Feiqi, 283n4
Liu Hezhen, 151, 169, 225, 230
Liu Jian'an, 63, 274n30
Liu Xian, 187–90, 203, 204, 218; illustrations by, 181, 187, 188, 195, 197, 198, 239, 244, 245; images of Ah Q by, 194, 195, 245; images of Kong Yiji by, 188, 189, 196, 245; portraits of Lu Xun by, 251
Liu Yazi, 165, 171
Liu Yukai, 7
Living China (anthology; Snow), 187, 191, 212, 246, 252
"The Loner" (fiction; Lu Xun), 25, 29, 44, 45, 144
Louie, Kam, 3
Lovell, Julia, 14, 269n17
Lu Shaofei, 213, 217, 242; images of Ah Q by, 201–2, 240; portraits of Lu Xun by, 253, 297n31
"Lu Xun" (woodcut print; Cao Bai), 189
Lu Xun (Zhou Shuren): adaptations of work of, 181–82, 191–92, 195–96, 201, 205, 219, 221, 232; on "Ah Q," 104–5, 107, 121; artists' connections with, 187, 188, 190–91; autobiographical writings of, 27–29, 31–33; biography of, 27–40, 123–33; CCP appropriation of, 3–6, 12, 15, 36, 38, 45, 52, 61, 144, 182, 184, 205–19, 231; cutting of queue by, 12, 39, 41, 48–49, 52, 57, 69, 75–77; death of, 3, 11, 19; diaries of, 101, 124, 126, 127, 128, 132, 153, 158, 170–71, 190, 254; education of, 29–30, 52–53; images of, 61–70, 122, 174–75, 181, 183, 184, 187–88, 199, 200, 206, 209, 210–13, 250–54; legacy of, 3–6, 12, 15, 50, 181–84, 191, 205–7, 231; name of, 270n27; personal life of, 9, 29–32, 37, 38; political militancy of, 72–74, 94–96, 153; productivity of, 38–39, 101–2; pseudonyms of, 22, 24, 28, 113, 238, 281n33; as public figure, 12, 28–29, 37, 38, 39, 51; reevaluation of, 6–8, 9–10, 14, 35–36; in textbooks, 9, 10, 23, 231, 267n38
Lu Xun Academy of Literature and Arts (Yan'an), 184
"Lu Xun and Gorky" (drawing; Wei Mengke), 252
Lu Xun and Modern Chinese History (Li Anbao), 226
"Lu Xun and Xianglin sao" (woodcut print; Cao Bai), 189, 247, 253
Lu Xun Chronology, 68, 75, 126, 132
Lu Xun's Societal Activities (Ni Moyan), 226

Lunacharsky, Anatoly, 212
Lunyu (periodical), 211, 251, 252
Luo Qingzhen, 188, 218, 252
Luo Zhenqing, 190
Luzhen theme park (Shaoxing), 10

M. K. Society, 214, 254
Ma Guoliang, 187, 217, 218, 240, 242, 250, 252
Ma Jian, 13
Macartney, Lord, 82
Magazines, 3, 8, 9, 17, 34; Lu Xun's founding of, 33, 37, 38; and New Literature, 1, 2, 20, 24–25, 37. See also *New Tide; New Youth; Zhejiang Tide*
Manchuria: Japanese invasion of, 43, 93, 184, 189; Russia in, 56, 85, 93; warlords in, 129
Manchus: defeat of Ming by, 92, 95, 113–14, 115; *vs.* Han Chinese, 90–91, 92, 94–95; and queue, 40, 41, 52, 59–60, 77, 79, 84, 88–91, 114, 199. See also Qing dynasty
Mandarin Ducks and Butterflies (Link), 8
Mangyuan (magazine), 174
Mao Dun, 2, 5, 25, 156, 242; on "Ah Q," 24, 130–31; and Lu Xun, 22, 37, 101; works by, 218, 219, 254
Mao Zedong, 4–5, 184, 212, 219, 286n52
"March of the Volunteers" (*Yiyongjun jinxingqu*; song; Tian Han), 186, 218
March 18th Incident (1926), 43; Lu Xun on, 26, 38, 45, 47–48, 73, 169, 225–26
Marxism, 38, 144
Masereel, Frans, 208, 291n11, 292n44
Massification (*dazhonghua*), 8, 144, 186, 205
Masuda Wataru, 74, 173
May Fourth Movement (1919), 7, 43, 94, 209, 219, 231; art in, 17, 217; and literature, 2–3, 20, 182–83, 232; and Lu Xun, 20, 56, 101, 144, 205, 220; new elite in, 12, 205; reevaluation of, 8–9
McDougall, Bonnie S., 3, 9
"Medicine" (fiction; Lu Xun), 23, 43, 44, 74, 133; death in, 135, 140, 141; illustrations for, 192, 194, 196
Meffert, Carl, 215
Meiji Emperor, 88
Meiji Restoration, 53
Memory, 12, 31, 40, 44–51, 179, 229–30; and poetry, 49–50; and queues, 49, 200–201, 225; and violence, 11, 45, 46, 100, 226
"Meshes of Law" (print series; Chen Tiegeng), 208
Metaphor: of iron house, 34; Lu Xun's life as, 28, 29; in Lu Xun's work, 19, 20, 22, 24; queue as, 221
Mickiewicz, Adam, 18, 268n54
Midnight (Mao Dun), 218
Mills, Harriet C., 226
Ming loyalists, 95, 113–14, 115
Ministry of Education, 136, 177, 280n9; Lu Xun in, 9, 30, 101, 127, 131, 132–33
Minzu bao (newspaper), 113
"Minzu de guomin" (essay; Wang Jingwei), 113
Les Miserables (Hugo), 53
"Misery" (print; Kollwitz), 207–8
"Miss Ah Q," 183
Modern Sketch (*Shidai manhua*; magazine), 240
The Monster That Is History (Wang), 40
Morning Post Supplement, 100, 113, 117
Morocco, 84
"The Most Unkindest Cut of All" (cartoon), 83
"Mr. Fujino" (essay; Lu Xun), 36, 66–67, 273n15

"Mr. Wang" (cartoon series; Ye Qianyu), 215, 217, 240
Muke jicheng (Record of Wood Engravings; Lu Xun), 190, 215, 220
Muling Woodcut Society, 218, 219
Munch, Edvard, 208
"My Theory of Manhua" (Huang Miaozi), 243

N (character; "A Story about Hair"), 75, 103, 109–12, 114, 126, 224, 230; and death, 43, 137–38, 140, 141, 142; name of, 115, 116
Nagao Kagekazu, 155
"Names" (essay; Lu Xun), 100, 115–16, 126
Nanjing, 30, 32, 52, 65, 136, 222
Nationalism: Japanese, 90; of Lu Xun, 42, 57, 58, 74, 179
Nationalist Party (Guomindang; GMD), 186; censorship by, 149, 184, 213; *vs.* Communists, 3, 43, 46, 47, 150, 169, 182, 227–28, 282n56, 284n9; and Five Martyrs, 12, 49, 152, 164, 180; and Lu Xun, 38, 206, 213
Natsume Sōseki, 37
New Culture Movement, 1, 25, 230
New Life (*Xin sheng*; magazine), 33–34
New Literature, 1–3; *vs.* classical poetry, 171; and film, 8, 9; and Lu Xun, 1–2, 19–20, 28, 39, 46, 101, 124, 133, 144, 220, 229, 230; and magazines, 1, 2, 20, 24–25, 37; *vs.* revolutionary literature, 182–83; and the West, 2, 16, 182
The New Literature of China: A Comprehensive Anthology, 8
New Masses (periodical), 156
New Tide (*Xin chao*; *Renaissance*; magazine), 24–25, 117, 204, 270n23

"New Year's Sacrifice" (Lu Xun), 25, 44, 45, 189
New Youth (*Xinqingnian*; magazine), 24–25, 75, 137, 222; Lu Xun's work in, 1–2, 22, 28, 30, 34, 100, 124, 238
Newspapers, 2, 3, 9, 88, 184, 186. See also *Shibao*; *Subao*; *Zhonghua ribao*
Ni Moyan, 9, 55, 92, 93, 226, 234, 248
1903 poem. *See* "Inscribed by the Author on a Small Likeness"
Nobel Prize in Literature, 14–15
Northern Campaign (Nationalist; 1927), 43
Northern Expedition Army, 136

Obara Eijirō, 172
Ōe Kenzaburō, 13, 16, 17
"Officials Capture Gamblers" (*Lingshi zhuo du*; lithograph), 81
Okamoto Shigeru, 158–59, 160, 161, 167, 168
Old Master Zhao (character; "Ah Q"), 117, 187, 194, 207, 240, 245
Old Tales Retold (*yanyi* collection; Lu Xun), 26, 102, 130, 269n17
"On Face" (essay; Lu Xun), 218
On Lu Xun and His Works (Tai Jingnong), 174–75
"On Minding Other People's Business, Etc." (essay; Lu Xun), 273n15
"On Radium" (essay; Lu Xun), 53, 176
Opium Wars, 1, 83
Origins of the Chinese Avant-Garde (Tang Xiaobing), 186
Ou Mei mingjia duanpian xiaoshuo congkan, 131
"Outline of Chinese Geology" (essay; Lu Xun), 53, 54, 55, 56, 176
"Outline of Science" (essay; Lu Xun), 272n5
Outpost (*Qianshao*; magazine), 156

Pamuk, Orhan, 16
"Die Passion eines Menschen" (Masereel), 208
Peng Xiaojie, 119
People's Liberation Army Daily, 73
Persimmon Oil Party (Freedom Party), 122, 123, 143
Petőfi, Sándor, 18, 54, 268n54; poems of, 154–55, 161
"Photograph with Hair Cut Short": *vs.* 1902 photograph, 64–68, 70, 233; and Lu Xun's militancy, 72, 73, 74, 94; and 1903 poem, 57–71, 75, 145–46, 174–75, 234; and queue cutting, 56, 97, 178–79, 223, 226, 233, 236; uniform in, 57, 60
Pigtail Army (*bianzi jun*), 99, 124, 127, 281n32
Poetry: of Lu Xun, 11, 12, 22–23, 27, 38, 65–66, 157–58, 170, 286n44; and memory, 44; and New Literature, 230; prose, 27, 34, 173; of Qu Qiubai, 159–60; and queues, 49, 56; vernacular, 22–23, 157, 230, 236, 238; and violence, 49–50, 173; of Zhang Binglin, 174, 177, 178, 180, 223, 224. *See also* "Inscribed by the Author on a Small Likeness"; *particular poems and collections*
Poetry, classical, 49–50, 51, 158, 165, 166, 227; of Lu Xun, 11, 23, 27, 38, 170; and 1903 poem, 50, 60, 147, 170–74; *vs.* vernacular, 157
Political activism: of Ah Q, 142–43; anti-Nationalist, 206; anti-Qing, 11–12, 42, 55, 74, 92–96, 109, 113–14, 115, 134, 147, 176, 180; and death, 134, 140–43; in Japan, 55, 89–94; of Lu Xun, 64, 72–74, 93–97, 153, 178, 226–27, 273n14; and 1903 poem, 179, 180

Politics: and art, 61, 184–186, 191, 206–207, 209–219; and Cao Bai, 141, 219, 291n13; and cartoons, 50, 206, 213, 216, 217, 219; and film, 217, 218, 242; leftist, 182–83, 206, 216–19; and literature, 182–83, 292n42; and Lu Xun, 7, 19–20, 55–56, 92, 129–33, 144, 149–50, 181–83, 217; and Lu Xun's legacy, 3–6, 12, 15, 182, 205–7, 231; and Lu Xun's portraits, 61, 213, 248, 251, 253; in Lu Xun's work, 106, 112, 229; and 1903 poem, 72, 73, 74, 94–96, 146, 153, 178–79, 235; of queue, 56, 59–60, 76–77, 90, 91, 96, 113, 114, 123, 134, 142–43, 225; and woodcuts, 43, 184, 191, 206, 213–19. *See also* violence, political
Pollard, David E., 21, 72, 74, 101
"Portrait of a Literary Tea" (drawing; Lu Shaofei), 253
Portrait of Gao Yongzhi at Age Twenty-eight (painting; Ren Yi, Hu Gongshou), 79, 80
"The Power of Mara Poetry" (essay; Lu Xun), 18, 272n5
"Preface to *Self-Selected Anthology*" (Lu Xun), 129–33, 227, 229
Pramoedya Ananta Toer, 18
Proust, Marcel, 39
"A Public Example" (fiction; Lu Xun), 141
Pushkin, Alexander, 4, 5, 18
Puyi, Emperor, 127

Qi Shoushan, 128
Qian Xingcun (A Ying), 45, 271n49
Qian Xuantong, 34, 35, 130
Qing dynasty: *vs.* Ming loyalists, 95, 113–14, 115; opposition to, 11–12, 42, 55, 74, 109, 147, 176, 180; overthrow of, 130; and queue, 40,

41, 52, 59–60, 77, 79, 84, 88–91, 114, 199; restorations of, 105, 106, 124, 127, 131
Qiu Jin, 42, 140, 283n64
Qu Qiubai, 118, 119, 223, 290n1; death of, 142; illustrations by, 119, 246–47; and 1903 poem, 159–60, 161, 179
Qu Yuan, 57, 60
Queue: abolition of, 41, 77, 82, 86–87, 294n1; in adaptations, 182, 201, 221; in "Ah Q," 41, 80, 81–82, 99, 100, 103, 117–23, 126, 135, 224; in art, 42, 50, 84, 85, 191, 196–201, 202, 225; artificial, 41, 91, 110, 111, 122; assimilation of, 79–80, 82, 84, 114; in Chinese culture, 79, 83–86, 114, 224–25; concealment of, 61–63, 66–67, 121; cultural history of, 52, 56, 76, 77–79; and death, 133, 134–35, 137, 139–40; in "Hair," 103, 109, 110, 126, 138; images of, 66–71, 80–86; Lu Xun on, 80, 81–82, 90–91, 97–98, 197; and Manchus, 40, 41, 52, 59–60, 77, 79, 84, 88, 89, 90–91, 114, 199; and memory, 49, 200–201, 225; and Pigtail Army, 99, 124, 127, 281n32; politics of, 56, 59–60, 76–77, 90, 91, 96, 113, 114, 123, 134, 142–143, 225; and Republican Revolution, 41–42, 84, 86–87, 100, 103, 121–22, 199, 223, 224; and "Storm," 41, 99, 100, 103, 124, 136; and Sun Yat-sen, 84, 87, 88–89; symbolism of, 77–89, 100, 225; as theme, 11, 40, 41–42, 51, 101–2, 103, 143; and violence, 41, 99, 100, 123; and the West, 82–86, 87, 88
Queue cutting: in "Hair," 75, 114, 134–35; by Lu Xun, 12, 39, 41, 48–49, 52–98; and 1903 poem and photograph, 56, 75, 97, 146, 178–79, 223, 226, 233–34, 236; politics of, 90, 91–93, 95, 96, 123, 177, 290n89; reasons for, 75–76, 84–86, 88–89; and Republican Revolution, 86–87; resistance to, 100; in "Storm," 87, 105–6, 134, 224; by Xu Shoushang, 63–64, 69, 75, 76, 77, 223; by Zhang Binglin, 60, 88, 223; by Zou Rong, 177, 223

"Rabbits and the Cat" (fiction; Lu Xun), 134
Reading "Call to Arms" (painting; Wang Junchu), 209, 248
Record of Wood Engravings (Muke jicheng), 190, 215, 220
Red Star over China (Snow), 212
"Regret for the Past" (fiction; Lu Xun), 26, 32, 109
"Remembering the Past" (fiction; Lu Xun), 125, 229, 276n76
"Remembrance in Order to Forget" (essay; Lu Xun), 13, 46, 286n52, 288n64; and classical poetry, 170, 173; and Five Martyrs, 150, 152, 155, 160, 180; and 1903 poem, 50, 145, 147, 150, 151, 154, 161–69, 179
"Remembrance" poem ("Though accustomed to"; Lu Xun), 147, 171, 174; and Five Martyrs, 161–69, 180; and 1903 poem, 164–67
Ren Yi, 79, 80
Renxue (Tan Sitong), 88
Republican Revolution (1911): and Lu Xun, 5, 43, 144; and Lu Xun's work, 24, 112, 126, 130, 133, 230; and queue, 41–42, 84, 86–87, 100, 103, 121–22, 199, 223, 224
Research Society on the Modern Woodcut, 218

Revolutionary Army (Zou Rong), 42, 75, 92, 96, 177
Rizal, Jose, 18, 268n54
"Roar, China!" (woodcut print; Li Hua), 188
Rolland, Romain, 14, 267n42
"Roses without Flowers (2)" (essay; Lu Xun), 270n19
Rou Shi: arrest of, 150; death of, 39, 43, 49, 73, 141, 142, 180, 227; in "Farewell to Mr. O. E.", 172; and Five Martyrs, 152, 169; and Lu Xun, 149, 150, 162, 168, 214, 226; mother of, 166–67; and 1903 poem, 147, 155–56, 161, 179
Runtu (character; "Hometown"), 63, 116, 187, 240
Russia, 4, 55, 65, 209; in Manchuria, 56, 85, 93; and "Sparta," 93–94
Russian language, 15, 250, 252
Russo-Japanese War (1904–5), 89, 91, 93; and beheading incident, 33, 35–37

"Sacrifice" (woodcut; Kollwitz), 156, 167
Satire: in "Ah Q," 108, 111; in cartoons, 213, 215; and language, 203; and Republican Revolution, 230; in "Storm," 103, 125, 135–36; and violence, 133
Science (*Kexue congshu*; series), 53
Second Revolution (1913), 43, 122, 130, 133, 136, 227
Second Supplement to the Collected Works (*Jiwaiji shiyi*), 147, 170
Seijō Academy (Japan), 72
"Self-Mockery" (poem; Lu Xun), 146, 165, 286n52
Semanov, V. I., 178
Semi-concession Anthologies (*Qiejie ji*; essay collection; Lu Xun), 27
Sendai Medical School (Japan), 29, 53, 54, 73–74; beheading incident at, 33, 35–37, 141
Seven-Pounds (character; "Storm"), 243, 280n14; and "Ah Q," 121, 135; images of, 194, 195, 245; vs. N, 137; name of, 115, 116; and queue, 41, 99, 103, 105–9, 143, 224
Seventy Years of Ah Q, 247
Shanghai, 27, 91, 217; arts in, 191, 218; CCP in, 149, 150–51, 288n69; Japanese attack on, 43, 138–39, 184, 228; Lu Xun in, 12, 30, 38, 43, 51, 219–20, 222; newspapers in, 53, 176, 177; in 1930s, 149–51, 180
Shanghai Sketch (*Shanghai manhua*; magazine), 215, 217, 240, 242
Shaoxing, 4, 10; Lu Xun in, 27, 29–30, 32, 41, 45, 52, 65, 102, 222; in Lu Xun's work, 45, 101, 122, 279n6; and Republican Revolution, 42, 43, 103, 140, 226–27, 230
Shaw, George Bernard, 211, 251
Shen Congwen, 163–64
Shen Diemin, 55
Shen Fei (Lu Xun), 281n33
Shen Jin, 176, 179
Shen Jin (Shen Yuxi), 177–78
Shi Lin, 271n40
Shibao (newspaper), 85, 86, 237
Short Story Monthly (*Xiaoshuo yuebao*), 8, 25, 37, 101, 134
Si Tang (Lu Xun), 132
"The Sight of Riches Spawns a Plan" (*Jian cai qiyi*; lithograph), 81, 277n85
Sima Qian, 96
"Sinking" (*Chenlun*; Yu Dafu), 31
Sino-Japanese War (1894–95), 1, 89–90
Situ Qiao, 240
Smedley, Agnes, 15, 152, 156
"Smell of Death" (woodcut; Munch), 208

Smith, Adam, 53
Snow, Edgar, 15, 187, 191, 212, 246, 252, 294n7
"Soap" (fiction; Lu Xun), 26, 280n14
Socialist realism, 4, 36, 206, 209–10
Society of Proletarian Painters, 219
"Some Dissent from 'The Wrong People Were Killed'" (essay; Lu Xun), 131–32, 282n44
"Song of the Xiang River Goddess" (poem; Lu Xun), 286n44
Songs of Chu. See *Chuci*
"Soul of Sparta" (essay; Lu Xun), 53–55, 60, 170, 176, 178, 235; and Lu Xun's militancy, 72–73, 74, 95–96; and Russia, 93–94
Soviet Union (U.S.S.R.), 4, 209. *See also* Russia
Spring Field Art Society (Chundi huahui), 214
"Storm" (*Fengbo*; fiction; Lu Xun), 49, 105–9; and "Ah Q," 102, 103, 106–9; and battles, 123–26; and "Hair," 106, 109–10, 137, 138; illustrations for, 187, 196, 197, 243, 244, 245; names in, 115–16; and political violence, 135–37; queue cutting in, 87, 105–6, 134, 224; queue in, 41, 99, 100, 103, 143, 224; as satire, 103, 125, 135–36; title of, 112
"Story about Hair" (*Toufa de gushi*; fiction; Lu Xun), 23, 49, 224, 230, 273n26; and "Ah Q," 102, 109–12, 113; death in, 137–40, 141, 142; illustrations for, 196; Lu Xun in, 110; names in, 115–16; publication of, 100; queue cutting in, 75, 114, 134–35; queue in, 103, 109, 110, 126, 138; and Republican Revolution, 43, 126; and "Storm," 106, 109–10, 137, 138; title of, 112–13

Student Lamp (*Xuedeng*; magazine), 100, 109, 126
Subao (newspaper; Shanghai), 53, 176, 177
Sullivan, Michael, 185, 186, 215, 216, 240, 292n44
Sun Fuyuan, 100, 104, 113, 117, 125
Sun Yat-sen, 92, 130; and queue, 84, 87, 88–89
Supplement to the Collected Works, 158, 170
"Surrendering in Life but Not in Death" (essay; Lu Xun), 100, 113–15, 126

Tagore, Rabindranath, 14, 15
Tai Jingnong, 158, 167–68, 174, 288n65
Taiping Rebellion, 78, 229–30
Tan Sitong, 53, 87–88
Tang Si (Lu Xun), 22, 238
Tang Xiaobing, 186, 205, 208
Tang Yingwei, 249
Tao Li qie (Plunder of Peach and Plum; film), 218, 239
Tao Yuanqing, 175, 192, 250
Theater (*Xi*; newspaper supplement), 217; and cartoons, 213; illustrations in, 186–87, 194, 197, 201, 239–43, 245; letters to, 190, 196, 201, 202; Lu Xun quoted in, 192, 198, 248
Theme parks, 10, 231
"Thinking to Myself" (*Ziyan ziyu*; feature; Lu Xun), 281n33
"This Too Is Life" (essay; Lu Xun), 51
Tian Han, 186, 290n3, 290n4
Tian'anmen Square Incident (1989), 9–10, 13, 267n38, 293n46
"To Detain Ding Yaoqing, a Couplet" (poem; Lu Xun), 274n37
"To the Front" (woodcut; Hu Yichuan), 206, 207, 214
"Tomorrow" (Lu Xun), 44, 196

Tongmenghui, 87, 89
Translations: by Lu Xun, 17, 37, 53–54, 101, 131, 138, 143; of Lu Xun's work, 14, 15, 140, 165, 221, 232, 248; from Western languages, 16, 154–55, 230, 250, 252
"True Story of Ah Q" (*Ah Q zhengzhuan*; fiction; Lu Xun), 39, 49, 102–9; accuracy in, 203–4; on China, 24, 108–9; death in, 139, 140–43; film adaptations of, 183, 281n29; and "Hair," 102, 109–12, 113; illustrations for, 118–20, 184–85, 192, 193, 196–98, 207–8, 210, 212, 217, 240–47; influence of, 19, 23; language of, 203–4, 205; and memory, 44–45; and "Names," 115; and politics, 12, 183; queue in, 41, 80, 81–82, 99, 100, 103, 117–23, 126, 135, 224; and Republican Revolution, 24, 112, 230; as satire, 108, 111; stage adaptations of, 118, 120, 121, 186–87, 203, 218, 242, 281n29, 290n3; and "Storm," 102, 103, 106–9; and "Surrendering in Life but Not in Death," 114–15; title of, 112–13; translations of, 14, 140, 232, 248
"Two or Three Things Brought to Mind by Mr. Zhang Taiyan" (essay; Lu Xun), 176, 273n26, 275n48, 278n105, 282n47

Uchiyama Bookstore, 151, 163, 168, 172, 220, 252
Uchiyama Kakichi, 215
Uchiyama Kanzō, 167, 171, 172, 215
Ukiyo-e, 215
"The Uneven Development of Culture" (essay; Lu Xun), 272n5
United States, Chinese students in, 86, 89, 269n4

Unlucky Star (*Huagai ji*; essay collection; Lu Xun), 27
Unnamed Publishers (Weiming she), 174
Unnamed Woodcut Society (Weiming muke she), 218, 244, 288n65, 291n16
"Upstairs at the Tavern" (fiction; Lu Xun), 25, 44, 45, 196
"The Uses of a Queue" (cartoon), 86

"Various Memories" (essay; Lu Xun), 226
Verne, Jules, 22, 53
"Village Opera" (fiction; Lu Xun), 44, 47, 196
Violence, political, 40, 42–43, 51; and art, 50, 191; and literature, 138–39, 143–44; and Lu Xun, 26, 49, 99, 123–33, 225–29; and memory, 11, 45, 46, 100, 226; and 1903 poem, 147, 156, 179; and poetry, 49–50, 173; and queue, 41, 99, 100, 123; and "Storm," 133, 134, 135–37
"The Violence of Observation" (Anderson), 40

Wakeman, Frederic, 43, 150
"Waking" (essay; Lu Xun), 47–48
Wales, Nym, 15, 246
Wang, David Der-wei, 40, 294n6
Wang Binzhang, 293n46
Wang Chi-chen, 20, 25
Wang Dehou, 7
Wang Dongfang, 89, 290n89
Wang Furen, 6
Wang Huazhu, 128
Wang Hui, 7, 54
Wang Jingwei, 113, 186
Wang Junchu, 190, 206, 209–10, 219, 248
Wang Shijia, 157

Wang Xiangrong, 89, 278n99
Wang Xiaoming, 6–7
Wang Xirong, 35–36, 37, 267n42
Warlords, 3, 43, 48, 129
Watts, George Frederic, 33
Wealth of Nations (Smith), 53
Weeds (*Yecao*; prose poems; Lu Xun), 27, 34, 130, 173; illustrations for, 187, 244
Wei Mengke, 187, 193, 209, 246, 291n22; cartoons of, 210–12; and politics, 206, 219; portraits of Lu Xun by, 251, 252
Wei Suyuan, 294n9
Wencong (periodical), 185
The West: and art, 17, 186, 199–200, 213, 214, 220; imperialism of, 43, 65, 83–86, 149, 222; and literature, 1, 2, 16, 17, 22, 116, 124, 133, 182, 230; Lu Xun studies in, 5, 6; and queue, 82–86, 87, 88; translations from, 16, 154–55, 230, 250, 252
"A Westerner Shows His Brutality" (*xiren chenxiong*; lithograph), 85
What Is World Literature? (Damrosch), 15
Whiskers Wang (character; "Ah Q"), 81, 119, 194, 245
"White Light" (fiction; Lu Xun), 44, 196, 244
Wong Young-tsu, 177
Woodcuts, 186, 239–54; exhibitions of, 188, 190, 213, 214, 218–19, 253, 254; as illustrations, 50, 185, 224, 239–49; and Lu Xun, 38, 54, 181, 183, 213, 214, 215, 220, 250; Nahan, 205, 206, 208, 249; and politics, 43, 184, 191, 206, 213–19; as portraits, 50, 184, 250–54; skill levels of, 188–89; societies for, 218, 219, 244, 288n65, 291n16; subjects of, 215; and war with Japan, 214, 215; Western models for, 150, 156, 167, 207–8, 214, 215; workshop on (1931), 190, 191, 208, 214, 215, 216, 218, 220, 245, 254. *See also* art, visual
Wooden Bell Society (Muling muke yanjiushe), 214
Wordsworth, William, 39
The World's Desire (Haggard and Lang), 53
Writers' Union, 4
Wu Haifa, 279n115
Wu Haiyong, 280n9
Wu Tingfang, 277n93
Wu Youru, 81. *See also Dianshizhai Pictorial*
Wu Yu, 24

Xiamen University, 47
Xiao D (character; "Ah Q"), 82, 119, 120–21
Xiao Hong, 38
Xiao Jun, 38
Xiaoshuo (fiction), 26, 38–39, 102
Xiaoshuo banyue kan. See Fiction semimonthly
Xinmin congbao (journal), 95
Xu Guangping, 9, 30, 37, 38, 47–48, 225; and Lu Xun's work, 160, 167, 170; on *shenshi*, 57, 235, 236
Xu Jishang, 128
Xu Lian, 249
Xu Shiquan, 199, 200, 250
Xu Shoushang, 47, 101, 152; assassination of, 97; in Japan, 54, 56, 276n67; on Lu Xun, 28, 92; and magazines, 33, 176; and 1903 poem, 57–59, 145–48, 158, 233–35, 283n4; and photograph, 289n83; and politics, 93, 94; and queue cutting, 63–64, 69, 75, 76, 77, 223; and "Remembrance" poem, 167, 171

Xu Xingzhi, 187, 201–2, 218, 242, 290n4

Yamamoto Hatsue, 167, 171, 288n64
Yan Fu, 1, 53, 60
Yan'an, 4, 184, 212
Yang, Gladys, 269n17
Yang Dequn, 225
Yang Jiyun, 170
Yang Keyang, 61
Yang Muzhi, 195, 217
Yang Quan, 43
Yang Xianyi, 269n17
Yang Yanli, 157, 234, 252
Yanyi (romances), 26, 102. See also *Old Tales Retold*
Yao Ke, 191, 252
Yao Wenfu, 75, 76, 290n89
Ye Lingfeng, 187, 194, 197, 201–2, 241, 295n6b
Ye Qianyu, 213, 215, 217–18, 240, 242, 290n4
Ye Shusui, 157, 252
Yellow Emperor, 57, 60, 68, 94–95
Young Chinese Scholar (painting; Alexander), 83, 277n87
Yu Cheng, 115
Yu Dafu, 31, 171
Yu Kunshan, 289n83
Yuan Muzhi, 186, 218, 239
Yuan Shikai, 12, 43, 93, 122, 124, 129; and Lu Xun, 130, 131–32, 133, 138
Yulun shishibao (newspaper), 84–85

Zhang Binglin (Zhang Taiyan): Lu Xun on, 176–78; and 1903 poem, 147, 176, 178, 179; poems by, 174, 177, 178, 180, 223, 224; politics of, 42, 91–92, 97, 132, 223; queue cutting by, 60, 88, 223; and Zou Rong, 176, 177–78, 179–80, 276n67

Zhang E, 187, 191, 216, 217, 218, 240, 242
Zhang Guangyu, 241
Zhang Mengyang, 183
Zhang Shizao, 276n67
Zhang Tianyi, 108
Zhang Xianzhong, 132, 282n45
Zhang Xiehe, 55
Zhang Xun ("Pigtail General"): coup by, 99, 126–28; and Lu Xun's fiction, 124, 125, 130, 131, 133, 135, 136
Zhang Yiping, 249, 296n21
Zhang Yunhong, 197, 243
Zhang Yunqiao, 218, 239
Zhang Zhengyu, 213, 217, 240
Zhang Zhongsu, 128
Zhang Ziqiang, 155, 159–60, 161, 163–64
Zhang Zuolin, 48
Zhang Zuying, 62
Zhao Yannian, 61, 119
Zhejiang Normal College, 54
Zhejiang Students Association, 55, 69–70
Zhejiang Tide (*Zhejiang chao*; magazine), 69, 94, 96, 176, 177, 178, 179
Zhong Buqing, 190, 215, 218, 250, 254
Zhongguo ribao (newspaper), 88
Zhonghua ribao (newspaper), 186, 241
Zhongshan University (Guangzhou), 47
Zhou Haiying (son), 30, 156–57, 158, 159, 160
Zhou Jianren (brother), 128, 153
Zhou Shuren. *See* Lu Xun
Zhou Yang, 183
Zhou Zuoren (brother): on "Ah Q," 24, 117; and Chen Duxiu, 281n34; diaries of, 126, 170; illness of, 102, 270n24; in Japan, 33, 37, 54, 89, 92; letters to, 75, 101; on Lu Xun, 31, 32, 66–67; on Lu Xun's queue, 67–68; and magazines, 34–35,

101; on names, 116; and 1903 poem, 94, 233; photographs sent to, 58–59, 64, 66, 68; poems sent to, 66, 68; on "Storm," 126; and violence, 127, 128, 137; work by, 8, 9, 177, 192; works with Lu Xun, 17, 54, 131, 133; on Yuan Shikai, 132

Zhu An, 30, 236

Zou Rong, 88, 90, 223, 276n67; death of, 97, 178; *Revolutionary Army* by, 42, 75, 92, 96, 177; and Zhang Binglin, 176, 177–78, 179–80, 276n67

ABOUT THE AUTHOR

EVA SHAN CHOU is Professor in the English Department at City University of New York, Baruch College. She is a graduate of Harvard College and received her Ph.D. from Harvard University. Chou has written on classical poetry as well as modern literature. Her study, *Reconsidering Tu Fu (712–770): Literary Greatness and Cultural Context*, was published by Cambridge University Press in 1996.

GPSR Authorized Representative: Easy Access System Europe, Mustamäe tee 50, 10621 Tallinn, Estonia, gpsr.requests@easproject.com

www.ingramcontent.com/pod-product-compliance
Lightning Source LLC
Chambersburg PA
CBHW030432300426
44112CB00009B/965